Best Drives in Maine, New Hampshire and Vermont

22 Tours in Northern New England

Kay and Bill Scheller

Jasper Heights Press   Waterville Vermont

First Edition
Copyright 2010

ISBN 978-0-9672682-5-5

Design by www.GreatBigGraphics.net
Front cover photograph: Fall foliage at Meredith, New Hampshire, taken from M/S *Mount
Washington* (courtesy Mount Washington Cruises)

Back cover photographs:
First Baptist Church of Bristol, Vermont
(courtesy Addison County Chamber of Commerce)

Portland Head Light, Cape Elizabeth, Maine
(courtesy Donald Dill / imagesbydonalddill.com)

Mount Washington Cog Railway
(courtesy Mount White Mountains Attractions Association)

Maps by Lara Craver

Special thanks to John Kitchener

Jasper Heights Press
438 Shipman Road
Waterville, Vermont
drivenewengland.com

Best Drives in Maine, New Hampshire and Vermont

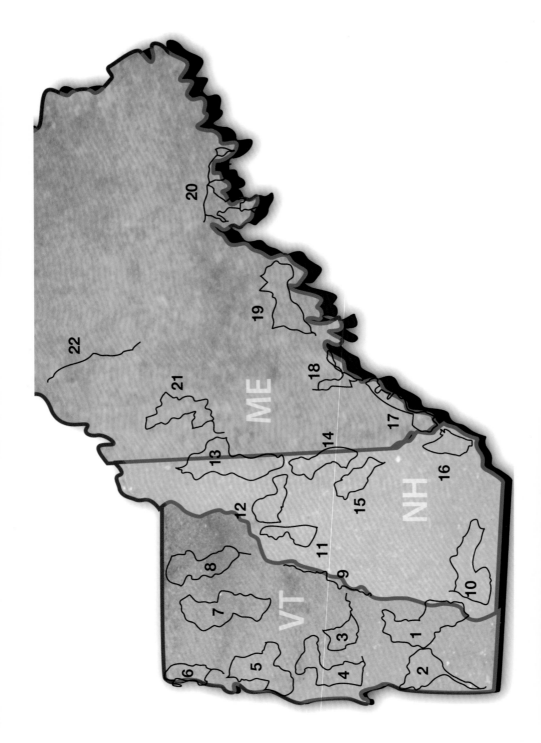

Introduction

For many travelers, the states of Maine, New Hampshire, and Vermont offer a real-life confirmation of the New England they've always imagined. That perception takes nothing away from the three states of the region's southern tier – but it credits the northern states' success at preserving an older and more bucolic realm, the New England of covered bridges, rolling pastures, White Mountain trails, the rock-bound coast of Maine, and the village that appears around the bend after miles of meadow and forest.

The drives described in this book bring together the best of the northern New England experience. We've strived to offer a balance of wild natural beauty, and the carefully crafted scenic character that comes from centuries of living in harmony with the landscape. Here are the people, the personality, and places that set these states apart from the rest of a world that changes at a far more frenzied pace.

To help with planning, each chapter begins with overall route mileage (not counting side trips), a brief sketch of the drive, and a list of major attractions along the way. Maps, which accompany each drive, are meant to be used in conjunction with the directions highlighted in the chapter. While these directions are clear and precise, it's always a good idea to carry a reliable road atlas and/or highway maps distributed free by state tourism agencies (see listings below). For maximum detail, we've always been partial to the series of individual state atlases published by the DeLorme Mapping Company in Freeport, Maine.

For the Lodgings listings, rate categories are keyed to dollar sign symbols, Rates are based on double occupancy:

$ = $100 or less
$$ = $101 - $175
$$$ = $176-$250
$$$$ = $251 and up.

When an establishment is listed as a bed and breakfast, breakfast is assumed as included in the rate. Private bath is assumed at places with higher rates, although it's always good to check before booking – even some high-end establishments have several rooms with shared baths, especially in expensive seaside areas. Remember that some places require a minimum two-night stay, particularly during holiday weekends and fall foliage season, and that a number of the more expensive b&bs and country inns allow children only over a certain age. And an increasing number of smaller, independently-owned establishments – very likely a majority by now – ban smoking entirely from their premises.

The dollar sign key for Restaurants is based on the price of a dinner entrée:

$ = under $10
$$ = $11-$17
$$$ = $18-$25
$$$$ = $26 and up.

We have made every attempt to include the latest information on lodgings, restaurants, attractions, and activities on each drive. However, we recommend checking in advance of a trip to determine lodging rates and policies, restaurant prices and days open, and opening/closing schedules for attractions and activities.

State Tourism Offices

Maine Office of Tourism
59 State House Station
Augusta, ME 04333
(888) 624-6345
visitmaine.com

New Hampshire Office of Travel and Tourism
P.O. Box 1856
172 Pembroke Road
Concord, NH 03302
(603) 271-2665
visitnh.gov

Vermont Department of Travel and Tourism
National Life Building, 6th floor
Montpelier, VT 05620
For brochure: (800) VERMONT
Other requests: (802) 828-3237
travel-vermont.com

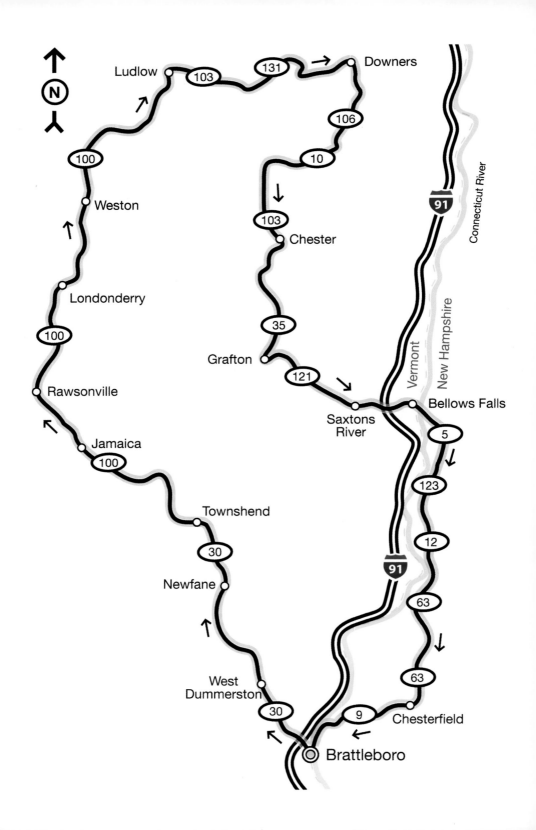

Drive 1

Brattleboro, West River Villages, and the Lower Connecticut Valley

130 miles

major **attractions**

- Brattleboro
- Newfane
- Chester
- Grafton
- Covered Bridges

$\mathcal{S}$tart out in Brattleboro, then follow the valley of the West River through a skein of inviting villages before winding back to the Connecticut Valley via Grafton, a once-forgotten town that now typifies Vermont's calendar-photo image. At the old railroad and canal center of Bellows Falls, pause to stroll through a small, reborn downtown, before crossing the Connecticut River and returning to "Brat" via quiet New Hampshire byways.

Brattleboro, nicknamed "Brat" (pronounced like the tot, not the sausage) is a melting pot for native Vermonters, aging counterculture types who arrived in the 60s and put down roots, and artists who have converted old brick factories into airy lofts. The result? A thriving downtown packed with bookstores, galleries, and ethnic restaurants and a lively cultural scene. It's anchored by the

Latchis Building, which houses the 1938 **Latchis Hotel** and its adjacent Latchis Theater, which together make up one of only two art deco commercial buildings in Vermont (the other is in Rutland).

> *In 1940 the Latchis Theater screened* Gone With the Wind, *making Brattleboro the first small town in America to see the film.*

One of the state's earliest white settlements was located near Brattleboro at Fort Dummer, which was completed in 1724 and served as a defense against hostile Indians as well as a scouting post and trading center. For its first two years the fort was under the command of Captain Timothy Dwight. His son Timothy, the first white child born in Vermont, later became an accomplished poet and president of Yale College. The fort was dismantled in 1763, and the land it stood on was later flooded by Vernon Dam on the Connecticut River. A granite marker about 1 1/2 miles south of town on Route 30 marks the approximate site.

In the 1840s, springs were discovered along Whetstone Brook in West Brattleboro, and the Brattleboro Hydropathic Establishment opened its doors a few years later. For more than thirty years it catered to wealthy patrons who flocked here to take the "water cure" -- a plunge into the generally icy waters.

The J. Estey Organ Company began production in Brattleboro during the 1850s, and eventually employed more than 500 people. In the days when families made their own evening entertainment, Estey spread Brattleboro's fame as the "organ capital of America," and manufactured parlor organs until the ascent of radio and phonographs in the 1920s. Several Estey organs are on exhibit at the **Brattleboro Historical Society**. The **Estey Organ Museum**, dedicated to the history and contributions of the company, is open Saturdays from June 20-October 12 from 1-4 p.m., with guided tours by advance reservation or at other times by appointment (call John Carnahan at 802-254-8398).

The Robert H. Gibson River Garden on Main Street is filled with plants and light, and has several restaurants and food carts. The outdoor terrace is a delightful spot to have lunch and enjoy one of the free summer concerts. Call the Chamber of Commerce (see "Information" below) for a schedule.

unlikely outpost of the Raj

In 1892, flush with his early literary success, 26-year-old Rudyard Kipling began building a handsome shingle-style home called **Naulakha** on a hillside in Dummerston, just over the town line from Brattleboro. Kipling had recently married an American woman, Caroline Balestier, whose family had long summered in the area, and the young writer quickly fell under the spell of rural Vermont. "The sun and the air and the light are good in this place and have made me healthy as I never was in my life," he wrote, and his literary output reflected this new invigoration: while living at Naulakha, Kipling wrote *The Jungle Book, The Day's Work, The Seven Seas,* and *Captains Courageous.* But the idyll was short lived: Kipling became caught up in a bitter feud with his eccentric brother-in-law, Beatty Balestier, and left Vermont for good in 1896.

His beautifully preserved house, together with much of its original furnishings, remains – it's the property of a British organization, The Landmark Trust, which rents it out for periods of a week or more (landmarktrustusa.org/naulakha). Once a year, there's an open house with guided tours for day visitors. If you want to just drive by for a look, head north out of Brattleboro on Route 5 for 2 1/2 miles, make a left at the sign for the SIT Graduate Institute (formerly known as the School for International Training: there's a Kipling marker here too), then turn right on Kipling Road. The house is up ahead on the left.

Head northwest out of Brattleboro on Route 30, following the West River. The Brattleboro Retreat, on the outskirts of town, opened in 1836 as the Vermont Lunatic Asylum, and was one of the first hospitals in the country designed exclusively for the treatment of mental illness (it's now a drug and alcohol abuse rehabilitation center). **Retreat Farm**, once a part of the hospital, is now part of a 475-acre historic site and recreation center owned by The Windham Foundation (see "Grafton".) Their Petting Farm, with more than 50 farm animals to feed and touch, is right next door to the new **Grafton Village Cheese Specialty Cheese & Wine Shoppe**, with lots of tasty samples and a great selection of Vermont products (including microbrews).

Just north of the village of West Dummerston is the West Dummerston Covered Bridge. Built in 1872 for $7,777.08 (and repaired in 1994 at a cost to the town of more than $600,000), this is the state's longest two-span covered bridge still used by cars (at 280 feet, it requires a central stone pier for support). There's a good swimming hole alongside the bridge.

along the West River Valley

The entire village of **Newfane**, one of Vermont's prettiest, is on the National Register of Historic Places. It has two elegant town greens and several noteworthy Federal and Greek Revival buildings, including the magnificent County Courthouse, built in 1825. Across the street is the Windham County Jail, once the most famous county jail in the country. For many years it served as both a jail and a hotel, lodging prisoners awaiting trial along with travelers who had business at the court. Seeing no reason to provide separate dining facilities for the two groups when the jail was already serving up "fair to middlin' vittles," the authorities gave travelers their meals in the jail's dining hall. The hotel's stationery was marked "Windham County Jail, Newfane, Vt."

Among Newfane natives was children's poet Eugene Field, who wrote "Wynken, Blynken, and Nod," and his father Roswell, who defended Dred Scott before the United States Supreme Court in 1856-1857. Economist John Kenneth Galbraith summered here.

Newfane is the home of several antiques shops, as well as the by-appointment-only shop of antiquarian horologist Ray Bates, "The British Clockmaker." Bates, who qualified as a master clockmaker under Britain's centuries-old apprentice system, specializes in the restoration and sale of antique timepieces. On his website (thebritishclockmaker.com) he lists clocks he does not work on. Among these: "cuckoo clocks, anniversary clocks, usually described as 'the one George brought back from Germany 40 years ago, has little balls that go around under a glass dome!', clocks made by your uncle, [and] clocks repaired by your uncle." At the more pedestrian end of the antiques business, visitors pack the **Newfane flea market** – one of the state's biggest – held just north of town on Route 30 on Sundays May-October.

Continue north through the once-thriving community of Harmonyville, nicknamed "Tin Pot" by the citizens of nearby **Townshend** circa 1830. In turn, Harmonyville-ites dubbed their neighbor to the north "Flyburg." Sticks and stones ...

Alphonso Taft, the father of President William Howard Taft, was born in Townshend, a charming village with a two-acre common and a long history. The Congregational Church was built in 1790; Townshend's Leland and Gray Union High School's antecedents go back to 1834. The Mary Meyer Stuffed Toys Factory Store, Vermont's oldest stuffed toy maker, began here as a family business more than seventy years ago. Their toys are sold at the Big Black Bear Shop, just north of town.

A bit further north and just off Route 30 is **Scott Bridge**, Vermont's longest single-span covered bridge ("single-span" means it isn't supported by a central pier, like the West Dummerston bridge, above). Built in 1870, the 277-foot structure was closed to traffic when engineers couldn't shore it up properly. Townspeople back in the 1950s – the Dark Ages of preservationism – didn't want to spend $20,000 for repairs and were prepared to put the bridge to the torch, but the chairman of the Townshend select board worked with the state to have ownership transferred, and in 1955 it was made a State Historic Site.

Just past the bridge is the entrance to **Townshend Lake Recreation Area**. Turn left and drive across the dam (built by the Army Corps of Engineers in 1961) and then turn right to the beach /recreation area. Much of the infrastructure here was built in the 1930s by the Civilian Conservation Corps; the headquarters lodge was constructed from stone quarried in the forest, and the handcrafted stone arch bridges were crafted by local masons. A steep trail with a vertical climb of 1,100 feet winds for 2.7 miles past waterfalls, chutes, and pools to the top of Bald Mountain.

The West River wraps around Jamaica, nestling in the shadow of 1,745-foot-high Ball Mountain to the north. The local Congregational minister, John Stoddard, never got to preach in the fine church built here in 1808. In 1799 he was fired after selling his wife to another man (local legend has it that she was delighted with the transaction).

Side Trip

Turn right off Route 30 onto Depot Street to reach 756-acre **Jamaica State Park**. The West River Railroad once ran through the park, and today the old railbed is a trail that leads along the West River to Ball Mountain Dam. Twice a year, in late April and late September, kayakers flock to the dam in anticipation of the U.S. Army Corps of Engineers' controlled release of water, which creates conditions for terrific whitewater paddling. A hiking trail leads to 120-foot Hamilton Falls, about a mile up Cobb Brook. (Note: Hamilton Falls are pretty to look at, but the pools and flumes are dangerous for swimmers.)

> *In Rawsonville, where Route 30 splits away from Route 100, pause at the fenced-in Rawson Monument to pay homage to Bailey Rawson, who founded the town in 1810-12. Before he fetched up here he made a name for himself selling sorrel seed to hopeful -- if naive -- farmers as "not clover seed." When disappointed planters brought him to court he said, "I sold the stuff for 'not clover seed'. If you can prove they are clover seed, I will pay the damage."*

Continue north on Route 100 through South Londonderry to Londonderry. If you're passing through on Saturday between 10 a.m. and noon, be sure to stop at the lively and copiously stocked **West River Farmers Market** at the intersection of routes 100 and 11.

Stay on Route 100 and continue to **Weston**, home of the Weston Playhouse and the Vermont Country Store (see Drive 2 for Weston information). North of Weston, Route 100 hugs the eastern border of the Green Mountain National Forest; an unpaved road (left) leads to the Greendale Recreation Area, with primitive campsites. Ahead, bear left at the fork with Route 155 to stay on Route 100 into **Ludlow**.

Ludlow is the primary service town for the Okemo ski resort, accessed off Route 100 just north of town. Most of the area's lodging, dining, and nightlife venues cluster near the resort; downtown Ludlow retains much of the workaday atmosphere that dates from the era when the retail and housing complex that dominates Main Street was a woolen mill and, later, a General Electric plant. Overlooking the town is the imposing brick Romanesque **Black River Academy,** built in 1889 and now housing a local history museum of the same name. Among its graduates was future president Calvin Coolidge, class of 1890.

From Ludlow, take Route 103 east to a left turn onto Route 131, which leads into Proctorsville, named for the family of marble-mining magnates that produced four Vermont governors. Proctorsville is one of two villages that make up the town of **Cavendish;** the other, Cavendish itself, lies just ahead on Route 131.

From 1976 to 1994, Cavendish played host to one of the 20th century's most famous literary exiles. Russian author Aleksandr Solzhenitsyn, who had been deported from the Soviet Union in 1974, settled here with his wife, three sons, and a stepson at a fenced-off rural compound where he continued writing his series of historical novels about the Russian Revolution. Solzhenitsyn, who addressed the Cavendish Town meeting in March, 1977, appreciated the privacy accorded him by local citizens – a famous sign on the door of the town's general store said, "No directions to Solzhenitsyn house." After the fall of communism, the author returned to his native land, where he died in 2008.

> *On September 13, 1848, an explosion drove an iron bar through the head of railroad construction foreman Phineas Gage while he was at work in Cavendish. Gage lived and worked for another twelve years, although his personality was changed. His skull – and the iron bar – are preserved at Harvard University.*

Route 131 east out of Cavendish follows the meandering Black River. Roughly five miles past Cavendish, look to the left for the Upper Falls Bridge, a 120-foot covered wooden span that carries Upper Falls Road across the river. It was built in 1840, and survived without major restoration until the 1970s. At that time, the bridge was raised 2½ feet to keep it out of reach of floodwaters. Inside are old advertisements, and some graffiti that date back more than a century.

Turn right onto Route 106 at Downers, which is little more than a four-corner intersection, and head south to **Perkinsville,** passing the turn-off for the Stoughton Pond Recreation Area on the left. At the top of Perkinsville's town green stands the handsome little Community Church, a 1932 stone structure with a fine Gothic window. A marker alongside the green tells of the 1947 crash of a B-29A Superfortress on nearby Hawks Mountain; straying off course in a severe storm, the bomber went down with the loss of all 12 crewmembers.

stone village..

At the intersection with Route 10 a few miles south of Perkinsville, turn right and follow Route 10 to Gassetts (no town here; just a country intersection), then turn left onto Route 103. Route 103 follows the deep valley of the Williams River, which appears on the right side of the road as little more than a creek. Continue into **Chester**, passing, as you come into town, a number of the stout stone houses which gave this part of town, today a historic district, its nickname, "Stone Village." It's an odd fact that in a state famous for its quarries, stone houses are a relative rarity; in his book *Old Vermont Houses,* the architectural historian Herbert Wheaton Congdon remarked on this curiosity, noting that "the shoemaker's children go barefoot." Chester has some 30 houses faced with gneiss and rough-hewn mica schist quarried from nearby Mt. Flamstead. The homes, built before the Civil War by two brothers, were used as safe houses on the Underground Railroad.

Chester also boasts a number of gingerbread-trimmed Victorian homes, and stately public buildings such as the 1871 Gothic Revival St. Luke's Episcopal Church, along both sides of the long, narrow green which splits Main Street.

The Victorian Chester Depot between Main and North streets, once used by the Rutland Railway, is now the northern terminus for the **Green Mountain Flyer**, an excursion train with restored, 1930s vintage cars that runs out of Bellows Falls (see below and "Activities").

a village preserved..

From Chester, turn south onto Route 35 to **Grafton**, a village deliberately plucked from obscurity and reborn as a picture-perfect rural community. Before the Civil War, Grafton was a thriving agricultural center, shepherding 10,000 merino sheep and supporting a large woolen mill. One of the country's largest soapstone quarries added to the town's prosperity. But one of every three of the town's menfolk went to war, and many who weren't killed in battle headed west when peace came, triggering Grafton's economic and physical decline.

It wasn't until 1963 that New York businessman Matthew Hall, with the help of a legacy left by his aunt, formed the nonprofit Windham Foundation with his cousin and co-heir, Dean Mathey. They began the monumental task of totally renovating an entire nineteenth-century village, and restoring its economic vitality.

Today's Grafton is testimony to the cousins' success. The Foundation owns fifty buildings and 3,000 acres in town, and its centerpiece is **The Old Tavern at Grafton**, which opened in 1801. In addition to the inn, Windham operates three museums, gives sheep-shearing demonstrations, and runs the **Grafton Village Cheese Company**, which manufactures award-winning cheddar using traditional methods. The popular Grafton Cornet Band performs on weekends throughout the summer.

Follow Route 121 east out of Grafton through Cambridgeport (named, like a lot of Connecticut Valley settlements, by emigrants honoring their home town in Massachusetts) and into Saxtons River. The latter is the home of the private Vermont Academy, founded in 1876. In 1910 the school's associate principal, James P. Taylor, a New York City transplant, hatched the idea for a statewide Green Mountain Club "to make Vermont mountains play a larger part in the life of the people." The **Long Trail** is an outgrowth of his efforts. (To visit Green Mountain Club headquarters, see Drive 7.)

Continuing on Route 121, cross under I-91 and head into **Bellows Falls**, settled in the 1780s. Like a lot of Vermont towns its size (small cities, by local standards), Bellows Falls is a place that has spent the past few decades coming to grips with its transition from an industrial community to a market town and tourist gateway. At one time, it was home to paper and farm machinery factories, and it was one of Vermont's first important rail centers. In 1802, work was completed here on America's first canal, designed to carry boat and barge traffic around a 50-foot falls, the largest natural drop on the Connecticut River. (Harking back to an even earlier era, there are Indian petroglyphs visible on the rocks along the river downstream from the Vilas Bridge.)

The canal's importance waned when the railroad arrived at Bellows Falls in 1849. When the first train pulled into town, the *Weekly Times* reported, "The engine came up in Grand Style and when opposite our village the Monster gave one of the most savage yells, frightening men, women and children considerable, and bringing forth deafening howls from all the dogs in the Neighborhood." The *Green Mountain Flyer* is carrying on the local railroad tradition, without causing quite as much commotion.

Hetty Howland Green (1834-1916) was an heiress to a New Bedford whaling fortune who married a Bellows Falls man, Edward Green, and lived in town for part of her life. She was one of America's richest individuals, and was known as the "Witch of Wall Street" -- although to be fair, she was no more a practitioner of the financial black arts than many male nabobs who were never accused of necromancy. She was, however, a legendary penny pincher. Her father had advised her, "never owe anyone anything, not even a kindness." When her son's leg became infected, she dressed as a beggar and brought him to the charity ward at Bellevue Hospital, where surgeons had to amputate. The same son later became adept at spending his late mother's fortune; her daughter married the great-grandson of John Jacob Astor.

At the power dam in downtown Bellows Falls is a **fish ladder and visitor center**, where a subsurface glass wall might offer a glimpse of passing shad or salmon during migration season. It's also worthwhile to stroll down Rockingham Street to Canal Street, which ends near the town's official visitors' center – built to somewhat resemble a railroad locomotive – and several historic depot structures (Amtrak's *Vermonter* still makes daily stops here). Along the way are several interesting new and used bookstores, a gallery or two, and the Hrafen Wood Café.

> *The Rev. John Williams preached the first Protestant sermon in what was to become Vermont in 1704 at the future site of Bellows Falls. Williams was one of more than 100 captives seized by Indians allied with the French in a raid on Greenfield, Massachusetts, and marched north to Canada.*

Side Trip

Head north on Route 5 to Route 103 north and follow signs to the National Historic Landmark **Rockingham Meeting House**. One of Vermont's earliest public buildings, built in 1787 and restored in 1907, the 2 1/2 story, white clapboard building perched on a hilltop is magnificent in its stark simplicity. The adjacent graveyard has some wonderful old stones. If you continue on Route 103, just past the turn-off for the Meeting House, you'll soon reach (left) the **Vermont Country Store's** Rockingham location.

into the Granite State

Cross the Connecticut River at Bellows Falls and turn left onto Route 12 in North Walpole, New Hampshire. On the left, just after you cross the bridge, are the shops of the Green Mountain Railroad, with a few ancient passenger cars standing idly on their sidings. Continue south through a somewhat built-up area; just past the intersection with Route 123 (stay on routes 12/123 south), look on the left for the Walpole Creamery, which serves its own ice cream, and on the right for Boggy Meadow Farm, makers and purveyors of farmstead Swiss cheese.

When Route 12 forks off to the left, bear right onto Route 63 to continue heading due south along the Connecticut River. Just past this intersection, on the left, Stuart and John's Sugar House serves pancake breakfasts on summer weekends, and sells their own maple syrup (no, Vermont doesn't have a monopoly on the stuff). As you continue south on Route 63, expansive views of the great valley of New England's longest river open on the right, with the hills of Vermont in the distance. Matching the natural surroundings in beauty is the charming little settlement of **Park Hill**, an array of Georgian white clapboard and brick houses clustered around a tidy little green that is dominated by the 1762 Park Hill Meeting House, moved here in sections by oxcart in 1779 and crowned with a majestic triple-tiered steeple, topped by an angel weathervane, in 1826. The bell in that steeple was cast in the Massachusetts foundry of Paul Revere.

The road winds south beneath a canopy of trees that make this an especially attractive route in autumn, and leads, in less than a mile, to the main settlement of the town of Westmoreland, where another pretty town green spreads before the white, steepled Westmoreland Town Hall. Continue south from here on Route 63, which still appears to tunnel beneath the broad branches of leafy hardwoods, passing Spofford Lake on your left. At the southern end of the lake, turn right onto Route 9 for the last leg of the drive, a seven-mile run to the Connecticut River bridge at Chesterfield, New Hampshire, and back to Brattleboro. (An entrance to I-91 is opposite the rotary on the Vermont side of the river.)

information

Brattleboro Area Chamber of Commerce (802-254-4565), 180 Main St., Brattleboro, VT 05301. brattleboro.com

Grafton Information Center (802-843-2255), Townshend Rd., P.O. Box 3, Grafton, VT 05146. Closed April. graftonvermont.org

Great Falls Regional Chamber of Commerce (802-463-4280), 17 Depot St., Bellows Falls, VT 05101. gfrcc.org

Greater Keene Chamber of Commerce (for NH towns on drive) (603-352-1303), 48 Central Sq., Keene, NH 03431. keenechamber.com

Londonderry Area Chamber of Commerce (802-824-8178), Mountain Marketplace Box 58, Londonderry, VT 05148. londonderryvt.com

Okemo Valley Regional Chamber of Commerce (802-228-5830), 57 Pond St., P.O. Box 333, Ludlow, VT 05149. okemovalleyvt.com

lodging

Andrie Rose Inn (802-228-4846), 13 Pleasant St., Ludlow, VT. 9 rooms and a two-fireplace suite in two buildings; dinner ($$$) might include confit of duck leg with white bean ragout. andrieroseinn.com $-$$$$

Boardman House B & B (802-365-4086), Village Green, Townshend, VT 05353. 19th-century farmhouse on the green, with 5 guest rooms and a 2-bedroom suite. southvermont.com/townshend/boardmanhouse $-$$

Cavendish Inn (802-226-7080), 1589 Main St., Cavendish, VT 05142. The Gothic Revival Glimmerstone mansion, built in the 1840s of shiny local gneiss and mica schist stone, houses this 9-room inn (2 with shared bath), which features an elegant dining room ($$$) and summer terrace dining. cavendishinnvt.com $-$$$

The Chester House (802-875-2205), Town Green, Chester, VT 05143. All 7 rooms at this c. 1780 National Register Historic Inn have phones, private baths and a/c; some have whirlpool baths and gas fireplaces. Breakfast served fireside in the keeping room. chesterhouseinn.com $$-$$$

Forty Putney Road B & B (802-254-6268), 192 Putney Rd., Brattleboro, VT 05301. French Provincial, 1930s estate with 4 guest rooms and a 2-room suite, all with TV and a/c; elegant gardens; pub. fortyputneyroad.com $$-$$$

Four Columns Inn (802-365-7713), 21 West St., Newfane, VT 05345. 1832 classic Greek Revival has 16 rooms and suites, some with gas-log fireplaces, 2-person Jacuzzis and/or decks. The restaurant ($$-$$$) fuses New American, Asian and French cuisines to offer dishes such as crispy panko scallops, and pan-seared breast of moulard duck. fourcolumnsinn.com $$$- $$$$

Fullerton Inn (802-875-2444), 40 The Common, Chester, VT 05143. More like an intimate country hotel, with more than 20 rooms and suites all with private bath. Full service restaurant and a cozy tavern. fullertoninn.com $$-$$$

Inn at Woodchuck Hill Farm (802-843-2398), 347 Woodchuck Hill Rd., P.O. Box 223, Grafton, VT 05146. 6 guest rooms (4 with private bath) in the c. 1790 main house, 2 barn suites, and an efficiency cottage with fireplace and wood stove. Situated on 200 hilltop acres west of town. Hiking, swimming pond, and sauna. woodchuckhill.com $$-$$$

Inn Victoria (802/875-4288), 321 Main St., Chester, VT 05143. This romantic c. 1851 B&B overlooking the town green has 7 elegantly furnished, antiques-filled rooms with private baths; several have gas fireplaces. A 3-course breakfast is served by candlelight. innvictoria.com $$-$$$$

Latchis Hotel (802-254-6300), 50 Main St., Brattleboro, VT 05301. A rare find, this downtown, art deco-style hotel has nicely-furnished and comfortable rooms at a bargain price. Rooms facing street can be noisy. Continental breakfast. latchis.com $-$$$

Londonderry Inn (802-824-5226), 8 Melendy Hill Rd., P.O. Box 206, South Londonderry, VT 05155. Rambling 1826 homestead with 24 guest rooms has been a haven for families for more than 50 years. Game room, outdoor pool, and light breakfast buffet. londonderryinn.com $-$$

Old Newfane Inn (802-365-4427), Rte. 30, Village Common, Newfane VT 05345. Chef-owned and operated since 1970, this 1787 inn has 10 antiques-filled rooms and a highly acclaimed restaurant ($$-$$$) specializing in classic French-Swiss cuisine, with specialties such as cream of garlic soup and breast of capon Cordon Rouge. oldnewfaneinn.com $$-$$$

Old Tavern at Grafton (802-843-2231), 92 Main St., Grafton, VT 05146. This historic, 1801 lodging has more than 60 rooms and suites in the inn and nearby buildings, as well as houses for rent. Upscale New England fare featuring vegetables and herbs grown at the inn ($$-$$$) is served in the formal dining room as well as a more casual restaurant. Sun. brunch and afternoon tea. X/C ski center, tennis, pub. Closed April. old-tavern.com $$-$$$$

Saxtons River Inn (802-869-2110), 27 Main St., Rte. 121, Saxtons River, VT 05154. 16 rooms in a handsome "downtown" 1903 inn. Tea is served in the garden when weather permits. Dishes with a Continental flair are served nightly in the lovely dining room ($$-$$$). There's also a Victorian pub. saxtonsriverinn.com $$

Stone Cottage Collectables (802-875-6211), 196 North St., Rte. 103, Chester, VT 05143. 1840, antiques-filled stone house in the historic district has 2 guest rooms including 1 with fireplace; available as suite with sitting room. stonecottagebb.com $$

Three Mountain Inn (802-874-4140), Rte. 30, Jamaica, VT 05343. Small, romantic 1790s country inn on the edge of Jamaica State Park has 15 guest rooms in the main and adjacent houses, and a private cottage. Dinner ($$-$$$) blends various cuisines and might include petite osso buco and New England fish stew. threemountaininn.com $$-$$$$

West River Lodge (802-365-7745), 117 Hill Rd., Newfane, VT 05345. Horse lovers and families feel particularly welcome at this farmhouse with 8 guest rooms (some with shared bath) adjacent to a riding stable (trail rides and English/Western lessons available). Private beach. westriverlodge.com $- $$

Windham Hill Inn, (802-874-4080), 311 Lawrence Drive, W. Townshend, VT 05359. "Upscale country" lodgings at an 1825 house on 160 acres. 21 guest rooms, some with soaking tubs, jacuzzis, and fireplaces. Pool and tennis. The menu ($$$-$$$$) might include an appetizer of Maine crab cakes and entree of roasted butternut squash and Vermont Camembert ravioli. windhamhill.com $$$-$$$$

off the drive

Putney Inn (802-387-5517), Depot Rd, Putney, VT 05346. Great care has been taken to preserve the charm and integrity of this 1790s farmhouse. The 25 guest rooms, all in a less historic adjacent building, are well appointed. The restaurant ($$-$$$) the restaurant earns accolades for classic New England fare. Pets welcome. putneyinn.com $$-$$$

restaurants

Baba-A-Louis Bakery (802-875-4666), 92 Rt. 11W, Chester, VT. Homemade soups, quiche, panini, and a salad bar; European-style breads, and fabulous pastries. Pizza Fri. 3-8 p.m., Tues.-Sat. 7 a.m.-6 p.m.

Boccelli's on the Canal (802-460-1190), 46 Canal St., Bellows Falls, VT. Italian favorites served in a cheerful setting; adjacent deli great for picnic supplies. L & D Wed.-Sat. Outdoor seating. $$

Country Girl Diner (802-875-2650), jct. Rtes. 11/103, Chester, VT. The crowds pack in for reliable, traditional diner eats. B & L daily; D weekends. $

Curtis' BBQ (802-875-6999), 908 Rte. 103S, Chester, VT. The daughter of Curtis (of Curtis' BBQ in Putney) has opened up her own place, and serves up all the traditional BBQ dishes. Sat. from 4-7 p.m., and Sun. from noon-3 p.m. for the all-you-can-eat buffet. L & D Wed.-Sun. $-$$$

Grandma Miller's Pies & Pastries (802-824-4032), 52 Hearthstone Lane, S. Londonderry, VT. Pies, pastries, cookies, and cakes made on site with Vermont's King Arthur flour. Grandma's grandson and his wife are the bakers. Closed Sun.

Miss Bellows Falls Diner, 900 Rockingham St., Bellows Falls, VT. A 1920s Worcester lunch car (here since '42) serves up burgers, hearty breakfasts, diner standbys, and all-you-can-eat Friday fish fries. B & L Sun.-Thurs.; D Fri.-Sat.

Peter Havens (802-257-3333), 32 Elliot St., Brattleboro, VT. Filet mignon with green peppercorn-bourbon sauce and house-cured gravlax are specialties of this bistro with an upscale, imaginative menu. Save room for homemade cheesecakes. D Tues.-Sat. $$-$$$

Stuart and John's Sugar House (603-399-4486), Rtes. 12 and 63, Westmoreland, NH. Pancakes with homemade maple syrup are the house specialty, but there are also lots of other tasty breakfast treats, as well as seafood, burgers, and 21 flavors of ice cream. B May-Sept., Sat. & Sun. 8 a.m.-1 p.m. L & D Memorial Day-Labor Day, Thurs.-Sun. 11 a.m.-8 p.m. $

T. J. Buckley's (802- 257-4922), 132 Elliot St., Brattleboro, VT. Gourmet fare in a tiny, 1920's, fire engine red diner. Appetizers such as a smoked trout tartlet followed by a choice of 4 entrees such as pan-seared halibut or Black Angus beef tenderloin. D Wed.-Sun; closed Wed. in winter. No credit cards. Reservations a must. $$$-$$$$

Three Clock Inn (802-824-6327), 95 Middletown Rd., S. Londonderry, VT. Superb French provincial cuisine (the chef is from Provence) – bouillabaisse, coq au vin, cassoulet and other classics. D; closed Mon. $$$$

attractions

Adams Grist Mill Museum (802-463-3706), Mill St., Bellows Falls, VT. Original machinery, tools, and memorabilia left when gristmill closed in the 1960s. July and Aug., Sat. and Sun. p.m.

Ball Mountain Dam (802-874-4881), off Rte. 30, Ball Mountain Lane, Jamaica, VT.

Black River Academy Museum (802-228-5050), 14 High St., Ludlow, VT. Housed in an 1889 Romanesque former school building, the museum is dedicated to the cultural history of the Ludlow area and Black River valley. Call for hrs.

Boggy Meadow Farm (603-756-3300), 13 Boggy Meadow Lane, Walpole, NH. Cheese-making tour; gift shop.

Brattleboro Farmers Market, Brattleboro, VT. May-Oct.: Sat., 9 a.m.-2 p.m. on Rte. 9 west of exit 2 off I-91. Wed., 10.a.m-2 p.m. at Co-op Plaza, off Main Street.

Brattleboro Historical Society (802-258-4957), Municipal Building, 230 Main St., Brattleboro, VT. Estey organs, historic photographs and voice recordings, and a walking tour brochure. Thurs. 1 p.m.-4 p.m., Sat. 9 a.m.-noon.

Brattleboro Museum & Art Center (802-257-0124), Union Railroad Station, 10 Vernon St., Brattleboro, VT. Thurs.-Mon.

Estey Organ Museum (802-246-8366), Estey Organ Company factory complex, Engine House, 108 Birge St., Brattleboro, VT.

Fletcher Farm School for Arts and Crafts Craft Shop (802-228-8770), 611 Rte. 103 S, Ludlow, VT. Handcrafted items by local artisans include ceramics, glassware, textiles, jewelry, and silver. Mid-June-mid-Sept.; closed Mon.

Grafton Village Cheese Co. (800-472-3866 or 802-843-2210), 533 Townshend Rd., Grafton, and 400 Linden St., Brattleboro, VT.

Historical Society of Windham County (802-365-4148), Rte. 30, Newfane, VT. Memorial Day-Oct., Wed. – Sun. p.m.

Hot Glass Works (802-874-4436), 3819 Main St. (Rte. 30), Jamaica, VT. Husband and wife Hank and Toby have been glass artisans for 30 years, and their showroom is filled with decorative and functional items, from hand-blown vases to stained-glass windows.

Jamaica State Park (802-874-4600), Rte. 30, Jamaica, VT. Camping, picnicking, tubing, swimming. Late April-Columbus Day.

Retreat Petting Farm (257-2240), 350 Linden St., Brattleboro, VT. Memorial Day-Columbus Day, Wed.-Sat., Sun. p.m., and Mon. holidays.

Rockingham Meeting House (802-463-3941), Meeting House Rd., off Rte. 103, Rockingham, VT. July and Aug. Donation.

Townshend Lake Recreation Area (802-365-7703), off Rte. 30, Townshend, VT.

Townshend State Park (802-365-7500), off Rte. 30, Townshend, VT. Camping, swimming, day use area. Late May-Columbus Day.

Vermont Artisan Designs (802-257-7044), 106 Main St., Brattleboro, VT. Vermont's largest contemporary American crafts gallery.

off the drive

Harlow's Sugar House (802-387-5852), Rte. 5, Putney, VT. Sugar house has pick-your-own fruit; watch syrup being made in season. March-late Dec.

Santa's Land (802-387-5550), Rte. 5, Putney, VT. May-Christmas.

activities

Belle of Brattleboro (802-254-1263), Marina on Rte. 5. Scenic cruises on the Connecticut River.

Bellows Falls Opera House (802-463-4766), 7 The Square, Bellows Falls, VT. Movies Fri.-Tues. nights at the handsome old Opera House, and ticket prices are rock bottom. The bill of fare usually runs to family films – just the thing for rainy vacation nights.

Big Black Bear Shop at Mary Meyer Stuffed Toys (802-365-4160), 1 Teddy Bear Lane, Rte. 30, Townshend, VT.

Brattleboro Bicycle Shop (800-254-8644), 165 Main St., Brattleboro, VT. Bike rentals.

Brattleboro Music Center (802-257-4523), 38 Walnut St., Brattleboro, VT. New England Bach Festival, held Sept.-Oct. at Marlboro College, as well as concerts and festivals throughout the year.

Green Mountain Flyer (802-463-3069), Union Station, Bellows Falls, VT. Scenic train rides on vintage equipment (not steam) between Bellows Falls and Chester, VT. May-Oct. (Also special excursion schedule including "Polar Express" in Dec.)

Latchis Theater (246-1500), 58 Main St., Brattleboro, VT. 3 screens show art and commercial films every week.

The Original Newfane Flea Market (802-365-4000 or 802-365-7710), Rte. 30, Newfane, VT. Vermont's biggest -- up to 200 dealers offer antiques, collectibles, crafts, books, and even fresh garden produce. Sundays May-Oct.

Robb Family Farm (802-254-7664), 827 Ames Hill Rd., W. Brattleboro, VT. Dairy farm offers "A Day on the Farm," hayrides and sleigh rides, maple sugaring, and barn tours.

Tom and Sally's Handmade Chocolates (802-254-4200), Rte. 30, Brattleboro, VT. Fabulous candies, toffee ... even chocolate body paint. Factory tours ($) Mon.-Sat. 10 a.m.-2 p.m. (Call ahead)

Townshend Auction Gallery (802-365-4388), 683 Rte. 30, Townshend, VT. Southern Vermont's oldest auction house runs a busy schedule, auctioning everything from furniture to jewelry to antique clocks.

Vermont Canoe Touring Center (802-257-5008), Veterans Memorial Bridge, 451 Putney Rd. (Rte. 5), Brattleboro, VT. Canoe and kayak rental; guided river trips.

Vermont Jazz Center (802-254-9088), 72 Cotton Mill Hill, Brattleboro, VT. Concerts and weekly jams.

off the drive

Marlboro Music Festival (802-254-2394), Parsons Auditorium, Marlboro College, Marlboro, VT. Musicians from around the world perform a 5-week chamber music concert series. Fri.-Sun. mid-July - mid-Aug. Advance tickets: 135 South 18th St., Philadelphia, Pa. 19103 (215) 569-4690). Tickets often available at door.

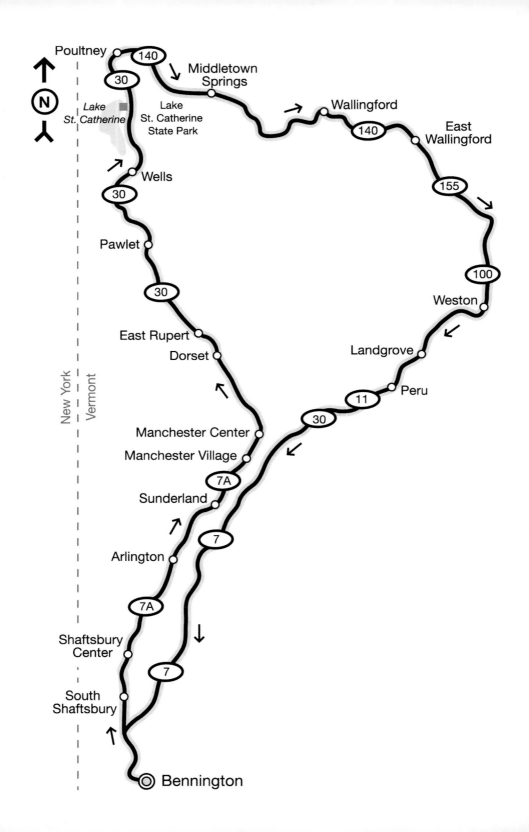

Drive 2

Bennington, Manchester, and the Valleys and Villages of Southwestern Vermont

137 miles

major attractions

- Bennington Battle Monument
- Bennington Museum
- Manchester Outlet Stores
- Hildene

- The Equinox
- The Orvis Company
- Weston
- Vermont Country Store

Starting in Bennington, a town steeped in early Vermont history, this drive follows a route between the Taconic and Green mountains to reach Manchester, one of the state's original resorts and today a lively retail outlet hub. The next portion of the drive takes in the scenic – and still heavily agricultural – Mettawee valley, before turning east into the Greens and the handsomely preserved village of Weston, home of distinguished summer theater and a country store that's become famous throughout America.

Begin the drive in Bennington, a town that looms large in Vermont's history as the site of a battle that actually took place somewhere else. The Battle of

Bennington, an engagement fought between British and American forces on August 16, 1777, happened just across the border in Walloomsac, New York. But "Battle of Walloomsac" lacks that fine alliterative ring – and besides, the Vermont town has the **Bennington Battle Monument**.

The granite obelisk erected in 1891 is still, at 306 feet, the tallest structure in Vermont. It commemorates the American victory over a British force that was attempting to seize a cache of military supplies at Bennington. "There are the Redcoats. Today they are ours or Molly Stark's a widow" was the exhortation supposedly uttered by Colonel (later General) John Stark, who had led a detachment of New Hampshiremen to Bennington over what is now called the Molly Stark Trail (Route 9).

Among the other American fighters that day were members of an informal local militia called the Green Mountain Boys, who along with their leader, Ethan Allen, had already struggled to secure Vermont's independence from the would-be enforcers of New York land claims. Bennington's Catamount Tavern (no longer standing: a marker on Monument Avenue indicates the site) was the Boys' frequent meeting place.

The Battle Monument and Catamount Tavern site are in the part of town called Old Bennington, a National Register Historic District. This neighborhood's most architecturally distinctive structure is the Old First Church (First Congregational Church), built in 1806. It's a graceful, late-Georgian gem with exquisite Palladian windows and one of the two or three finest steeples in the state. Its adjacent burial ground contains the graves of five Vermont governors as well as that of poet Robert Frost.

> *Robert Frost's gravestone is inscribed with a line of his verse, "I had a lover's quarrel with the world."*

In addition to its connections with the birth of Vermont and the struggle for American independence, Bennington has links to two other proud traditions: liberal education and hand-made pottery. Bennington College, founded in 1932, occupies a bucolic campus on the outskirts of town, and has long been noted for its writing, modern languages, and performing arts programs. And **Bennington Potters** represents the modern revival of an old-time local industry; its high-quality stoneware is renowned for its solid simplicity. The trigger mug – two finger holes in the handle – is a signature Bennington design. **Bennington Potters Yard** (see "Attractions" below) has an excellent selection.

Bennington pottery, along with many other examples of regional art and artisanship, make up the collection of the **Bennington Museum**. The museum possesses the largest public collection of Grandma Moses paintings; landscapes and portraits by lesser-known local artists; and local furniture and glassware. The "Grandma Moses schoolhouse" is the actual country school attended by Anna Mary Moses, nee Robertson, in the 1860s; it was moved here from its original site just over the border in New York State. Also among the exhibits are the Bennington-made Wasp, the only automobile ever produced in Vermont, and a flag carried at the Battle of Bennington that is believed to be the oldest surviving example of the Stars-and-Stripes design.

along the valley of Vermont . . . .

Head north out of town on Route 7A, following the Valley of Vermont that separates the Taconic from the Green mountains, to the Shaftsburys, which were settled in the 1760s by emigrants from Rhode Island and Connecticut. In 1920 Robert Frost bought the c. 1769 Stone House, on Route 7A in **South Shaftsbury**. It was here that he wrote the poem "New Hampshire," with its concluding line, "At present I am living in Vermont," as well as "Stopping by Woods on a Snowy Evening," referred to by the poet as "my best bid for remembrance. " The Friends of Robert Frost bought the house and opened it as the **Robert Frost Stone House Museum**, with one floor dedicated to the poet, and another to changing exhibits. Daily poetry readings are scheduled for 2:00 p.m. in season. Woodcuts by J.J. Lanke, who did much of the art for Frost's books, are also on exhibit.

In **Center Shaftsbury** the 1846 Greek Revival **Baptist Meeting House**, still in use today, houses the Shaftsbury Historical Society's collection of more than 6,000 artifacts, including tools used by the Eagle Square Manufacturing Company, makers of the first steel carpenters' tools. The village was home to Revolutionary War Captain Jonas Galusha, who served nine terms as governor of Vermont. His handsome white colonial home, with its unique trinity window above the entrance, still stands in the village.

The beach at twenty-six-acre Lake **Shaftsbury State Park** *is a delightful spot for cooling off on a hot summer day. There are boat rentals and a picnic area.*

Arlington stands alongside the Batten Kill (sometimes spelled "Battenkill," a legendary trout stream ("kill" is Dutch for stream or small river; this is its only use in Vermont and shows the influence of nearby Dutch-settled New York). Located between the Taconic Range and the Green Mountains, Arlington has been home to many noteworthy Vermonters. The town's early history differed from other Vermont communities in that it was shaped not by typical New England Calvinism, but by the more liberal precepts of the Anglican Church. This religious anglophilia was, during Revolutionary days, accompanied by a Tory bent in politics – the town was in fact known as Tory Hollow in the early 1770s.

Nevertheless, Arlington loomed large in the affairs of the 1777-1791 Independent Republic of Vermont, as it was the home of the first governor, Thomas Chittenden, who, after election, opened his office and conducted affairs of state from here. The renovated 1759 home of Ira Allen (Ethan's brother), on the shores of the Batten Kill, is a state historic site and now **The Ira Allen House** – a lovely B&B.

Arlington has been home to numerous artists and writers over the years. Writer Dorothy Canfield Fisher's family lived in the red brick building that housed Vermont's first medical school, which opened in 1790 (corner of Route 7A and Fisher Road). Mrs. Fisher lived in a home on Arlington's green for many years, and loved Vermont and its people. Among her more than fifty books was *Vermont Tradition, The Biography of an Outlook of Life.* Mrs. Fisher's home is now the **Martha Canfield Library**.

Arlington was also home to two famous artists named Rockwell: Rockwell Kent, who drew inspiration for many of his works from the woods of nearby Red Mountain; and Norman Rockwell, who lived here from 1939 to 1953 and used many of the townspeople as models for his illustrations. One of his most famous was of country doctor George A. Russell, an Arlington resident from 1879 to 1968. His extensive collection of books, letters, photographs and other mementos is preserved at the **Dr. George A. Russell Collection of Vermontiana** in the library. Many of Rockwell's Saturday Evening Post covers and other works are displayed in the **Norman Rockwell Exhibition and Gift Shop**.

Although the present St. James Episcopal Church dates to 1829, the first church was built here in 1787, and the walled cemetery is one of the state's oldest. Among those interred here is Ethan Allen's first wife, Mary Brownson (his second wife, Fanny, is buried in Elmwood Cemetery in Burlington, while Ethan himself lies in Burlington's Greenmount Cemetery.)

Side Trip

Turn left onto Rte. 313 and follow alongside the Batten Kill River to **West Arlington**, home to the 1852 West Arlington Covered Bridge (a great place for a dip) and the **Inn on Covered Bridge Green**, Mr. Rockwell's last Vermont home. Ethan Allen mustered his Green Mountain Boys on the Green across from the inn.

Continue north on Route 7A. About four miles from Arlington, turn left to climb 3,816-foot **Mount Equinox** via five-mile **Skyline Drive** ($). Much of Mount Equinox is owned by an order of Carthusian monks, whose monastery is visible from the top of Skyline Drive. There are also hiking trails to the summit, and a web of short and scenic trails to follow once you get up there.

Back on Route 7A, continue north a few miles to **Hildene**. In the summer of 1863, Abraham Lincoln's son, Robert Todd, first visited The Equinox Resort (see below) with his mother, Mary Todd. Forty years later, after he had made his money in the railroad car industry, he purchased land on the outskirts of Manchester Village and built a summer home. Lincoln, and afterwards his descendants, lived in the twenty-four-room Georgian Revival mansion until 1975.

Since then the home has been preserved, complete with many of the Lincoln family's furnishings and possessions. Visitors are treated to a concert played on the 1,000-pipe Aeolian organ, installed in 1908. The formal gardens, with many of their original plantings, are a favorite part of the tour. Guests are invited to enjoy a picnic and/or take a walk on one of the trails that crisscross the 412-acre estate. Hildene is sumptuously decorated for Christmas, and the cross-country ski trails are open all winter.

It's not surprising that The Equinox, which first opened its doors to guests in 1769, should have a few ghosts lurking about. But Mary Todd, the wife of Abraham Lincoln? She and her children spent two summers here, and had planned to return in 1865, but changed their plans when the president was assassinated. Some speculate that Mrs. Lincoln's shade may be trying to recreate happier times.

Just a bit farther to the north, **Manchester Village**, in the shadow of Mount Equinox, is one of Vermont's earliest summer resort towns and an architectural gem: beautifully-preserved colonial and early Federal period buildings line the shade-dappled main street (Route 7A), which is flanked by sidewalks made of marble slabs. Manchester Village's premier resort, **The Equinox Resort**, has hosted luminaries such as Ulysses S. Grant and Theodore Roosevelt. Ethan Allen and the Green Mountain boys met here to plan Vermont's independence.

The landmark hostelry – a 19th-century successor to earlier inn structures – is characterized by a long, colonnaded veranda. Guinness, the brewing titan that purchased the inn in the 1980s, has renovated the Equinox's superb golf course, and introduced programs such as The British School of Falconry and the Land Rover Driving School.

In 1993 The Equinox bequeathed 850 acres of land on Mount Equinox to the Vermont Land Trust, so the tract could be kept "forever green." The preserve, which abuts the resort, is a wonderful spot for taking a short walk or a vigorous hike. It's supervised by the Vermont Institute of Natural Science (see Drive 3), which offers natural history programs. If you've only time for a quick stroll, the gentle 1.2-mile loop around Equinox Pond is ideal.

fly fishing, fine art, and factory outlets . . . .

Before continuing north on Route 7A, take West Road out of the center of Manchester Village and follow signs up the long, winding drive to the **Southern Vermont Art Center.** The twenty-eight-room Georgian revival mansion on a slope of Mt. Equinox was built in 1917 as a summer home, and has been an art center since the 1950s. Contemporary and near-contemporary works (many for sale) by local artists are displayed in ten galleries and in an outdoor sculpture garden. The 400-seat Arkell Pavilion hosts concerts, lectures and theatrical performances. The Café serves lunch, and dinner on performance nights. The Manchester Music Festival performs here Thursday evenings in season.

Return to Manchester Village and take Route 7A north to **Manchester** (sometimes called Manchester Center). In its early days, it was a bustling mill town called Factory Point.

The **Charles F. Orvis Company,** which began making bamboo fishing rods in 1856 and became the country's first mail order company, has a strong presence in the area to this day. Its 23,000-square foot flagship store, billed as "Vermont's largest retail attraction," features indoor and outdoor trout ponds and houses the world's largest rod shop. It's the place to outfit yourself for a stylish safari – or to splurge on a superbly balanced fly rod crafted of the finest Tonkin cane, which you can try out on Orvis's own casting pond. If you want to learn from the folks who wrote the book, the Orvis Fly Fishing School runs 2 1/2-day schools twice a week from April through early October. An upland game-shooting course is also offered. (There's an Orvis **Outlet Store** just up the road at 4382 Main Street.)

Many Orvis artifacts, along with a huge collection of other memorabilia, are on exhibit at the nearby American Museum of Fly Fishing, which documents the evolution of the sport.

Manchester has also become legendary for another industry: outlet shopping. Big-name retailers including Giorgio Armani, Brooks Brothers, Ralph Lauren, J. Crew, and Burberry sell discounted merchandise in chic shops that line the main road. Take time, though, to look beyond the outlets: Manchester's Main Street looks much as it did 100 years ago, except for the names of the businesses. There are some handsome old buildings: the mansard-roofed **Northshire Bookstore** – Vermont's largest independent book and music seller, with used and antiquarian volumes in its Next Chapter annex – occupies the 1872 Colburn House, once Manchester Center's main hotel.

Head north out of Manchester on Route 30 as designer outlets quickly give way to rolling farmland. Watch for the **H.N. Williams Store,** a classic general store that began as a harness shop in 1840. It has been a family run business for six generations.

Upscale **Dorset,** which received its charter in 1761, was at one time a major trading place for farmers throughout this corner of Vermont. The country's first marble quarry was opened here in 1785, and supplied marble for New York City's Public Library. In 1776, at the first convention of the New Hampshire Grants in the now-defunct Cephas Kent's Tavern on the main street (Route 30), the Green Mountain Boys declared Vermont an independent state. The **Dorset Inn**, a National Historic Site on the town's trim little green, opened its door to travelers just twenty years later, and is the state's oldest continuously operating hostelry. The entire village is on the National Register of Historic Places.

Be sure to stop at the United Church of Dorset, constructed of Dorset marble. The stained glass windows portray scenes of the surrounding valley. A professional acting troupe performs at the Dorset Playhouse, one of Vermont's oldest summer theaters.

the lovely Mettawee Valley.........................

Continue north on Route 30 to East Rupert. It was near here, in 1785, that Reuben Harmon minted the first copper coins for the Republic of Vermont. If you ever see a coin with the inscription, *Vermontensium Res Publica 1786,* snap it up: Reuben isn't making them any more.

Between East Rupert and Pawlet, Route 30 follows the Mettawee River. The river, which first comes into view at a state-maintained access area about a mile north of East Rupert (right) and dodges back and forth from one side of the road to the other, drains a valley that is home to some of Vermont's most picturesque dairy farms. Much of this agricultural land is legally preserved – many local farmers have arranged conservation easements through the Vermont Land Trust, assuring that their acres will never be developed.

Pawlet is a quiet village with memories of an industrial past; the Mettawee and its tributary, Flower Brook, once turned the wheels of local commerce. Over the years, once-workaday Pawlet has metamorphosed into one of Vermont's prettiest hamlets. The main street (Route 30) is lined with art galleries and craft studios. But don't let their allure keep you from stopping in at **Machs' Market and Brick-Oven Bakery**. The rambling old emporium (it carries everything from eye drops to eye bolts) extends out over Flower Brook, and that gave original owner Johnny Mach an idea. He installed a viewing window in an elevated platform in one of the store aisles, and to this day visitors can look down at water raging through a dramatic rock formation some fifty feet below.

Side Trip

For one last look at the Mettawee River (it's bound for New York State, where it empties into the Champlain Canal), turn left onto Button Falls Road between North Pawlet and

Wells. Go down a few hundred yards and park at the bridge, where the river plunges through a series of rapids in a deep, stone-walled gorge.

Continue north on Route 30 through tiny **Wells**, in the shadow of the Taconic Mountains. Little Pond at the south end of town is actually the southernmost portion of Lake St. Catherine. A few miles ahead is the entrance to **Lake St. Catherine State Park**, on the 930-acre lake. There's a pleasant little sand beach here, as well as rowboat rentals – just the ticket for anglers, as the lake teems with large- and smallmouth bass, yellow perch, and lake and rainbow trout.

Poultney was settled in 1771 by Ethan Allen's cousins and his brother Heber. For many years the town's primary industry was slate, and today many of the quarries are once again open for business. Take a stroll down Main Street, a National Register thoroughfare that ends at the campus lawns and trim brick buildings of Green Mountain College, founded in 1836 by the Methodist Episcopal Church, but today a secular institution.

From Poultney, take Route 140 east to **East Poultney**, a tiny crossroads with a big history. During the late 1820s, New York Tribune founder Horace Greeley learned how to set type when he worked as a printer's devil at the *Poultney Gazette,* behind the elegant, 1805 Old Baptist Church on the town green. The fellow who apprenticed with him, a Poultney-born man named George Jones, went on to found *The New York Times* with Henry J. Raymond in 1851.

Greeley boarded for several years at the Eagle Tavern (don't stop in for a drink; it's a private home), built circa 1790 as a stagecoach stop. The tavern is forty feet square, but is saved from having anything like a blunt, blocky appearance by the two-story columns that support the gently hipped roof and create a graceful portico on two sides. In his 1940 book *Old Vermont Houses,* Herbert Wheaton Congdon tells us: "When the frame of the building was raised the usual keg of rum was provided to refresh the workers, and there are hints in the architecture that it was frequently refilled." Among the evidence Congdon cites for his conclusion is the fact that of the twelve columns, "... no two are the same distance apart." You can't miss the place – it's yellow, and stands right on the green. Right nearby is the East Poultney General Store, as genuine as its name and a good place to stock up on picnic provisions. Also near the green is the Old Cemetery, where Heber Allen is buried.

The **Poultney Historical Society** owns three historic buildings on the green: the Victorian Schoolhouse (1896), the Union Academy (1791), and the Melodeon Factory, which during the middle of the 19th century was the largest manufacturer of melodeons outside Boston or New York. Since 1954 it has served as the Society's museum.

a long-ago spa

Continue east on Route 140, following the Poultney River to **Middletown Springs**. It was in the 1770s that Native Americans first told settlers that mineral springs here had restorative powers. More than 100 years later, hordes of health-conscious tourists were flocking to the springs to partake of the iron- and sulfur-laden waters. A family of local entrepreneurs named Gray built an ornate hotel – the Montvert – near the springs to accommodate 250 guests, and then began to bottle and sell their natural elixir. They eventually sold the operation to an out-of-state group, which dismantled the hotel in 1906 when people lost interest in "taking the waters." Then, in 1927, a flood covered the springs under a mound of gravel and dirt.

The Grays were more than hotel keepers and bottlers. A.W. Gray invented "horsepowers," treadmills on which horses walked to run machines that cut corn and sawed wood (smaller animals were hitched up to accomplish smaller jobs). But the advent of gasoline engines slashed the demand for horsepowers, and the factory closed just before World War I.

Today, a core group of Middletown boosters is working hard to breathe new life into the old resort. The springs have been uncovered, and visitors can once again sample the waters at a replica of a Victorian springhouse at Mineral Springs Park. The town's fascinating history is recounted at the **Historical Society Museum** on the green.

Continue east on Route 140 through a sparsely populated region to the tiny village of Tinmouth, where, in the early 1800s, furnaces and forges processed iron. A few miles ahead, on the right, is a turnoff for small Elfin Lake, where there is a swimming beach. Just ahead is **Wallingford**, the childhood home of Paul Harris, founder of Rotary International. The town also has a long history in the hand tool business: Lyman Batcheller started a garden tool factory here in 1836; its modern outgrowth is a branch manufacturing plant of True-Temper.

Stay on Route 140 as it passes through the intersection with Route 7 at the center of Wallingford. Leaving town, the road twists and climbs, soon passing (right) the access for **White Rocks National Recreation Area** in the Green Mountain National Forest. A trail here leads to a treeless mountainside where well-shaded rock formations hold ice throughout the summer months. Just beyond the White Rocks access road, the Long Trail, Vermont's "Footpath in the Wilderness," crosses Route 140.

At the hamlet of East Wallingford, **turn right to head south on Route 155.** Tarbellville Road, on the left a few miles down, takes a quick jog to the pretty little village of Belmont, where you can pick up supplies at the general store and picnic alongside lovely Star Lake, where a dam powered a sawmill as early as 1790.

Stay on Route 155 until it ends at Route 100, and continue south on 100. An access road for the national forest's Greendale Recreation Area, with primitive campsites, is on the right, and soon after, also right, is the turnoff for the **Weston Priory**, a small Benedictine monastery. The brothers welcome visitors to their daily services, which include a lovely sung liturgy. A gift shop on the premises sells handmade items and products from the priory farm.

Weston was one of the first Vermont towns to trade on its beautiful location, serene atmosphere, and architectural harmony. Writer Vrest Orton, a Vermont native who fondly recalled the general stores of his youth, helped put the town on the map in the late 1940s when he opened the **Vermont Country Store**, although by that time outsiders already had been drawn here for more than a decade to attend performances at the **Weston Playhouse**, one of America's oldest summer theaters. Today the town – with its cast-iron-fenced green, Victorian bandstand, historic homes, and interesting assortment of shops – is one of Vermont's most popular tourist destinations. With murals (done by WPA artists) and artfully arranged exhibits, curators at the restored **Farrar-Mansur House**, built as a tavern in 1797, recapture life in a Vermont community two centuries ago. The **Kinhaven Music School**, perched on a hill outside of town, offers free concerts on summer weekends. And, of course, the Vermont Country Store carries on its mission of offering sturdy clothing, hard-to-find practical items (many of which you thought they'd stopped making years ago), an astounding variety of penny candy, and a full line of Vermont edibles (lots of samples).

It was in Weston, on November 10, 1774 – twenty months before the issue was taken up by the Continental Congress in Philadelphia – that local citizens issued a Declaration of Independence stating that "all the acts of the British Parliament tending to take away Rights of Freedom ought not to be obeyed."

a village reborn

Turn right just after the Weston Town Green onto Lawrence Hill Road to head out of town towards Landgrove, making sure to bear left at the fork onto Landgrove Road just ahead. The road skirts the Green Mountain National Forest, soon arriving in a village that was literally brought back from oblivion. **Landgrove** was a typical busy hill town of the nineteenth century, surrounded by small farms; by the 1930s, though, it was all but a ghost town. Enter Sam Ogden, who in the depths of the Depression bought most of the houses in the core village for about $6,000, and began a one-man restoration program. Ogden sold off the houses as he fixed them up, and Landgrove was reborn.

After passing through "downtown" Landgrove (don't expect to encounter any businesses, other than the **Landgrove Inn**), **turn right onto on Hapgood Pond Road**, which leads (left) past the **Hapgood Pond Recreation Area** entrance. The area features a pleasant swimming beach, and a nature walk around the pond. Continue on Hapgood Pond Road into the village of **Peru**. At the village green (church on your right; general store straight ahead), **turn right to reach Route 11 and bear right (west) on 11.** Route 11 passes **Bromley Mountain**, one of Vermont's oldest ski areas. Gravity also works here in the summer: At the Thrill Zone are America's longest alpine slide, the Northeast's only Parabounce, The Trampoline Thing, scenic chairlift rides, miniature golf, and a climbing wall.

As you head west on Route 11, you're looking directly ahead at Mt. Equinox; off to your left, across the valley, you can see the trails of Stratton Mountain, another huge ski resort. **Follow Route 11 into Manchester Depot and pick up Route 7 south**, the limited-access alternative to Route 7A that will take you south back to Bennington.

information *All area codes are (802) unless otherwise indicated.*

Bennington Area Chamber of Commerce (447-3311), 100 Veterans Memorial Dr., Bennington 05201. bennington.com

Dorset Area Chamber of Commerce (867-2450), P.O. Box 121, Rte. 30, Dorset 05251. dorsetvt.com

Manchester & the Mountains Regional Chamber of Commerce (362-2100), Rte. 7A N., Manchester Center 05255. manchestervermont.net

Poultney Area Chamber of Commerce (287-2010), P.O. Box 151, 63 Main St., Poultney 05764. poultneyvt.com

lodging

Alexandra B&B Inn (802-442-5619), 916 Orchard Rd., Bennington 05201. Luxury and comfort are hallmarks of this handsomely landscaped inn with 6 spacious rooms in the main house and 6 in a recent addition. All have a/c and TV, some have fireplaces. A 4-course, prix fixe dinner is served to guests by reservation. Breakfast is included. $$-$$$

The Arlington Inn (802- 375-6532), Rte. 7A, Arlington 05250. Antiques-filled 1848 Greek Revival mansion has 5 rooms in the main house, 6in the carriage house, and 6 in the Old Parsonage. Dinner ($$$-$$$) in the elegant dining room might include grilled filet mignon or pan-fried rainbow trout. B&B and MAP available. arlingtoninn.com $$-$$$$

The Aspen (802-362-2450), Rte. 7A N, PO Box 548, Manchester Center 05255. Modern, clean, and comfortable motel with colonial furnishings set on spacious grounds well back from the busy highway. 22 units and several housekeeping cottages perfect for families. Outdoor pool. theaspenatmanchester.com $-$$

Barrows House (867-4455), Rte. 30, Dorset 05251. Small, laid-back resort on 11 acres in the heart of the Historic District has 28 classic rooms on the second floor of the 1804 main inn and more luxurious accommodations in 8 historic outer buildings. Tennis courts, outdoor pool, sauna, and bicycles. Dishes such as crab cakes and roast duck are served in the historic dining room ($$-$$$$) as well as the cozy tavern. barrows-house.com $$$

The Bentley House (287-4004), 399 Bentley Ave., Poultney 05764. 1895 Queen Anne Victorian across from Green Mountain College has 4 antiques-filled guest rooms with private baths, and a guest kitchen. bentleyhouse.com $$

Bromley Mountain Resort (824-5522), Box 1130, Manchester Center 05255. Fully equipped slopeside condominiums. Two-night minimum. bromley.com $

Colonial House Inn & Motel (824-6286), 287 Rte. 100, Weston, VT 05161. Comfortable, family-friendly property has 9 motel units and 6 rooms with shared baths in the inn. Game room. Full breakfast; dinner available weekends. Pets welcome in motel. cohoinn.com $-$$

Dorset Inn (867-5500), Church St. (Rte. 30), Dorset 05251. Country charm and sophistication mesh nicely at Vermont's oldest continuously operating inn, a National Register of Historic Places property established in 1796. The award-winning dining room ($$-$$$), a member of the Vermont Slow Food Network, specializes in comfort food, with specialties including turkey croquettes, and mushroom and broccoli pasta. Tavern menu. Pets welcome. dorsetinn.com $$-$$$

The Equinox Resort & Spa (362-1595), Rte. 7A, Manchester Village 05254. Landmark historic resort with 195 rooms in 4 unique buildings. Fitness center and spa, indoor and outdoor pools, stocked trout pond, tennis court, and 18-hole golf course. Sunday brunch in the formal Colonnade dining room is a local tradition. Hungry? Tuck into the 24-ounce porterhouse at The Chop House ($$$$). equinoxresort.com $$$

The Four Chimneys Inn & Restaurant (802-447-3500), 21 West Rd. (Rte. 9), Old Bennington 05201. Beautifully restored, 1910 Colonial Revival home has 11 elegant rooms with some fireplaces and/or Jacuzzis. Continental fare in the elegant dining room, with entrees such as crispy seared duck breast, and mushroom and leek risotto. Breakfast included. fourchimneys.com $$-$$$

Hillbrook Motel (447-7201), Rte. 7A, Shaftsbury. 16 nicely appointed ground-level units (4 efficiencies) on 5 acres set well back from highway; pool, picnic area. All rooms have refrigerators and microwaves. Pets welcome ($). $

Inn at West View Farm (867-5715), Rte. 30, Dorset 05251. Romantic full service inn in an 1870 farmhouse has 10 guest rooms with 4-poster beds and sitting rooms (some with fireplace; 1 with TV; none with phones). The restaurant serves American cuisine with French influences, with appetizers such as arborio-crusted sweetbreads, and entrees including sautéed skate. Breakfast included. innatwestviewfarm.com $$-$$$

The Inn at Weston (824-6789), Rte. 100, Weston, VT 05161. Romantic hideaway offers 13 guest rooms and 2 suites with some balconies, fireplaces, and 2-person whirlpools. Imaginative, contemporary regional fare ($$$) might feature an appetizer of tuna tartare with mango chutney, and an entree of grilled loin lamb chops with minted zucchini noodles. Extensive wine list. Lovely gardens; orchid-filled greenhouse. Children over 12. innweston.com $$-$$$$

Inn on Covered Bridge Green (375-9489), 3587 River Rd., Arlington 05250. The one time home of Norman Rockwell is right on the Batenkill River. There are 6 rooms (4 with fireplaces and spa tubs), and two cottages. The Norman Rockwell studio is in a private setting and has 2 bedrooms; the Honeymoon Cottage sleeps 2. coveredbridgegreen.com $$-$$$

The Ira Allen House (362-2284), Rte. 7A, Arlington 05250. One of Vermont's oldest inns, a State Historic Site, was built by Revolutionary War heroes Ethan and Ira Allen. An addition was built in 1846. The 5 guest suites are spacious and several are perfect for families. The inn is on the Batten Kill River, and ½ mile south of Skyline Drive. iraallen.com $$-$$$.

Landgrove Inn (824-6673), Landgrove 05158. Red clapboard, family-oriented country inn built in 1810 has 18 rooms with air conditioning, antique colonial furnishings; all but 2 have private baths. Facilities include a heated pool, tennis, trout pond, hiking trails, and horse-drawn sleigh and hay rides. Specialties in the candlelit dining room, open Wed-Sun, ($$) include grilled pork tenderloin and rack of lamb. landgroveinn.com $-$$$

Palmer House Resort Motel (362-3600), Rte. 7A, Manchester Center 05255. 22-acre resort has spacious and well-equipped rooms; facilities include a 9-hole, par-3 executive golf course, indoor lap pool, outdoor pool, tennis courts, and a stocked trout pond. New England favorites are specialties at the adjacent Ye Olde Tavern ($$-$$$). Continental breakfast included. palmerhouse.com $-$$$

Paradise Inn (442-8351), 141 W. Main St., Bennington 05201. Well off the highway, there are 77 nicely appointed rooms and suites, some with private balconies and Jacuzzis. Outdoor pool, tennis, fitness room, and laundry. vermontparadiseinn.com $-$$$

Reluctant Panther Inn & Restaurant (362-2568), West Rd., Manchester Village 05254. Superb accommodations and gourmet fare make the inn – along with several adjacent buildings – one of the area's most popular. Rooms and suites are spacious and luxurious; several have sitting rooms, two fireplaces, and private entrances. Regional American fare ($$$-$$$$) is served in the candlelit restaurant, and the pub. reluctantpanther.com $$$-$$$$

West Mountain Inn (375-6516), River Rd., Rte. 313, Arlington 05250. Country elegance is the hallmark of this inn/llama ranch on 150 acres. Rooms in the main inn, cottage, and renovated mill are antiques-filled and luxurious (some have fireplaces and private porches). A 5-course, prix fixe ($$$) dinner by candlelight might include pistachio-encrusted pork medallions or lamb ragout. Breakfast included. westmountaininn.com $$$-$$$$

White Rocks Inn (446-2077), Rte. 7, Wallingford 05773. National Register of Historic Places property, a Greek Revival farmhouse built in 1845, has 5 antiques-filled guest rooms and 2 secluded housekeeping cottages. All have gas fireplaces and air conditioning; the cottages have TVs and whirlpool or spa tubs. Full breakfast. whiterocksinn.com $$-$$$

restaurants

Alldays & Onions (447-0043), 519 Main St., Bennington. A casual, family-friendly spot in town features "create your own" sandwiches at lunch (Mon.-Sat.); and a dinner menu of American favorites such as roast turkey, as well as creative fish and pasta dishes. B Sat.; Brunch Sun.; D Thurs.-Sat. Children's menu. $$

The Barn Restaurant & Tavern (325-3088), Rte. 30, Pawlet. A cheerful and family-friendly spot with solid American fare, including hand cut steaks and burgers, as well as a tavern menu ($). Chicken Mettowee is a house classic. D. $$-$$$

Bistro Henry (362-4982), 1942 Route 11/30, Manchester. An eclectic menu and award-winning cuisine have made this bistro an area hot spot. The menu has a Mediterranean flair with southern French and Northern Italian highlights, with house specials such as Merlot braised lamb shank, and a bevy of fabulous fresh baked desserts. D; June-Oct, Tues.-Sun., Nov.-Apr., Tues-Sat. $$$-$$$$

Blue Benn Diner (442-5140), Rte. 7N, Bennington. Breakfast (killer berry pancakes) and sandwiches are served all day in this landmark 1940s Silk City diner; there may be long weekend waits for tables, but there's usually space at the counter. B & L, Mon., Tues., Sat. and Sun.; B, L, & D Wed.-Fri. $

The Bryant House Restaurant (824-6287), next to Vermont Country Store, Rte. 100, Weston. Traditional New England dishes, afternoon tea; sandwiches and homemade pies. Crackers and milk with Vermont cheddar – where else? L Mon.-Sat.; "supper" Fri.-Sat. $-$$

Café at the Falls (824-5288), Weston Playhouse, on the Green, Weston. Bistro cuisine served overlooking a stream on theater nights. Reservations suggested. $$-$$$

Chantecleer (362-1616), Rte. 7A, East Dorset. Classic continental cuisine with an accent on Swiss specialties and tableside service in a renovated dairy barn. Among specialities: escargots, rack of lamb, and a fabulous selection of home baked desserts. Reservations. D Wed.-Sun. $$$-$$$$

Garden Café (366-8298), Southern Vermont Arts Center, 930 West Rd., Manchester. Salads, sandwiches, and desserts indoors or on the covered deck overlooking the lovely grounds. May, Thurs.-Sat., & Wed. weather permitting; June Tues.-Sat., July & Aug., Tues.-Sun., Sept. Tues.-Sat., & Sun. during foliage, weather permitting. Dinner on performance nights. $-$$

Jonathan's Table (375-1021), Rte. 7A, Arlington. Ask for a river view at this cozy, casual spot behind the Sugar Shack. House specialties include prime rib, veal, and seafood; the lobster ravioli and sautéed mushrooms are a hit, too. D Thurs.-Tues. $$-$$$

Little Rooster Café (362-3496), Route 7A South, Manchester Center. The corned beef hash alone hauls in patrons from near and far, but the hash browns with Vermont cheddar and the buttermilk pancakes are also terrific. B & D daily. $

Pangaea (442-7171), 1 Prospect St., North Bennington. Chef Bill Scully set out to create an upscale bistro that would rival any in New York City, and has, by all accounts, succeeded admirably. Offerings such as seared diver scallops, Thai green curry stir fry, and steak pommes frites are handled deftly, and the wine list is superb. The outdoor terrace is a delight; lighter fare is served in the lounge. D Tues-Sat. $$$

Perry's Main Street Eatery (287-5188), 18 Main St., Poultney. Solid diner fare, with tasty sandwiches (try the Perry burger), daily specials, and Sat. prime rib. B, L, & D (closes 2 PM Sun.) $-$$

Up for Breakfast (362-4204), 710 Main St., Rte. 7A, Manchester. One of the area's most popular breakfast spots serves creative omelettes, homemade hash, and baked goodies. B & L. $

attractions

American Museum of Fly Fishing (362-3300), 4104 Main St. (Rte. 7A), Manchester. Houses the world's largest collection of angling and angling-related items, and documents the evolution of the sport. Tues.-Sun.

Baptist Meeting House, Shaftsbury Historical Society Museum (447-7488), Center Shaftsbury. Mid-June-mid-Oct. Tues.-Sun.

Bennington Battle Monument (447-0550), 15 Monument Ave., Bennington. Elevator. Mid-April-late Oct.

Bennington Museum (447-1571), 75 Main St. (Rte. 9), Bennington. Open Thurs.-Tues.; daily Sept. & Oct.

Bennington Potters Yard (800-205-8033 or 447-7531), 324 County St., Bennington. First-quality and seconds; self-guided walking tours.

The Dr. George A. Russell Collection of Vermontiana (375-6307), Martha Canfield Public Library, Arlington. Call for hrs.

Farrar-Mansur House (824-8190), Village Green, Weston. June-mid-Oct. daily 1 p.m.-5 p.m.

Gallery Northstar (362-4541), Rte. 7A, Manchester Village. Regional artists' works are exhibited in one of Vermont's oldest art galleries.

Hapgood Recreation Area (362-2307) Mount Tabor Rd., Peru. Camping, swimming, boating, hiking trails.

Hildene (362-1788), Rte. 7A South, Manchester Village. Mid-May-Oct., 1-hour guided tours every half hour.

H.N. Williams Store (867-5353), 2732 Rte. 30, Dorset.

Lake St. Catherine State Park (287-9158), Poultney. Swimming, fishing, camping, boat rental. Mid- May- Columbus Day.

Lake Shaftsbury State Park (375-9978), Rte. 7A. Swimming, nature trail, boat and canoe rental. Late May-Labor Day.

Middletown Springs Historical Society Museum, on the Green, Middletown Springs. Memorial Day-Oct. Sun. p.m.

Norman Rockwell Exhibition (375-6423), Rte. 7A, Arlington. In an 1800s church.

Old First Church, Church St. and Monument Ave., Bennington.

The Orvis Store (362-3750), 4180 Main St. (Rte. 7A), Manchester.

Park-McCullough House (442-5441), Cor. Park and West sts., North Bennington. Mid- May-mid Oct. Tours on the hour.

Poultney Historical Society (287-5252), East Poultney Town Green. Memorial Day-Labor Day 1-4 p.m. and by appointment.

Robert Frost Stone House Museum (447-6200), Historic Rte. 7A, Shaftsbury. May-Dec., Tues.-Sun.

Skyline Drive (362-1114), Rte. 7 South, Manchester Village. May-Nov.

Southern Vermont Art Center (362-1405), West Rd., Manchester Village. Botany trail. Tues.-Sun.

Vermont Country Store (824-3184), Rte. 100, Weston; and Rte. 103, Rockingham (463-2224).

Weston Priory (824-5409), Rte. 100, Weston.

activities

Bromley Mountain Thrill Zone (824-5522), Rte. 11, Peru. Late May-mid-June, weekends; mid-June-Labor Day, daily; after Labor Day-Columbus Day, weekends.

Battenkill Anglers (362-3184), Rte .7A, Manchester. Thomas & Thomas sponsored fly fishing school; guide, instruction, and outfitter.

Battenkill Sports Cycle Shop (362-2734), jct. Rte. 7/ 30, Manchester Center. Mountain, hybrid and road bike rentals.

Battenkill Canoe Ltd. (362-2800), River Rd., Arlington. Day trips, rentals, instruction, and inn-to-inn tours.

Dorset Playhouse (867-5777), 104 Cheney Rd., Dorset. Schedule: dorsettheatrefestival.org

Horses for Hire (297-1468), 893 South Road, Peru. 1-hr. and ½-day trail rides; winter sleigh rides.

Kinhaven Music School (824-4332), 354 Lawrence Hill Rd., Weston. Free student concerts early July through mid-August: Fri. at 4 p.m.; faculty concerts Sat. at 8 p.m. Picnics welcome.

Manchester Music Festival (362-1956), West Rd., Manchester Center. Tickets sold at Northshire Bookstore, Manchester.

Northshire Bookstore (362-2200), 4869 Main St., Manchester.

Oldcastle Theatre Company (447-0564), Rte. 9 & Gypsy Lane, Bennington. Professional theater troupe performs at the Bennington Center for the Arts Theatre. Schedule: oldcastletheatreco.org

Sailing Winds Marina, Inc. (287-9411), Rte. 30, Lake St. Catherine. Sailboat, motorboat, bass boat, paddle boat, sailboards, and kayak rentals late June-Labor Day.

Weston Playhouse (824-5288), 703 Main St. (on the Green), Weston, VT. Schedule: westonplayhouse.org

White Rocks National Recreation Area (362-2307), Manchester Ranger District, Rte. 11/30, Manchester Center.

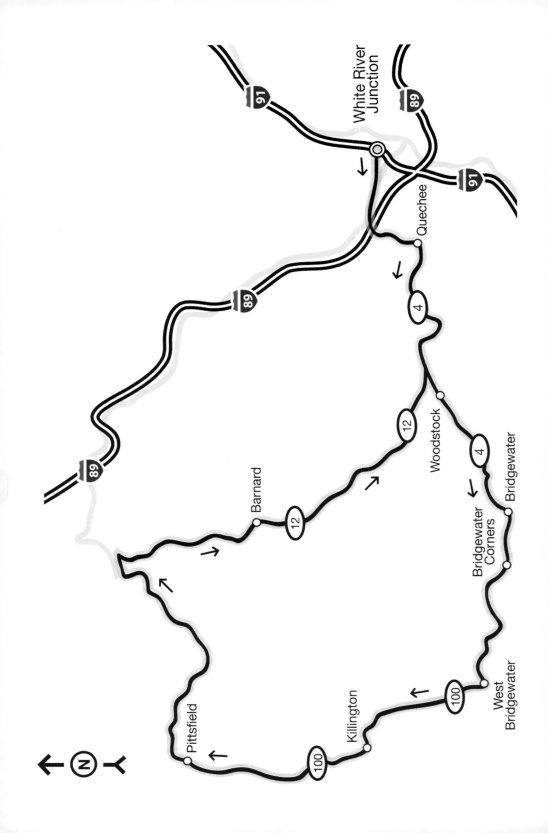

Drive 3

Woodstock, Route 100, and the White River Valley

80 miles

major attractions

- Quechee Gorge
- Billings Farm and Museum
- Killington Resort

- Marsh-Billings-Rockefeller National Park
- President Calvin Coolidge State Historic Site

*B*eginning at the rim of Vermont's deepest gorge, this drive takes in one of Vermont's most attractive small towns, and then continues westward to the village that forged the character of an upcountry Yankee who became president of the United States. After skirting the boundaries of the Green Mountain National Forest in the shadow of lofty Killington Peak, the route follows the swift-flowing White River before dropping south through gently rolling farmland.

(Note: If you're heading to the beginning of this drive from I-89, take exit #1 and head west on Route 4 toward Quechee and Woodstock.)

Begin in Quechee, where the dramatic **Quechee Gorge** was created by a glacier more than 13,000 years ago. As the ice receded, meltwater ate away at the bedrock, eventually carving out Vermont's "Little Grand Canyon." Today, the river that runs through the gorge is called the Ottauquechee, a Native American word meaning "swift mountain stream" or "cattails or rushes near a swift current." The Route 4 bridge over the gorge, built on the site of a former railroad bridge which was at one time the highest in the East, spans the river at a height of 165 feet. An easy 1 ½-mile round-trip hike into the gorge begins behind the gift shop near the **Quechee Gorge Recreation Area**. Maps are available at the Chamber of Commerce information booth near the gorge. If you're ready for a dip, this is the place to ask for directions to the great swimming hole at the west end of the bridge.

Follow signs into Quechee Village, where, throughout the 19th and well into the 20th century, the Ottauquechee supplied power for the large woolen mills that lined its banks. One of the mills, J.C. Parker & Co., produced some of the country's finest white baby flannel. Today the mill houses **Simon Pearce Glass**, which is using the river's power to keep its furnace roaring. Pearce, a glassmaker from Ireland, converted the abandoned mills into an attractive studio, retail operation and restaurant. Visitors can watch glass being blown daily.

Another Quechee attraction is the **Vermont Institute of Natural Science** (VINS), near the gorge on Route 4. Bald eagles, peregrine falcons, snowy owls, and more than 20 other raptor species live at the preserve, and there's a changing series of natural history exhibits and live animal programs daily in season.

Back on Route 4, continue west past Quechee Village and Quechee Gorge State Park to Taftsville, home of the 1840 Taftsville Country Store and the Taftsville Covered Bridge. The 1836 bridge, built at a cost of $1800 to link the villages of Quechee and Taftsville with communities and farms to the north and east, measures 189 feet and is one the state's oldest and longest. A bike path parallels River Road from the bridge to Woodstock village.

From Taftsville, stay on Route 4 for four miles to Woodstock, one of the handful of towns most frequently taken by outsiders – rightly or wrongly – to be emblematic of Vermont. What began as an unassuming village on the banks of the Ottauquechee has been a popular tourist destination since mineral springs first brought summer visitors in the late 1800s. Woodstock's next big boost came in 1934, when a group of skiers hobnobbing at a local inn started lamenting the fact that every run had to be preceded by an exhausting uphill climb. They built Vermont's first ski lift – a rope tow powered by an old Model T. Woodstock soon became a chic ski capital – a role in which it has long since been eclipsed by Killington and Stowe, but which is nicely commemorated in the final few feet of a mural in the downtown post office. The painting goes from Native Americans to settlers to schussboomers in one neat WPA sweep. (There's still skiing nearby, on the short but steep slopes of the **Woodstock Inn's** Suicide Six Resort.)

conservation and philanthropy

Woodstock boasts a disproportionate number of famous native sons. Sculptor Hiram Powers (1805-1873) garnered immense Victorian-era popularity via works such as *The Greek Slave*. George Perkins Marsh (1801-1882) was a congressman and diplomat whose landmark book *Man and Nature* was a founding text of the conservation movement; he also helped make the Smithsonian Institution a reality. Marsh's great admirer Frederick Billings, who made his fortune with the Northern Pacific Railroad, put the conservationist's principles to work in the reforestation of his Woodstock estate and the 1871 founding of his model farm, now the **Billings Farm and Museum**. Billings' operation continues as a working farm, as well as a museum of agriculture and rural life.

The skein of influence that began with Marsh continues into our own time with the recent establishment of **Marsh-Billings-Rockefeller National Park**, a 500-acre-plus tract on the outskirts of town. The property, Vermont's first and only national park, and the only park in the system to concentrate specifically on conservation, was the gift of the late Laurance Rockefeller. Rockefeller's wife, Mary, was Frederick Billings' granddaughter. For years a part-time Woodstock resident, the conservationist and resort developer counted among his properties the luxurious Woodstock Inn.

Park visitors can tour the mansion, which houses personal effects of former residents Billings and Rockefeller as well as paintings by Thomas Cole and Albert Bierstadt; take a guided walk on the carriage roads; and explore the professionally-managed forest stands and hiking trails of Mount Tom.

Visitors to the **Woodstock Historical Society's** 1807 Dana House are offered a view of village life in the days before rope tows and Rockefellers.
The Society publishes several excellent publications to help visitors exploring the area, including "Woodstock: A Walking Guide." It's available at the Dana House, Chamber of Commerce, and local bookstores. Highlights include the 1809 Georgian Colonial Johnson House; the Richardson Romanesque 1885 Norman Williams Public Library; and the 1808 Old White Meeting House, with a Bulfinch tower and a Paul Revere bell. Revere bells also grace the Universalist, Christian and Episcopal churches.

The Dana Brothers, who published The Elm Tree Monthly in Woodstock in the early 1900s, wrote, "Woodstock Village is the best village in Vermont. Few doubt this and none can prove it isn't true. ... Woodstock has more good people in more comfortable homes than any village of its size in the world. ... The library is better than we need, but not above our tastes. The natives are of good old Yankee stock, with enough Canadians, Italians, and Negroes to give a little zest."

> One of the nation's earliest medical schools, the Clinical School of Medicine (later Vermont Medical College) operated in Woodstock from 1827 until 1856.

As you head west through Woodstock on Route 4, watch on the right for Middle Bridge, a handsome Town lattice-design covered bridge erected in 1969 by Milton Graton, the self-described "last of the covered bridge builders." (Developed by 19th-century bridge builder Ithiel Town, the Town lattice employs crisscross side frames.) Lincoln Bridge, three miles further west on Route 4, was built in 1877 and is the only covered bridge in the country that incorporates the wood-and-iron truss designed by T. Willis Pratt.

Continue west on Route 4 to **Bridgewater**, where one of the vast, rambling woolen mills that manufactured the popular "Vermont Tweeds" in the 1800s now houses the **Bridgewater Mill**, with its shops and craft galleries. Bridgewater was the birthplace of geologist and naturalist Zadock Thompson (1796-1856), who wrote an almanac of flora and fauna to raise tuition money to attend the University of Vermont. His later works included the 700-page *Civil, Natural History, Gazetteer, Botany and Geology of Vermont*.

At Bridgewater Corners, take a tour of one of the state's first craft breweries, the **Long Trail Brewing Company**. It's also housed in one of the Ottauquechee valley's old textile mills.

birthplace of a president

Turn left onto Route 100A and continue past the entrance to Coolidge State Park and Forest to **President Calvin Coolidge State Historic Site** in **Plymouth Notch**. Looking like nothing so much as Vermont's version of Brigadoon, the Broadway-musical Scottish village lost in the mists of time, Plymouth Notch is the birthplace and boyhood home of Calvin Coolidge, thirtieth president of the United States. It has remained virtually unchanged since 1923, when, at 2:47 a.m. on August 3, Coolidge's father, a justice of the peace, administered the presidential oath of office to the then-vice-president when word arrived of the death of President Warren G. Harding.

Alone among America's presidential birthplaces, the Plymouth Notch site preserves not only an individual home, but an entire village. Among the hill town's Coolidge-related sites are the birthplace home itself; the house in which the oath was administered (the parlor the Coolidges stood in still contains the kerosene lantern that lit it that night); the general store Coolidge's father ran; the village church; and the cheese factory founded by the president's father (under a lease arrangement with the state, a private cheesemaking firm still turns out cheddar here). There's also a carriage barn, filled with antique horse-drawn vehicles (we like the postman's snug, stove-heated sleigh), and a new visitor center with exhibits interpreting the Coolidge era. "Silent Cal" himself now lies with the rest of the silent majority in the village cemetery.

> *The rustic space above the Coolidge store in Plymouth Notch served as the presidential mailroom during Calvin Coolidge's summer sojourns in his home village.*

Side Trip

It was at Buffalo Brook in nearby Ludlow, in 1855, that Matthew Kennedy's discovery of a gold nugget launched Vermont's short-lived, and mostly non-lucrative, gold rush. If you want to try your luck, at the intersection of routes 100A and 100, detour south on Route 100 to **Camp Plymouth State Park.** Prospectors have also plucked gold nuggets and dust from streams near the abandoned town of Five Corners in **Coolidge State Park and Forest.** Ask at the park office for directions.

Green Mountain playground

Continue south on Route 100A to the junction with Route 100, then turn north on 100 through West Bridgewater to **Killington.** The largest ski area in the East is also a major summer resort: it boasts two championship golf courses, 42 miles of mountain biking trails, 50 miles of hiking trails, alpine slides, horseback riding and a spa. The K1 Express Gondola whisks visitors to the top of Vermont's second-highest peak (4,241 feet), where, in 1763, the Reverend Samuel Peters is said to have stood when he dubbed the state "Verd-Mont."

Almost 200 years later, in 1946, more than 3,000 acres of forest were purchased by the state for less than $7 an acre, and surveyed as a possible ski area. Connecticut resident Preston Smith leased land from the state and opened Killington in 1958. The resort is merged with neighboring **Pico Peak,** a pioneer Vermont ski area that was founded by the parents of the late Olympic gold medalist skier Andrea Mead Lawrence.

After years of confusion, Killington and the town in which it is located now share the same name. At their 1999 town meeting, Sherburne residents voted to change the name of their municipality back to Killington, the original name under which it was chartered in 1761.

Continue north on Route 100 to Gifford Woods State Park. The 2,100-mile **Appalachian Trail** passes through the park (it meets up with the **Long Trail** about 1 1/2 miles from the campground; the two become one between here and the Massachusetts border) and provides access to several rewarding hikes, including a trek up Deer Leap Mountain, and to a waterfall along the Thundering Brook Trail. The seven-acre old-growth natural hardwood stand at **Gifford Woods Natural Area**, across from the campground, is a National Natural Landmark and a State Fragile Area. (There's a closer trailhead to the top of Deer Leap Mountain at the **Inn at Long Trail**, on Route 4 in Sherburne Pass).

Anglers may want to try their luck at hooking bass, sunfish – and stocked rainbow and brown trout early in the season – from the man-made, 71-acre Kent Pond, just off Route 100 on the right. There's a Fish and Wildlife Department public launch site here. The Appalachian Trail crosses Route 100 near the pond, and offers day hikers a pleasant ramble along its south shore. Golfers can opt for a round at the award-winning **Green Mountain National Golf Course**.

the White River Valley

Follow Route 100 north along the Tweed River through tiny Pittsfield (settled by pioneers from Pittsfield, Massachusetts) to the junction with Route 107. **Head east (right) on 107:** Soon you'll be paralleling the White River, which along with its many tributaries forms one of the major watersheds of eastern Vermont. With its primary source on the eastern slope of Battell Mountain in Ripton, the White has its outlet at the Connecticut River near White River Junction. It thus forms part of the drainage system which ultimately empties into Long Island Sound – as opposed to the system on the western slope of the Green Mountains, which drains into the Atlantic Ocean via Lake Champlain and the St. Lawrence River. (There's also a watershed in southwestern Vermont emptying into the Hudson, and thence into New York harbor.)

Side Trip

At the intersection with Route 107, detour north on Route 100 for a short distance to **Peavine State Forest**. The White River valley has been used as a travelway for almost 12,000 years: there is evidence that nomadic Paleoindians passed through as early as 10,000 B.C. Today the area hosts transients of a different sort – it's on the migration path for many bird species. For details, stop at the interpretive site in Peavine, so nicknamed because of the short, crooked route of the defunct White River Railroad.

> *The portion of the White River flowing along Route 107 is informally known as the "Tubing Capital of Vermont." Vermont River Tubing, on Route 100 in Stockbridge, offers tube rentals and shuttle service in summer. See "Activities" below for information.*

Continue east on Route 107 to Bethel. As you come into town, watch for **the White River National Fish Hatchery**. Each year it produces about 400,000 newly hatched salmon fry as part of the Atlantic Salmon Restoration Program, which aims to reintroduce the fish which thrived in the White River before dams built on the Connecticut blocked their route to the sea.

Bethel, which bills itself as "A Real Vermont Town" (where does this leave all the others?), was in 1779 the first town to be chartered by the newly formed Republic of Vermont. At the turn of the century, the town's economy was firmly based on granite: it supplied $2,000,000 worth of "Bethel White" for buildings such as Washington, D.C.'s Union Station and the Western Union Building in New York City. Today, the town's tiny Main Street is lined with antique shops, and only its handsome public buildings and banks hearken back to its glory days. Before leaving town, head north over the bridge on Route 12 to see the fine 1816 United Church, originally called the Old Brick Church.

Backtrack to the junction of Route 12 and head south. Approximately six miles out of town, look on the right (by a white house with green trim) for a small plaque mounted on a large rock. This marks the site of Fort Defiance, built in 1780 after an Indian raid.

Continue south to **Barnard**, whose "downtown" at the outlet of Silver Lake consists of little more than the Barnard General Store (well-stocked with necessities and treats, and boasting a genuine old-time soda fountain). The "beach" across from the store is a popular swimming spot. **Silver Lake State Park**, just beyond the village center, has a beach and boat rental.

Barnard has long been popular among summer visitors, including writers Sinclair Lewis (1885-1951) and his wife, journalist Dorothy Thompson (1894-1961), who liked the area so much they settled here at a property called Twin Farms during the 1930s. Another visitor had a less pleasant stay: the last eastern mountain lion killed in the state was shot here in 1881, and is now in the collection of the State Historical Society museum in Montpelier (see Drive 7). Ms. Thompson and her third husband, Czech artist Maxim Kopf, have a more private resting place: they're buried in the Barnard cemetery.

Side Trip
About four miles south on Route 12, turn right onto Lakota Road, park in the lot, and hike for 45 minutes to Lucy's Lookout on the Appalachian Trail: the views from the top are outstanding. (Note: this area can be tricky. Best ask at the Barnard General Store for a map.)

Back on Route 12, continue south to return to Woodstock. An historic marker on the outskirts of town commemorates the site where those far-sighted and forgivably lazy weekenders built that primordial rope tow. For better and for worse, it did more than anything else to pull Vermont into the 20th century.

information *All area codes are (802) unless otherwise indicated.*

Green Mountain National Forest (747-6700), U.S. Forest Service, 231 North Main St., Rutland 05701. Rochester Ranger District (767-4261), 99 Ranger Rd., Rochester 05767. fs.fed.us/r9/forests/greenmountain

Hartford Area Chamber of Commerce (295-7900), 100 Railroad Row, White River Junction, VT 05001. Quechee Gorge information booth mid-May-mid-Oct. hartfordvtchamber.com

Killington Chamber of Commerce (773-4181), 2046 Rte. 4, (P.O. Box 114), Killington 05751. killingtonchamber.com

Woodstock Area Chamber of Commerce (457-3555), 18 Central St., PO Box 486, Woodstock 05091. Information booth on the Green. woodstockvt.com

lodging

Casa Bella Inn and Restaurant (877-746-8943 or 746-8943), 3911 Rte. 100, Pittsfield 05762. Eight snug rooms decorated with antiques, all with private bath. Big front porch overlooks the village green. Restaurant menu ($$-$$$) reflects the innkeeper's Italian heritage. $-$$

Cobble House Inn (234-5458), 1 Cobble House Rd., Gaysville 05746. Hilltop Italianate mansion on the White River, with 4 cozy rooms – all with private bath – decorated with Victorian antiques. Full breakfast buffet features eggs from the inn's own hens. $$

Farmbrook Motel (672-3621), Rte. 100A, Plymouth 05056. Tidy 12-unit lodging by a brook 3 mi. from the Historic District. farmbrookmotel.net $

Grey Bonnet Inn and Restaurant (775-2537), 831 Rte. 100 North, Killington. 41-room inn on 25 wooded acres, with indoor and outdoor pools, tennis, Jacuzzi, sauna, exercise and game rooms. Hiking trails. greybonnetinn.com $-$$$

Inn at Long Trail (775-7181), 709 Rte. 4, Sherburne Pass, Killington 05751. Rustic country inn popular in winter with skiers has 14 traditional rooms whirlpool rooms, and 6 fireplaced suites. Fieldstone fireplace, hot tub, restaurant ($$-$$$), and Irish pub with live music. Pets with approval. innatlongtrail.com $-$$

Jackson House Inn (457-2065), 114-3 Senior Lane, Woodstock 05091. 1890 has 9 luxuriously furnished rooms, and 6 suites with gas fireplaces. The restaurant ($$$-$$$$) serves New American cuisine, with a choice of fixed-price menus: a 2-course + dessert; a 6-course vegetable tasting menu; and a 6-course chef's tasting menu. Spa & steam room; 5 acres of gardens. jacksonhouse.com $$-$$$$

Kedron Valley Inn (457-1473), 10671 South Rd. (Rte. 106), South Woodstock 05071. Rooms with fireplaces or wood burning stoves, Jacuzzis, canopy beds, and patios. The candlelit dining room (Thurs.-Sun.; $$-$$$) offers seasonal menus that might include steamed Maine mussels with grape tomatoes and basil, and grilled Angus beef filet with local tomatoes and greens. A tavern menu is also offered. Trail rides (see "Activities" below). Pet friendly. kedronvalleyinn.com $$-$$$$

Maple Leaf Inn (234-5342), 5890 Rte. 12, Barnard 05031. The "pillow library", where guests choose their own, best sums up the lengths the owners go to please guests at this reproduction Victorian-style farmhouse on 16 acres. Each of the 7 guest rooms has a sitting area and king-size bed with handmade quilts; most have fireplaces and whirlpool tubs. mapleleafinn.com $$-$$$$

The October Country Inn (672-3412), 362 Upper Rd., (jct. Rte. 4 and 100A), Bridgewater Corners 05035. 10 guest rooms (8 with private baths), a swimming pool, and meals featuring ethnic specialties served family style, make this farmhouse a popular overnight retreat. MAP or B & B. octobercountryinn.com $$-$$$

Ottauquechee Motor Lodge (672-3404), 529 Rte. 4, Woodstock 05091. 15 comfortable units with fridges, color TV and a/c; and a 3-room fireplaced suite overlooking the Ottauquechee River. ottauquechee.com $-$$

Quechee Inn at Marshland Farm (295-3133), 1119 Quechee Main St, Quechee 05059. The 18th-century restored farmhouse of the state's first lieutenant governor has 22 handsome guest rooms with TV and a/c. Guests have access to Quechee Lakes Country Club. Dinner ($$$$) might include an appetizer of scallops gratinee with fresh sage, followed by maple stout braised short ribs. A lighter menu is also offered. Home to Wilderness Trails (see "Activities" below). quecheeinn.com $$-$$$$

Red Clover Inn (775-2290), Rte. 4, Killington 05751. 1840s country inn on 13 acres has 14 meticulously furnished rooms and suites, some with fireplaces, whirlpools for 2, and views. Dinner in the fireplaced dining room ($$$; open Mon.-Sat., Sun in foliage and holidays) might include pan-seared shrimp in spiced garlic cream; and herb-basted chicken with sweet corn risotto. redcloverinn.com $$-$$$$

Shire Motel (457-2211), 46 Pleasant St., Woodstock 05091. Comfortable in-town motel with 42 nicely furnished rooms and suites overlooking the Ottauquechee River. shiremotel.com $-$$$

Twin Farms (234-9999), Barnard 05031. Vermont's most exclusive lodging, on 300 acres, features 10 suites and 10 cottages, all with exquisite décor; superb cuisine, a 26,000-bottle wine cellar, and a host of activities, including a ski lift, fly-fishing, fitness center, and mountain biking. twinfarms.com $2000-$3000 double occupancy includes meals, wine and all other beverages, and all activities and recreation equipment. $$$$

The Woodstock Inn and Resort (457-1100), 14 The Green, Woodstock. 142 elegantly appointed rooms and suites. 3 restaurants include the formal dining room ($$$-$$$$), serving an "innovative interpretation of classic American and New England fare," with offerings such as oysters Rockefeller (Laurance's favorite), and grilled sea scallops with Maine lobster risotto. Sunday brunch is a standout. Full resort activities, including championship golf course, indoor/outdoor tennis, and health and fitness center. woodstockinn.com $$-$$$

restaurants

Allechante (457-3300), 61 Central St., Woodstock. Fresh breads and pastries; daily soup specials; sandwiches ranging from yellowfin tuna to pulled pork. Scones and own yogurt among breakfast offerings. Baked goods to go. B & L. $-$$

Barnard Inn Restaurant (234-9961), Rt. 12, Barnard. Venison carpaccio or house-cured grav-lax might precede winter vegetable gnocchi or chili and sesame encrusted ahi tuna at this elegant 1796 inn with several fireplaced dining rooms. A lighter tavern menu is available. D Wed.-Sun. $$$-$$$$

Bentley's Restaurant & Cafe (457-3232), 3 Elm St., Woodstock. Good, solid American fare amidst comfortable Victorian surroundings. Lighter menu in cafe. Dancing Fri. and Sat.; live music Thurs. L, D and Sun. brunch. $$-$$$

Blanche and Bill's Pancake House (422-3816), 586 Rte. 4, Bridgewater Corners. Pancakes and waffles are legendary at this popular restaurant, which also serves up great burgers and sandwiches. B (served all day) & L Wed.-Sun. $

Casey's Caboose (422-3795), 2841 Killington Rd., Killington. A popular family restaurant (in a real caboose) with an extensive menu including steaks, burgers, ribs, seafood, Italian special-ties, served in cheery ski pub surroundings. Closed early May. D; L weekends and holidays. $$$

Creek House Diner (234-9191), 1837 River St., Bethel. Locals rave about the breakfasts, burg-ers, and sandwiches; lots of classic comfort foods, also specials such as pasta with summer vegetables. B, L, D daily. $

The Farmers' Diner (295-4600), Route 4, Quechee. The "locavore" movement has a home in this classic 1946 diner: more than half of menu items come from small-scale local produc-ers – everything from organic yogurt to pasture eggs served up with hash and potatoes. B & L daily. $-$$

Hemingway's Restaurant (422-3886), 4988 Rte. 4, Killington. Consistently rated one of Ver-mont's finest, the restaurant in an 1860 country house features fireside dining, handcrafted American cuisine, and a wine tasting menu. D Wed.-Sun.; closed early Nov. and mid-April to mid-May. $$$$

Pane e Salute (457-4882), 61 Central St., Woodstock. Authentic Italian osteria menu built around fresh local ingredients and "slow food" principles. Wine bar. Reservations recom-mended. D Thurs.-Sun. Closed Nov. and April. $$-$$$

The Parker House Inn and Restaurant (295-6077), Main Street, Quechee. Even if you're not staying at this lovely 1857 Victorian overlooking Quechee dam, don't miss Alexandra Lanou-Adler's superb cuisine. Maine lobster bouillabaisse, spinach and Asiago cheese in puff pastry, roasted pork short ribs with maple demi-glace are recent standouts. $$$-$$$$

Peavine Family Restaurant and Thirsty Bull Pub (234-9434), Rte. 107, Stockbridge. Steak, chops, Italian dishes, and special treatment for the kids. Friday night is fresh seafood night: Saturday specials are prime rib and BBQ ribs. Live music Sat. L Sat.-Sun.; D daily. SS-SSS

The Prince and the Pauper (457-1818), 24 Elm St., Woodstock. A Woodstock institution for more than 20 years, the owner-chef serves gourmet Continental cuisine. A selection of appe-tizers for the 3-course, prix fixe menu might begin with apple cider onion soup and include an entree of carre d'Agneau "Royale" (boneless grilled rack of lamb baked in puff pastry). A lighter bistro menu ($$$) is offered. D. $$$$

Simon Pearce Restaurant (295-1470), The Mill, 1760 Quechee Main St., Quechee. Hearty yet sophisticated American, British, and continental fare served at the glassworks and show-room, in contemporary surroundings overlooking the Ottauquechee River and falls. Terrace seating in summer. L, D, & Sun. brunch. $$$$

Sugar & Spice (773-7832), 43 Rte. 4 East, Mendon. Fluffy pancakes, cinnamon French toast – all served with maple syrup from the on-site sugarhouse. Omelettes, burgers, and sand-wiches too. L & D. $

Tozier's (234-9400), 2678 River St. (Rte. 107), Bethel. Light meals, sandwiches, and ice cream in a pleasant setting overlooking the White River. L & D. $

attractions

Billings Farm and Museum (457-2355), Rte. 12 and River Rd., Woodstock. May- late Oct., daily. Limited winter hours.

Bill's Country Store (773-9313), Rte. 4, Killington. Vermont products such as maple syrup, cheeses, cob smoked ham, and homemade jams, Rat Trap store cheese, general merchan-dise, and gifts.

Bridgewater Mill (672-3332), Rte. 4, Bridgewater. Charles Shackleton Furniture/Miranda Thomas Pottery are among the specialty shops, gourmet foods, arts and crafts dealers, book-store, and antiques shop in this historic woolen mill.

Camp Plymouth State Park (228-2025), 2008 Scout Camp Rd., Ludlow. Off Rte. 100 on the shores of Echo Lake. Popular day use park. Swimming, boat and canoe rental, hiking trails. Late May-Labor Day.

Coolidge State Park and Forest (672-3612), Rte. 100A, Plymouth. The 16,166-acre preserve stretches through 7 towns; the park has hiking trails, a campground, and picnic area. Park: Late May –mid Oct.

The Dana House (457-1822), Woodstock Historical Society, 26 Elm St., Woodstock. Wed.-Sun., late May-Oct.

Gifford Woods State Park (775-5354), Rte. 100, Killington. Late May-Columbus Day.

Killington K1 Express Gondola (422-6232) and Mountain Bike Center (422-6232), Rte. 100, Killington.

Long Trail Brewing Company (672-5011), 5520 Rte. 4, Bridgewater Corners. Tours, tastings, and pub fare daily from 11 a.m-6 p.m.

Marsh-Billings-Rockefeller National Historical Park (457-3368), 54 Elm St. (off Rte. 12), Wood-stock. Visitor Center open ate May- Oct. 31. Advance reservation for tours; grounds open year-round.

Ottauquechee Valley Winery (295-9463), 5573 Woodstock Rd., Rte.4, Quechee Gorge Village, Quechee. Free tastings of wine made from locally grown fruit.

Peavine State Forest, Rte. 100, Stockbridge: see Green Mountain National Forest in "Information," above. Interpretive site, wildlife viewing site, picnic area, hiking trails, and fishing.

Pico Peak Alpine Slide and Mountain Resort Attractions (800-621-6867), Rte. 4, Killington. Memorial Day-Columbus Day. Take the triple chairlift up 3,410 ft, and the slide down (you control the speed). Climbing wall; "Pico Power Jump" ride. Mountain bike rentals.

President Calvin Coolidge State Historic Site (672-3773) off Rte. 100A, Plymouth. Mid-May-mid-Oct. daily.

Quechee State Park (295-2990), Rte. 4, Quechee. Camping and hiking on 611 acres perched above the gorge. Late May-Columbus Day.

Quechee Gorge Village (295-1550), Rte. 4, Quechee. Country store; arts & crafts center; and large antiques mall. Toy and train museum.
Silver Lake State Park (234-9451), North Rd., Barnard. Picnicking, camping, swimming, fishing, boat rental. Late May-Labor Day.

Sugarbush Farm, Inc. (457-1757), Hillside Rd., Woodstock. Working farm has a sugar house self-guided tour, nature trails, farm animals, and store with a full line of cheeses and maple products made on the premises: call ahead for directions.

Taftsville Country Store (457-1135), Rte. 4, Taftsville. One of – if not the – biggest selections of Vermont cheeses, and an excellent assortment of moderately priced wines; fresh baked breads and pastries.

The Vermont Institute of Natural Science Nature Center (359-5000), Rte. 4, Quechee. Late May-Oct.

White River National Fish Hatchery (234-5400), Rte. 107, Bethel.

Woodstock Farmers' Market (457-3658), Rte. 4 W, Woodstock. Home baked goodies, deli, soups, lattes, and sandwiches to go.

activities

Balloons of Vermont (291-4887 or 369-0213). Hot air balloon trips over Queechee Gorge and the Upper Valley area of Vermont and New Hampshire. balloonsofvermont.com

The Cyclery Plus (457-3377), 36 W. Woodstock St., Woodstock. Bike rentals.

Green Mountain National Golf Course (422-4653), 476 Barrows Towne Rd., Killington. Rated #1 in Vermont by Golf Digest, May 2009.

Hawk Inn and Mountain Resort (672-3811), Rte. 100, Plymouth. Guided scenic trail rides; fly fishing school.

Kedron Valley Stables (457-1480), Rte.106, S. Woodstock. Trail rides; carriage and sleigh rides; riding lessons.

Killington Music Festival (773-4003), P.O. Box 386, Rutland 05702. Internationally acclaimed musicians, teaching faculty, and students join together to perform "Music in the Mountains" Sun. in summer at the Ramshead Lodge on Killington Rd. killingtonmusicfestival.org

Simon Pearce Glass (295-2711), The Mill, 1760 Main St., Quechee.

Vermont River Tubing (746-8106), Rte. 100, Stockbridge. Tube rentals and shuttle service along the White River.

Wilderness Trails (295-7620), 1119 Quechee Main St., Quechee. Bike and canoe rental, guided trips on Connecticut and White rivers, fly fishing school, hiking maps, mountain and hybrid bike rentals and trails; winter activities.

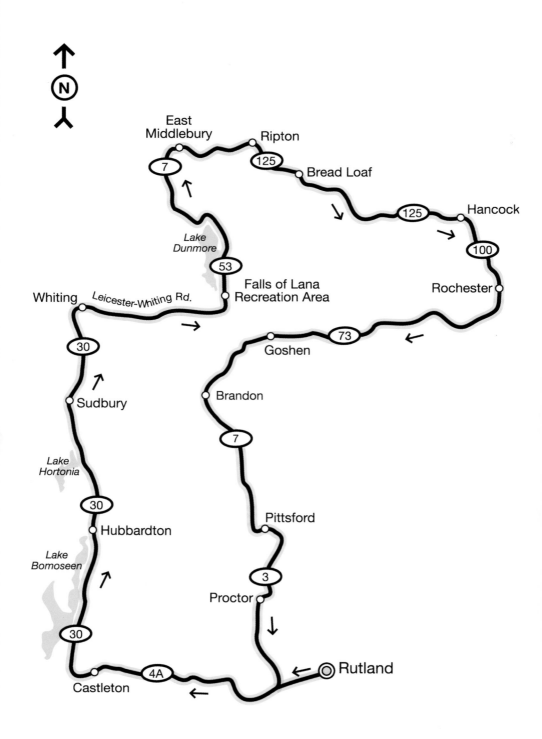

Drive 4

Rutland, the Western Lakes, and the Green Mountain Gaps

105 miles

major attractions

- Robert Frost Wayside Area
- Middlebury and Brandon Gaps
- Vermont Marble Museum
- Chaffee Art Center
- Wilson Castle
- Lake Bomoseen

Starting in Vermont's "second city," this drive heads west through the college town of Castleton and follows the eastern shore of Lake Bomoseen. By way of lakes Hortonia and Dunmore, it winds to the north and east to reach the Green Mountain National Forest and a pair of roller-coaster roads through natural "gaps" in the steep, forested hills. The return route to Rutland is via the handsome streets of Brandon and the heart of Vermont's marble country.

If things had worked out differently – if it weren't for Burlington's superb lakeside location and the presence of the University of Vermont – **Rutland** might well have become the state's largest city. Actually, it did briefly claim that title, when an economic and population boom in the 1880s sent it into the number one spot. Rutland's location on Otter Creek, at the crossroads of central Vermont, was in those days mightily reinforced by the rise of the marble industry and the Rutland Railroad.

Compact it may be, but Rutland's downtown still has the look of an urban center, Vermont style. Local businesses occupy premises with a mid-20th century, Edward Hopperesque cast about them; one edifice, the Service Building on Merchants Row, is a squat mini-skyscraper that has the honor of being one of only two sizable art deco buildings in the state (the other is the Latchis Hotel in Brattleboro; see Drive 1). And Rutland hosts the Vermont State Fair, held at the fairgrounds on the south side of the city each September. Rutland also has the *Rutland Herald*, a proudly independent, Pulitzer Prize-winning daily newspaper that has been printed continuously since 1794.

Any walk through Rutland should take in not only the downtown commercial blocks, but the fine array of Victorian homes that stretches along Main Street (Route 7). This is where marble money liked to settle, back before this broad thoroughfare was taken over by cars.

The **Chaffee Art Center** is housed in a grand 1896 Queen Anne Victorian that is a work of art in itself. Listed on both the State and National Register of Historic Places, it was one of the first homes in the city to have central heating, gas lighting, and indoor plumbing. The center is now the home of the Rutland Area Art Association, which curates up to 15 exhibitions of works by Vermont artists each year.

> *Vermont's first pizza was served at Rutland's Palms restaurant in 1949.*

Head west out of Rutland on Route 4A (note – this is "old" Route 4; don't get confused with the new one, which is a limited-access road on the outskirts of town). Just past the junction with Route 3, turn right onto West Proctor Road and follow signs to **Wilson Castle**, a thirty-two-room mansion complete with towers, turrets, balconies, stained glass, and thirteen fireplaces. It was built by a doctor for his wife, an English noblewoman, in 1888, and there is no Gilded Age monument quite like it in Vermont.

Return to Route 4A and head west to Castleton. To the left is Bird Mountain, named for Castleton's first settler, Colonel Bird, who died so soon after building a sawmill that the first boards were used to make his coffin. A marker on the outskirts of town commemorates the Battle of Hubbardton (see below), the only Revolutionary War engagement actually fought in Vermont (see Drive 2 regarding the Battle of Bennington, which was fought in New York); and Fort Warren, built in 1779 to defend the northern frontier.

Castleton's Main Street is lined with a series of elegant, pillared houses designed by Thomas Royal Dake, who arrived here in 1807 and stayed for fifty years, following the trade of an architect-builder. Among the finest are the 1833 Langdon-Cole House, with its unusual inverted portico; and the 1833 Federated Church, with its Greek Revival Manse, at the east end of the village.

Another historic marker, just past the vintage **Birdseye Diner**, proclaims that Castleton State College, Vermont's first college and the eighteenth oldest in the nation, opened here in 1787. In its early days, the college boasted the largest and best equipped medical school in New England. It moved to its present location, just off Main Street, in 1833.

Lakes Bomoseen and Hortonia – and revolutionary side trips . . . .

Turn right from Route 4A onto Route 30 at Castleton Corners, and head north as the road hugs the eastern shore of **Lake Bomoseen**. The territory surrounding the one-and-a-half-mile-wide, eight-mile-long lake was once the home of a small band of Algonkian Indians called the Obom Sawin. In the 1920s and 30s, the lake's Neshobe Island sheltered a more exotic band: critic Alexander Woollcott bought the island and made it a summer outpost of New York City's legendary Algonquin Hotel Round Table. Woollcott and his friends (among them Harpo Marx, who was known to paint himself blue with crayon and walk along the shore naked to frighten picnickers) used Neshobe for their own special brand of R & R, including martini-fueled cutthroat croquet matches.

Lake Bomoseen also attracted a more sedate tourist clientele to a string of rambling Victorian waterfront hotels, all vanished now. The bass fishing those old-time sojourners enjoyed is still excellent, although fishermen and others who care about Bomoseen are attempting to fight off an invasion of Eurasian milfoil. Down near the lake's southern end, you may see one or more of the floating machines that rip up and haul away the fast-growing aquatic weed. Boat rentals are available at the **Lake Bomoseen Marina** (see "Activities" below).

Side Trip
In Hubbardton, at the northern end of Lake Bomoseen, turn off onto Monument Hill Road and follow signs for six miles to **Hubbardton Battle Monument and Museum**. A granite shaft marks the spot where, on July 7, 1777, Colonel Seth Warner and his Green Mountain Boys were camped while protecting the retreat of American General Arthur St. Clair from nearby Mount Independence. Early in the morning they were attacked by a superior British force. The English won the battle, but Warner and his men, aided by Massachusetts militiamen and a regiment from New Hampshire, inflicted such heavy losses that the enemy had to give up their pursuit of St. Clair.
Continue north on Route 30 through Hubbardton Gulf and past the eastern shores of

Lake Hortonia (note: Beebe Pond, not Hortonia, is the first body of water to appear on your left after Lake Bomoseen). Hortonia is a popular anglers' lake, with bass as well as rainbow and lake trout the prime quarry. Boat launch points can be reached by turning left (west) onto Route 144 at the northern tip of the lake.

The next community is Sudbury, which overlooks the Lemon Fair River valley. There are several stories that venture to explain how the river got its name. One of the most popular tells of a massacre of settlers by Indians along the banks of the river. The event was described as a lamentable affair, which over the years evolved into "Lemon Fair." Another version offers the same etymology, but bases the description on the somewhat less lamentable loss of a horse in quicksand. Probably more reliable is the suggestion that the river's name is a derivation of "limon faire," French for "making silt," but the likeliest origin might simply be a corruption of *"les monts verts"* – green mountains. The Lemon Fair is a slow, meandering stream, popular with canoeists and birders.

Side Trip

Turn west on Route 73 and continue for approximately 12 miles (follow the signs) to Mount Independence State Historic Site, on a headland overlooking Lake Champlain. The defensive fort, which was connected to New York State's Fort Ticonderoga by a floating bridge, garrisoned 12,000 American troops during the brutal winter of 1776-77. From here they marched to battle and defeated the British at Saratoga. Exhibits here recount their grueling winter and the battle that helped win the Revolution.

In Whiting, there's an interesting old cemetery in back of the 1811 Whiting Community Church.

In 1775, when Ethan Allen wanted to round up his Green Mountain Boys for their attack on Fort Ticonderoga, he sent as his courier Whiting native Samuel Beach, who ran sixty-four miles through the countryside with the summons.

Turn right in the center of Whiting onto the Leicester-Whiting Road, one of Vermont's prettiest country byways. The mountains straight ahead are part of the **Green Mountain National Forest** (GMNF) and include Hogback (2,285 feet), Romance (3,140), Cape Lookoff (3,360), and Mount Horrid (3,216). **When the road ends at a T intersection, turn left and then bear right for Leicester, cross Route 7, and continue onto East Road/Fern Lake Road. Continue to the intersection of Fern Lake and Lake Dunmore roads, and turn left (north) onto Route 53.** You'll now be riding along the edge of a tiny portion of the 350,000-acre GMNF – which stretches over two-thirds of the length of the state and is laced by more than 500 miles of trails – and along the eastern shore of **Lake Dunmore**.

Lake Dunmore was named for the Earl of Dunmore, described in one account as "a rapacious Scottish peer." History notes that "Lord Dunmore and his party came up the Leicester River to the site of Salisbury village, and from thence on foot over to the lake where the Earl waded into the water a few steps, and pouring upon the waves a libation of wine, proclaimed, 'Ever after, this body of water shall be called Lake Dunmore, in honor of the Earl of Dunmore.'" Two Indians spread the branches of a small tree and stuck the empty bottle in it, making the naming official (all the while, we imagine, rolling their eyes at each other). The Lord, "as proof of his industry ... in the short space of eight months granted to speculators four hundred and fifty thousand acres of Vermont lands and received fees for the same, and also had granted to himself in the name of others fifty-one thousand acres more."

While following Lake Dunmore's eastern shore, watch for signs for the Green Mountain National Forest's **Silver Lake/Falls of Lana Recreation Area**. Follow the moderately difficult (some steep sections) Silver Lake Trail about ½ mile to the falls (there are rumored to be some good swimming holes below the cataract). Several trails branch off from the falls, including a continuation of the Silver Lake Trail to remote Silver Lake. There's good swimming at the north end of the lake, near the foundation stones of a grand hotel that burned in the 1940s. The lake is classified by the state as a semi-primitive campsite.

Campers are strongly cautioned not to leave their cars in the recreation area parking lot overnight – there have been problems with vandalism – but to pay the entrance fee to **Branbury State Park**, just past the Silver Lake parking lot, and leave their cars there. Fortunately, not everyone involved in the history of these parts was as greedy as Lord Dunmore. In 1945 multimillionaire philanthropist Shirley Farr donated land to the state for this 64-acre park at the base of Mount Moosalamoo on Lake Dunmore. The facility has a sandy beach, boat rentals, a nature museum, and trails, include one that passes the Falls of Lana.

At the end of Route 53, turn right (north) onto Route 7 for a few miles to the junction with Route 125, and then turn right (east) on 125 toward East Middlebury. The Waybury Inn, a short distance from the turn, was the setting for the outdoor shots of the inn on television's *Newhart*. To take a dip in East Middlebury Gorge, turn right about 1 ½ miles after turning onto Route 125, cross a small bridge, park, and walk back across the bridge. A 10-foot waterfall feeds a narrow channel below the bridge, making it a delightful spot for cooling off.

Robert Frost country ·

Follow Route 125, one of Vermont's two designated Scenic Routes (the other is Route 108 through Smuggler's Notch; see Drive 7), also called the Robert Frost Memorial

Highway, to **Ripton**. Vermont's favorite adopted son, Robert Frost, bought a summer home here in 1939; ten years later he made Ripton his legal address. The **Chipman Inn** was built in 1833 for Middlebury College co-founder Daniel Chipman.

Side Trip

Just east of Ripton, take a right onto Forest Route 32, the access road for **Moosalamoo National Recreation Area**, a 20,000-acre semi-wilderness of mountains, lakes, forests, valleys, and streams. Moosalamoo, an Abenaki word believed to mean "the moose departs" or "he trails the moose," was used as a winter encampment by the Missisquoi band of the Abenaki more than 300 years ago. This is also the turnoff for **Blueberry Hill Inn and Cross-Country Ski Area**.

Continue east on Route 125 to the **Robert Frost Wayside Area and Trails**. A marker honors Frost, a "Vermonter by preference, poet laureate of Vermont, first citizen of the town of Ripton ..." Poems by Frost line the gentle, mile-long trail that winds through woods and meadows to the Middlebury River. The first 3/10 of a mile is a barrier-free boardwalk. There's an interesting old cemetery on the right, just past the rest area.

The **Spirit in Nature Interfaith Path Center**, adjacent to the Robert Frost Trails, is a work in progress spearheaded by Unitarian Universalist minister Reverend Paul Bortz. A web of 10 different faith paths totaling six miles – each representing various religions' ideas about the environment – wind through 70 acres of woods, apple orchard, and along the river and meet in a clearing known as the "Sacred Circle." Signs en route quote philosophy, bits of scripture, and poetry from the spiritual traditions represented.

Further east, perched high on a hill overlooking the vast Moosalamoo tract, is Middlebury College's **Bread Loaf** campus, long famous as the site of the Bread Loaf Writers' Conference held each August. The complex was originally developed as an inn by Colonel Joseph Battell, a Middlebury newspaper editor and horse lover who established the national headquarters for developing purebred Morgan horses here (see Drive 5 for the Morgan's current Middlebury-area connections).

Joseph Battell loved horses, and he loved the tranquil pace of a vanishing way of life. Not surprisingly, he hated automobiles. Each week he offered the readers of his weekly newspaper, the Middlebury Register, a generous sampling of grisly auto accident reports. Nor would he let visitors drive to his farm: they had to leave their cars at Ripton Hollow and come by horse the rest of the way.

Continue east past the **Middlebury College Snow Bowl** and **Middlebury Gap** (elevation 2,149 feet), which marks the divide between the Lake Champlain and Connecticut River watersheds. The **Long Trail** crosses here, and then climbs to the **Breadloaf Wilderness**, a 21,480 acre tract that is the largest wilderness in the Green Mountain National Forest (the area takes its name from 3,835-foot Breadloaf Mountain). The road wends its way down through a scenic valley, past the turn-off for **Texas Falls**, a dramatic cascade complete with flumes and potholes. A boardwalk and stone steps descend to the falls, where there are wonderful views into the ravine. To continue on the easy, 1 2/10-mile interpretive **Texas Falls Trail** loop, cross over Texas Brook and follow the signs. Pick up a brochure at the registration box.

over the gap to Brandon ....

In Hancock, at the end of Route 125, turn right (south) onto Route 100 and follow alongside the White River to **Rochester**. Stop at the Green Mountain National Forest District Ranger Office just north of town for information on camping and/or hiking in the area. **Just south of Rochester, turn right and head west on Route 73 toward Goshen.** As the road climbs up Goshen Mountain to **Brandon Gap** (elevation 2,170 feet), there will be numerous turnoffs for National Forest roads and trails. Among them are Forest Road 42 (Bingo Road), right, which meanders along a stream leading past a trove of cellar holes, 19th-century cemeteries, and swimming holes; Forest Road 45 (Chittenden Brook Road), left, which leads to the difficult, 7 1/2 mile Chittenden Brook Trail and its intersection with the Long Trail; and the Mount Horrid Great Cliff Trail, right, a steep 1 4/10 mile route from Brandon Gap to the top of the "Great Cliff" on 3,216-foot Mount Horrid. *(Note: This trail is closed when peregrine falcons, which disappeared in the 1950s and were reintroduced by the state in the 1980s, are nesting in the cliffs.)*

The turnoff for Recreation Route 32 and Goshen – once famous for Goshen potatoes – is on the right as you descend the Gap (if you follow this road to its end, you'll head past the Blueberry Hill Inn and through Moosalamoo Recreation Area, ending up back on Route 125 in Ripton). **Continue on Route 73 through Forest Dale**, where a plaque commemorates the iron works which thrived here from 1810 until 1865.

Head into downtown Brandon on Route 73, and turn right onto Park Street. This broad, maple-shaded avenue was once a military parade ground. Park Street ends at the town center, whose entire core of 243 buildings is listed on the National Register of Historic Places. Even if you're not staying at the 1786 **Brandon Inn**, stop for a look at the comfortably elegant lobby, which seems to have been frozen in time.

Just north of downtown, turn left off Route 7 onto Pearl Street and continue for 1 3/10 mile to the 132-foot **Sanderson Bridge**, built circa 1840. This bridge over Otter Creek was closed to vehicles in 1987, and was slated for renovations. But because the creek was a known Indian route, and the state requires an archaeological investigation of any possibly sensitive area before construction begins, the University of Vermont conducted a dig in 1993. To the west of the bridge they found remains dating back 5,000 years; to the east were Woodland Indian remains approximately 1,600 years old. It is believed that there may have been a permanent Woodland settlement here – the only one ever found in Vermont. The bridge has been reopened for vehicles.

Head back into Brandon and drive north a short distance on Route 7 to the white cottage next to the Baptist Church. It's the **birthplace of Stephen A. Douglas,** "The Little Giant" of Lincoln-Douglas Debate fame. The Brandon Chamber of Commerce has an information booth here, where you can pick up a copy of the brochure, "Map & Guide for Brandon and Surrounding Area." The birthplace also houses the new **Brandon Museum,** which focuses on the history of the community and its relation to the abolitionist movement.

In 1851, Stephen A. Douglas remarked that "Vermont was a good state to be born in provided one migrated early." Oddly, the occasion was his receipt of an honorary degree from Middlebury College.

Turn around and continue south on Route 7 into Pittsford. A marble monument on the right marks the site where Caleb Houghton was killed by Indians in 1780, and where Fort Vengeance, named by his friends, was erected. The **New England Maple Museum,** "the world's largest maple museum" (and a mighty big gift shop, too), tells the story of maple sugaring from sap to syrup.

Pittsford is home to four covered bridges, including the 139-foot **Hammond Covered Bridge,** now a State Historic Site. To get to the bridge, turn right onto Kendall Hill Road approximately 1 1/10 mile north of town and continue for 3/10 mile. If you're at the bridge in late April or May, look for fiddlehead ferns, one of Vermont's most popular native delicacies. If you're camping, or have cooking facilities (or an obliging B&B host), all they need is a quick steaming and sautéing in butter (they're edible only before the "fiddlehead" has unfurled).

The Hammond Covered Bridge is one of Vermont's better-traveled historic spans, having taken a mile-long journey down Otter Creek during the Great Flood of 1927. It was brought back to its proper site by the clever means of floating it on empty steel barrels and hauling it upstream with a team of horses.

Salmon and trout are hatched at the U.S. Fish and Wildlife Service's **Pittsford National Fish Hatchery,** on Furnace Road just south of town off Route 7.

a town built on marble......................................

At the junction of routes 7 and 3, turn south onto Route 3 to Proctor, "Marble Center of the World." Marble was first quarried here in 1836, and for more than 100 years the town was home to the Vermont Marble Company, established by Redfield Proctor, one-time state senator, governor, and U.S. secretary of war. In its heyday, in addition to its home state, Vermont Marble had quarries in Colorado, Tennessee, and Alaska. Proctor marble (and some from nearby Danby) went into Washington D.C.'s U.S. Supreme Court building and the Lincoln Memorial.

Marble is in evidence everywhere in Proctor – at the bridge into town, in public buildings, on signs, and in cemeteries. The **Vermont Marble Museum**, the world's largest marble museum (just off Route 3, after the town library), features a fascinating, hands-on geology exhibit, demonstrations by resident carvers (with marble items for sale), and a walk to the now-inactive Sutherland Falls Quarry.

Before leaving town, be sure to stop at the roaring, 128-foot Sutherland Falls, named for an early settler who harnessed the falls' cascade to power a sawmill and gristmill.

Back on Route 3, continue south to Route 4 and Rutland.

information *All area codes are (802) unless otherwise indicated.*

Brandon Area Chamber of Commerce (247-6401), Stephen A. Douglas Birthplace, 4 Grove St. (Rte. 7), P.O. Box 267, Brandon 05733. brandon.org

Green Mountain National Forest, USDA Forest Service. Manchester Ranger District (362-2307), Rtes. 11/30, Manchester Center 05255. Rochester Ranger District (767-4261), Rochester 05767. fs.fed.us/r9/gmfl

Rutland Region Chamber of Commerce (773-2747), 256 N. Main St., Rutland 05701. Info. booth: Memorial Day weekend-Columbus Day weekend, Main St. Park, cor. Rte. 4/ 7. rutlandvermont.com

lodging

Note: There are numerous chain and independent motels on Rtes. 4 & 7 on the outskirts of Rutland.

Blueberry Hill Inn (247-6735), 1307 Goshen-Ripton Rd., Goshen 05733. Antiques, quilts and – in winter – hot water bottles to warm the beds are trademarks of this lovely 11-room inn in the Green Mountain National Forest. Activities include hiking and mountain biking, and x-country skiing. Menus change nightly; 4-course dinners (BYOB) are preceded by cheese tastings. MAP available. blueberryhillinn.com $$$

Brandon Inn (247-5766), Village Green, Brandon 05733. 39 spacious rooms with period furnishings, private baths, and a/c; TV only in lounge. Secluded pool. Rates include breakfast. D only when groups are booked. historicbrandoninn.com $$

Brandon Motor Lodge (247-9594), 2095 Franklin St. (Rte. 7), Brandon 05733. 25 comfortable units. Pets welcome ($10). Breakfast available summer and fall. brandonmotorlodge.com $-$$

The Chipman Inn (388-2390), Rte. 125, Ripton. Traditional 1828 inn with 7 rooms and 1 suite, all with private bath; most with a/c. Bar (beer and wine). Closed Apr. and Nov. chipmaninn.com $$-$$$

Edgewater Resort (468-5251), Rte. 30, Lake Bomoseen 05732. 50 motel, inn, and condo rooms with a/c, TV, and fridges; 24 housekeeping units and cottages. Many units on lake. Pool, game room, restaurant, golf course next door. Weekly rates available. edgewatervermont.com $-$$

Harvest Moon B&B (773-0889), 1659 North Grove St., Rutland 05701. Vt. State Register of Historic Places, 1835 farmhouse overlooking the Green Mountains has 2 guest rooms – 1 with a 4-poster bed, another with a claw-foot tub. Vegetarian breakfast. Heirloom gardens. harvestmoonvt.com $$

The Inn at Rutland (773-0575), 70 N. Main St. (Rte. 7), Rutland 05701. 1889 Victorian mansion has 8 individually decorated rooms with private bath and TV; some with a/c. 3-course breakfast. innatrutland.com $$-$$$

Inn on Park Street (247-3843), 69 Park St., Brandon 05733. 5 rooms and a suite with private baths and Victorian furnishings in a c. 1865 Italianate home. Home-baked treats at breakfast; desserts nightly in the living room. Weekend cooking class packages. theinnonparkstreet.com $$-$$$

Lilac Inn (247-5463), 53 Park St., Brandon 05733. 1909 National Register mansion on 2 landscaped acres has 9 luxurious and elegantly furnished guest rooms, 3 with wood burning fireplaces, ideal for a romantic interlude. Fabulous honeymoon suite; and a cottage that sleeps 4. 3-course breakfast. 2-night minimum summer and fall weekends (3 nights holiday weekends). Pet friendly ($35). lilacinn.com $$-$$$$

Motel at Mendon Mountain Orchards (775-5477), Rte. 4 E, Rutland. 12 pleasant non-housekeeping rooms with cable TV and a/c nestled in Vermont's oldest working apple orchard. Pool. Pets welcome ($5). Also, a farm store with gifts and homemade pies. mendonorchards.com $

restaurants

Birdseye Diner (468-5817), Main St., Castleton. Restored 1949 Silk City diner features homemade muffins and pastries; daily specials. B, L, & D. $

Café Provence (247-9997), 11 Center St. (Rte. 7), Brandon. Hearty salads, soups, sandwiches and quiche at lunch; dinner might include thin tomato pie with Vermont blue cheese, and marinated grilled lamb chops on ratatouille. Tapas menu. L, D, & Sun. brunch. $$$

The Palms (773-2367), 36 Strongs Ave., Rutland. This Italian restaurant has been chef-owned and family-operated – five generations – for more than 75 years. Classic southern Italian menu. D; closed Sun. $-$$

Panda Pavilion (775-6682), 283 Rte. 4, Rutland. Popular Chinese restaurant serves authentic Szechuan, Hunan, and Mandarin specialties. L & D. $

Patricia's Restaurant (247-3223), 18 Center St., Brandon. Traditional country fare includes pork chops and fried haddock; daily specials. L, D, and Sun. brunch. $

Seward Family Restaurant (773-2738), 224 N. Main St., (Rte. 7), Rutland. The former dairy bar, in operation since 1946, serves up its own brand of ice cream as well as sandwiches and dinner platters. B, L, & D. $

Sugar & Spice Restaurant & Gift Shop, Rte. 4, Mendon. If you're there in spring, you can watch maple syrup being made. But homemade maple walnut ice cream, pancakes, waffles and other breakfast favorites are always in season (and served up at breakfast or lunch), along with lunchtime sandwiches. The gift shop features Vermont-made products. B & L. $

Table 24 (775-2424), 24 Wales St., Rutland. Sophisticated comfort food such as meatloaf with wild mushrooms, along with less traditional offerings including wild mushroom ravioli, and tamari glazed trout, served in a casually upscale spot in town. L & D Mon.-Sat. $$-$$$

Three Tomatoes (747-7747), 88 Merchants Row. Cheerful downtown *trattoria* features reliable chicken, veal, and pasta dishes that rise above the usual red-sauce offerings; try the sausage and gnocchi. D. $$

attractions

Branbury State Park (247-5925), Lake Dunmore. Campground; lean-tos. Beach on Lake Dunmore. Late May - mid-Oct.

Brandon Museum (247-6401), 4 Grove St. (Rte. 7), Brandon. Daily summer and fall; call for hours.

Breadloaf Wilderness: see Green Mountain National Forest in "Information" above.

Chaffee Art Center (775-0356), 16 S. Main St., Rutland. Open Wed.–Sat., Sun. p.m. Closed winter. Donation.

Hubbardton Battle Monument and Museum (759-2412), 5696 Monument Rd., off Rte. 30, Hubbardton. Late May-Columbus Day, Thurs.-Sun.

Mount Independence State Historic Site (759-2412; 948-2000 in season), 497 Mount Independence Rd., 6 mi. W. of Rte. 22A, Orwell. Visitors Center, hiking trails. Memorial Day-Columbus Day.

New England Maple Museum (483-9414), Rte. 7, Pittsford. Mid-March-Dec. Admission to museum only.

Norman Rockwell Museum of Vermont (773-6095), Rte. 4, Rutland. Magazine covers, advertisements and other published illustrations document the artists' career from 1912 to 1978. Gift shop.

Pittsford National Fish Hatchery (483-6618), Furnace Rd., Pittsford.

Rocking Horse Country Store (773-7882), 1307 Rte. 4, Rutland. 3 floors of Vermont foods, homemade wine, antiques, and gifts.

Stephen A. Douglas Birthplace (247-6401), 4 Grove St. (Rte. 7), Brandon. (See Brandon Museum, above.)

Vermont Marble Museum. (459-2300), 52 Main St., Proctor. Mid-May-Oct.; gift shop open year-round.

Wilson Castle (773-3284). West Proctor Rd., Proctor. Memorial Day-Columbus Day.

activities

Moosalamoo National Recreation Area (747-7900). moosalamoo.org

Pond Hill Ranch (468-2449 or 468-0578), 1683 Pond Hill Rd., Castleton. Trail rides, riding lessons on a 2,000-acre ranch. Rodeos Sat. eve. July-Labor Day.

Robert Frost Wayside Area and Trails (388-4362), Rte. 125, Ripton.

Spirit in Nature Interfaith Path Center (388-7244), Rte. 125, Ripton; (mailing address: P.O. Box 253, East Middlebury 05740.)

Woodard Marine (265-3690), Lake Bomoseen Marina, 615 Creek Rd., Hydeville. Power boat (including ski and pontoon boats) and kayak rentals.

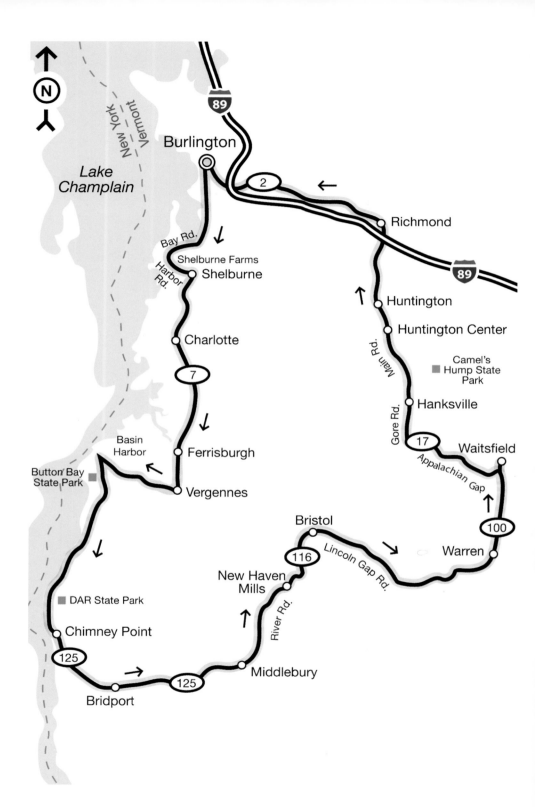

Drive 5

From Lake Champlain Shores to Middlebury and Lincoln Gap

137 miles

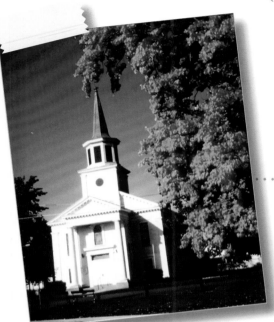

major attractions

- Shelburne Farms
- Shelburne Museum
- Lincoln Gap
- Lake Champlain Maritime Museum
- Middlebury

Follow the shoreline of Lake Champlain south from Burlington (see Drive 6 for Burlington), stopping along the way to learn the role of this "Sixth Great Lake" in American history. Meander east through prime dairy country to the college town of Middlebury, and then climb through Lincoln Gap before descending into Mad River Valley ski country. Head back to Burlington via the tortuous Appalachian Gap, skirting – or maybe conquering on foot – a prominent mountain peak with a history of colorful animal names.

Begin in Burlington (see Drive 6) and head south on Route 7 (Shelburne Road), navigating your way through one of the (thankfully) few parts of

Vermont that truly deserves the label "urban sprawl." It's also the home of the state's worst rush-hour traffic. Suburban Route 7 does offer a choice of inexpensive chain and independent motels and restaurants, but other than that it will appeal to you only if your idea of a Vermont souvenir is a dining room set or a new car.

Turn right onto Bay Road in Shelburne, just over the town line from South Burlington, **and follow along the south shore of Lake Champlain's Shelburne Bay.** It was here, during the War of 1812, that the "poor forlorn looking [American] squadron" under the command of Thomas Macdonough wintered in 1812-13 before moving south to Vergennes.

legacies of the gilded age

Just ahead is Shelburne Farms, the 1880s retreat of railroad magnifico William Seward Webb and his wife, Lila Vanderbilt Webb. The 1,400-acre estate overlooking Lake Champlain was landscaped by Frederick Law Olmsted, and was originally nearly three times as large as it is today. Webb's descendants now maintain the property as a model farm, agricultural education center, and cheese making operation – its cheddar has won awards – complete with bucolic footpaths and a barnyard where children can meet farm animals.

The Webbs' 1889 110-room summer "cottage" is now the elegant Inn at Shelburne Farms, but perhaps the property's greatest architectural attractions are its monumental barns. The restored Farm Barn, built in an Arcadian version of Richardson Romanesque, is, at more than 400 feet in length, actually large enough to house a polo match, were anyone inclined to stage one. In addition to the regular program of tours, Shelburne Farms' grounds are open for a variety of seasonal special events, including Vermont Mozart Festival and Vermont Symphony Orchestra concerts (see Drive 6 for information).

> *Built in 1891, the Breeding Barn at Shelburne Farms was once the largest open-span wooden structure in the U.S.*

Leaving Shelburne Farms, turn right onto Harbor Road, and continue to Route 7. Turn right on Route 7, and continue south through the tidy Shelburne Village Historic District to one of the Vermont's premier attractions, the **Shelburne Museum.** The forty-five-acre complex contains thirty-seven buildings, most of them representative late-eighteenth and early-nineteenth-century structures moved here from sites around New England.

The museum's collection of fine and folk art, and of Americana ranging from quilts to farm tools to hand-carved decoys to toys to horse-drawn carriages – some 80,000 objects in all – had its origins in the vast trove bequeathed by its founder, the late Electra Havemeyer Webb, a sugar heiress who married J. Watson Webb of the Shelburne Farms Webbs.

Highlights include a Gilded Age private railroad car (a princely indulgence that makes a corporate jet look like a flimsy and inconsequential toy); shops at which artisans demonstrate old-time trades; and everyone's favorite, the SS Ticonderoga, last of the side-wheeler steamships to ply Lake Champlain. (It was moved to its high-and-dry location nearly fifty years ago, on railroad tracks specially constructed for the task, and has just been given a keel-to-wheelhouse restoration. The Museum also maintains a circa-1950 suburban ranch house, still in its original location adjoining the grounds. Museum visitors can tour the house, which is authentic to its era right down to the canned goods in the cupboards.

Plan to spend at least a half-day at the museum.

Next door to the museum, on Bostwick Road, is the National Museum of the Morgan Horse, which celebrates the life and times of Justin Morgan, the schoolteacher who first introduced the doughty breed to Vermont, and of course the horses themselves. (The original Morgan Horse was also called Justin Morgan – more on both of them when we get to Weybridge, down near Middlebury.)

Continue south on Route 7. If you're traveling with kids, they'll love a tour of the **Vermont Teddy Bear Factory**, a short distance ahead on the left. There's a museum of teddy bear history, and a work area where you can make your own bears.

vistas preserved . . . .

Continue south on Route 7 through Charlotte: As you travel toward Charlotte, you'll notice the open, rolling rural landscape, with views across Lake Champlain to the Adirondack Mountains in New York State. Back in the 1990s Dr. Stephen Rockefeller, a professor emeritus of religion at Middlebury College, decided that he wanted to do something to preserve the view that he had enjoyed so often when driving along Route 7. He joined with the Conservation Fund to form The Demeter Fund (named for the Greek goddess of grain, fertility and agriculture) to purchase and conserve 850 acres. Today the **Charlotte Park and Wildlife Refuge** encompasses Mr. Rockefeller's panoramas as well as trails, wetlands, forest lands, and more than 500 acres of preserved farmlands. To get to the park, turn right just past the Shelburne Museum onto Bostwick Road, past the Morgan Horse Museum, to the entrance on Greenbush Road.

As you continue south into Charlotte, you'll understand what Professor Rockefeller was afraid of. The fields of the one-time farming community have sprouted posh homes on the 10-acre lots that have come to symbolize upscale sprawl. But there's relief at the **Vermont Wildflower Farm**, six luminous acres of wildflowers where pathways punctuated with explanatory plaques thread through fields and glades. The seed shop will get you started on transforming your own back forty.

> *In 1849, railroad workers laying track in Charlotte uncovered the fossil of a beluga whale, dating back 12,500 years to when Lake Champlain was connected with the Atlantic Ocean. "Charlotte" is now the official Vermont State Fossil.*

In **Ferrisburgh**, a cluster of historic buildings houses the **Ferrisburgh Artisans' Guild**. The renovated complex features arts and crafts by more than 130 juried Vermont artists and houses artists' studios. The **Starry Night Café**, one of the area's most popular restaurants, opens its outdoor deck in nice weather.

A bit further south, on the left-hand side of Route 7, is **Rokeby**, the home of one of Vermont's favorite authors, Rowland Robinson (1833-1900). Robinson, who is noted for his stories written in upcountry Yankee and French-Canadian dialect, was a Quaker and a passionate abolitionist, and his farmhouse is believed to have been a stop on the Underground Railroad. In his book A Study of Independence, he reported that "[the railroad] held its hidden way through Vermont along which many a dark skinned passenger secretly traveled, concealed during the day in quiet stations, at night passing from one to another, helped onward by friendly hands until he reached Canada ..." At Rokeby, Robinson's books and illustrations are exhibited along with memorabilia of the four generations of his family who lived here.

Bear right off Route 7 onto Route 22A past **Kennedy Brothers Marketplace**, an old creamery complex housing dozens of shops selling crafts and Vermontiana. Now you're in **Vergennes**, Vermont's oldest city, founded in 1788. The downtown area is a tidy, compact district of Victorian homes and public buildings. Main Street slopes down to Otter Creek Falls, where, during the War of 1812, furnaces and forges turned out 170 tons of cannonballs. It was just below the falls, in 1814, that Thomas Macdonough oversaw the building of three ships – including the 734-ton Saratoga – in the incredibly short span of forty days, enabling him to seize victory over the British at the battle of Plattsburgh and earn his memorial on Vergennes' green.

When Thomas Macdonough took command of the Lake Champlain naval squadron in October of 1812, it was a sad assemblage of small, poorly armed vessels manned by untrained crews. Two years later he commanded a sizable fleet and a crack fight-

ing force. Still, he knew that it would be folly to meet the British on the open waters of the big lake. So he strategically placed his ships in the harbor at Plattsburgh, on the New York side, and waited for the enemy to come to him. They did, on September 11, 1814. The ensuing battle ranks with Perry's Lake Erie victory, in the same war, as one of the most swiftly decisive engagements ever fought by the United States Navy on fresh water. It decimated His Majesty's fleet, forced the British army to retreat into Canada, and assured that the Great Lakes would remain in American hands.

Side Trip

Head east on Route 17 seven miles to the 2,858-**acre Dead Creek Wildlife Management Area**, home to a wealth of bird and animal life including black bear, wild turkey, and several species of ducks. The 1,000-acre Waterfowl Area serves as a major stopover for snow geese on their southerly migration. The marshy tract is popular with canoeists, birders, and, in season, duck hunters.

history on land and lake

Just west of Vergennes, turn right onto Panton Road to Basin Harbor Road and the Lake Champlain Maritime Museum. The museum, which serves as a conservation center for artifacts brought up from the lake bottom (a spectacular find was one of Benedict Arnold's Revolutionary War gunboats) offers exhibits chronicling the military, mercantile, and recreational history of Lake Champlain. Maps and vintage watercraft tell the lake's story, from the era of the Indians and French explorers, down through its role as the birthplace of the American Navy in the eighteenth century and its later importance in the freight and passenger trade ... not to mention Prohibition-era bootlegging. Moored in a cove adjacent to the museum is a modern replica of another Arnold gunboat, the Philadelphia. Clamber aboard, and conjure up this far outpost of the days of fighting sail.

Many historic shipwrecks have been preserved in the cold, deep waters of Lake Champlain – but they're increasingly susceptible to encrustation by zebra mussels, a nuisance invasive species.

Back on Basin Harbor Road, continue directly to the 700-acre Basin Harbor Club, a serenely luxurious old resort on Lake Champlain which has it has its own airstrip, and still asks gentlemen to wear jackets and ties at dinner. **Or turn left onto Button Bay Road to Button Bay State Park**, one of the loveliest public-access areas on Lake Champlain. The name of the park comes from the little button-shaped stones, oddly pierced at their centers, which turn up on the beach here. The stones, which have become more rare in recent years, were formed when sediment collected around the stems of prehistoric vegetation.

At the fork, bear right onto Arnold Bay Road and follow along the shore of Lake Champlain past Arnold Bay. Here in October of 1776, Benedict Arnold, pursued by the British after the battle of Valcour Island (see Drive 6), ran his flagship Congress and four other vessels ashore and burned them – with colors flying – rather than let them be captured by the British.

Continue south along the lakeshore, following Arnold Bay Road as it turns into Lake Road past Yankee Kingdom Orchard, and then onto Lake Street, which merges with Route 17. Continue south on 17 to the turnoff for **DAR State Park** and the **John Strong Mansion**. This handsome Georgian house, built in the 1790s with bricks fired on site, stands near the location of Strong's original home, burned by the British in 1777. Check out the four "hidey holes": historians are unsure whether they were meant to hide family members during Indian attacks, to protect them from bears (one had entered Strong's first house looking for food), or both.

Just past the park, at the junction of Routes 17 and 125, in the shadow of the bridge to New York State, is **Chimney Point State Historic Site**. Some say that Samuel de Champlain stood here on July 30, 1609, and named the lake after himself. In 1690 a party of French colonists from the vicinity of modern-day Albany, New York, established what became a vital outpost here. The French fled in 1759, shortly before Mohawk raiders torched the settlement. All that remained were blackened chimneys; hence the name.

The site's museum, which traces the area's Native American and French heritage, is housed in a late eighteenth-century tavern and inn that was built on the remains of a prehistoric Indian campsite and the French settlement. According to legend, Green Mountain Boys Ethan Allen and Seth Warner were surprised by the British in the inn's taproom (the Boys knew every taproom in Vermont) and narrowly escaped capture. However, architectural evidence points to the present structure having been built after the time of the alleged incident.

Cross the Crown Point Bridge into New York State for a look at the Champlain Lighthouse, restored for the 2009 celebration of the 400th anniversary of the explorer's arrival in Vermont. Of particular note is a bronze relief plaque by Auguste Rodin, "La France," set in the lighthouse base.

Turn left (east) onto Route 125 to the tiny village of **Bridport**, where 125 takes a short jog to the south along Route 22A before heading east again on its own. Approximately three miles from the village, watch on the left for the tiny cemetery near the intersection with Snake Mountain Road. There are several interesting old headstones here, including one for Mr. Benedict, who "was slain by apoplexy without warning and entered into spirit life 6/20/1881."

a classic college town . . . .

Continue on Route 125 into Middlebury, passing the campus of **Middlebury College** before reaching downtown. Middlebury, an esteemed liberal arts institution with no present-day religious affiliation, was founded in 1800 as a godly alternative to the University of Vermont, then just getting off the ground itself but suspect because of its nominal association with the freethinking Allen brothers. The college's chief benefactor was local squire Gamaliel Painter – his Federalist mansion still stands downtown – for whom the oldest campus building, the elegantly simple Painter Hall (1816), is named.

The Middlebury campus building of greatest interest to visitors (aside from those heading for the admissions office) is the college's **Museum of Art.** Highlights of the collections include sculptures by Auguste Rodin and the nineteenth-century Woodstock, Vermont native, Hiram Powers; as well as ancient Cypriot pottery and works by contemporary painters.

Middlebury's downtown, which bustles with the shops and restaurants of a typical New England college community, clusters against the banks of Otter Creek. At this point, the "creek" is more of a full-fledged river complete with a lovely waterfall. The town's historic district has almost 300 buildings that were built during the eighteenth- and early-nineteenth centuries, when it was a major wool-processing center and site of Vermont's first major marble quarrying operation (1803). An 1829 marble merchant's home houses **the Henry Sheldon Museum of Vermont History** and its superb collection of nineteenth-century Vermont paintings, furniture, decorative arts, household items and farm tools, as well as the contents of an old-time pharmacist's establishment. Another marble-era relic is the **Historic Marble Works,** off Elm Street just north of downtown. The complex, which is actually built of marble, now houses shops, offices, and restaurants.

> *Amun-Her-Khepesh-Ef, an Egyptian prince who died in 1883 B.C. at the age of two and was mummified, has had a long, strange trip, indeed. In 1886, when the eclectic collector Henry Sheldon was amassing the many and varied objects that would later be in his museum, he heard that the prince's mummy was being sold in New York for $20. He had it shipped to Middlebury, where it arrived in ill repair. Sheldon paid $10 and put the mummy in his office, and then in his attic. In 1945, the museum's curator found the mummy in even worse shape. The museum's board had it cremated, then laid the prince's remains to rest in Middlebury Cemetery (also called West Cemetery). His headstone isn't hard to spot – it's the one with a Christian cross, an Egyptian ankh, and a bird on it.*

Downtown Middlebury's most distinctive structure is the 1809 **Congregational Church,** on the north side of the Green. With its arched doorways, magnificent Palladian window, and 136-foot, four-tiered spire incorporating an octagonal belfry, the church joins Bennington's First Congregational (see Drive 2) and Strafford's Town House as perhaps the most graceful ecclesiastical structures in Vermont. Also worth a look, or a stroll through the lobby, or even a night's stay, is the **Middlebury Inn**, an inviting 1830 brick hostelry facing the Green. At the Vermont Folklife Center you can listen to recordings of Vermonters' reminiscences and folktales.

There are two covered bridges in Middlebury: **Pulp Mill Bridge**, built between 1808 and 1820; and Vermont's highest, the 1824 **Halpin Bridge**, built to carry wagon loads of marble forty-one feet over the Muddy Branch of the New Haven River. Ask in town for directions to both bridges, which are on the northern outskirts.

Side Trip

Located just four miles north of Middlebury, **the University of Vermont Morgan Horse Farm** is dedicated to the breeding and promotion of Vermont's state animal. All Morgans are descended from a horse called Figure, who lived at the beginning of the nineteenth century and was owned by a Vermont schoolteacher named Justin Morgan. Figure (later himself known as Justin Morgan), who was most likely descended from Thoroughbred and Arabian stock, was a "genetic sport" – an animal showing significant changes from its parental stock. In Figure's case, the new characteristics were compactness and clean-lined limbs, along with powerful neck muscles, shoulders, and quarters. Now prized by recreational equestrians, Morgans were formerly a mainstay of the U.S. Cavalry, for which they were raised on this 150-acre farm. The University of Vermont facility offers tours of its barns and a presentation on Morgan history.

From Middlebury, take Route 125 west to Route 23 (Weybridge Street) north, and follow signs.

into the Green Mountains

Leaving Middlebury, head north on Route 7 for just under three miles and turn right onto River Road toward New Haven Mills. This once-thriving community on the banks of the New Haven River was devastated by the 1927 flood. But one building – a Victorian Italianate structure perched high on a hill in town – was left unscathed and now stands out like a sore thumb in this farm country. This former schoolhouse was the gift of native son Curtis Miranda Lampson, who left Vermont in his early years, made a fortune in the fur trade as an associate of John Jacob Astor, and was knighted by Queen Victoria for helping to finance the first transatlantic telegraph cable. The school was built in 1868, with Lampson's $8,000 donation. Lampson School served the community until World War II, and has been restored after years of neglect.

Turn left (north) at the intersection with Route 116 (which soon merges with Route 17) to reach Bristol. The tidy little community with its red brick, vest-pocket downtown today calls itself the "Gateway to the Green Mountains," but it once had a less glamorous nickname. It was known as the "Coffin Community" back when the National Casket Company was one of the wood products enterprises that took advantage of Bristol's proximity to a vast sea of lumber. Several are still in business, though coffins are no longer part of the picture.

As you continue east out of Bristol on Route 116/17, watch for the Lord's Prayer Rock. A Buffalo physician named Joseph Greene, who grew up near Bristol, recalled teamsters swearing mightily as they cracked their whips to coax overworked horses up the muddy hill. In 1891, Dr. Greene had the rock inscribed as a counter to the teamsters' profanity.

A short distance from town, at the Squirrel's Nest Restaurant, bear right onto Lincoln Gap Road, which twists and turns alongside the New Haven River as it descends through the **New Haven River Gorge** in a series of rapids, cascades, and waterfalls. There are two wonderful swimming holes along the road: **Bristol Falls**, on the right immediately after the turn-off (one of the best pools is at the upper waterfall, approximately 4/10 mile up the road); and, a short distance up the road, also on the right, **Circle Current**.

Side Trip

Bristol is the gateway to Bristol Cliffs Wilderness, one of central Vermont's most intriguing natural areas. At Bristol Cliffs, a 3,740-acre tract of the Green Mountain National Forest maintained as a roadless area off-limits to logging and mechanized travel, vertical crags rise from the rugged shoulder of South Mountain to tower 1,500 feet above the Champlain valley. One protrusion, Devil's Pulpit, is a bulging mass of quartzite that may have been used for Indian arrowheads. Although the peripheral parts of the present-day wilderness were once logged, the deep interior of the parcel is covered by what is believed to be one of Vermont's few old-growth virgin forests. Both Lower Notch Road, which extends south from River Street in downtown Bristol, and Lincoln Gap Road off Route 116/17 east of town offer access to Bristol Cliffs trailheads. Hikers should note, however, that in keeping with the tract's wilderness status, trails peter out; and the use of compasses and topographical maps is recommended.

threading through Lincoln Gap . . . .

Lincoln, settled by Quakers more than 200 years ago, retains the look and feel of a frontier logging town. In fact, the **Old Hotel B&B** was built in 1820 to house lumberjacks. One note of sophistication is the brick Burnham Library, which was refurbished after sustaining extensive flood damage in 1997.

The road through **Lincoln Gap** (closed in winter) is the highest automobile route in the state, cresting at an altitude of 2,424 feet. It snakes through a steep, narrow pass surrounded by mountains, including Mt. Ellen, Vermont's third highest (4,135 feet). The Long Trail crosses the highway near the top, where there are sweeping panoramas of the Green Mountain Range, the Champlain Valley, and the Adirondacks. A moderately difficult 1.25 mile trail at the top passes through the **Bread Loaf Wilderness**, a 21,480-acre primitive tract which is the Green Mountain National Forest's largest wilderness and offers expansive views that include Warren to the east, Mount Abraham to the north, Bristol and the Bristol Cliffs to the west, and Mount Grant to the south.

Side Trip

The moderately difficult but nevertheless popular Battell Trail (4 6/10 miles) climbs to the Battell Shelter, which sleeps eight. From the shelter, which is maintained by the Green Mountain Club and the U.S. Forest Service, a steep 8/10- mile trail leads to the open summit of Mount Abraham (there's a connection here with the Long Trail) and fabulous views of the White Mountains, Bristol Cliffs, Lake Champlain, and the Adirondacks. Be sure to watch where you walk on the summit: it shelters a variety of rare, arctic-alpine plants. To reach the Battell Trail, head north out of Lincoln village on Quaker Street, then turn right on Elder Hill Road. Bear right at the fork and follow signs for trail parking.

The road through Lincoln Gap descends to Route 100, the main street of the Mad River valley. The surrounding region is home to two of Vermont's major ski areas – **Sugarbush** and **Mad River Glen**. **At the intersection with Route 100, turn left (north) for a short distance, and then take the second right, Covered Bridge Road, for Warren village.** The road crosses the Mad River through the 1879-1880 **Warren Covered Bridge**. Most of the town's Greek Revival homes were built much earlier, when Warren was a thriving mill village. Today it exists primarily as a service town for the ski areas, and is home to the elegant **Pitcher Inn**. Enjoy a home baked pastry or lunch on the deck overlooking the waterfall at the historic **Warren Store**, across from the inn.

Side Trip

If you're thinking more about swimming than skiing in the Mad River Valley, detour south on Route 100 for a few miles to Warren Falls, one of the state's most popular swimming holes. Park in the lot on the right by the sign that reads, "43rd Infantry Division Memorial Highway."

Head north on Route 100, past one of the access roads to Sugarbush, to the junction with Route 17. To visit **Waitsfield**, the main service area for the ski resorts, continue north on Route 100 for about a mile. The Chamber of Commerce distributes an excellent brochure entitled "Waitsfield Village Historic District Walking Tour," which provides information on the town's many historic buildings. The 1833 **Village Bridge**, most likely the state's second oldest covered bridge, and one of the few with an attached walkway, is on Bridge Street. Graton Associates, the company that restored the bridge in 1973, was committed to using only wood, rather than adding the steel I-beam supports found in many rehabbed covered bridges. Look for their craftsmanship in the roof bracing, which incorporates "ship knees" – right-angle timbers cut from the junctures of branches and trunks on large trees.

a gap, a gore – and Camel's Hump . . . .

Backtrack to Route 17 and continue west, past access roads for Sugarbush and Mad River Glen – the former a modern, two-mountain mega-resort, and the latter a proud, cooperative-owned throwback boasting Vermont's only no-snowboard policy and the last single chairlift in operation in the U.S.

The road now ascends through a tortuous series of switchbacks into unorganized **Buels Gore** (2000 population: 12) and crests the **Appalachian Gap** at 2,365 feet in the shadow of Baby Stark Mountain. Just as abruptly, Route 17 begins its descent into the Champlain valley, with outstanding westward views at the summit and along the way.

Several small and remote pieces of land in Vermont have the word "Gore" in their names. What's a gore? No, it's not a place where an especially bloody battle was fought. The word's closest related use is in tailoring, in which a gore is a triangular piece of material inserted between two larger pieces to alter or expand a garment's shape. Similarly, a gore on the map is a triangular or nearly triangular parcel of land that was left over when two more uniformly shaped townships were surveyed.

At the bottom of the gap, turn right onto Gore Road, which soon changes names and becomes Main Road, and head north toward Hanksville and Huntington Center. In Huntington Center, turn off at the sign for **Camel's Hump State Park** and 4,083-ft. **Camel's Hump,** one of the Vermont's most popular hikers' destinations. The summit offers a look at examples of subalpine vegetation, along with views that range over hundreds of square miles and take in the highest peaks of three states: Vermont's Mount Mansfield (north); New York's Mount Marcy (west, across Lake Champlain); and New Hampshire's Mount Washington (east, among the other summits of the Presidential Range). There are several trails, of varying degrees of difficulty that meet the Long Trail near the summit of Camel's Hump. The best source of information is the Green Mountain Club, in Waterbury (see Drive 7) and its Guide Book of the Long Trail.

In 1944, an Army Air Corps B-24 crashed on the side of Camel's Hump, killing nine of the ten crewmembers on board. A section of the aircraft's wing remains on the mountain, visible from the Alpine Trail.

Samuel de Champlain called Camel's Hump le lion couchant – the couching lion – because he felt its ridgeline resembled just that when seen from the east or west. On Ira Allen's 1798 map, it was called "Camel's Rump," but Vermont gazetteer compiler Zadock Thompson, no doubt sensing the Victorian era just around the corner, changed the name to Camel's Hump – in any event, a more pronounced feature of the beast. We are glad no one is renaming the mountain in our own indelicate time.

Back on Main Road, continue north through Huntington, a former logging and dairying town that is now an outlying bedroom community for Burlington commuters. Just ahead are the **Green Mountain Audubon Nature Center** and the adjacent **Birds of Vermont Museum**. Visitors to the 230-acre nature center can wander a network of trails through woodlands, meadows, and apple orchards, and alongside beaver ponds.

Continue on to Richmond, home of the **Old Round Church**. The sixteen-sided structure with its octagonal belfry, completed in 1813, was a joint undertaking of five sects, who held services here until they each eventually broke away. The building served as the town hall for several years. The interior still has the original pews, pulpit, and gallery. Richmond itself has suffered two calamities: a fire destroyed the entire business section in 1908, and nineteen years later, in the Great Flood of 1927, much of the village was inundated when the Winooski River roared over its banks. Today, the thriving center, home to several businesses and restaurants, is frequently praised as an example of how even a small community can have a well planned, working downtown, despite all the trends to the contrary.

Turn left on Route 2 to return to Burlington via Williston (the latter part of this route is heavily commercialized), or hop onto I-89 northbound.

information *All area codes are (802) unless otherwise indicated.*

Addison County Chamber of Commerce (388-7951), 2 Court St., Middlebury 05753. midvermont.com

Green Mountain National Forest (767-4261), U.S.D.A. Forest Service, RD #1, Box 108, Rochester 05767. fs.fed.us/r9/forests/greenmountain

Lake Champlain Regional Chamber of Commerce (863-3489), 60 Main St., Suite 100, Burlington 05401. vermont.org/chamber

Mad River Valley Chamber of Commerce (496-3409), Rte. 100, P.O. Box 173, Waitsfield 05673. madrivervalley.com

lodging

Basin Harbor Club (475-2311), Basin Harbor Rd., Vergennes 05491. Lakefront resort has 38 rooms in the main inn and 2 lodges; and 74 1-3-bedroom cottages (some with fireplaces, decks, and porches). The dining room ($$-$$$) serves classic American fare such as pan-roasted breast of duck. Jackets and ties required in the restaurant and common rooms after 6 p.m. in summer. 18-hole golf course, pool, beach, children's programs. Pets welcome in cottages ($). Mid-May-mid-Oct. basinharbor.com $$$

Firefly Ranch (453-2223), 80 Bull Run Rd., (Lincoln) Bristol 05443. Horse lovers (and others) will enjoy this country b&b with its own pasture so you can bring your own horse. Small pets welcome. fireflybb.com $

Inn at Mad River Barn (80 496-3310), 2849 Mill Brook Rd. (Rte. 17), Waitsfield 05673. 15 guest rooms with TVs and some steam baths in a laid back, down-home environment. Dinner in winter. madriverbarn.com $-$$

Inn at Shelburne Farms (985-8498), 1611 Harbor Rd., Shelburne Farms, Shelburne 05482. The Webbs' 45-room, lakefront mansion has 24 rooms (17 with private bath) of varying size and amenities, and 2 cottages. The formal Marble Room serves contemporary regional dishes made with beef, lamb, and produce raised at Shelburne Farms. Sunday brunch is a treat, and includes admission to the grounds. Tennis courts, boats, and beach. Mid-May-mid-Oct. (no heat or air conditioning). shelburnefarms.org $$-$$$

Inn at the Round Barn Farm (496-2276), 1661 E. Warren Rd., Waitsfield 05673. The barn houses a lap pool and greenhouse; some of the 12 antiques-filled guest rooms and suites in the farmhouse have fireplaces and steam showers or Jacuzzis. Children 15 + welcome. X-c ski trails. roundbarninn.com $$-$$$$

The Inn on the Green (388-7512), 71 South Pleasant St., Middlebury 05753. Gracefully restored 1803 National Historic Register Landmark Federalist on the Green has 11 elegant rooms and suites. Breakfast included. innonthegreen.com $$-$$$$

Lemon Fair B & B 758-2699), Crown Point Rd., Bridport 05734. 4 comfortable guest rooms (2 with private bath) in a 1796 home. "We'll put a pie in the oven if we know you're coming," say the proprietors. $

Middlebury Inn (388-4961), 14 Court Sq., Middlebury 05753. All 55 rooms in the inn, as well as those in the contemporary motel and Victorian-era Porter House Mansion, are furnished with period pieces and have TVs, phones, and hair dryers. Rooms facing the front can be a bit noisy. The restaurant ($$) serves traditional Yankee fare and afternoon tea with home baked treats. B, L Mon.-Fri., D Wed.-Sun., & Sun. brunch. middleburyinn.com $$-$$$

Millbrook Inn and Restaurant (496-2405), Rte. 17, Waitsfield. 7 guest rooms with hand stenciling, antique bedsteads and handmade quilts; the 2-bedroom Octagon House ($$$) sleeps 4-5. Dinner ($-$$) specialties include five-peppercorn beef, three-cheese fettuccini, and Indian dishes. MAP available. Pets by arrangement. millbrookinn.com $$

The Old Hotel B&B (453-2567), 233 E. River Rd., Lincoln 05443. The recently renovated historic inn has 6 2nd-floor guest rooms with shared bath. Whole house rental available; also adjacent house by day or week. oldhotel.net $-$$

Pitcher Inn (496-6350), 275 Main St., Warren 05674. Each of the 9 rooms and 2 2-bedroom suites— all with Jacuzzis and many with steam showers and fireplaces – was designed by a different architect. The restaurant ($$$) serves contemporary American dishes such as lobster and corn chowder, and sesame crusted ahi tuna. The wine list is spectacular. B, D & Sun. brunch. pitcherinn.com $$$$

Richmond Victorian Inn (434-4410), 191 E. Main St., Rte. 2, Richmond 05477. Beautifully restored 1880's Queen Anne b&b has 6 antique-furnished guest rooms. Children 12+. richmondvictorianinn.com $$

The Wait Farm Motor Inn (496-2033), 4805 Main St., Waitsfield 05673. Tidy in-town motel has standard units and efficiencies. waitfarmmotorinn.com $-$$

restaurants

American Flatbread (496-8856), Lareau Farm, Rte. 100, Waitsfield. The pizzas, baked in a wood-fired clay oven, have crisp crusts and only the freshest toppings, and the chicken is oven roasted. D Fri. & Sat. $-$$

Buono's Italian Restaurant (985-2232), 3182 Shelburne Road (Rte. 7 next to the EconoLodge), Shelburne. Pizza and southern Italian classics. D. $$

Cafe Shelburne (985-3939), Rte. 7, Shelburne. One of the most popular upscale restaurants in the area has been serving delicious French bistro cuisine for over 35 years. D; closed Sun. and Mon. $$$-$$$$

The Common Man Restaurant (583-2800), 3209 German Flats Rd., Warren. Romantic restaurant in a 19th-century barn, serving dishes such as seared beef carpaccio and local cider and sage braised pork shank. D; closed Mon. $$$

De Pasquale's Delicatessen (388-3385), Marbleworks, Middlebury. Italian subs, fresh fried fish, salads, Italian meats, cheeses and wine for take-out. $

Fire & Ice (800-367-7166 or 388-7166), 26 Seymour St., Middlebury. Prime rib, steaks, fish, and a great salad and bread bar. Special "kids' room" to entertain the small ones while parents dine. L Tues.-Sat., D; Sun. from 1 p.m. for dinner. $$$

Mary's at Baldwin Creek (453-2432), 1868 Rte. 116 (at Rte. 17), Bristol. A highly creative chef, and a 1790s farmhouse dining room with a fieldstone fireplace and pewter oil lamps keep the crowds coming. Among specialties are cream of garlic soup, and lobster risotto. Also, 4 2nd-floor guest rooms ($$-$$$) and a 2-room suite. D Wed.- Sun., Sun. breakfast. $$$-$$$$

Harrington's of Vermont (985-2000), Rte. 7, across from Shelburne Museum, Shelburne. Gourmet goodies, cob-smoked bacon and ham, and the "World's Best Ham Sandwich." $

Roland's Place (453-6309), 3629 Rte. 7, New Haven Junction. In a beautifully restored 1796 house, French chef Roland prepares hearty entrees using fresh local products. "Early bird" specials are a deal. Also a b&b. D & Sun. brunch. $$$

Rosie's Restaurant (388-7052), Rte. 7S, Middlebury. Hearty family-style meals, homemade pies and soups. B, L, D. $-$$

Sonoma Station (434-5949), Bridge St., Richmond. New American cuisine in a laidback atmosphere. Specialties include duck liver pate and coriander-crusted pork loin. D Tues.–Sat. $$$

The Starry Night Café (877-6316), 5467 Rte. 7, Ferrisburgh. European and American cuisine with an innovative twist. D Wed.–Sat. $$$

Warren Store (496-3864), Warren Village. Bakery, sandwiches, picnic goodies. $

attractions

Birds of Vermont Museum (434-2167), 900 Sherman Hollow Rd., Huntington. Carvings of more than 150 bird species; wild bird viewing area, carving demonstrations, nature trails (open year round). May-Oct.

Bixby Memorial Library (877-2211), Vergennes. Mon.-Fri.

Button Bay State Park (475-2377), Vergennes. Camping, pool, boat rental, picnic tables, playground, hiking, nature center. Late May-Columbus Day.

Camels Hump State Park, Huntington. Information: Vermont Department of Forests, Parks and Recreation (241-3655), 103 South Main St., Waterbury.

Chimney Point State Historic Site (759-2412), Rtes. 17 & 125 (Lake Champlain Bridge), West Addison. Memorial Day-Columbus Day, Wed.-Sun.

Dakin Farm (425-3971), Rte. 7, Ferrisburgh. Cob smoked ham, cheese, maple syrup, and other specialty foods – and plenty of free samples.

D.A.R. State Park and John Strong Mansion (759-2354), Rte. 17, West Addison. Picnic area, and shale beach. Late May-Columbus Day.

Green Mountain Audubon Nature Center (434-3068), Sherman Hollow Rd., Huntington. Visitor Center closed Sun., and some Sat.; trails open daily.

Henry Sheldon Museum of Vermont History (388-2117), 1 Park St., Middlebury. Closed Sun.

Kennedy Brothers Marketplace (877-2975), Rte. 22A, Vergennes. Almost 200 crafts and antiques booths, Ben & Jerry's Scoop Shop, deli, Vermont foods and syrup. Play area.

Lake Champlain Ferry (864-9804), Charlotte. Schedule: ferries.com

Lake Champlain Maritime Museum (475-2022), 4472 Basin Harbor Rd., Vergennes. May-mid-Oct.

Middlebury College Museum of Art (443-5007), Center for the Arts, Middlebury. Closed Mon.

Mt. Philo State Park (425-2390), 5425 Mt. Philo Road, Charlotte. Mid-May-mid-Oct.

National Museum of the Morgan Horse (985-8665), 122 Bostwick Rd., Shelburne. Call for hrs. morganmuseum.org. Donation.

Robert Compton Pottery (453-3778), 2662 Rte. 116N, Bristol. Japanese wood fired kiln, raku, pit fired and stoneware pottery, clay fountains and aquariums, and hand woven textiles. By chance or appointment.

Rocky Dale Gardens (453-2782), 62 Rocky Dale Rd., Bristol. 3 acres of display gardens showcase perennials, dwarf conifers, and unusual trees and shrubs. Closed Tues.

Rokeby Museum (877-3406), Rte. 7, Ferrisburgh. Mid-May-mid-Oct., Thurs.-Sun. Guided tours 11 a.m., & 12:30 and 2 p.m.

Shelburne Farms (985-8686), Harbor Rd., Shelburne. Mid-May-mid-Oct. Farm store, visitor center, and walking trails year-round (no fee Nov.-Apr.)

Shelburne Museum (985-3346), Rte. 7, Shelburne. Late-May-mid-Oct. Mid-Oct.-late May, guided tour of selected buildings daily at 1 p.m., weather permitting, exc. holidays. Store open year round.

Sugarbush Resort (583-2381), Warren. Chairlift rides late June-mid-Oct.

UVM Morgan Horse Farm (388-2011), off Rte. 23, Middlebury. May-Oct.

Vermont Bookshop (388-2061), 38 Main St., Middlebury. One of the region's finest collections of current and out-of-print Vermont authors, including the works of Robert Frost.

Vermont Folklife Center (388-4964), 3 Court Square, Middlebury. Traditional arts and folkways center. Gallery closed Sun. and Mon.

Vermont Teddy Bear Company (985-1319), Rte. 7, Shelburne. Tour, museum, and factory store.

Vermont Wildflower Farm (425-3641), Rte. 7, Charlotte. Early Apr.-late Oct.

activities

Bike and Ski Touring Center (388-6666), 74 Main St., Middlebury. Bike rental. Call ahead on Sun.

Green Mountain Cultural Center (496-7722), Joslyn Road Barn, Waitsfield. Summer concerts and art exhibits. Also a venue for the Green Mountain Opera Festival in June.

Vermont Icelandic Horse Farm (496-7141), 3061 North Fayston Rd., Waitsfield. Trail rides and inn-to-inn treks on pony-sized, smooth-gaited horses described as "the most comfortable riding horses in the world." Skijoring.

Yankee Kingdom Orchard (759-2387), 2789 Lake St., West Addison. Pick-your-own apples, strawberries and pumpkins, or buy them – fresh or baked into treats – at the country store. Petting zoo.

off the drive

Chipman Point Marina (948-2288), Rte. 73, Orwell. Houseboat rentals.

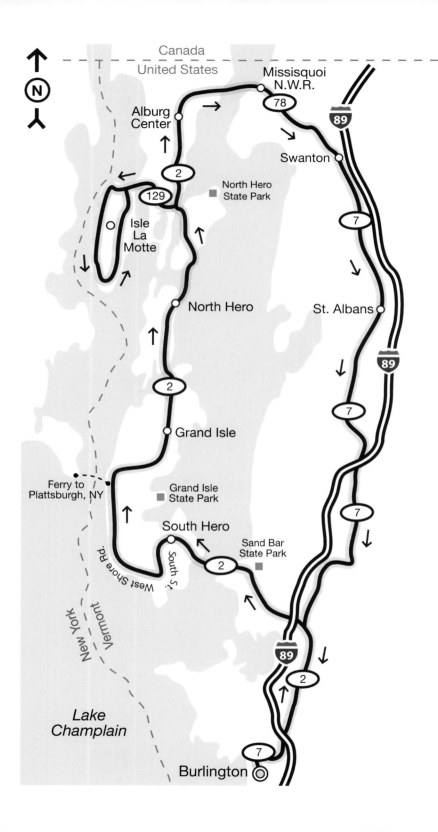

Burlington, the Champlain Islands, and St. Albans

110 miles

major attractions

- Burlington and the University of Vermont
- Sand Bar State Park
- South Hero's Orchards and Winery
- St. Anne's Shrine
- Fisk Quarry
- Missisquoi National Wildlife Refuge
- St. Albans

This is a drive that begins in Burlington, Vermont's lakeside "Queen City," and continues through the Champlain Islands, the archipelago that forms Grand Isle County, before rejoining the Vermont mainland. It's a heroic trip, you might say, since the lake's two main islands are called South Hero and North Hero, after those celebrated titans of Vermont's frontier days, Ethan and Ira Allen. Leaving the islands and their scenic string of state parks, visit a national wildlife refuge on the way to historic St. Albans, a onetime railroad hub that was an unlikely player in a Civil War drama.

Begin the drive in Burlington, which is best explored on foot (see following pages). Leaving the city via I-89 (entrance off Route 2 in South Burlington), take Exit 17, the Champlain Islands exit, turning west on Route 2.

South Hero and North Hero, along with Isle La Motte and the Alburg peninsula, come as somewhat of a surprise for those who think of Vermont as a mountain state. There are no mountains out here – but there are few places as perfect for viewing them. Look across the vast northwestern arm of Lake Champlain called the "Inland Sea," and take in the peaks from Camel's Hump to Jay; turn in the other direction, and there are the northern Adirondacks. In between, surrounded by all that water, is gently rolling orchard and dairy country, slowly suburbanizing towards the southern end of South Hero Island but still largely bucolic and serene, with a handsome scattering of state parks offering plenty of shoreline access.

Burlington highlights

While it's a metropolis by Vermont standards, Burlington is the smallest largest city of any state. With four colleges, Burlington is right up to date, but its history goes all the way back to Ethan Allen, and the merchants who made Lake Champlain a major avenue of trade. Here are a few highlights of the "Queen City," to enjoy before – or after – a drive north through the Champlain Islands. *(Note: Unless provided here, practical information for the places listed below can be found under "Attractions" or "Activities" at the end of this drive.)*

The park just behind City Hall is the site of a popular Farmers' Market from late spring through fall.

The 1930 Art Deco Flynn Center for the Performing Arts, 153 Main St., is a former movie palace splendidly restored in the 1980s to serve as the city's premier performing arts venue.

The Church Street Marketplace is Burlington's grand promenade and favorite place for people-watching. Closed to vehicles, the four-block stretch between Main and Pearl streets bustles with boutiques, restaurants, sidewalk cafés, and musicians.

The Firehouse Center for the Visual Arts, on the Church Street Marketplace between Main and College streets, showcases works by Vermont artists in various media.

Burlington's waterfront is the site of a marina, the Community Boathouse (sailboat rentals) and cruise ship docks. The Burlington Recreation Path extends along the waterfront, providing bicycle and walking access to city parks. Cyclists can ride north to the end of a former railroad causeway in Colchester, roughly 10 miles distant; on summer weekends, a bike ferry links the route with the Champlain Islands (bike rentals at Local Motion.) The car and passenger ferry to Port Kent, New York leaves from King Street dock.

ECHO at the Leahy Center for Lake Champlain, on the waterfront at Main Street, focuses on the history and ecology of the Lake Champlain region, and houses more than 2,200 live animals in 30,000 square feet of space. Aquarium tanks display lake fish and other aquatic life, and there are plenty of hands-on activities for children.

The University of Vermont campus stands on a hilltop overlooking downtown and the lake. UVM founder Ira Allen, brother of Ethan, is commemorated in the 1927 Ira Allen Chapel, a colonial revival structure with a lofty campanile housing a carillon. Alongside the chapel on the campus's University Row is the 1886 Billings Library, a Romanesque masterpiece designed by Henry Hobson Richardson. Just to the south is the 1896 Williams Science Hall, which boasts intricate terra-cotta detailing. Next along the row is the Old Mill, the oldest building on campus. Its cornerstone was laid in 1825 by the Marquis de Lafayette. Directly behind the Ira Allen Chapel is the Robert Hull Fleming Museum, which houses UVM's art and ethnography collections. (To sign up for a tour of the UVM campus, offered in summer and early fall, visit uvm.edu/historictour.)

Just off Route 127, three miles north of downtown Burlington, the Ethan Allen Homestead is a restoration of the farmhouse to which Vermont's greatest hero moved in 1787, and in which he died two years later.

North Beach Park, off North Avenue two miles north of downtown, has a swimming beach, camping and picnic sites, and access to the Burlington Recreation Path.

After Burlington, the first major attraction of this drive isn't really on the Champlain Islands, but on their mainland threshold. **Sand Bar State Park** offers one of Vermont's best swimming beaches. There's a smooth, sandy shore and gorgeous vistas of the lake and Adirondack Mountains beyond. With changing rooms, picnic tables and grills, a snack bar, and windsurfer, paddleboat and canoe rentals, Sand Bar is the perfect setup for a summer day. It's so perfect, in fact, that it can get quite crowded on weekends. Get there early, or opt for a weekday evening and enjoy the magnificent sunset.

The center of **South Hero** is four miles ahead at the intersection of Route 2 and South Street, marked on the left by an imposing early nineteenth-century stone structure, once an inn and now a bank branch. **Turn left onto South Street**, and keep an eye out (on the right) for a curious little stone castle, about four feet high, in a yard alongside a private home. The castle, one of several in the area, was the handiwork of an early twentieth-century custodian for some of the island's summer homes.

apples and wine

Rich soil and the moderating effect of Lake Champlain on island temperatures make South Hero prime apple-growing country. In early autumn, you can pick your own apples at **Allenholm Farm** and **Hackett's Orchards**, both on South Street. The orchards are the centerpieces of South Hero's Applefest, held each year in early October. Although the festival has in recent years gotten a little too heavy on the yard sales, it's still worth a visit if you can get there during the cider-pressing competition, or for the cricket match, featuring an expert Jamaican cricket team drawn from the hardworking migrant apple pickers who arrive each summer to help bring in South Hero's apple crop. They play the local Burlington cricket club, and invariably win.

If you continue to the end of South Street, you'll reach a quiet residential community at the southern tip of South Hero Island. Here, on summer weekends, bicyclists can ride out onto an old railroad causeway and hop a ferry to reach the causeway's continuation in Colchester, and a connection with the Burlington Bike Path. Contact Local Motion for information.

About a mile past the orchards, take a right onto West Shore Road to **Snow Farm Vineyard and Winery,** an enterprise that has proven that what mild island temperatures can do for apples, they'll do for grapes. Cold-hardy reds and whites are grown, and the Vidal Blanc ice wine is superb. If you visit Snow Farm on a Thursday in summer, pack a picnic and enjoy a free concert on the lawn from 6 to 8 p.m.

Beyond the winery, West Shore Road wanders north past some of Vermont's choicest real estate, where lakefront property owners enjoy magnificent views of the Adirondacks.

At the Grand Isle town line, West Shore Road merges with Route 314 (as of this writing, there's no sign for Route 314). A right turn here will take you back to Route 2, on the island's east side. If you continue directly ahead (north), though, you'll soon reach the Grand Isle - Plattsburgh Ferry at Gordon Landing. Park your car and hop aboard for an inexpensive, 40-minute round trip lake cruise.

lake life . . . .

Almost directly opposite the ferry landing, turn right onto Bell Hill Road to visit the **Ed Weed Fish Culture Station**, where a self-guided tour of the state-run facility shows how trout and salmon are raised to release size. You can even help raise them; alongside one of the raceways are vending machines that sell fish food.

The hatchery also displays information on perhaps the greatest threat currently faced by the Lake Champlain ecosystem – the zebra mussel, a fingernail-sized freshwater mollusk released into the Great Lakes and St. Lawrence River system by foreign tankers disposing of ballast water. The mussels have begun to encrust the lake bottom, and even threatened the viability of the hatchery by clogging intake pipes. It was saved after installation of expensive measures for filtering out the mussels and their spawn.

To learn more about zebra mussels and the lake's ecology in general, stop in at the **Lake Champlain Basin Program**, housed in an 1824 stone house just past the entrance to the ferry.

Continue north on Route 314, which soon veers to the right and leaves West Shore Road. Within a mile it intersects with Route 2: turn left here. Continue north (the official designation of Route 2 is E-W, but you're heading north), past the right-turn entrance to **Grand Isle State Park** (camping only) to the **Hyde Log Cabin**. Revolutionary War veteran Jedediah Hyde, Jr. built his 20 foot x 25 foot home out of locally-felled cedar in 1783. Often cited as the oldest surviving log cabin in the country, the doughty little structure contains furnishings and exhibits documenting everyday life on what was once New England's wild frontier.

Side Trip

At the northern tip of Grand Isle, turn right at the blinking yellow light onto East Shore Drive North and continue past the town beach to the **Grand Isle Lake House** overlooking Pearl Bay. Built in 1903 as the Island Villa Hotel, the building was purchased in 1956 by The Sisters of Mercy for a girls' camp, which closed in 1993. In 1997 the property was donated to the Preservation Trust of Vermont, which rents it for events. (There are overnight guest rooms on the second floor.) Visitors are invited to tour the building as long as there is no function in progress and a caretaker is on the premises.

If you're not planning to visit the Hyde Log Cabin, after leaving the Lake House turn right and follow East Shore Drive as it loops around the "Inland Sea", past one of Vermont's few remaining round barns, and then rejoins Route 2.

battle stations! . . . .

The drawbridge that connects the islands of South Hero and **North Hero** marks the spot where the British fleet anchored in October, 1776, before encountering four ships that Benedict Arnold dangled in front of them as bait to lure them toward Valcour Island, near the New York shore of Lake Champlain, where the American fleet was waiting in ambush.

After a night of furious battle, Arnold and a small contingent of ships once again lured the enemy away from the major part of the American fleet, allowing it to escape to Ticonderoga and thus delay the English advance for another year. When the British were about to overtake Arnold's small, retreating force, he ran his boats aground and burned them on the Vermont shore, rather than allow them to be captured. By surviving the battle, of course, Arnold lived to turn sides and become a synonym for treachery and treason.

on to North Hero . . . .

Immediately after crossing the bridge onto North Hero Island, turn left for the entrance to **Knight Point State Park.** A 54-acre day-use facility (no camping), Knight Point has a sandy beach, boat rentals, a picnic area with cooking grills, and foot trails that meander through meadow and forest comprising a designated state natural area. It is home to the **Island Center for Arts & Recreation**, which brings a host of cultural events to the park, including presentations by the Vermont Shakespeare Company and the Vermont Mozart Festival. The park is located at the site of the original ferry crossing between North and South Hero islands. The ferry stopped running with the opening of the first bridge in 1892. The building that now serves as park headquarters is a vivid reminder of the old ferryboat days: the brick section dates to 1845, while the wooden addition is a reconstruction of Knight Tavern, a 1790 inn at which travelers would stop for a dram while awaiting transportation.

The town of North Hero is the shire town of Grand Isle County and the Islands' prettiest settlement. At the village center, wooded points of land create a natural harbor, grandiosely called "City Bay." Dominating the "city" are the stately Grand Isle County Courthouse, built in 1824 of marble from nearby Isle La Motte; the **North Hero House,** with gracious lakefront rooms and a fine restaurant; and **Hero's Welcome**, one of those omnium-gatherum Vermont emporia where you can buy bait, made-to-order sandwiches, and a decent Zinfandel. The store also rents canoes and kayaks, and City Bay is a delightful place to paddle around – you might even want to make your way around Hibbard Point to tiny Hen Island.

Follow Route 2 north beyond the narrow neck of land called the Carrying Place (the name harks back to Indian portages). (Bear right at the fork to visit **North Hero State Park**.) The drawbridge spans Alburg Passage, a narrow channel that separates North Hero Island from the Alburg peninsula, which extends southward from the Canadian border and is at no point connected to the U.S. mainland.

Vermont's faraway isle...........................

Turn left onto Route 129 to reach the most remote and bucolic corner of the Lake Champlain archipelago, two-by-five-mile **Isle La Motte**. Just past the bridge, look left for a bit of history: a monument here commemorates the spot where two Green Mountain Boys, Seth Warner and Remember Baker, camped with General Montgomery in 1775 on their way to attack Montreal.

> *Captured during the ill-fated American attempt to seize the city in 1775, Ethan Allen spent the next three years as a British prisoner of war.*

Side Trip
The 625-acre Alburg Dunes State Park is a little bit of Cape Cod in a Lake Champlain setting, with sand dunes created by centuries of erosion of glacially-deposited material, and the relentless action of the wind. The dunes comprise a barrier between the lakefront and an interior cedar swamp; within these shifting hillocks of sand are stands of rare Champlain beach grass and beach pea. Although the fragile dunes themselves are fenced off, the day-use-only park has a sandy swimming beach as well as bicycle and pedestrian paths. To reach the park, turn left at the State Park sign onto Route 129. Turn left again onto Route 129 Extension/Sand Beach Road, and then onto Coon Point Road to the park entrance.

Follow signs and bear right to **St. Anne's Shrine**, at Isle La Motte's northwestern tip. The French, under the Sieur de la Motte and accompanied by a contingent of Jesuits, put ashore here in 1665 and built a fort as a defense against hostile Mohawk Indians, thus creating Vermont's first (if not permanent) European settlement. The priests celebrated the state's first Roman Catholic mass here on July 26, 1666. (La Motte with his soldiers and Jesuits weren't the first whites to land here, however: on July 2 and 3, 1609, Samuel de Champlain and his party beached their canoes, hunted, and camped on this yet-unnamed island "three leagues long" in Champlain's eponymous lake.)

Developed and maintained for the past 100 years by the Society of Saint Edmund, St. Anne's features an outdoor pavilion and small indoor chapel where daily masses are celebrated, along with outdoor stations of the cross, a cafeteria, and a swimming beach with a boat dock. Among the shrine's statuary is a 15-foot representation of Our Lady of Lourdes, exquisitely gilded through the bequest of an anonymous donor; and a statue of Champlain sculpted in the Vermont Pavilion of the 1967 World Exposition in Montreal by Vermont artist D.W. Webb. Candlelight processions are held here in summer; contact the Shrine for dates.

To make a short but interesting circuit of Isle La Motte, **head south from the Shrine, keeping the lake on your right.** The most enticing views are west across the water to the New York shore, but about two-thirds of the way south along the island, keep an eye out on the left for the stone ruins of the estate of one-time Vermont lieutenant governor Nelson Fisk. It was here, while attending a luncheon of the Vermont Fish and Game Club in September of 1901, that Vice-President Theodore Roosevelt learned that President William McKinley had been shot.

Next door is historic **Fisk Farm**, a B&B whose weekly rentals include a stone cottage built in the 1700s. On Sunday afternoons in July and August, and on one Saturday evening each month in June, July, and August, Fisk Farm hosts free concerts sponsored by the Isla La Motte Preservation Trust. The Trust owns and manages the Fisk Quarry Preserve, a 20-acre site with remnants of the 450-million-year old Chazy Fossil Reef, adjacent to the Farm.

Just past Fisk Farm (left) is the entrance to **Fisk Quarry**, which recalls Isle La Motte's most famous industry, but is now better known as one of the world's most significant geological sites. The island has long been known for its supply of a limestone that is almost but not quite marble, and in particular for a black variety of this stone available at only a few other sites on the globe.

A close examination of the exposed rock surfaces in the quarry, and at several of the island's other exposed outcrops, reveals the fossils of prehistoric sea creatures. These animals, primitive bryozoa and stromatoporoids, once inhabited a warm tropical sea that covered Isle La Motte some 400 million years ago. They form part of what is considered the oldest fossil reef in the world – a reef so old, in fact, that only the more recent of its petrified specimens can properly be called corals, which evolved long after the reef began to form. This portion of the reef was threatened by a reopening of the quarry, until concerned citizens led an effort to buy the site and set it aside under the auspices of the Isle La Motte Reef Preservation Trust, which has installed walkways and interpretive signs.

Isle La Motte's distinctive black stone has been used in the U.S. Capitol, in New York's Radio City Music Hall, and in Vermont's State Capitol.

Finish your Isle La Motte exploration by bearing left at the southern end of the island and heading north on The Main Road, which passes the little Isle La Motte Historical Society museum (just beyond, in a field on the right, is another reef outcrop), and heads through the village with its handsome library and two churches, all made of local stone. The Main Road soon rejoins Route 129.

Retrace your route to return to Route 2, and then continue north to the junction with Route 78 at Alburgh Center. (Note: Depending on where you are in town, the name is spelled with or without the "h.")

Side Trip
If you like cheese – and if you have your passport or enhanced driver's license with you – head north from Alburgh Center on Route 225 to the U.S.-Canada border crossing, less than two miles distant. Just after crossing the border, watch for small signs that say "*Fromagerie*" – they'll lead you to the establishment of **Fritz Kaiser,** a master cheesemaker who works his magic with milk from nearby farms.

mouth of the Missisquoi . . . .

At Alburgh Center, turn right onto Route 78 and head east over the causeway, past the West Swanton Orchard and Cider Mill, to the **Missisquoi National Wildlife Refuge,** which includes much of the marshy estuary of the Missisquoi River as it empties into Lake Champlain's Missisquoi Bay. The refuge is a haven for waterfowl, ospreys, and other wildlife, and harbors a huge great blue heron rookery on Shad Island. In all, some 201 avian species have been identified on the 6,729-acre refuge since 1943. The refuge headquarters, located right on Route 78, can supply information, maps of foot trails and canoe routes … and the occasional frog license. That's right. If you're visiting between July 15th and September 30th and have a hankering for frog's legs, you can harvest up to 12 tree leopard frogs a day along Route 78 and Mac's Bend Road (license required).

In 1835, a lead tube was found alongside the Missisquoi River. Inside was a document which read: "Nov. 29. A.D. 1564 – This is the solme day I must now die this is the 90th day since we lef the Ship all have Parished and on the Banks of this River I die to farewell my future Posteritye know our end – John Graye."

A theory once held that this odd document was written by the last survivor of one of Martin Frobisher's sixteenth-century voyages, but it is now thought to have been a nineteenth-century hoax. The tube has long since disappeared (it's rumored to be somewhere at the University of Vermont), but a copy of the document survives at the Highgate Historical Society museum, located on Route 78 in nearby Highgate (open from May-Oct., 10 to 2 on the first and third Sunday of each month).

Swanton, a Missisquoi riverside city whose fortunes have ebbed and flowed over the years, served as a campsite for Native Americans as early as 6,000 B.C., and is thus Vermont's oldest known community. The tribe later known as the St. Francis Indians lived in the area before the French arrived about 1700. Many of their descendants, grouped under the tribal designation Abenaki, still reside here. The **Abenaki Tribal Museum** exhibits tribal artifacts such as traditional garb, woven baskets, beadwork, and a birch bark canoe.

> *The swans in Swanton Park are descendants of Betty and Sam, who were given to the city by Queen Elizabeth II in 1961. They were flown here from Norfolk, England.*

In the cemetery just south of Swanton Park, look for the large monument with an angel bearing a cross. This is the burial place of Lieutenant Stephen F. Brown of the 17th Regiment of Vermont Volunteers, a Swanton native who, as the inscription tells it, arrived on the battlefield at Gettysburg without a sword, and wielded a hatchet while defending the Union position during Pickett's charge until he got hold of a Confederate sword. His statue adorns the regiment's memorial at Gettysburg.

shades of the Civil War

Route 78 intersects with Route 7 in downtown Swanton. Finish your drive by heading south on Route 7 to **St. Albans**, settled by emigrants from Vermont's lower Connecticut Valley and formally organized as a town in 1788. Shortly after its incorporation, Ethan Allen's Tory brother, Levi, laid claim to so much of the town's land that he addressed his wife in a letter as "Duchess of St. Albans." He could not validate his claims, however, and was forced to leave town.

In earlier days the lifeblood of St. Albans was the Central Vermont Railway (now New England Central), which maintained extensive yards and shops here. Although the glory days of the Iron Horse are commemorated by little more than an Amtrak stop (northern terminus of the **Vermonter** service from Washington, D.C.), it remains a handsome old Victorian city, with much of its brick downtown blocks rehabbed. The stately row of civic buildings along Taylor Park include the **St. Albans Historical Museum**, which houses a fully-equipped turn-of-the-twentieth-century doctor's office and railroad memorabilia.

St. Albans earned its place in more than local history on October 19, 1864, when 22 Confederate soldiers staged the St. Albans Raid, the most northerly engagement of the Civil War. Dressed in civilian clothes, they simultaneously held up all of the banks in town and escaped to Canada with $201,000, killing a man as they fled. They were caught and tried in Canada, but acquitted on the grounds that the raid had been a legitimate act of war. (Just to assuage strained cross-border feelings, though, Canada reimbursed the banks $50,000.) The raid had been meant to throw a scare into the North, but it backfired: Union Army enlistments increased. Every year, the raid is reenacted in Taylor Park. Each April, St. Albans is also the site of the **Vermont Maple Festival**, a weekend-long tribute to the state's signature sweet, much of which is made here in Franklin County.

From St. Albans, return to Burlington via either Route 7 or I-89.

information *All area codes are (802) unless otherwise indicated.*

Lake Champlain Islands Chamber of Commerce (372-8400), 3537 Rte. 2, P.O. Box 213, North Hero 05474. champlainislands.com

Lake Champlain Regional Chamber of Commerce (863-3489), 60 Main St., Suite 100, Burlington 05401. Closed weekends. vermont.org

St. Albans Chamber of Commerce (524-2444), 2 North Main Street, PO Box 327, St. Albans 05478. stalbanschamber.com

Swanton Chamber of Commerce (868-7200), P.O. Box 237, Swanton 05488. swantonchamber.com

Vermont State Parks (241-3655), 103 South Main St., Waterbury 05671. Seasonal. vtstateparks.com $

lodging – Burlington

Note: there are many moderately priced chain and independent motels south and north of Burlington on Route 7, and to the east along Rte 2.

Hawthorn Suites Hotel (860-1212), 401 Dorset St., S. Burlington 05403. 1- and 2-bedroom suites with full kitchens; fireplace and Jacuzzi suites. Indoor pool, hot tub and fitness center. hawthorn.com $$-$$$

Hilton Burlington (658-6500), 60 Battery St., Burlington 05401. Overlooking the lake and within walking distance of Church Street, the non-smoking chain hotel has a fitness center and all the modern conveniences. hilton.com $$$

Lang House (652-2500), 360 Main St., Burlington 05401. Restored 1881 Eastlake Victorian just up the hill from downtown has 11 well-appointed rooms with period furnishings. langhouse. com $$$

Marriott Courtyard Burlington Harbor (864-4700), 25 Cherry St., Burlington 05401. New downtown hotel facing Lake Champlain. All rooms with flat screen TV; some have 2-person Jacuzzis; some balconies with lake and mountain views. Casual dining. $$$$

Sheraton-Burlington Hotel & Conference Center (865-6600), 870 Williston Rd., Burlington 05403 . The modern, sprawling hotel on the fringe of downtown and within walking distance of UVM has 309 rooms, indoor pool, fitness center, and Jacuzzis. sheraton.com $$-$$$

Sunset House B&B (864-3790), 78 Main St., Burlington 05401. Restored, downtown Historic Queen Anne-style, c. 1854 boarding house has 4 air- conditioned guest rooms with shared baths. sunsethousebb.com $$

Willard Street Inn (651-8710), 349 So. Willard St., Burlington 05401. Historic, intown three-story 1881 Victorian brick mansion with lake views has 14 elegant rooms with private baths. Breakfast is served in the solarium. Children 12+. willardstreetinn.com $$-$$$

lodging – along the drive

Back Inn Time B&B (527-5116), 68 Fairfield St., St. Albans. Antiques lovers will love with this meticulously-restored, 1860 Victorian. 2 of 6 guest rooms have fireplaces; full breakfast is served in the formal dining room or overlooking the English gardens. Dinner ($) and high tea by reservation. backinntime.com $$

Charlie's Northland Lodge (372-8822), Rte. 2, North Hero. Lakefront housekeeping cottages, and rooms with shared bath in the 19th-century house; boat and motor rentals, fishing licenses and supplies. charliesnorthlandlodge.com $-$$

Fisk Farm (928-3364), West Shore Rd. (next to Fisk Quarry Preserve), Isle La Motte 05463. Two cottages for rent by the week include the late 1700s Stone Cottage ($900), and the one-room Shore Cottage ($700). fiskfarm.com $$

High Winds B & B (868-2521), Hog Island, Campbell Bay Rd., W. Swanton 05488. 2 rooms with private baths in the 1800s farmhouse of a dairy farm overlooking the Missisquoi River. Canoes and boats. April-Nov. $

North Hero House Inn & Restaurant (372-8237), Rte. 2, N. Hero 05474. Many of the 24 rooms in the main inn and three annexes overlook the lake; all have private baths, phones, and TVs (some have Jacuzzis and fireplaces). The dining room ($$-$$$) serves fare such as brandied lobster bisque, and Dijon crusted rack of lamb. Small beach, sauna, hot tub and boat rental. Breakfast included. northherohouse.com $$-$$$

Ransom Bay Inn (796-3399), 4 Center Bay Rd., Alburg 05440. 4 pleasant rooms in a handsome 1795 stone, one-time stagecoach stop just off Rte. 2. Dinner ($) by reservation. Breakfast included. $- $$

Ruthcliffe Lodge (928-3200), Old Quarry Rd., Isle La Motte. 7 of the 9 simply furnished motel units (no TVs) face the lake; the restaurant ($$) serves Italian fish and pasta specialties, as well as classics like rack of lamb, in a knotty pine dining room or on the waterfront deck. D. Boating, swimming, fishing. Breakfast included. ruthcliffe.com $$

Shore Acres Inn and Restaurant (372-8722), Rte. 2, N. Hero. Set well back from the highway, 19 of the 23 pleasant motel units are lakefront; 4 in the garden house have lake views. Tennis courts and private beach. The lakefront restaurant ($$-$$$) serves specialties such as homemade grilled polenta, and Apple Island chicken. shoreacres.com $$-$$$

Terry Lodge (928-3264), 54 West Shore Rd., Isle La Motte 05463. Family-friendly lakefront accommodations include 7 rooms in the lodge (2 with private bath), 4 motel units, a housekeeping cottage, and an apartment. Family-style dinner available to guests (others by reservation). Private swimming beach, dock, and raft. Open May 15-mid-Oct. $$

Thomas Mott Homestead B & B (796-4402), 63 Blue Rock Rd., Alburg 05440. Four simple and very tidy guest rooms of varying sizes with private baths in an 1838 Shaker farmhouse overlooking Lake Champlain. Private dock and canoes. Kids 12+. thomas-mott-bb.com $$

restaurants – Burlington

Al's French Frys (862-9203), 1251 Williston Rd. (Route 2), Burlington. Folks may disagree about who makes the area's best French fries, but nobody can dispute that this +50-year-old "diner" is the queen of the Queen City's fast food eateries. L & D. $

Bove's (864-6651), 68 Pearl St. Unpretentious family-run eatery has been serving up good, plain Neapolitan fare for more than 60 years. The meatball sandwich is a bargain. L & D Tues.-Sat. $

Leunig's Bistro (863-3759), 115 Church St. European bistro menu and ambience – "the panache of Paris and the value of Vermont." Bar; outdoor seating. Special low pricing early and late. Live jazz Tues. - Thurs. L & D; open until midnight. $-$$

Nectar's (658-4771), 188 Main St. Legendary for its French fries with gravy and as the place the band Phish was launched. Solid, diner-type fare and evening entertainment. $

Penny Cluse Café (651-8834), 169 Cherry St. Popular with college kids, who know where to find a good deal. Healthy and hearty fare, including homemade soups, vegetarian specials, and huge breakfasts. Be prepared to wait. B & L. $-$$

Sakura (863-1988), 2 Church St. Authentic Japanese fare right on Church Street: the tempura is terrific, the bento boxes heroic, and the sushi is off-the-boat fresh. Outdoor seating. L Mon.-Fri., D nightly. $$

A Single Pebble (865-5200), 133 Bank St. The place for classic Chinese cuisine: traditional clay pot, wok, noodle and dumpling specialties. The "Tasting Lunch" is an adventure. L & D Tues.-Sun. $

Souza's Churrascaria-Brazilian Steakhouse (864-2433), 131 Main St. Heroic amounts of barbecued meats on skewers, and an extremely creative international salad bar. Sun. brunch (9 a.m.-2 p.m.) is an event. $$

Splash (658-2244), at the Boathouse, foot of College St. A casual waterfront spot, with outdoor seating and bar, and a grand view of Lake Champlain. Ribs, burgers, crab cakes, lobster rolls, salads; Tex-Mex offerings include a tasty fish taco. L & D Late May–Sept. $-$$

Sweetwaters (864-9800), 120 Church St. Creative sandwiches, local micro brews, hamburgers, buffalo burgers and more, in a former bank building. Great sweet potato fries. Patio seating. L & D, Sun. brunch. $-$$

Trattoria Delia (864-5253), 152 St. Paul St. Authentic Italian trattoria specialties include handmade pastas and hardwood grilled entrees. D. $$-$$$

Beansie's Bus, Battery Park. L spring-fall. $

restaurants – along the drive

Blue Paddle Bistro (802-372-4814), 316 Rte. 2, South Hero. Creative and tasty dishes such as Gorgonzola stuffed meatloaf, and mushroom stuffed ravioli, in a cheerful, unfussy, and very popular spot; the second floor offers a quieter ambiance. D nightly, Sun brunch. $-$$

Chow! Bella Café & Wine Bar (524-1405), 28 N. Main St., St. Albans. Intimate restaurant housed in an historic building serves Italian Trattoria fare including creative pasta dishes and pizzas, sandwiches, salads, and seafood entrees. L & D Mon.-Sat. $-$$

Jacob's Restaurant (868-3190), 73 First St., Swanton. Solid fare with an Italian touch at a down-home, family-friendly spot. B & L Wed.-Mon.; D Wed-Sun. $

Jeff's Maine Seafood Market (524-6135), 65 N. Main St., St. Albans. Restaurant/market/deli serves fresh seafood specialties, fabulous chowders, and a fair selection of meat entrees. L & D Mon.-Sat. $-$$

Margo's (372-6112), Rte. 2, Grand Isle. Bakery-cafe serves up tasty baked goods and sandwiches. $

Thai House (802-524-0999), 359 Lake St., St, Albans. All the classic favorites, including crispy calamari, Pad Thai, tom ka soup, delicious curries, duck salad with fresh mint and cilantro. Tell them how spicy you like it. Dessert: fried ice cream. L Mon.-Sat.; D nightly. $-$$

attractions – Burlington

Burlington Farmers' Market, City Hall Park. Seasonal Saturdays 10 a.m.- 2 p.m.

ECHO at the Leahy Center for Lake Champlain (864-1848), 1 College St. Mid-June-Labor Day, 11 a.m.-5 p.m.; rest of the year, weekend and school vacation afternoons. $

Ethan Allen Homestead (865-4556), off Route 127, Burlington. Mid-May-mid-Oct. daily. $

Firehouse Center for the Visual Arts (865-7166), Church St. Open daily.

Flynn Center for the Performing Arts (863-5966 for tickets; 863-8778 for tours and information), 153 Main St. $

North Beach Park (865-7247).

Robert Hull Fleming Museum (656-0750), 61 Colchester Ave. Tues.-Sun. $

University of Vermont (656-3480), 85 South Prospect St. Maps available at information office in Waterman Building, student center, library, and bookstore.

attractions – along the drive

Abenaki Tribal Museum (868-2559), 100 Grand Ave., Swanton. Mon.- Fri. Donations.

Champlain Basin Program (372-3213), 54 West Shore Rd., Rte. 314, Grand Isle. Open weekdays.

Ed Weed Fish Culture Station (372-3171), Bell Hill Rd., Grand Isle.

Fromagerie Fritz Kaiser (450-294-2207), Noyan, Quebec, Canada. Mon.-Sat.

Grand Isle Lake House (372-5024 or 865-2522), East Shore Drive North, Grand Isle.

Grand Isle-Plattsburgh Ferry (864-9804), Lake Champlain Ferries, Gordon Landing, Grand Isle. $

Hyde Log Cabin (372-5440), Route 2, Grand Isle. July 4 -Labor Day, Thurs.-Mon., 11 a.m.-5 p.m. $

Lakes End Cheeses/Shoreline Chocolates (796-3730), 212 W. Shore Rd., Alburg. Delicious goats' milk cheeses at this family-owned dairy, which also makes candy. They're sold, along with ice cream and hot dogs, at the scoop shop.
Missisquoi National Wildlife Refuge (868-4781), Route 78, Swanton.

St. Albans Historical Museum (527-7933), Taylor Park, St. Albans. Mid-May-mid-Oct., Tues.-Sat. Donations.

St. Anne's Shrine (928-3362), West Shore Rd., Isle La Motte. Mid-May-mid-Oct.

activities – Burlington

Burlington Community Boathouse (865-3377), foot of College St. Hourly Laser and Rhodes sailboat rentals, powerboat and canoe rentals, fishing charters, captained day sails. Late May-Oct.

Champlain Valley Flyer (463-3069), Union Station, cor. of Main and Battery Sts. Sat. excursions to Charlotte between July 4-late Aug., and early Sept.-mid-Oct., with stops on the return trip at Shelburne and Magic Hat Brewery. rails-vt.com $

Lake Champlain Chocolates (864-1807), 750 Pine St. Watch chocolates being made and sample the wares; factory seconds. Retail store at 63 Church St.

Lake Champlain Cruises (864-9669), King Street Dock. Excursions on *Northern Lights*, a handsome replica of 19th century lake cruiser; lunch, brunch, and dinner cruises.

Lake Champlain Ferries (864-9804), King Street Dock. Seasonal ferries from Burlington to Port Kent, NY and Charlotte to Essex, NY; year-round from Grand Isle to Plattsburgh, NY.

Local Motion (652-2453), 1 Steele St. Source of information on everything relating to cycling in the Burlington area; operates bike ferry weekends in summer linking Burlington Bike Path with Champlain Islands. Bike and blade rentals. localmotion.org

Magic Hat Brewery (658-2739), 5 Bartlett Bay Rd., South Burlington. The city's favorite microbrewery opens its Growler Bar and offers self-guided tours Mon-Sat and Sun p.m. Guided tours Thurs & Fri. at 3, 4 and 5 p.m.; Sat. noon, 1, 2 and 3 p.m.; gift shop and free samples.

Moonlight Lady (863-3350), 348 Flynn Ave. Overnight (and longer) cruises aboard a replica 1920s-era inland waterway cruiser. The 65-ft. cruiser has just 8 cabins and sails as far north as the inland waterways of Quebec.

Pizza Putt (862-7888), 1205 Airport Parkway, S. Burlington. Imaginative indoor miniature golf course, pitching machines, arcade, and small kids' playground make this a good destination for a rainy day.

Spirit of Ethan Allen III, Lake Champlain Shoreline Cruises (862-8300), Burlington Community Boathouse, College St. Scenic lunch, sunset dinner, and Sun. brunch cruises aboard the 500-passenger Spirit. May-mid-Oct.

True North Kayak Tours (860-1910), 53 Nash Place. Day paddles around Lake Champlain, as well as wilderness trips (lodging arranged): day trips; no experience required. vermontkayak.com

Vermont Mozart Festival (862-7352), 110 Main St. Mid-July - early-Aug. World-class classical, jazz and other musical events at venues throughout Northern and Western Vermont. Schedule: vtmozart.org

Vermont State Craft Center/Frog Hollow on the Marketplace (863-6458), 85 Church St. High-end crafts by some of the state's finest artists. Mon.-Sat., Sun. p.m.

Waterfront Boat Rental (864-4858), Perkins Pier (53 Lavalley Lane). Rentals of rowboats, kayaks, canoes, aluminum boats, skiffs, and Boston Whalers by hr. or day.

Whistling Man Schooner (598-6504). Next to ECHO Center. Daily sailing cruises; half and full day private charters aboard a Maine-built, 31 ft. Friendship sloop. Late May-Oct.

Winds of Ireland (863-5090), Burlington Community Boathouse. Sailboat cruises, charters (28 ft.-41 ft.) and bareboat charters.

Vermont Lake Monsters (655-6611). Single-A Washington Nationals farm club plays in summer at UVM's Centennial Field, Colchester Avenue. $ (Note: As of this writing, the Monsters' survival depends upon a league-mandated upgrade of Centennial Field.)

activities – along the drive

Allenholm Farm (372-5566), 111 South St., S. Hero. Farm store, petting paddock, bicycle rental (including tandems, kids', and tag-alongs.), and a B&B.

An Bradon Fishing Charters (654-9282), 23 Sunrise Dr., S. Hero. 4, 6 or 8 hr. fishing charters on Lake Champlain with Capt. Tony Bushway. April-Sept.

Charlie's Northland Lodge (372-8822), Rte. 2, North Hero. Boat rental; fishing supplies and maps.

Hackett's Orchard (372-4848), 86 South St., South Hero. Pick your own apples; syrup, pies, cider donuts.

Henry's Sportsman's Cottages (796-3616), 218 Poor Farm Rd., Alburgh. Motorboat rentals.

Hero's Welcome (372-4161). Rte. 2, North Hero. Gifts, sandwiches, picnic supplies, wine (and this book). Kayak, canoe and bicycle rentals.

Snow Farm Vineyard and Winery (372-9463), 190 West Shore Rd., South Hero. Tasting room and guided tours at 11 a.m. and 2 p.m. May-Oct.; self-guided tours year-round. Free concert series Thurs. evenings in summer.

Vermont Shakespeare Company (877-874-1911). Islands Center, Knight Point State Park, North Hero. vermontshakespeare.org

West Swanton Orchard & Cider Mill (868-7851), Rte. 78, West Swanton. Working cider mill, pick-your-own apples, fresh fruits and vegetables.

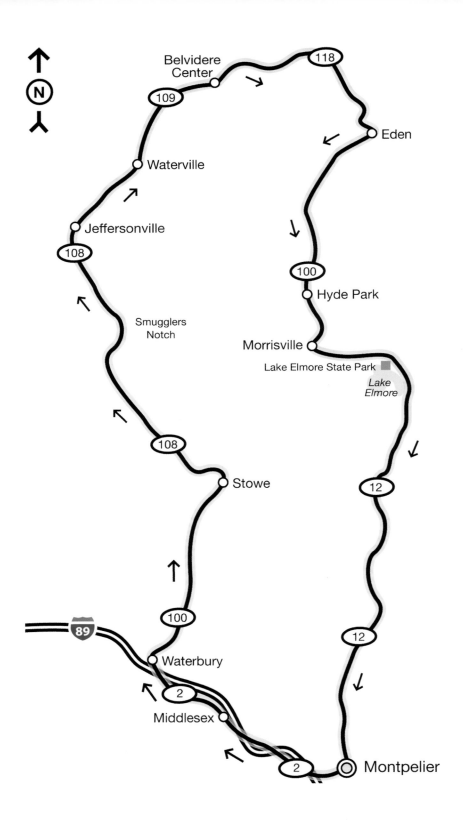

Drive 7

Montpelier, Mount Mansfield, and the Covered Bridges of Lamoille County

102 miles

major attractions

- Vermont State House
- Ben & Jerry's Ice Cream Factory
- Stowe
- Mount Mansfield Toll Road
- Stowe Aerial Gondola
- Vermont Historical Society Museum
- Smugglers Notch
- Covered Bridges

his drive begins in Vermont's capital, and then follows the Winooski River valley before swinging north to the celebrated ski town of Stowe and the lofty passage through Smugglers' Notch. Farther north still, in Waterville and Belvidere, the route takes in five examples of that most characteristic expression of Vermont folk engineering, the covered bridge. Return to Montpelier via the Worcester Range, where fall colors are spectacular.

Begin in Montpelier. With a population of fewer than 8,000, it's the smallest state capital in the U.S. State government may be what puts Montpelier in the newspapers, but the town has a flavor of its own, and it's decidedly not vanilla. It owes its personality more to a lively, quirkily independent, and often activist population than to the presence of the governor and the legislature. An example? You can search far and wide in downtown Montpelier for a fast food franchise, but you won't find one. The city kept the burgers at bay by raising the question of litter, which they thought would follow in the franchises' wake. The real reason, of course, is that Montpelierites thought that the clowns and kings who hawk quick eats would lend a tawdry note to a business district that draws its character from shops selling used vinyl records and locally designed clothing; from small ethnic restaurants, independent bookshops, and a theater showing art films … and from the one chain operation nearly all Vermonters approve of, Ben & Jerry's.

The **Vermont State House,** though, is the main attraction for visitors. Built in 1836 of Barre granite, Vermont's capitol is, on the outside, a demure Greek Revival expression of agrarian democracy -- right down to the statue reputed to be of Ceres, the Roman goddess of agriculture, atop its golden dome. Inside, things get a bit more ornate, as a fire resulted in an 1859 Victorian remodeling (a meticulous 1990s restoration has preserved that style). A tour, guided or self-guided, takes in the House and more intimate Senate chambers, the lobbies where legislators conduct business with constituents (they don't have private offices), and the Cedar Creek Room, dominated by a splendid painting depicting Vermont troops in one of their major Civil War engagements. If you're visiting between January and mid-April, while the legislature is in session, you're welcome to sit in.

The brick Victorian edifice with the mansard roof that stands next to the State House is the **Pavilion Building.** If it looks like an old-time hotel, there's a good reason: it was a hotel in its last incarnation. The original structure, which was a virtual dormitory for out-of-town legislators, was torn down in the 1970s, and replaced with a near-replica.

Today's Pavilion Building contains state offices rather than hotel rooms, and is the home of the **Vermont Historical Society** and its **museum.** The Society's permanent exhibit, "Freedom and Unity" (the Vermont motto), chronicles the state's history from 1600 to the present, using collections that range from an Abenaki wigwam to a replica 19th-century railroad station with working telegraph. Temporary exhibitions are built around various Vermont themes.

The **T.W. Wood Gallery and Arts Center,** four blocks east on the Vermont College Campus. Founded by Montpelier-born artist Thomas Waterman Wood (1823-1903), a well-known portrait and genre painter who contributed his art collection to the city in 1895, the gallery's holdings run heavily to 19th-century landscapes and portraits, but also include paintings done by WPA artists such as Joseph Stella and Reginald Marsh. A contemporary gallery highlights Vermont artists of today.

Another Montpelier campus nurtures creativity of a decidedly different sort. The **New England Culinary Institute**, a nationally-renowned institution for training chefs, showcases its students and instructors' skills at a pair of restaurants in the capital: the **Main Street Grill & Bar** and **La Brioche Bakery & Cafe**.

Side Trip

Take Route 2 to Route 302 east from Montpelier to **Barre** (pronounced "Barry"), one of the granite capitals of the world. Just south of town are the vast quarries of the **Rock of Ages** company (see "off the drive" below), where tours take in quarrying and carving operations. Many elaborate examples of the sculptor's art decorate the city's **Hope Cemetery,** a mile from downtown on Route 14. The Monument to Barre's Italian stonecutters, at the intersection of North Main Street and Maple Avenue, is a handsome and poignant tribute to the immigrants who built this city.

Head west out of Montpelier on Route 2, which follows the course of the Winooski River. The Winooski – the name means "Onion River" in Abenaki – is one of three major streams flowing west through northern Vermont to empty into Lake Champlain. The others are the Lamoille and the Missisquoi, both farther north. All three rivers actually predate the Green Mountains. As the mountains rose, the rivers kept to their ancient courses, carving deep, fertile valleys across the range.

> *In March 1992, the Winooski River rose behind an ice dam that blocked its course through Montpelier, inundating the city's downtown with waist-deep water.*

Continue west along Route 2 and the Winooski valley to **Waterbury**, perhaps with a stop at the **Red Hen Bakery** in Middlesex for a fresh-baked snack or loaf of artisan bread for a picnic. For many years, Waterbury was home to the sprawling Vermont State Hospital complex, now mostly converted into state offices. Downtown Waterbury, somewhat overshadowed by the red brick campus, occupies a compact cluster of blocks recently enlivened by new pubs and restaurants, and **by Green Mountain Coffee Roasters'** conversion of the town's little Victorian railroad station into a spiffy visitor center and café (the station still serves its original purpose, as Amtrak's *Vermonter* rumbles in twice each day). Chef Eric Warnstedt, named one of the country's 10 best new chefs by *Food & Wine Magazine* in 2008, presides over the kitchen at **Hen of the Wood**, in an old gristmill just off Main Street.

Just past the center of town, head north on Route 100. For the next 10 miles, between here and Stowe, you'll be in tourist paradise: pick and choose your stops with care, if you hope to finish this drive before "snow flies," as they say hereabouts. (If it's already flown, you are probably headed for Stowe and aren't stopping anywhere.)

First up is **Ben & Jerry's Ice Cream** Factory and Tour. If you don't want to stop, make sure to cover the kids' eyes before they see the Disneyesque building flanked by a herd of ersatz cows. The wait for the tour – and/or an ice cream cone – can be interminable, because common consensus now has it that a trip to Vermont isn't complete without a stop to see the wonderful world built by two jolly 60s souls from Long Island who ... well, you'll hear it all on the tour. Suffice it to say that all this and a couple of other plants, along with hundreds of jobs and the utilization of a significant percentage of Vermont's dairy output, began with a hand-cranked ice cream machine in a barely-converted Burlington gas station a little over 30 years ago. Tours last 30 minutes, are given frequently, and, on Sunday, do not include a visit to the production line. The ice cream elves get a day of rest.

Also along this stretch of Route 100:

 – **The Cabot Annex Store**, which houses Green Mountain Chocolates, a Vermont Teddy Bear outlet, Snow Farm Vineyard Tasting Room (see Drive 6), the Cabot Cheese Annex (lots of wonderful samples), Green Mountain Coffee Roasters, and several other retail operations.

 – **Cold Hollow Cider Mill,** with a year-round cider pressing operation, a bakery specializing in mouth-watering donuts and apple-cheddar squares, a huge gift shop featuring local specialty foods, a fudge shop, and Grand View Winery's tasting room.

 – **Waterbury Center State Park**, on a reservoir which is Vermont's ninth largest body of water, was created in the 1930s to control flooding along the Winooski River Valley. It has a sandy beach, picnic area, nature trail, and boat rental (handled by Umiak Outfitters: see "Activities" below).

 – **Green Mountain Club Headquarters**, on the left side of Route 100 about a mile past the cider mill, has maps, guidebooks, and the latest information on the **Long Trail** and other footpaths. Roughly three miles north of Waterbury, look to the northwest for your first glimpse of **Mount Mansfield** (4,393 feet), Vermont's highest mountain. Mount Hunger (3,620 feet), the highest peak in the Worcester Range, is to the east.

Side Trip

For the past half-century, Americans have been captivated by the story of a certain Austrian expatriate family with a talent for singing. To visit the **Trapp Family Lodge**, turn left across from the Burgundy Rose Motel onto Moscow Road, past **Little River Hot Glass Studio**, and follow the signs. Still owned by descendants of Baron and Baroness Georg and Maria von Trapp, heroes of *The Sound of Music*, the resort is a famous cross-country ski venue and a reminder that if you look in the right place, you can find a place that looks, well, sort of like home.

the famous ski capital......................................

For decades, **Stowe** has been one of Vermont's premier destination resorts, a place synonymous with skiing in the Green Mountains. In 1914, a Dartmouth College librarian named Nathaniel Goodrich set tongues clucking in this quiet hill farm community by making the earliest recorded descent of Mount Mansfield on skis. Within 20 years Civilian Conservation Corps (CCC) crews were cutting the mountain's first ski trails, precursors of the "Front Four" and other legendary runs at **Stowe Mountain Resort**, which sprawls across Mount Mansfield and nearby Spruce Peak. The resort's magnificent, $400 million luxury resort hotel, completed in 2008, is the first big luxury hotel to be built in New England in more than 50 years.

But for all its winter sports fame, Stowe at heart is still a small town – the cheery, busy village itself runs for only a few blocks, and most of the shopping, dining, and lodging (there are plenty of choices, but we're not talking Aspen or Gstaad here) are strung along the Mountain Road (Route 108), which leads north out of town to the narrow defile at the crest of Smugglers Notch and the ski resort of the same name on the other side.

For just taking in the scenery, you can't do better than to grab a bicycle, a pair of rollerblades, snowshoes, or just your walking shoes and take to the 5 1/2-mile **Stowe Recreation Path**, which begins downtown right behind the sharp-spired Stowe Community Church and follows roughly the same route as the Mountain Road (there are a number of other access points along the way). Mount Mansfield, always in view, looms sublimely above the valley floor through which the path meanders; from the right angle, you just might be able to make out the reclining human profile that the summit ridge is said to resemble, and which gave its peaks the names "Nose," "Chin," "Forehead," and "Adam's Apple."

A number of trails, including the Long Trail, ascend Mount Mansfield from Stowe, Cambridge (Smugglers Notch), and Underhill. All are described in the Green Mountain Club's Long Trail Guide, available at bookstores and the Club's headquarters (see above).

Take Route 108 (the Mountain Road) north out of Stowe village. Among the Stowe Mountain Resort attractions accessible along the road, once you get past the shops, inns, and restaurants, are the **Toll Road** for automobiles, which ends just under the Nose and doubles as a gentle ski trail in the winter; and the **Gondola**, a cable-suspended ski lift operating during summer and foliage season as well as in winter (the casually elegant **Cliff House**, at the upper terminal, serves lunch, and occasional Saturday evening dinners, with a spectacular view). On Spruce Peak, opposite Mount Mansfield, an **Alpine Slide** – individual rider-controlled sleds on a concrete chute served by a chairlift – operates in summer and early fall and proves that skiers don't have a monopoly on gravity-based thrills.

Side Trips

To view **Moss Glen Falls**, one of Vermont's highest waterfalls, head north from Stowe Village on Route 100 for approximately 3 2/10 miles. Turn right onto Randolph Road, and then right onto Moss Glen Falls Road to the sign for the falls. Follow a short path to see cascades of water plummet more than 100 feet to a gorge below, creating a cooling, if shallow, swimming hole. (Don't confuse this site with the other Moss Glen Falls, off Route 100 in the town of Granville.)

Another nice spot for a dip is **Bingham Falls,** a short walk from a small parking area just past the entrance to Smugglers Notch State Park on the Mountain Road. A waterfall here, in the West Branch of the Waterbury River, cascades through a deep ravine: even if you don't want to swim, the scenery is worth the approximately 1/3 mile trek down a well-worn dirt path.

into the Notch . . . .

Smugglers Notch Scenic Highway in **Smugglers Notch State Park** is one of Vermont's three official designated scenic routes (the others are Route 125, Middlebury Gap State Scenic Road – see Drive 5; and Route 131 Cavendish Road – see Drive 1). Take the RV ban seriously: the road to the top is narrow and very steep, with fiddler's-elbow turns that graze gigantic boulders. The 2,162-foot summit is crowded on both sides by towering cliffs and dark, beetling ledges where reintroduced pairs of peregrine falcons nest.

The Notch was used by smugglers during the War of 1812 when trade with Canada was forbidden; as an escape route to Canada for slaves during the days of the Underground Railroad; and by bootleggers smuggling liquor from Canada during Prohibition. One caveat: this is one of the state's major attractions, and traffic to the top on a fine summer day can be maddeningly slow. If you want to experience the Notch's grandeur in relative solitude, try to travel in the early morning or evening. Once the first snowfall arrives – and until the drifts finally melt in early May – you won't be traveling through the Notch at all. The road is simply too narrow and tortuous to plow.

Several popular hikes begin at the crest of the Notch, including one of our favorites, a short (1 2/10 mile) but strenuous climb to trout-stocked Sterling Pond, the highest significant body of water in Vermont. Be sure to continue past the pond a short distance to Sterling Mountain look off; Smugglers Notch Resort, the Lamoille Valley, Jay Peak, and Canada (in exactly that order of distance) are all directly ahead to the north.

Head down the north side of the notch on the flank of 3,640-foot Madonna Mountain, past **Smugglers Notch Resort**, consistently rated one of the country's top family resorts. As you parallel the Brewster River, watch for the turnoff for Old North Road: here, at the junction, waterfalls plummet into Brewster River Gorge. A bit farther north, at the intersection with Canyon Road, the 85-foot Grist Mill Covered Bridge, built in 1919, spans the river.

Continue into tiny **Jeffersonville,** a popular artists' retreat for more than 50 years. The **Bryan Memorial Art Gallery** exhibits the works of regional artists throughout the season**. At the intersection with Route 15, turn right (east) and continue a short distance to Route 108. Turn left onto 108** and cross the old steel truss bridge over the Lamoille River near a small streamside picnic and fishing access area. This bridge, which is scheduled for replacement in the near future (word has it that it may be salvaged to carry a bike path across the Missisquoi River north of here) was built in 1931 to replace a wooden covered bridge, which burned when a farmer's cigarette ignited his horse-drawn load of hay. **Continue a short distance to the intersection with Route 109. Turn right (north) onto Route 109 toward Waterville.**

Side Trip

At the intersection of routes 108 and 15, turn left onto Route 15 and head three miles to Cambridge to visit Boyden Valley Winery (just the other side of Cambridge village), which offers tours (11:30 a.m. and 1 p.m.), tastings ($), and a gift shop featuring locally-made crafts and foods. The winery also makes maple syrup and sells its own organic beef.

In all the world, there's only one Lamoille River – or Lamoille anything. Must be a French word, right? Wrong. According to the most plausible theory, the name came about because of Samuel de Champlain's careless handwriting: on a map detailing his explorations, Champlain supposedly named the river La Mouette – the Gull. But the father of New France forgot to cross his Ts, and his "e" looked like an "i." So Lamoille it is.

covered bridge country. . . . .

Continue north on Route 109 to Waterville (our hometown). Waterville has three covered bridges, all just off Route 109 and all spanning the North Branch of the Lamoille River. The Village Bridge (1887 or 1895, depending on your source) carries Church Street over the river; it's on the left just past the Waterville Market in the village center. The 1887 Montgomery Bridge is off to the right 1 1/5 miles north of the center; and the circa 1877 Jaynes, or "Kissing" Bridge, also on the right, is approximately 1/2 mile past the Montgomery Bridge. Below each bridge is a swimming hole.

Where was Chester A. Arthur born? Fairfield, Vermont claims the 21st president for its own – but many believe Arthur (1830-1886) was born in Waterville. His birth, they say, was registered in Fairfield after his mother brought him there as an infant to join his itinerant preacher father.

A little more than four miles north of Waterville village center, after you've crossed a highway bridge into the little hamlet of Belvidere Junction, turn left onto Back Road to reach the 1895 queenpost Mill Bridge, one of two in the town of Belvidere (both, like the Waterville bridges, cross the Lamoille's North Branch). The foundations of two 19th-century mills that gave the bridge its name remain along the riverbank. Drive through the bridge and continue to bear right, keeping an eye out on the right for the 1887 Morgan Bridge. Drive through it back onto Route 109, turn left and continue north. (If you want to skip the bridges, just continue north on Route 109 from Waterville to Belvidere).

In **Belvidere Center**, which lies just ahead beyond the cemetery and school, be sure to stop at Tallman's general store, one of the most authentic, least "cutesified" mercantile time capsules in New England. Here in downtown Belvidere, it's easy to recall that this stretch of Route 109 was the last portion of state highway in Vermont to be paved. That happened in 1981, and not everyone hereabouts was happy about it.

Route 109 ends at the intersection with Route 118; continue straight onto 118 South. Serene little Belvidere Pond, also called Long Pond, lies just ahead on the left. Its wooded shoreline is totally undeveloped, and is state-owned to assure that it remains that way. The road along the marshy area leading up to the pond is a good place to spot moose, especially around dusk – and also a good place to cut your speed, since the moose is the giant sport utility vehicle of the deer family.

Side Trip

If you turn left onto Route 118 instead of heading straight, it's an eight-mile drive to **Montgomery Center**. Log onto the town's website, montgomeryvt.us, to download a map showing the locations of the town's six covered bridges (a seventh is just over the Enosburg line) along with their history, or ask at the town clerk's office on Main Street. Several are just a quick turnoff from the main road.

If you'd rather not backtrack to this drive's main route, you can take Route 53 – the Hazen's Notch Road (closed in winter) from Montgomery Center through deep woods with great views of majestic Jay Peak to the north, to Lowell, then take Route 100 south to rejoin the drive at Eden.

Continue on Route 118 past Belvidere Pond, and watch for markers for the **Long Trail**, which crosses the road just ahead. If you have time for a hike, take the trail south (on the left; parking is on the right) for a gentle, 1 7/10- mile ascent to a lookout over pretty little Ritterbush Pond. A more strenuous hike of 2 ½ miles leads from the parking area to the summit of Belvidere Mountain, where an abandoned fire tower offers fine views. Ahead, Route 118 ends at a T intersection with Route 100, where there is a well-stocked general store and service station. **Turn right onto Route 100** and head south. The views ahead, as you pass through rolling farmland alternating with stands of birch and pine, are of Mount Elmore and the peaks of the Worcester Range. Continue through the hamlet of North Hyde Park, and – if the kids are along – watch on the right for **Common Acres**, a campground that has a miniature golf course and go-kart track.

back door to Montpelier . . . .

Route 100 joins Route 15 in Hyde Park (the village, which is the "shire town" – county seat – of Lamoille County) is set back from the highway, a few blocks to the south. **Turn left onto Route 100** and continue to **Morrisville**, the county's largest town. **Turn right at the traffic light** – one of the very few in the county – and **follow signs for Route 100**, passing a shopping center and threading through the downtown business district. **This will involve making a left at a T intersection, crossing a bridge, turning right at the movie theater, then left onto Main Street at the end of Portland Street to get onto Route 12 south.** (Alternate route: If you turn right onto Main Street, you can continue directly back to Stowe on Route 100 instead of taking the scenic route to Montpelier.)

A few miles south of Morrisville on Route 12, watch on the left for **Lake Elmore State Park**, which has a swimming beach with a gentle drop-off on the lake, which lies in the shadow of Mount Elmore. There is a fairly rigorous hiking trail to the summit, where there is a disused fire tower.

Beyond Lake Elmore, Route 12 heads into a heavily wooded, thinly populated upland, with the 3,000-foot-plus sentinels of the Worcester Range rising to the west. Farmland reappears around the village of Worcester, which lies on the North Branch of the Winooski River. Stowe is only 10 miles distant, but there has never been a road between the two towns – 3,539-foot Mount Hunger, and a lot of rugged terrain, lies between them.

Finish the drive by following Route 12 towards the Winooski River valley and the northern suburbs (if a town this small, even a state capital, can have suburbs) of Montpelier. From here, you can continue east or west on Route 2, or take I-89 (accessible via Route 2 west of town) to Burlington or points south.

information *All area codes are (802) unless otherwise indicated.*

Central Vermont Chamber of Commerce (229-4619), P.O. Box 336, Barre 05641. cvchamber.com

Green Mountain Club (244-7037), Rte. 100, Waterbury Center 05766. greenmountainclub.org

Lamoille Valley Chamber of Commerce (888-7607), 43 Portland St., Morrisville 05661. lamoillevalleychamberr.com

Smugglers' Notch Area Chamber of Commerce (644-8232), P.O. Box 364, Jeffersonville 05464. smugnotch.com

Stowe Area Association (253-7321), Main St., Stowe 05672. gostowe.com

Waterbury Tourism Council, P.O. Box 468, Waterbury 05676. waterbury.org

lodging

Betsy's B & B (229-0466), 74 E. State St., Montpelier 05602. 12 nicely furnished rooms and suites with TVs and phones (some with kitchens) occupy 2 adjacent Victorian homes in the Historic District. Bike and weight machine. betsysbnb.com $-$$

Capitol Plaza Hotel & Conference Center (223-5252), 100 State St., Montpelier 05602. 56 tastefully furnished rooms and 3 suites in full-service downtown hotel; J. Morgan's Steakhouse (B, L, D & Sun. brunch: $$-$$$) and shops on premises. capitolplaza.com $$

Comfort Inn & Suites at Maplewood (229-2222), 213 Paine Turnpike North, Berlin (exit 7 off I-89). Well-appointed chain motel close to the highway has 89 rooms and 18 suites with kitchens. comfortinnsuites.com $-$$$

Deer Run Motor Inn (644-8866), Rte. 15 Jeffersonville. Nicely updated, 2-floor motel has 25 rooms with baths, TV, a/c, fridges, coffee makers (you supply coffee), and an in-ground pool. deerrunmotorinn.com $

Donomar Inn B&B (644-2937), 916 Rte. 108S, Jeffersonville 05464. Overlooking Mt. Mansfield, the 1865 home has 6 guest rooms with shared or private baths: some have fireplaces and Jacuzzis. The outdoor hot tub is a magical spot on a starry night. donomarinn.com $-$$

Edson Hill Manor (253-7371), 1500 Edson Hill Rd., Stowe 05672. One of Stowe's finest inns/ restaurants has 9 rooms – most with fireplaces – in the manor house, and 4 carriage houses, each with 4 fireplaced units. American cuisine, served in a dining room ($$-$$$) resembling a trellised garden, includes appetizers such as smoked duck French toast, and entrees including seared rare tuna loin. Stable and trout pond. B&B and MAP available. edsonhillmanor.com $$-$$$

English Rose Inn (326-4391), 195 Rte. 242, Montgomery Center 05471. 14 rooms with private baths in an 1850s, 25-room farmhouse 3 mi. from Jay Peak Ski Area. MAP includes a 4-course dinner in the on-site Paddington's Restaurant. Breakfast included. englishroseinnvermont.com $-$$

1836 Cabins (244-8533) Box 128T, off Rte. 100, Waterbury Center 05677. Secluded, modern housekeeping cabins (some with fireplaces) sleep 2-6, set in the woods on 200 acres in back of the Green Mountain Club. stowecabins.com $$

Green Mountain Inn (253-7301), 18 Main St., Stowe 05672. 1833 village inn has 100 rooms and suites, many with canopy beds, fireplaces and Jacuzzis. Year-round outdoor pool and health club; and restaurant. greenmountaininn.com $$-$$$

The Inn at Montpelier (223-2727), 147 Main St., Montpelier 05602. This handsome, two-building historic downtown complex has 19 rooms with private baths, TV, a/c/, and phones; deluxe rooms have wood burning fireplaces. Breakfast baked goods are made by La Brioche Bakery & Café (part of NECI). innatmontpelier.com $$-$$$

The Inn at Turner Mill (253-2062), 56 Turner Mill Lane, Stowe 05672. 10-acre complex close to Mt. Mansfield has 4 rooms and 4 1- and 2-bedroom suites with kitchens. Some fireplaces. Swimming hole, pool, snowshoe rental, x-c trails. Breakfast summer & fall. turnermill.com $-$$$

Nye's Green Valley Farm B&B (644-1984), 8976 Rte. 15, Jeffersonville 05464. A lovingly re-stored early 1800s stagecoach tavern—now a private home, farm, and garden center – has 3 air-conditioned rooms (2 with shared bath). nyesgreenvalleyfarm.com $

Old Stagecoach Inn (244-5056), 18 N. Main St., Waterbury 05676. Renovated 1826 stage-coach stop has 8 comfortable guestrooms (2 with shared bath; some with a/c and phone), and 3 apartments perfect for kids and pets. Breakfast included. oldstagecoach.com $-$$$

Phineas Swann B&B Inn (326-4306), Main St., Montgomery Center 05471. This beautifully landscaped and elegantly furnished inn bills itself as New England's "most romantic pet-friendly inn." 3 rooms and 2 carriage house suites, all with private baths, TV, and a/c, are amply comfortable for people, too. Breakfast included. phineasswann.com $$-$$$$

Smugglers' Notch Resort (644-8851), Rte. 108, Smugglers' Notch 05464. Sprawling, self-contained ski/summer resort village consistently wins top ranking for family programs. Restaurants, pools and slides, tennis, canoe and fishing trips; children's programs. smuggs.com $$-$$$

Sterling Ridge Suites & Cabins (644-8265), 1073 Junction Hill Rd., Jeffersonville 05464. Inn/log cabin complex on 80 acres overlooking Mt. Mansfield has 8 guest rooms (4 with private bath), 1- 2-and 3-bedroom housekeeping log cabins with fireplaces, and an elegant custom log home. Several offer seclusion. Hot tub, outdoor pool, canoes and mountain bikes. vermont-cabins.com $$-$$$

Stone Hill Inn (253-6282), 89 Houston Farm Rd., Stowe 05672. One of the area's most romantic lodgings, set well off the Mountain Rd., offers 9 beautifully-furnished rooms with fireside bedrooms and baths, and 2-person Jacuzzis. Lovely landscaped grounds. Candlelight breakfast included. stonehillinn.com $$$$

Sunset Motor Inn (888-4956), 160 Rte. 15, Morrisville 05661. Classic motel has 55 units with TV, phones, hair dryers; some with whirlpool baths and fridges. Outdoor pool and play area. Some pet friendly rooms. $-$$

Stowe Motel and Snowdrift (253-7629), 2043 Mountain Road, Stowe 05672. Comfortable motel rooms; also, apartments, suites, and houses. Heated pools, hot tub, tennis; mountain bike and snowshoe rentals. stowemotel.com Motel: $-$$

Stowe Mountain Lodge (253-3560), 7412 Mountain Rd., Stowe 05672. All 139 rooms at the resort's new, $400 million 6-story luxury lodging feature bamboo bed linens, feather beds, goose down comforters, relaxation tubs, and oversize windows with balconies. The dramatic lobby is decorated with locally made crafts; facilities include a 21,000 sq. ft. spa, boutiques, restaurant, and bar. stowemountainlodge.com $$$$

Thatcher Brook Inn (244-5911), Rte. 100 N, Waterbury 05676. 22 well-appointed rooms ranging from classic b&b to luxury suites (fireplaces and Jacuzzis) in c.1899 Victorian inn complex close to I-89. Breakfast included. thatcherbrook.com $-$$$$

Topnotch at Stowe Resort & Spa (253-8585), 4000 Mountain Rd., Stowe 05672. A 23,000 sq. ft. spa, year-round tennis, a highly rated restaurant (see "Restaurants" below), and an assortment of accommodations make this plush resort on 120 acres a popular retreat. Year-round tennis. topnotchresort.com $$$-$$$$

Trapp Family Lodge (253-8511), Luce Hill Rd., Stowe 05672. 116 rooms 2,800-acre resort popular with bus tours offer a variety of lodging options. The main dining room (see "Restaurants" below) serves European-style cuisine. Extensive trail network, tennis courts, indoor pool, and sports center. Children's programs. trappfamily.com $$-$$$

restaurants

The Bee's Knees (888-7889), 82 Lower Main St., Morrisville. At breakfast, omelettes dozens of ways; hearty sandwiches at lunch; "supper" might include Atlantic salmon, or seared pork loin with sweet and sour maple sauce. Local microbrews, organic wine. Live music most nights. Closed Mon. B, L & D. $$

Blue Moon Cafe (253-7006), 35 School St., Stowe. Contemporary American dishes inspired by Asia and the Mediterranean are elegantly served in a bistro environment. House specials include blue corn crusted sea scallops and roast duck. D. $$$-$$$$

Cliff House (253-3500), atop Mount Mansfield. The view is magnificent (on a clear day); the food – particularly the burger – is tasty and substantial, with an accent on local ingredients. You can buy a one-way gondola ticket (or even better, hike both ways) and walk off your meal if you wish. Seasonal. L; special Sat. dinners (reservations required). $$-$$$

Green Mountain Coffee Visitor Center and Café (882-2700), 1 Rotarian Place, Waterbury. Coffee, of course, along with sandwiches, salads and quiche, all prepared off-site. 7 a.m.-7 p.m. $

Hen of the Wood (244-7300), 95 Stowe St., Waterbury. The award-winning chef and his talented crew emphasize fresh, local ingredients, an extensive boutique wine list, and local cheeses in an intimate 19th-century gristmill. D, closed Sun. $$-$$$

Michael's on the Hill (244-7476), 4182 Stowe-Waterbury Rd., Waterbury. Fine Swiss cuisine in an 1820 farmhouse, with Swiss-born chef Michael turning out dishes such as a Gouda cheese tart appetizer, and entrees such as skillet chicken with buttermilk Vidalia onion rings or "Michael's veal" with mushrooms and a white wine cream sauce. D, closed Tues. $$$

The New England Culinary Institute of Montpelier has two downtown restaurants: the Main Street Grill & Bar (223-3188), 110 Main Street, an upscale American bistro; and La Brioche Bakery & Café (229-0443), 89 Main St., with pastries, breads, and sandwiches. $-$$$

Red Hen Bakery (223-5200), 961B Rte 2, Middlesex. Delicious breads, along with goodies such as ham and cheese croissants and sticky buns, as well as salads, soups, and sumptuous sandwiches. On summer Sunday afternoons, local musicians perform; kids' play area. Mon.-Sat. 7 a.m.-6 p.m.; Sun. 8 a.m.-6 p.m. $

Sarducci's (223-0229), 3 Main St., Montpelier. The casual and bustling bistro-style restaurant serves well-prepared Italian cuisine featuring wood-fired pizza and imaginative pasta dishes. Patio overlooking river. L Mon.-Sat., D. $-$$

The Shed (253-4364), Mountain Rd., Stowe. "The mighty Shed burger" is the star, but the extensive menu includes lots of favorites including BBQ ribs, Southern fried chicken, and chili, as well as more extensive dinner entrees. L & D. $-$$$

Norma's Restaurant, Topnotch at Stowe Resort & Spa (253-8585), 4000 Mountain Rd., Stowe 05672. Casual, family-friendly bistro with an open kitchen specializes in an eclectic menu of thoughtfully prepared spa cuisine dishes utilizing fresh, local ingredients. B, L, & D. Children's menu, and Fri. and Sat. bistro menu. $$-$$$$

Trapp Family Lodge (253-8511), Luce Hill Rd., Stowe 05672. Three restaurants, including the main dining room (B & D, $$$-$$$$) serves European-style cuisine, with entrees such as Wiener schnitzel and phyllo wrapped halibut. Also, the Lounge ($-$$, L & D) and the Deli Bakery ($-$$, B & L).

attractions

The Artisans' Hand (229-9492), 89 Main St., Montpelier. Cooperative gallery displays and sells works of more than 100 local artisans. Closed Sun.

Ben & Jerry's Ice Cream (244-8687), Rte. 100, Waterbury.

Bryan Memorial Art Gallery (644-5100), 180 Main St., Jeffersonville. May-Oct. Donation.

Cabot Annex Store (244-6334), 2653 Waterbury-Stowe Rd., Rte. 100, Waterbury. Vt. wines, microbrews, specialty foods, and lots of samples.

Cold Hollow Cider Mill (244-8771), Rte. 100, Waterbury Center.

Little River Hotglass Studio (253-0889), 593 Moscow Rd., Moscow. Original pieces by Michael Trimpol include perfume bottles and paperweights. Closed Tues.

Morse Farm Sugar Works (223-2740), 1168 County Rd., Montpelier. One of Vermont's oldest maple sugar farms has a maple museum, tours and tastings, a video theater, store, and crafts emporium.

Stowe Mountain Resort (253-3000), Mountain Rd., Stowe. Alpine Slide Mid-June-Labor Day; after Labor Day-Columbus Day, weekends; Gondola, mid-June-mid-Oct.; Toll Road, mid-May-mid-Oct.

T.W. Wood Gallery & Arts Center (828-8743), Vermont College, College Hall, 36 College St., Montpelier. Closed Mon.

Vermont Historical Society Museum (828-2291), Pavilion Building, 109 State St., Montpelier. Closed Sun.

Vermont Ski Museum (802-253-9911), 1 Main St., Stowe. Ski technology and history, period clothing, local history, and special exhibits. Closed Tues.

Vermont State House (828-2228), State St., Montpelier. Tours on half hour July-Oct. Closed Sun. Free.

Waterbury Center State Park (244-1226), 177 Reservoir Rd., Waterbury. Memorial Day-Labor Day.

Ziemke Glass Blowing Studio (244-6126), 3033 Waterbury-Stowe Rd. (Rte. 100), Waterbury Center. Glenn Ziemke's exquisite hand-blown art glass, on exhibit and for sale; observe glassblowing.

activities

Bert's Boats (644-8189 or cell 802-730-2216), 73 Smugglers View Rd., Jeffersonville. Rentals, guided tours include Boyden Valley Winery; overnight camping tours.

Common Acres Campground(888-5151), 1781 Rte. 100, Hyde Park. Miniature golf and go-karts.

The Fly Rod Shop/Fly Fish (253-7346), 2703 Waterbury Rd. (Rte. 100), Stowe. Free fishing maps, fly rod and reel rental, fishing and hunting licenses; 1- and 2-day drift boat trips; guide service.

Green Mountain Troutfitters (644-2214), 233 Mill St., (Rte.108), Jeffersonville. Fly-fishing outfitter also offers clinics and classes, rental equipment, and a guide service.

Green River Canoe (644-8336), Rte. 15, Jeffersonville. Canoe rental/shuttle on the Lamoille River.

Lajoie Stables (644-5347), 992 Pollander Rd., Jeffersonville. Vermont's largest horseback facility offers year-round 1- to 3-hr. trail rides; also sleigh and pony rides.

Lost Nation Theater (229-0492), City Hall Arts Center, 39 Main St., Montpelier. Comedies, drama, musicals and, in foliage season, Shakespeare, performed by resident professional company. June-Oct. Schedule: lostnationtheater.org

Mountain Sports and Bike Shop (253-7919), 580 Mountain Rd., Stowe. Mountain bike, in-line skate, and baby jogger rentals.

Stowe Soaring/Whitcomb Aviation (888-7845), Rte. 100, Morrisville. Glider and airplane rides.

Umiak Outfitters (253-2317), 849 S. Main St. (Rte. 100), Stowe. Kayaks and canoe sales and rentals; sea kayaking instruction; guided river trips.

off the drive

Boyden Valley Winery (644-8151), Rte. 104, Cambridge.

Butternut Mountain Farm (635-2329), Main St., Johnson. Maple syrup and products, Vermont crafts and cheeses, books.

Rock of Ages (476-3119), 558 Graniteville Rd., Graniteville. Visitors center open May-Oct.; guided tours June-mid-Oct. Mon.-Fri.; manufacturing facility Mon.-Fri.

Vermont Maple Outlet (644-5482), Rte. 15, Jeffersonville. Maple syrup and products – including the local specialty, maple creemees; also local cheeses, specialty foods, and crafts.

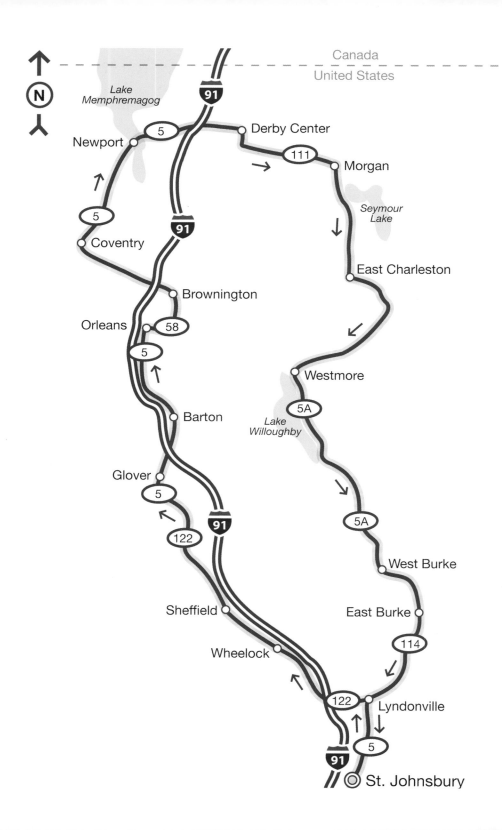

Drive **8**

St. Johnsbury and the Northeast Kingdom
. . . .
100 miles

major attractions

- St. Johnsbury Athenaeum
- Fairbanks Museum and Planetarium
- Dog Mountain

- Bread and Puppet Museum
- Crystal Lake State Park
- Lake Willoughby

*T*his drive ventures deep into the heart of what Vermont's late Governor George Aiken christened the "Northeast Kingdom" – a remote, thinly populated, and ruggedly scenic part of the state characterized by deep blue lakes, vast forests, and peaks that stand apart from the central range of the Green Mountains. At opposite ends of the route, the small cities of St. Johnsbury and Newport invite travelers to park their cars and stroll historic downtown streets.

Begin the drive in St. Johnsbury, shire town of Caledonia County and the largest community in northeastern Vermont. "Saint J," which lies at the confluence of the Passumpsic, Moose, and Sleepers rivers, was named for Hector St.

Jean de Crevecoeur, the French émigré commentator on early American life and first popularizer of the "melting pot" idea, and is the only St. Johnsbury in the world.

Although the city was first settled in 1786, its history really began in 1830, when Thaddeus Fairbanks filed for a patent on his revolutionary platform scale. Over the next 40 years St. Johnsbury's population tripled, as Fairbanks Scales were shipped to the four corners of the globe. Long the city's first family, the philanthropic Fairbanks clan contributed to the building of many of the city's grandest structures, including the handsome, Second Empire **St. Johnsbury Athenaeum**, one of only fifteen libraries in the nation to be declared a National Historic Landmark. Horace Fairbanks intended the Athenaeum not only as a place of study, but of visual delight: a substantial rear wing of the building houses an art gallery whose collection – mostly landscapes and still lifes – has been kept unchanged as a precise record of the artistic tastes of a century and a quarter ago. But there's more than historic interest here: the splendid Eastlake-style gallery's centerpiece is Albert Bierstadt's 10' x 15' "The Domes of the Yosemite," a landmark work of the Hudson River School.

Thaddeus Fairbanks was knighted by the emperor of Austria in honor of his development of the platform scale. His brother Erastus, with whom he ran the family business, had to be satisfied with serving as governor of Vermont.

Fairbanks money also made possible St. Johnsbury Academy, an unusual but highly regarded hybrid of private preparatory school and public (for St. Johnsbury and a couple of surrounding towns) high school; and the handsome Richardson Romanesque **Fairbanks Museum and Planetarium**, a great gallimaufry of ethnographic and natural history exhibits from all over the world, with special emphasis on Vermont and the Northern Forest. Museums like this were how people saw the world before the Discovery Channel: here are more than 175,000 objects including mounted birds, mammals and reptiles, as well as old toys, weapons, fossils, general exotica … and Fairbanks scales. There's also a children's area, with hands-on exhibits and a full schedule of special programs. The planetarium is tiny, but it does offer accurate star shows. Also quite accurate – everyone hopes – are the weather reports issued each day from the meteorological center in the basement of the museum and broadcast throughout the state on Vermont Public Radio.

Catamount Film and Arts, a nonprofit organization that has served the Northeast Kingdom and northern New Hampshire for more than 25 years, stages performances through the North Country. Throughout the year, at its St. Johnsbury headquarters in a former Masonic Hall on Eastern Avenue, the organization hosts regional film premieres, foreign and independent films, and a Sunday jazz series. It also exhibits the work of local artists in its galleries.

St. Johnsbury was once an important rail center, home of the St. Johnsbury & Lake Champlain Railroad, nicknamed by some wags "Slow, Jerky & Late Coming." But downtown St. J still has the look of an old railroad town, its sturdy brick business blocks paralleling tracks that still see Canadian Pacific freight traffic. The passenger station? It's now a restaurant. On Railroad Street, the **Moose River Lake and Lodge Store**, purveyors of Great Camp Adirondack furniture and accouterments, will make your house look like the kind of place where the butler has to chase away raccoons.

Just a short distance to the east on Route 2, **Maple Grove Farms**, the oldest and largest maple sugaring operation in the country, earns St. Johnsbury the title of "Maple Center of the World." There's a guided tour of the factory, a museum, and a fine gift shop.

to the dogs. . . . .

If Stephen Huneck has his way, St. Johnsbury could also become known as "Dog Haven of the World." The artist and dog lover, known for the whimsical canines that populate his prints and bizarre furniture designs, has created **Dog Mountain**, an art center/sculpture garden where dogs and their humans can soak up a little culture, and then retreat for meditation to a chapel complete with stained glass windows done in dog themes ("All Breeds, All Creeds, No Dogmas Allowed"). Turn onto Spaulding Road off Route 2 across from Fairbanks Scales and follow signs. If you'll be visiting Stowe, be sure to visit his gallery on Central Street (Drive 7).

Head north out of St. Johnsbury on Route 5 toward Lyndonville. There are five covered bridges in the Lyndon/Lyndonville area, including several along or just off our route. Pick up a brochure giving directions to the bridges at the Lyndonville Information Booth or at the town's Cobleigh Library, 14 Depot Street.

As you follow what passes in Caledonia County for suburban sprawl, watch for the **Miss Lyndonville Diner** on the right. Although not a diner in the true architectural sense, it serves up classic roadside fare, including breakfasts hefty enough to stoke a Northeast Kingdom logger, and fresh strawberry pie in season. On the left, **Trout River Brewing Company** makes all-natural, unfiltered ales and lagers using traditional methods and will be glad to let you sample the wares ($) at their retail store.

During the 1860s, **Lyndonville** was the headquarters and terminus of the Passumpsic Division of the Boston & Maine Railroad, and its days of prosperity, though long past, are still evident in the handsome Victorian architecture along Depot Street. Today the town is home to enterprises as diverse as Lyndon State College, home of an appropriately-sited degree program in meteorology; and the Dairy Association Company, manufacturers of Bag Balm, the ointment in the little green tin which was developed in 1899 as a soothing unguent for cows' udders and is now used to soothe the chapped hands and dry skin of humans, many of whom have never had an actual bovine encounter. Balm for the intellect is available at **Green Mountain Books**, which has a terrific selection of new and used Vermont titles.

As you continue north on Route 5, watch for the town green and bandstand. One of the region's oldest musical ensembles, the Lyndonville Band, plays here on Wednesday evenings in the summer.

The covered Sanborn Bridge spans the East Branch of the Passumpsic River just south of the intersection of Route 5 and routes 122 and 114. The open-sided bridge, built in 1867 to a design called the Paddleford truss, is on the property of the **Lynburke Motel**. It was moved here from another Lyndonville location in 1960, when it was threatened with demolition.

Just north of Lyndonville, turn left onto Route 122, which follows alongside the Miller River through **Wheelock**, named after President John Wheelock of Dartmouth College. In the 1700s Vermont's General Assembly granted the township to the impoverished school, and rental incomes paid by the townspeople helped to keep it solvent. In 1930, Dartmouth voted full tuition scholarships to all Wheelock residents who qualify for admission – a tradition still honored today.

Tiny **Sheffield** is a battleground between concerned citizens and the state's Public Service Board: a private enterprise wants to construct 16 400-foot-high wind turbines on the ridges above the town and in nearby Sutton. A group of citizens united as the Ridge Protectors believe that the windmills will be an economic, visual, and ecological blight on the landscape, and are fighting the development … as of this writing, unsuccessfully.

Continue on Route 122 to Glover, home to the **Bread and Puppet Museum.** The huge puppets on display here are the creation of Peter Schumann, and have long been a common sight at political and social justice rallies throughout New England. Performances (and museum tours) are given throughout the summer (see "Attractions" below).

When Route 122 ends at Route 16, turn right (north) on Route 16 through the village of Glover, past **Labour of Love Public Gardens**, where more than 400 varieties of hardy perennials are in bloom from April until frost. Visitors are invited to picnic by the river and visit the restored 1880s Greek Revival home, filled with antiques and a hand-weaving studio. The tiny and quaint Pete's Busy Bee Diner grills a fine hotdog; grab a cookie at the Wooden Spoon Bakery.

The fair-sized and rather plain town of **Barton**, at the north end of **Crystal Lake**, was once a thriving industrial community. During the heyday of passenger rail service, six trains a day delivered fun seekers to Barton on their way to Crystal Lake and Willoughby. But industry has left, the trains stopped arriving, and today Barton is at its liveliest in early August when it hosts the Orleans County Fair on the outskirts of town. The old fashioned soda fountain in The Marketplace is a fun place for a light lunch or coffee.

To visit **Crystal Lake State Park,** bear to the right up the hill in town and then turn left onto Route 16 for less than a mile: the entrance is immediately ahead on the right. The glacially-formed, three-mile long, 100-foot-deep lake is a favorite of fishermen as well as swimmers: the water is sparkling clean, the mountain views superb, the beach sandy, and, unlike many other Vermont lakes, the lake bottom is clear of sticks and weeds.

Continue north out of Barton on Route 5 alongside the Barton River to **Orleans,** where the Barton and Willoughby Rivers merge on their way north to Lake Memphremagog. **At the intersection of routes 5 and 58, turn right and continue into town.** The huge Ethan Allen furniture factory on your right is the town's principal employer. **Turn right onto Church Street and then left onto Brownington Street toward Brownington.**

If you're visiting between the last week of April and the second week in May, be sure to stop at **Willoughby Falls Wildlife Management Area,** just 1/10-mile after the Brownington turn, to look for rainbow trout struggling upstream over the raging Willoughby Falls on their way to spawn in the clean gravel beds of the Willoughby River and its feeder streams. The annual "rainbow run" begins downstream – in this case, to the north – at Lake Memphremagog.

a stone monument to learning . . . .

For many visitors, tiny **Brownington Village** has the feel of a rural Shangri-La. It's hard to imagine that the sleepy hill town surrounded by farmlands and distant mountains was a thriving community on the main stage route between Boston and Montreal in the early part of the 19th century. But the handsome homes and public edifices built in the village's heyday – now the National Register of Historic Places Historic District – are testament to past glories.

Brownington's **Old Stone House Museum** is a monument to the determination and hard work of Alexander Twilight, who built the four-story granite structure he called Athenian Hall in 1836 to serve as both a dormitory and classroom for the Orleans County Grammar School, which he served as headmaster. The building now houses the 18th- and 19th-century collections of the Orleans County Historical Society, which sheds light not only on Twilight and his impressive academy, but also on all the vanished bustle of what has become a gorgeous backwater. Twilight's Greek Revival home directly across the road from the museum, serves as a visitor center and headquarters.

Alexander Twilight (1795-1857), Middlebury College class of 1825, is believed to have been the first African-American to have graduated from an American college. Elected to the Vermont General Assembly in 1836, he was the state's first African-American legislator.

Before leaving Brownington, be sure to climb up the wooden observatory in the meadow behind the church for a wonderful view of the distant hills. A walking tour booklet is available at the museum.

Head north from the center of town on Hinman Road into North Brownington, and turn left onto Brownington Road, which crosses under I- 91. Bear to the right as the road turns into Airport Road and cuts through **Barton River Marsh**, a 500-acre section of the 1,559-acre **South Bay Wildlife Management Area** at Lake Memphremagog's southern end. The area is a nesting area for osprey and black terns, and also harbors bald eagles, great blue and green herons, American bitterns, and painted and snapping turtles; and is one of New England's most pristine large, shallow freshwater marshes.

lake port on the border . . . .

When the Airport Road ends at the intersection with Route 5, turn right onto Route 5 and head north (bearing to the left at the fork to stay off the truck route) into **Newport**, Vermont's northernmost city, situated on a sloping promontory at the southern end of **Lake Memphremagog**. The Algonquin and Abenaki Indians who first lived in this area gave the lake its name, which translates as "beautiful waters." Only five of the 33 miles of the lake are in the U.S. The northern end, which splits into east and west forks, extends as far north as Magog, Quebec, and summer weekends bring many French-speaking boaters to Newport's downtown marina. The island-dotted lake is 350 feet deep in places, and teems with lake, brown and rainbow trout, landlocked salmon, pickerel, walleye, pike, large- and smallmouth bass, perch, smelt, bullheads ... and the requisite monster that no one ever really sees, in this case bearing the obvious and unlovely name Memphre. Heavily wooded mountains, most notably 3,360-foot Owl's Head (named for an Indian chief), hem in the shoreline north of town.

The first documented white visitors to the southern shores of Lake Memphremagog were Rogers' Rangers, returning from their successful raid against the Quebec home base of the St. Francis Indians in 1759. (In Northwest Passage, *Hollywood's version of this epic French and Indian War adventure based on Kenneth Roberts' fine novel of the same title, Spencer Tracy played the redoubtable Major Rogers.)*

During the 19th century, vast surrounding forests and good railroad connections made Newport an important lumber town. Its firm of Prouty and Miller was one of the biggest timber companies in the east, and Lake Memphremagog's South Bay was choked with logs awaiting the sawmills. The railroads also made Newport a resort destination, bringing passengers from Boston to the now-vanished, 400-room Memphremagog House and its hot springs spa.

For a great view of the lake, drive up Prospect Hill to St. Mary, Star of the Sea Roman Catholic Church, a twin-towered harbinger of the monolithic granite churches that dot the landscape of Quebec. After heading back downtown, park and take a stroll down Main Street, the best place to gauge the progress Newport has made in its transition from a forest products economy to one based on tourism and other post-industrial pursuits. It hasn't been an entirely smooth ride – you'll probably see an empty storefront or two – but all in all the old lakeshore city has picked itself up quite handily, and now boasts an attractive assortment of restaurants and shops.

Just a block away, the formerly industrial waterfront has become a focus for civic improvements. The docks at the handsome Gateway Center are a fine place for a stroll, especially on a summer's day. If the farther vistas of Lake Memphremagog are more tempting, you can rent a runabout or pontoon boat at **Newport Boat Rentals**, a short distance from downtown (see "Activities" below). And in late July, the city's Summerfest pulls downtown and the lakefront together with fiddlers, fireworks, an antique boat show, and a torchlight canoe parade. (Note: hopefully, the new cruise boat *Newport Belle* will be giving tours.)

Newport's city seals bears an image of the Lady of the Lake, *a passenger steamer that shuttled up and down lake Memphremagog at the turn of the 20th century.*

Free concerts are held at the bandstand in Gardner Park on Wednesday evenings throughout the summer. The park is also the site of a Farmers' Market on summer Wednesdays and Saturdays. Prouty Beach, named for the late Vermont senator and Newport native Winston Prouty, is just east of the city. It has a swimming beach, picnic area, and campground.

In 1996, at the behest of local citizens, Citizens Utilities removed the 100-foot-long, 20-foot-high concrete Dam #11 that for 40 years had prevented salmon from swimming freely between Lake Memphremagog and the Clyde River, where they spawn. The salmon are back once again, and the best time to catch them is usually the first week of October.

Head north out of Newport on Route 5 to the intersection with Route 105 in Derby Center, putting Newport's last few strip malls and the modest studios of quaintly-named WMOO Radio behind you. Those aren't cows, though, grazing behind the **Derby Cow Palace Restaurant**. In 1992, dairy farmer Doug Nelson decided to diversify, and began raising American elk, also known as wapiti, which were long ago native to this area. The low-fat meat of the handsome creatures is a specialty of the restaurant.

Side Trip

If you head north (instead of south, our direction) on Route 5, you'll soon reach Derby Line, on the U.S.-Canada border. And we do mean on the border. At the late 19th-century **Haskell Opera House**, the audience sits in the U.S., and the stage is in Canada. (There's a program of plays, concerts and musicals from mid-April to mid-October.) Downstairs, in the town library, you can cross the international border by walking from one room to another.

lake country . . . .

At the T intersection by the Cow Palace Restaurant, turn right off Route 5 onto Route 5A/105, and then left (east) onto Route 111. That's **Lake Salem** on your right a few miles after the turnoff; as the lake disappears from view, a lovely roller-coaster stretch of Route 111 cuts through pretty dairy country on its way to the tiny settlement of **Morgan** on **Seymour Lake**, one of the largest bodies of water lying entirely within Vermont's boundaries. The lake is popular among anglers seeking lake trout and landlocked salmon. That's one of the trout, weighing in at 25 pounds, in the picture hanging above the post office window in the Morgan store; he's posing with the fellow who caught him in 1956. If you want to try for a 26-pounder, **Clyde River Recreation** in nearby West Charleston rents and delivers canoes, kayaks, and other small boats (see "Activities" below).

Turn right at the Morgan store onto the Morgan Charleston Road, a dirt road that turns into Echo Lake Road, then Echo Pond Road, and finally West Echo Lake Road as it hugs the shore of Echo Lake (bear right at each fork). At the intersection of West Echo Lake Road, and Church Hill Road, bear to the right onto Church Hill Road. At the stop sign in East Charleston, turn left onto Route 105. The tiny village, originally named Navy by Revolutionary naval officer (and grantee of the town) Commodore Whipple, once boasted a thriving lumber mill.

About two miles out of East Charleston, turn right onto Hudson Road, then, at approximately 1/4 mile, left onto Westmore Road. Bear right as the road turns into Hinton Road, then Hinton Hill Road, and climbs up out of the woods until spread directly below you is beautiful, fjord-like **Lake Willoughby**, set between the steep slopes of Mount Pisgah (east shore) and Mount Hor (west shore, set further back). The 1,692-

acre lake was formed more than 12,000 years ago, when glaciers gouged a trough in the underlying granite, and with a maximum depth of 312 feet it is the deepest in the Northeast Kingdom. The cold waters provide some of the best fishing in the region – again, the top species are landlocked salmon and lake trout; in winter many fine specimens of the latter are taken through the ice.

At the stop sign where Hinton Hill Road ends at the lake, turn left onto Route 5A to continue this drive and/or to head towards **Willoughby State Forest** (see below). To get to the small public beach at the northern end of the lake and/or the **WilloughVale Inn**, turn right at the stop sign.

The sheer cliffs of Mounts Pisgah and Hor have been designated a National Natural Landmark, and lie within the 7,300-acre Willoughby State Forest. The forest, much of which was planted with Norway and white spruce and red and white pine by the CCC during the 1930s, offers hiking, cross country skiing, and snowmobile trails. Six cold-water ponds within its boundaries are stocked annually with brook and rainbow trout.

For superb views of the area, and possibly a glimpse of some of the cliffs' resident peregrine falcons, plan a hike up Mount Pisgah. The trailhead for the moderately difficult 3 1/2-mile route to the summit is on the left side of Route 5A, just past the southern tip of the lake; there's a parking lot on the right. (An interesting footnote: the original "south" trail up the mountain has been in use for almost 200 years.) The falcons returned here in 1985, after a 30-year hiatus. They come back each spring, nest during the summer, and generally leave by August. The best time to view them is in the early morning and late afternoon.

Although the summit of Mount Hor is wooded, there are splendid views from several vantage points on the cliffs. To reach the trailhead, continue through the parking area for Mount Pisgah, and up a gravel road at the right side of the parking area. Bear right at the fork to the parking area, and follow the blue-blazed trail. Total hiking distance is 3 ½ miles, and the rating is easy to moderate. For the best views, follow the East Branch Trail to the East Lookout Trail to Prospect Rock (if you're there in late August, stop and pick some of the plump raspberries that grow along the way).

Continue south on Route 5A to West Burke. (The Burkes were named for British statesman Edmund Burke, the British parliamentarian who though renowned as a conservative was sympathetic to the American colonists.) **In town, turn left toward Burke Hollow.** That's **Burke Mountain Ski Area** directly in front of you. **Bear right at the intersection**, past the 1825 Unionville Meeting House, **to the intersection with Route 114.** Turn left to the center of **East Burke** – a bustling little spot with the **River Garden Café**, **Bailey's & Burke General Store**, and the **Pub Outback**. It's also the headquarters for **Kingdom Trails**, with more than 100 miles of mountain biking (and in winter, cross country skiing and snowshoeing) trails. **East Burke Sports** rents both bikes and canoes and kayaks (see "Activities" below).

For unparalleled views of the region, take the winding **toll road** to the top of **Burke Mountain**.

Continue south on Route 114 back to the junction with Route 5, and south back to St. Johnsbury.

information *All area codes are (802) unless otherwise indicated.*

Barton Area Chamber of Commerce (525-1137), P.O. Box 403, Barton 05822. centerofthekingdom.com

Burke Area Chamber of Commerce (626-4124), P.O. Box 347, East Burke 05832. burkevermont.com

Kingdom Trails Association (626-0737), P.O. Box 204, E. Burke 05832. Maintains extensive network of mountain bike/ x-c trails. kingdomtrails.org

Lyndon Area Chamber of Commerce (802-626-9696), 51 Depot St., Lyndonville 05851. Information booth: Broad St. across from Lyndonville Savings Bank (Memorial Day-Labor Day). lyndonvermont.com

Northeast Kingdom Chamber of Commerce (748-3678), 51 Depot Square, St. Johnsbury 05819. nekchamber.com

Travel and Tourism Association of the Northeast Kingdom: (626-0737). travelthekingdom.com

Vermont's North Country Chamber of Commerce (334-7782), 246 The Causeway, Newport 05655. vtnorthcountry.org

lodgings

Note: there are a number of moderately-priced motels in and around downtown St. Johnsbury; contact the Northeast Kingdom Chamber of Commerce (above) for a listing. Also, there are numerous cottage colonies along Lake Willoughby.

Albro Nichols House (751-8434), 7 Boynton Ave., St. Johnsbury 05819. 3 cozy rooms with baths in a handsomely restored 1846 farmhouse privately situated off Main St. nekchamber. com/albronicholshouse. $

Burke Vacation Rentals (888-327-2850), Rte. 114, East Burke 05832. Slopeside accommodations at Burke Mt. include studio to 5-bedroom units, all with full kitchens. burkemill.com $$-$$$

Cliff Haven Farm B&B (334-2401), 5463 Lake Road, Newport Center 05857. 1800s post and beam farmhouse on 300 acres overlooking Lake Memphremagog. Swimming pond. cliffhavenfarmbedandbreakfast.com $-$$$

Estabrook House (751-826), 1569 Main St., St. Johnsbury 05819. Classic Victorian "painted lady" just ¼ mi. from I-91 has 4 charmingly decorated 2nd-floor rooms. The shared bath has an antique claw-foot soaking tub. Breakfast included. estabrookhouse.com $-$$

Fairbanks Inn (748-5666), 401 Western Ave., St. Johnsbury 05819. 45 nicely decorated rooms and suites in a 2-story motel near town. Heated pool. Continental breakfast. Pet-friendly rooms. stjay.com $$-$$$

Inn at Mountain View Farm (626-9924), Box 355, East Burke 05832. 440-acre retreat has 14 antiques-filled rooms and suites in a handsome Georgian colonial building and adjacent farmhouse. Breakfast included. Mid-May-Oct. innmtview.com $$$

Lake Salem Inn (766-5560), 1273 Rte. 105, Derby 05829. Romantic inn on 7 private acres overlooking the lake has 4 handsomely appointed rooms with queen-size beds (no cots) and private baths. The owner (former owner of an Italian restaurant) serves dinner by reservation; breakfast included. lakesaleminn.com $$

Lakeview Cabins (525-4463), 662 South Barton Rd., Barton 05822.
A classic, 1950s 1- and 2-bedroom cottage colony on Crystal Lake. Linens are supplied (but not towels). May-Oct. lakeviewcabinsvacation.com $-$$

Lynburke Lodge and Motel, (626-3346), 791 Main St., Lyndonville 05851. Classic motel on the Passumpsic River has standard rooms and family suites. lynburkelodge.com. $-$$

Newport City Motel (334-6558), 974 East Main St., Newport 05855. Well-kept, 2-story motel close to town has 82 rooms, including a new building with extended stay rooms. Business center; coin-operated laundry; indoor pool, hot tub, and fitness center. vermonter.com/ncm $-$$

Pinecrest Motel & Cabins (525-3472), Rte. 5N, Barton. 10 basic, tidy riverside cabins (5 housekeeping) and 5 motel rooms right off the road. Pool. Pets welcome. $

Seymour Lake Lodge (895-2752), 28 Valley Rd., Morgan 05853. Waterfront lodge has 8 basic but homey rooms with private and shared baths, including a 2-room suite with a TV and fridge. Guests have kitchen privileges and free use of canoes, kayaks, and rowboats. Powerboats ($). Pets welcome. seymourlakelodge.com $-$$

Super 8 Motel (334-1775), 4412 Rte. 5, Newport 05855. Just off I-91, the chain motel offers basic but comfortable rooms. Continental breakfast included. super8.com $

Vermont Sportsman Lodge (895-4209), 6111 Rte. 111, Morgan 05853. 4 rooms with shared baths, and a 3-room suite with private bath; TV in Great Room. Owner/guide Bob Beaupre (see "Activities" below) is a knowledgeable hunter and fisherman. No credit cards. $

The Village Inn of East Burke (802-626-3161), 606 Rte. 14, E. Burke 05832. Sprawling intown b&b has long been a favorite for folks looking for classic, comfortable, no- frills lodging. 6 rooms, and a 3-bedroom apartment that sleeps up to 12. Pets welcome. Breakfast included. Guide service available. villageinnofeastburke.com $

WilloughVale Inn (525-4123), Rte. 5A, Westmore 05860. Lakefront inn has 10 rooms in the main building (some with water views), 4 lakefront housekeeping cottages, and 4 lakeview cottages set back on a hill. The restaurant (D Wed-Sun in season: $$-$$$) serves dishes such as stuffed chicken breast and filet mignon. Canoe and kayak rental. willoughvale.com $$ -$$$$

off the drive

Rabbit Hill Inn (748-5168), Lower Waterford Rd., Lower Waterford 05848. Just 11 mi. from St. Johnsbury and well worth the ride for elegant accommodations and first-rate cuisine in an incomparable setting. Many rooms have fireplaces and double whirlpool tubs. MAP and B&B available. rabbithillinn.com $$$-$$$$

restaurants

Anthony's Restaurant (802-748-3613), 50 Railroad St., St. Johnsbury. Solid American fare at this casual, family spot includes tasty hamburgers and homemade potato chips; daily specials. B, L, & D. $

B & W Snack Bar, Rte. 5, Barton. Open summer and fall for snacks, creemees, sandwiches, and terrific french fries. $

Derby Cow Palace Restaurant (766-4724), 3111 Rte. 5, Derby. A 1-lb prime rib with salad bar, elk and beef burgers, seafood, and pasta are served up in a cheerful wood-paneled room overlooking an elk ranch. $-$$

East Side Landing (334-2340), 25 Lake St., Newport. Classic Yankee fare, ample portions, and a festive atmosphere make this one of the area's most popular spots. Antiques and VT products. B Sat. & Sun.; L, & D. $-$$

Elements (748-8400), 98 Mill St., St. Johnsbury. Housed in a renovated mill, this very popular restaurant serves creative comfort food such as smoked trout and apple cakes, and seafood sausage and grits. The daily blue-plate specials are a bargain. Children's menu. D Tues-Sat. $$-$$$

Kham's Thai Cuisine (751-8424), 1112 Memorial Drive (Rte. 5), St. Johnsbury. Classic dishes such as pad Thai are well executed using the freshest ingredients. L & D. $

Lago Trattoria (334-8222), 95 Main St., Newport. A large selection of well-prepared Italian dishes in a sophisticated yet casual setting. Try the caramelized sweet onion with sausage and the ricotta-stuffed ravioli. Homemade pizza. L Fri., D Tues.-Sun. $$

Montgomery's Café (334-2626), 66 Main St., Newport. Homemade breads, tasty desserts and a creative assortment of soups and entrees in the café next door to a natural foods store. B & L. $

River Garden Café (626-3514), 3111 Rte. 5, East Burke. A most pleasant surprise in rural surroundings, it's no surprise that the owners are refugees from Manhattan. Look for artichoke dip, pepper crusted lamb, duck breast, and homemade desserts. L & D Wed-Sun, and Sun. brunch. $$-$$$

St. Jay Diner (748-9751), Memorial Drive, Rte. 5 N, St. Johnsbury. Solid diner fare. B, L, & D. $

Thai Tanic Restaurant (334-8788), 501 Pleasant St., Newport. Master chef Chay Senesombath prepares classic Thai dishes (spiced according to patrons' tastes. There's a fine assortment of duck items, as well as offerings such as crispy fried tofu and Massaman curry. L & D. $

attractions

Bread and Puppet Museum (525-3031), 753 Heights Rd. (Rte. 122), Glover. Museum (free) June-Oct. Dirt Cheap Money Circus and Pageant early July-Aug. Sun. 3 p.m; Lubberland National Dance Co. performs mid-July-Aug. Fri. at 8 p.m. Museum tours Fri. at 6 p.m. and Sun. at 1 p.m. on performance days.

Catamount Film and Arts (748-2600), 139 Eastern Ave., St. Johnsbury. Schedule: catamountarts.org

Crystal Lake State Park (525-6205), Rte. 16N, Barton. Memorial Day-Labor Day. Snack bar; changing room, picnic area.

Dog Mountain (748-2700), Spaulding Rd., St. Johnsbury. June-Oct. daily; other times by appointment.

Fairbanks Museum & Planetarium (748-2372), Main St., St. Johnsbury. July-Aug.; weekends Sept.-June.

Labour of Love Public Gardens, Antiques and Crafts (525-6695), Rte.16, Glover Village. Gardens daily; antique shop Thurs.-Sat.

Maple Grove Farms of Vermont (748-5141), 1052 Portland St., St. Johnsbury. Weekdays except holidays; gift shop and sugar house open May-Oct. $ tour.

Methodist Episcopal Church, Central St., St. Johnsbury, houses the memorial window, "Annunciation to the Shepherds" by Louis C. Tiffany.

Moose River Lake & Lodge Store (748-2423), 69 Railroad St., St. Johnsbury. Rustic furnishings, pack baskets, fishing creels, moose antlers, old taxidermy, wines, vintage canoes, and lots more.

Northeast Kingdom Artisans Guild (748-0158), 430 Railroad St., St. Johnsbury. Co-operative shop for Northeast Kingdom artists. Closed Sun.

Old Stone House Museum (754-2022), Brownington. Mid-May-mid-Oct, Wed.-Sun.

South Bay Wildlife Management Area (748-8787), Coventry St., Newport.

St. Johnsbury Athenaeum (748-8291), 1171 Main St., St. Johnsbury. Closed Sun.

Sugarmill Farm Maple Museum (525-3701), Rte. 16, Barton. Sugarhouse, exhibits, gifts, syrup, and an ice cream parlor.

activities

Burke Mountain Toll Road: May-Oct.

Clyde River Recreation (895-4333), 2355 Rte. 105, West Charleston. Kayak, canoe, paddle, and fishing boat rentals.

East Burke Sports (626-3215), Rte. 114, East Burke. Bicycle, canoe, and kayak rentals; also ski and snowboard rentals.

Fishing/Hiking Guide (895-4209), Vermont Sportsman Lodge, Rte. 111, Morgan Center (see "Lodgings" above). Bob Beaupre offers a fishing and hiking guide service.

Haskell Opera House and Library (819-876-2020), Derby Line. Late April-mid-Oct.

Kingdom Trails (see "Information" above).

Newport Boat Rentals & Marine Services (334-5911), Farrants Point, Newport. ½- and full-day motor and pontoon boat rentals.

Village Sport Shop (626-8448), 511 Broad St., Lyndonville. Lots of helpful information on fishing and boating, as well as canoe and kayak rentals and sales.

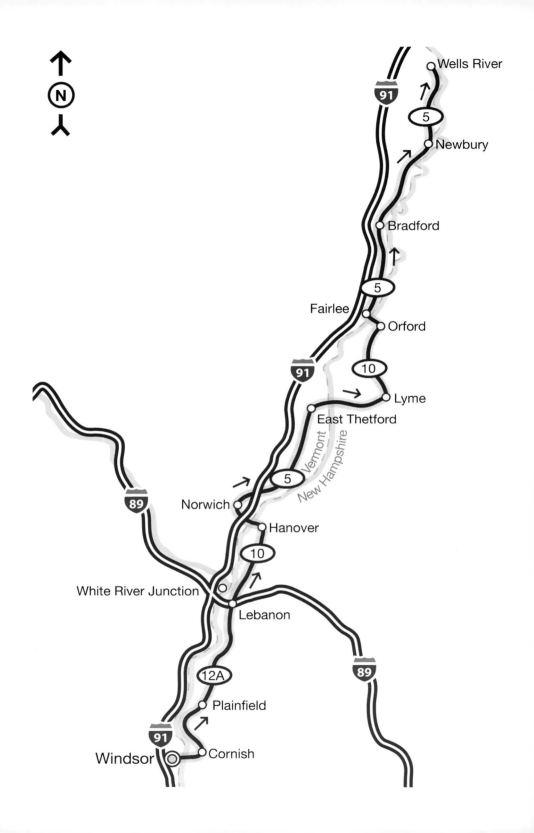

Drive 9

The Upper Connecticut Valley

50 miles

major **attractions**

- American Precision Museum
- Windsor-Cornish Bridge
- Cornish Colony Museum
- Dartmouth College
- Saint-Gaudens National Historic Site
- Montshire Museum of Science

*I*t's difficult to decide which bank of the upper Connecticut River boasts the prettiest scenery, the handsomest small towns, or the most sites that exemplify the region's history and special character – so this drive weaves back and forth across the river, taking in the best of the Vermont and New Hampshire sides. Begin by crossing a landmark covered bridge, then visit a famous sculptor's rural retreat, a classic college campus, and a very kid-friendly science museum, before delving into what is perhaps the loveliest stretch of New England's longest river valley.

Begin this drive in Windsor. "The Birthplace of Vermont" earned its sobriquet in July of 1777 when delegates from the New Hampshire Grants gathered at Elijah West's tavern to create an independent Republic of Vermont. Using as a model Benjamin Franklin's constitution for Pennsylvania, they wrote the first constitution in America that banned slavery, gave voting privileges to all males, and mandated a public school system. The story is told in the tavern, renamed the **Old Constitution House** and moved to its present location.

> *While delegates were busy hammering together the new republic's constitution at Windsor on July 8, 1777, reports of British General John Burgoyne's incursion into the Lake Champlain valley caused such consternation that the assembly very nearly broke up. They decided to stick with their task, though, when a sudden thunderstorm made a virtual island of their meeting place. Thus the representatives gathered at Vermont's birthplace had help from an unexpected midwife – the weather.*

Today, it's hard to imagine that in 1820 this quiet little town was the largest in Vermont, and just 30 years later, a thriving industrial center. The town was fertile soil for tinkerers, too: it was the home of more inventions, and inventors, than any other community in the state. Interchangeable parts were first produced for everyday use at the 1846 Robbins and Lawrence Armory – now the National Historic Landmark **American Precision Museum**.

At one time Windsor had a less flattering nickname. From 1809 until it closed in 1975, "Prison Town" was home to the Vermont State Prison. The last person to be executed by the State of Vermont went to the electric chair here in 1952.

an art colony, and a bridge dethroned . . . .

Artist Maxfield Parrish, who lived just across the river in New Hampshire from 1898 until his death in 1966, was a familiar sight on the streets of Windsor. He was attracted to the area by Augustus Saint-Gaudens (see below), and became a part of the Cornish Colony, one of the earliest art colonies in the country. Some of his finest paintings were of landscapes he saw every day, including 3,320-foot Mount Ascutney. His works are the anchor at the **Cornish Colony Museum**. Other artists' works on exhibit include Willard Metcalf, Henry and Edith Prellwitz, and Bessie Potter Vonnoh.

The graceful, white **Old South Church** on Main Street, built in 1798, was designed by Asher Benjamin, a well-known architect who lived in Windsor for several years. If you're a diner aficionado, plan a stop at the **Windsor Diner**, a 1950 classic from the workshops of the Worcester Lunch Car Company.

Side Trip

Head north on Route 5 a short distance to visit **Harpoon Brewery,** which offers free in-depth tours (and samples for all those 21 years of age and older) at 3 p.m. on Fridays and Saturdays. At other times, there's a viewing platform. Lunch is served daily in summer in the Beer Garden. **Simon Pearce** (see Drive 3) has a store close by, and demonstrates glassblowing and pottery-making daily.

Turn east onto Bridge Street and cross over the Connecticut River into New Hampshire on the 460-foot-long Town Lattice 1866 **Windsor-Cornish Bridge.** Once the longest covered bridge in the country (it was eclipsed in 2008 by a new bridge in Ohio), it's still the world's longest two-span covered bridge. It cost $9,000 to build.

The Windsor-Cornish span is the fourth bridge built at this site. The first, which opened on November 8, 1796, was described that year in the local newspaper, Rising Sun: "...[i]t embraces the Connecticut River with two most beautiful arches, each 184 ft. 4 in. long, with a pier in the center ... it comes sufficiently above high water mark so as to defend and break off the ice." Unfortunately, the newspaper was being overly optimistic: the bridge was destroyed by a flood in 1824, as were successor spans in 1848 and 1866.

Head north a short distance on Route 12A to **Saint-Gaudens National Historic Site.** The sculptor of works including the *Standing Lincoln,* Madison Square Garden's *Diana,* and the Robert Gould Shaw Memorial on Boston Common summered in Cornish from 1885, and lived here year-round from 1900 until his death in 1907. The story has it that he first was steered toward New Hampshire while researching his *Standing Lincoln.* A New York friend told the sculptor that he would find "plenty of Lincoln-shaped men in the Granite State to use as models."

Whether or not he found any appropriate Lincolns, he did find beautiful sunsets over Mt. Ascutney, and an old brick tavern on a hilltop to watch from. He named his estate "Aspet" after his father's native village in France, and remodeled it into the imposing mansion now preserved, along with his gardens and studios.

Continue north on Route 12A. The old building on the right just outside Plainfield's village center was named for Blow-Me-Down Brook, a corruption of the name "Blomidon" bestowed on it by Charles C. Beamann. He was a New York lawyer who bought a summer home in Plainfield over a century ago, and continued to purchase property until, at one point, he owned 23 homes. Beamann sent out the word that the area was a good climate for artists and writers: among the first to arrive was Saint-Gaudens.

In **West Lebanon,** Route 12A passes a sprawl of big box stores, fast food restaurants, and malls. One of the largest, Power House Mall, has more than 40 shops, including Anichini Company Store (luxury linens) and an L.L. Bean outlet. There's a New Hampshire State Liquor Store tucked into the Shaw's Plaza on the right just past the I-89 intersection.

Side Trip

Just across the river in Vermont, **White River Junction** is a once-important railroad town where the tracks took their cue from the junction of the White and Connecticut rivers. The downtown is a National Register Historic District: pick up a walking tour brochure at the Chamber of Commerce (see "Information" below). Highlights include the **Briggs Opera House**, a venue for productions by Northern Stage, a professional regional theater company; and the 1926 Hotel Coolidge (named for the president's father, John Coolidge), a rare example of a surviving "railroad hotel," just across from Union Depot. Preserved at the depot – which is still served by Amtrak's "Vermonter" – is a restored 1892 4-4-0 steam locomotive, formerly No. 494 of the Boston & Maine Railroad. The **Green Mountain Railroad** runs the *White River Flyer* in summer and fall to the Montshire Museum of Science (see below), and farther north to Thetford, from the depot. (See "Activities" for details.)

Side Trip

Turn right onto Route 4 to Route 4A to visit the **Enfield Shaker Museum**. The Shakers' village at what they called their "Chosen Vale" on the southern shore of Lake Mascoma was founded in 1793 and survived until 1923. Today a non-profit organization preserves the sect's legacy in eight buildings, including the centerpiece Great Stone Dwelling, the largest of its type ever built by a Shaker community. At the time of its construction in 1840, the massive, four-story building fashioned of stones quarried at nearby Canaan was the most expensive in New Hampshire except for the State Capitol. There's also a gift shop and gardens. The Mary Keane Chapel, a tiny gem built by the Missionaries of La Salette between 1930 and 1931, houses a Casavant organ and magnificent German stained glass windows.

bastion of the Ivy League

From West Lebanon, continue north on Route 10 to Hanover. "It is a small college," Daniel Webster once said in a landmark court case regarding the charter of **Dartmouth College**, his alma mater, "but yet there are those who love it." Indeed there are – many more so now than in 1818, when he spoke. But beloved though Dartmouth still may be, it is "small" only by the standards of the giant institutions with which it makes up its Ivy League brethren. For a small New England town like Hanover, Dartmouth is big enough, and old enough, to have obscured any distinction between the campus and the community. To outsiders, Dartmouth *is* Hanover, and Hanover Dartmouth.

The town does predate the school, although not by very many years. In 1761 Governor Benning Wentworth, that prolific creator of colonial New Hampshire towns (generally to his own benefit, as he was in the habit of keeping the choicest acreage for himself) issued a charter for a tract of 22,400 acres on the east bank of the Connecticut River where Hanover now stands.

Meanwhile, in Lebanon, Connecticut, Reverend Eleazar Wheelock was contemplating a move of his own, one that would forever change the fledgling village of Hanover. He ran a Christian school for young Indians, and had been busy raising funds with which to relocate and expand his mission. He sent one of his former pupils, a Mohegan preacher named Samson Occom, on a speaking tour of England to solicit contributions for this venture. Occom must have been a persuasive fundraiser – he came back with a pledged endowment of £11,000 sterling (over $1,000,000 in today's currency) and the patronage of the Earl of Dartmouth.

With his funding secure, Reverend Wheelock began to entertain invitations from a number of communities that wanted to host the new school. Hanover won, through successful use of the same tactic a modern town might use to lure a corporate headquarters to its new office park: it offered land (3,000 acres), money, lumber, and the manpower of its citizens. What the yeomen hoped for in return were prestige and improved real estate values. Little did they suspect they were in for a medical school, a ski jump, a winter carnival, an art museum, the **Hanover Inn**, and one of the great libraries of North America.

King George III granted Reverend Wheelock the charter for Dartmouth in 1769, and the following year he began holding classes in a log cabin. But despite Wheelock's original intentions, few Indians ever showed up, and before long Dartmouth was a white man's college. It graduated four students at its first commencement exercise in 1771. For that occasion, Governor John Wentworth, Benning's nephew and successor, arrived via a 75-mile road he had built for the occasion from his summer residence in Wolfeboro (see Drive 15).

> *Dartmouth's Latin motto is* Vox Clamantis in Deserto, *"A Voice Crying in the Wilderness."*

A tour of the campus need not stray from the Green, as most of the buildings of architectural or historic interests border it almost directly. Be sure to visit **Baker-Berry Library**, the central library. Its holdings include: 150 volumes of incunabula (books printed before 1501); the Hickmott Shakespeare Collection, including copies of all four folios, nearly 40 quarto volumes, and all known pre-1700 editions of *Macbeth*; a comprehensive Melville collection; and the first three volumes of the enormous "elephant folio" edition of John James Audubon's Birds of America once owned by Daniel Webster (speculation is that Webster didn't own Volume Four because he didn't pay Audubon for the first three).

In the basement reading room, Mexican artist Jose Clemente Orozco painted a series of murals illustrating his critical view of the triumph of Western civilization in the New World. He did the work between 1932 and 1934, while he was teaching in the art department.

The other not-to-be-missed attraction at Dartmouth is the **Hood Museum of Art**. Among the collections are American 18th-century portraits, works by Italian masters, an abstract by Dartmouth grad Frank Stella, and Picasso's *Guitar on the Table*. In front of Parkhurst Hall on North Main Street is the school's landmark 94-foot Parkhurst Elm.

Before leaving Hanover, stop in at the local **League of New Hampshire Craftsmen**. Established in 1932 to preserve traditional hand craftsmanship (see Drive 15), the League represents hundreds of craftspeople whose works are juried and on display for sale at locations throughout the state (others are in Concord, North Conway, Meredith, Wolfeboro, Littleton, and Center Sandwich.

Cross over the Connecticut River to Norwich, Vermont and the **Montshire Museum of Science**, a manageably sized yet fascinating trove of informative hands-on exhibits for kids of all ages. The building is surrounded by 110 acres of woodland and nature trails along the Connecticut River. Most of the trails pass through Science Park, a two-acre outdoor hands-on exhibit center.

a postcard town ... with flour.....................

Manicured **Norwich** is often held up as an example of what the perfect Vermont village is supposed to look like; truth be told, however, much of its polish derives from its status as a bedroom community for Dartmouth College. Regardless of who's paying the bills, the town is still a visual treasure, filled with magnificent late 18th- and early 19th-century homes. On your stroll along Main Street, stop in at Jasper Murdock's Alehouse in the 1794 **Norwich Inn** for a pint of their home brew.

Head north out of town on Route 5. Bakers will want to make a pit stop at the **King Arthur Flour Baker's Store**. The Vermont-based, employee-owned firm – established in Boston in 1790 and now the country's oldest flour company – has grown over the years to national proportions. Their *Baker's Catalogue* offers more than 1,000 baking tools and ingredients, many which are sold at their retail store.

Head north on Route 5 through Pompanoosuc, where the Ompompanoosuc River meets with the Connecticut, and **East Thetford**, home to another successful company that began as a cottage industry. The handmade furniture business that Dwight Sargeant started in his home some years back is now known as **Pompanoosuc Mills**, and ships its clean-lined hardwood wares around the world.

Side Trip

Brian Boland has set numerous world records, won national championships, and has flown all over the globe since he started ballooning more than 30 years ago. He's head-quartered at a 50-acre antique airport just a short jaunt west off Route 5 via Route 244 in **Post Mills**, Vermont, and takes passengers on exhilarating, three- to 15-mile, one -hour rides (allow three hours total). Even if you don't want to soar, plan to visit the private **Experimental Balloon and Airship Museum**, Brian's collection of more than one hundred balloons, airships, special interest and antique vehicles and "other interesting, rusty, dusty stuff."

In East Thetford, turn right and cross the river into Lyme, chartered in 1761 and once the sheep-raising capital of New England. The village is clustered around a big, grassy Common whose centerpiece is the elegantly spired, 1812 Lyme Congregational Church. The bell, cast by Paul Revere, rings on the hour. Behind the church is an old cemetery, worth a brief stroll. Next to the church is the longest line of contiguous horse sheds in New England. Built in 1810 by the son of the church's builder, they once numbered 50; 27 remain. From the outside **Stella's Italian Kitchen & Market** looks small and unprepossessing. But the shelves are filled with tasty treats, there's a take-out for picnics, and the large, spacious restaurant serves up moderately priced dishes such as eggplant Parmesan, vodka rigatoni, and white bean *cassoulet*. Take a stroll along the Common, and then tuck in for the night at the **Dowd Country Inn.**

Continue north on Route 10 to Orford, regarded by many as the loveliest of all the Upper Valley towns. Washington Irving said, "In all my travels in this country and Europe I have never seen any village more beautiful than this. It is a charming place; nature has done her utmost here." The town's outstanding architectural feature is the string of seven white mansions, built between 1773 and 1839, which line "The Ridge" above Route 10 and the river. One, the circa 1815 General John B. Wheeler House at the southern end of the row, was designed by Asher Benjamin during his association with Charles Bulfinch. The oldest house belonged to inventor Samuel Morey.

Yankee ingenuity

Head back across the Connecticut River to Fairlee, Vermont, nestled in the lee of a 600-foot rock barrier called the Palisades. Fairlee is the service town for cottagers around Lake Morey, named for the inventor Samuel Morey who experimented with a steamboat 14 years before Robert Fulton launched his Clermont. Many a fine day Mr. Morey could be seen chugging up and down the Connecticut or across the lake in his contraption. Later, bitter at Fulton's fame, the inventor is said to have cried, "curse his

Venturing beyond steam, Samuel Morey built a boat named Aunt Sally, propelled by an internal combustion engine, and operated it on Fairlee Pond, renamed Lake Morey about 1820.

Continue north on Route 5 to Bradford, the next town of any size along the Vermont side of the Connecticut. Several years ago it got some publicity when *Travel and Leisure* magazine listed its downtown thoroughfare as one of the top ten Main Streets in America, commenting that this string of utilitarian blocks is "so ordinary it's extraordinary." Bradford was home to some not-so-ordinary citizens, though. James Wilson was a local farmer and self-taught engraver, who in the early 1800s created America's first geographical globes. Admiral Charles Clark, born here in 1843, commanded the battleship *Oregon* during its rush around Cape Horn to victory at Santiago Bay, Cuba in the Spanish-American War. (Landlocked Vermont, by the way, had the unlikely distinction of supplying two naval heroes in that conflict. Admiral George Dewey, who sank the Spanish fleet at Manila Bay, was a Montpelier boy.)

Not content to rest on its Main Street laurels, Bradford also hosts one of the state's finest wild game suppers every year on the Saturday before Thanksgiving, serving up delicacies including wild boar, bear, and venison. To receive a brochure write: Game Supper Committee, Bradford, VT 05033 or call 802-222-5913.

Side Trip

Turn right onto Route 25 to visit **Farm-Way, Inc.,** "Complete Outfitters for Man & Beast." The sprawling, family-owned store, housed in an old feed and grain company, sells "top quality, brand name, American-made products for people, places and their animals ... [and promises that] though our staff is friendly, they won't call you 'dahling' no matter how good you look in those spiffy new jeans."

Farther north on Route 5, in Newbury, the Connecticut River goes through a tortuous series of loops called "oxbows," one of which makes a near-circle of four miles before winding up half a mile from where it began. The Abenaki Indians were attracted to the fertile meadowlands and fine fishing grounds created by the oxbows, and had a permanent settlement here long before Revolutionary War General Jacob Bayley and his party made their way north from Newbury, Massachusetts in the early 1760s to establish the then-furthermost northern outpost on the Vermont side of the Connecticut.

General Bayley was also on hand to organize and oversee the building of the first 14

miles of the Bayley-Hazen Military Road, from Newbury to Peacham. He promised his 110 men the equivalent of $10 a month plus food, and a half-pint of rum a day; they finished the job in just 45 days. Unfortunately, the Continental Congress was unable to pay the bill that Bayley presented. We hope the men did get their rum; they had built the first real road in Vermont.

Newbury is a classic Vermont village of post-colonial homes and graceful churches, with the 1794 Congregational Church a particular standout. One distinctive local structure, however, has not survived: the 1805 Bedell Bridge between Newbury and Haverhill, New Hampshire had been battered mercilessly by storms over the years, and was re-built no fewer than four times. In the late 1970s, local citizens contributed to finance a thorough restoration of the 396-foot span, which was rededicated and opened to foot traffic in July, 1979. The banners had barely been taken down when, on September 15, violent winds tore the bridge to splinters. It could have been much worse: a wedding was to have taken place on the bridge the following day. All that remains of the Bedell Bridge are its piers, visible at the end of a dirt road off Route 5.

As you head north out of Newbury on Route 5, watch for the Ox-Bow Cemetery. It's the final resting place of Old Joe, the Indian guide who lived in nearby West Danville and befriended early settlers. According to one account, "Old Joe had no passion for war himself, but he was a great Whig and rejoiced in the defeat of the British whom he could never forgive the slaughter and dispersion of his tribe [the St. Francis] in Nova Scotia … "

The next town to the north on Route 5, Wells River, is a curious place: it's a small Vermont community that feels like it would be more comfortable alongside its more work-aday mill town sisters across the river in New Hampshire. But it has a sort of utilitarian dignity, and maybe *Travel and Leisure* should take a look at it. We could well imagine Jimmy Stewart walking down Main Street on his way back to the bank after lunch.

The town had its glory days during the 19th century, when steamboats chugged up-stream to dock at this northernmost navigable point on the Connecticut River. Later, it was a thriving railroad junction. Its present-day link to the transportation industry is the **P & H Truck Stop**, the only 24-hour diner in northeastern Vermont, and a mecca for hungry teamsters barreling up and down I-91.

information

Greater Lebanon Chamber of Commerce (603-448-1203), Village House, 1 School St., Lebanon, NH 03766. lebanonchamber.com

Hanover Area Chamber of Commerce (603-643-3115), 47 S. Main St., Hanover, NH 03755. hanoverchamber.org

Hartford Area Chamber of Commerce (802-295-7900), 100 Railroad Row, White River Junction, VT 05001. hartfordvtchamber.com

Lower Cohase Regional Chamber of Commerce (802-757-2549), P.O. Box 35, Wells River, VT 05081. (Newbury and Bradford, VT) cohase.org

Windsor-Mt. Ascutney Region Chamber of Commerce (802-674-5910), 3 Railroad Ave., Windsor 05089. windsorvt.com.

lodging

Chase House B&B (603-675-5391), Rte. 12A, Cornish, NH 03745. All 9 antiques-filled rooms and suites at this National Historic Landmark inn have views; several have 4-poster beds and private balconies. 2 night minimum stay. chasehouse.com $$-$$$

The Dowds' Country Inn (603-795-4712), On the Common, Lyme, NH 03768. 22 nicely furnished rooms with private baths in a handsome 1780 inn and carriage house. Breakfast included. dowdscountryinn.com $-$$

The Gibson House (603-989-3125), 341 Dartmouth College Highway, On the Green, Haverhill, NH 03765. 3 lovingly decorated and luxurious antiques-filled guest rooms in a meticulously restored 1850 National Register home overlooking the Connecticut River Valley. gibsonhousebb.com $$-$$$

Hanover Inn (603-643-4300), Box 151, The Green, Hanover, NH 03755. Dartmouth College's 4-story hotel has 92 rooms and several restaurants, including the Daniel Webster Room (see "Restaurants" below). hanoverinn.com $$$

Juniper Hill Inn (802-674-5273), 153 Pembroke Rd., Windsor, VT 05089. Secluded hilltop mansion has 16 guest rooms (11 with fireplaces), a pool, gardens, and grand common rooms. Dinner ($$$-$$$$) might include macadamia nut crusted rack of lamb or lobster "mac" & cheese. juniperhillinn.com $$-$$$

Lake Morey Inn Resort (802-333-4311), Clubhouse Rd., Fairlee, VT 05045. 600-acre 4-season resort has 137 guest units, a championship golf course, indoor and outdoor pools, a spring-fed lake, tennis, boating, and kids' programs. lakemoreyresort.com $$-$$$

Loch Lyme Lodge (603-795-2141), 70 Orford Rd., Rte. 10, Lyme, NH 03768. Resort on 120 acres has 21 basic cabins (some with kitchens.) Private beach, rowboats, canoes, windsurfer, tennis courts. Meals are served in the 1784 lodge. Pets welcome. lochlymelodge.com $-$$

Nootka Lodge (603-747-2418), jct. rtes. 302/10, Woodsville, NH 03785 (just across the river from Wells River). 34 spacious units: the second floor rooms have cathedral ceilings and balconies. Pool, barbecue pit, Jacuzzi, game and exercise rooms. Pets in some rooms. nootkalodge.com $-$$

The Norwich Inn (802-649-1143), Main St., Norwich, VT 05055. 16 guest rooms in the inn, 4 efficiency suites in the Vestry, and 7 motel units: all with antiques, phones and TVs. norwichinn.com $-$$

Peach Brook Inn B & B (866-3389), Doe Hill (off Rte. 5), Newbury, VT 05051. Colonial home overlooking the Connecticut River has 3 rooms with shared or private baths. Children 10+. $

Silver Maple Lodge & Cottages (802-333-4326), 520 Rte. 5, Fairlee, VT 05045. Rambling, 1855 farmhouse has 8 pleasant guest rooms (6 with private bath), and 7 cottages (some with kitchens and fireplaces). Biking, and hot air balloon and canoe packages. Pets allowed in cottages. Continental breakfast. silvermaplelodge.com $-$$

Trumbull House B&B (603-643-2370), 40 Etna Rd., Hanover, NH 03755. 5 luxuriously-appointed rooms and a cottage at a 16-acre country inn. Amenities include an outdoor pool, basketball half-court, and target golf course. trumbullhouse.com $$-$$$$

White Goose Inn (353-4812), Rte. 10, Orford, NH 03777. Thoughtfully restored and modernized 1766 brick house has 10 guest rooms with period furnishings; some with shared baths. whitegooseinn.com $-$$

restaurants

Carpenter and Main Restaurant (802-649-2922), 326 Main St., Norwich, VT. Owner/chef Bruce MacLeod uses locally raised, seasonal ingredients to prepare dishes such as rabbit three ways, and artichoke gnocchi. D Wed.-Sun. $$-$$$

Colatina Exit (222-9008), 164 Main St., Bradford, VT. A genuine Italian trattoria – with candles and red-checkered tablecloths no less – in the heart of Vermont. The menu includes 7 kinds of pasta with 12 different sauces, and hearth baked pizzas. D. $-$$

Hanover Inn, (603-643-4300), Main St., Hanover, NH. B, L and Sun. brunch are served in the elegant Daniel Webster Room; Zin's winebistro (L & D; $$$-$$$) emphasizes American cuisine, which specialties such as ginger & lemon grass glazed salmon, and olive dusted rack of lamb. *Al fresco* dining on The Terrace (L & D) in season.

Harpoon Brewery Beer Garden (802-674-5491), 336 Ruth Carney Dr., Windsor, VT. Open daily in summer; Tues.-Sun. rest of year. $

Jesse's (603-643-4111), Rte. 120, Hanover, NH. An extensive salad bar, homemade bread, a fine selection of steaks, and BBQ ribs share the menu with seafood and poultry dishes. Children's menu. D nightly. $$-$$$

Lou's Restaurant & Bakery (603-643-3321), 30 S. Main St., Hanover, NH. Since 1947 a local favorite for hearty breakfasts, lunches, and home baked treats. Lunch includes gyros and quesadillas, as well as classic American fare. B & L. $

The Norwich Inn (802-649-1143), 325 Main St., Norwich, VT. The dining room ($$-$$$) smokes its own meats and poultry, and serves dishes such as grilled twin beef tournedos. Jasper Murdock's Alehouse ($) serves English-style ale brewed on premises and a pub menu.

P & H Truck Stop (429-2141), Rte. 302 near I-91, 3 mi. west of downtown Wells River, VT. Home baked bread and desserts, terrific breakfast specials, homemade meatloaf, and hot turkey sandwiches. B, L, & D. $

Perfect Pear Café (802-225-5912), 48 Main St., Bradford, VT. Sunlit by day, candlelit by night, this cozy spot in an old gristmill serves well-prepared contemporary American fare. L Tues.-Sat., D Tues.-Sun. $$-$$$

Polka Dot Restaurant (295-9722), 1 N. Main St., White River Jct., VT. Classic diner fare in a classic down home spot once popular with train passengers. Open from 5 a.m. to 3 p.m. Tues.-Sun. $ Stella's Italian Kitchen & Market (603-795-4302), 5 Main St., Lyme, NH. L & D Mon.-Sat. Market open Mon.-Sat. $-$$

Tip Top Café (802-295-3312), 85 N. Main St., White River Junction, VT. American bistro fare in a casual downtown spot. Try the tomato basil bisque, and pork & ginger meatloaf. L & D Tues.-Sat. $$-$$$

Warner's Gallery Restaurant (429-2120), 2284 Rte. 302, Wells River, VT. The "home of the sticky buns" serves up prime rib, along with fish, poultry, and a huge salad bar in a large, family-friendly establishment. D Tues.-Sun. & Sun. brunch. $$-$$$

Windsor Diner (674-5555), 135 Main St., Windsor, VT. Homemade clam chowder and pies, daily specials, and diner favorites including fried liver and onions. Daily 7 a.m.-8 p.m. $

attractions

American Precision Museum (674-5781), 196 Main St., Windsor, VT. Open daily late May-Oct.

Cornish Colony Museum (674-6008), 147 Main St., Windsor, VT. Memorial Day weekend-late Oct., Wed.-Sun. Call for off-season schedule.

Dartmouth College (603-646-2808), Hanover, NH: Baker-Berry Library, 1 Elm St., open daily; Hood Museum of Art, Wheelock St., open Tues.-Sat., Sun. p.m. Free.

Enfield Shaker Museum (603-632-4346), 447 Rte. 4A, Enfield, NH. Mon.-Sat., Sun. p.m.

Farm-Way, Inc. (800-222-9316), Rte. 25, Bradford, VT. Closed Sun.

Harpoon Brewery (802-674-5491), 336 Ruth Carney Drive, Windsor, VT.

King Arthur Flour Baker's Store (649-3361), Rte. 5, Norwich, VT.

League of New Hampshire Craftsmen (603-643-5050), 13 Lebanon St., Hanover, NH. Mon.-Sat.

Montshire Museum of Science (802-649-2200), Montshire Rd., Norwich, VT.

Old Constitution House (802-672-3773), 16 N. Main St., Windsor, VT. Late May-Mid Oct., Sat. & Sun. Pompanoosuc Mills (802-785-4851), Rte. 5, East Thetford, VT.

Saint-Gaudens National Historic Site (603-675-2175), Rte. 12A, Cornish, NH. Late May-Oct. Visitor Center Nov.-late May Mon.-Fri. Concerts July & Aug. Sun. at 2 p.m. Grounds dawn-dusk.

Simon Pearce (802-674-6280), 109 Park Rd., Windsor, VT.

activities

Ascutney Mountain Resort (802-484-3511), Brownsville, VT. Mountain bike rentals.

Briggs Opera House (802-296-7000), 58 N. Main St., White River Junction, VT. Schedule: northernstage.org

Fairlee Marine (802-333-9745), Rte. 5, Fairlee, VT. Pontoon, speedboats, rowboats (with small motors), kayak, and canoe rental; fishing supplies.

Green Mountain Railroad (463-3069), Union Depot, White River Junction, VT. The *White River Flyer* Thurs.-Sun. July-Labor Day between White River Junction and Thetford, with a stop at the Montshire Museum.

Ledyard Canoe Club (603-643-6709), off Wheelock St., Hanover, NH. Dartmouth's historic boating club has cruising canoes and 1-person sea kayaks for rent hourly or daily. Open when Connecticut River is warmer than 50 degrees; may be closed Sept. 1-15 – call ahead.

Lebanon Opera House (603-448-0400). 51 North Park St., Lebanon, NH. Opera North and plays in a restored, 1924 theater. Schedule: lebanonoperahouse.org

Morningside Flight Park (603-542-4416), 357 Morningside Lane, N. Charlestown, NH. Hang gliding and paragliding; introductory courses.

North Star Canoe Rental (603-542-6929), 1356 Rte. 12A, Cornish, NH. Self-guided canoe, kayak and rafting trips; shuttle. Memorial Day-Columbus Day, Wed.-Mon.

Norwich Farmers' Market, Rte. 5S, Norwich, VT. May-Oct., Sat. a.m.

Post Mills Airport (802-333-9254), Robinson Hill Rd., Post Mills, VT. Hot air balloon rides at 6 a.m. or 2 hrs. before sunset. Package flights/B&B lodgings with Silver Maple Lodge and Cottages.

Storrs Pond Recreation Area (603-643-2134), off Rt. 10, Reservoir Rd., Hanover, NH. Swimming in a man-made, 13-acre pond with a sandy beach or in a heated Olympic-sized pool. Picnicking, nature trails. Mid-May-mid-Sept.

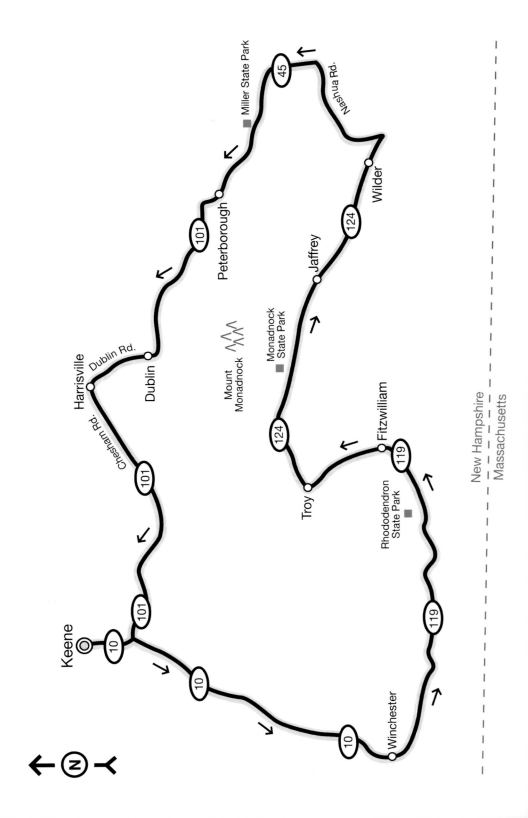

The Monadnock Region

70 miles

major attractions

- Horatio Colony Museum
- Peterborough
- Monadnock State Park
- Rhododendron State Park
- Cathedral of the Pines
- Harrisville

his jaunt through New Hampshire's southwestern corner winds through a countryside rich in covered bridges, antique shops, rhododendrons, and mountain trails. The region's most distinctive peak and an open-air "cathedral" stand along the route, which also takes in a town that has assumed mythic proportions on the American stage.

Begin in Keene, the region's largest city (population 22,000). Founded in the 1730s, it was abandoned a few years later because of Indian attacks, and re-settled in the 1750s. Throughout its history, Keene has been a mill town: two prominent families opened Faulkner and Colony Mill in 1838 to weave wool gathered from surrounding sheep farms. When the looms finally shut down in 1953, it was one of the oldest continuously operating mills in the country under original management. Other products made here over the years included chairs, shoes, glassware, and even golf tees.

Today, most of the mills have closed and the city on the Shallot River serves primarily as a market center for surrounding communities, and as the home of Keene State College. But several old factories have been restored and now house shops and restaurants: the sprawling **Colony Mill Marketplace** is one of the state's most successful renewal projects.

In 1770 the trustees of Dartmouth College held their first meeting at a Main Street tavern built by Captain Isaac Wyman in 1762. On an April day five years later, 29 Minutemen under the command of Captain Wyman set out from the tavern for Lexington and Concord. The restored **Wyman Tavern Museum**, maintained by the Historical Society of Cheshire County, documents Keene's history from 1770 to the 1870s. The **Horatio Colony Museum**, another trove of local lore, occupies the 1806 Federal-style home of several generations of the mill-owning Colony family, and is filled with heirlooms and treasures accumulated by world traveler Horatio Colony, a 20th-century author who was the last of the clan to live here. The United Church of Christ, with its graceful wedding-cake spire gracing the northern end of Main St., was built in 1787.

a wealth of covered bridges . . . .

Head south out of Keene on Route 10. Between 1827 and 1912, more than 300 covered bridges were built throughout New Hampshire. Today approximately 54 survive, including four in Swanzey, the "Covered Bridge Capital of New Hampshire." Three are Town lattice truss (named for architect Ithiel Town, who devised the lattice framework in the early 1800s): **Slate Bridge**, built in 2001, is east of Route 10 on Westport Village Road; the 1859 **Cresson Bridge** on Sawyer's Crossing Road a mile north of Route 32; and the 1832 **Thompson Bridge** alongside Route 10, which has a handsome outside walkway; the queenpost **Carleton Bridge**, built in 1869, is off Route 32 on Carleton Road. Watch for the covered bridge signs along Route 10. The **Swanzey Historical Museum** is an excellent place to get information and directions.

> *A kingpost covered bridge frame has one central upright; a queenpost has two, with a horizontal timber between them.*

Just before the junction with Route 119 in Winchester, watch for the Evergreen Cemetery. It's the burial place of P.F.F. Albee (1836-1914), the first Avon Lady. She was hired by Daniel H. McConnell, Sr., who founded the California Perfume Company in 1883 and needed help with sales. Ms. Albee took to the road with her sample case, and began knocking on doors. The firm, which became Avon Products, dubbed her the "Mother of the Company" and named its highest sales award after her. Her stone is near the front of the cemetery.

Continue south on Route 10 to Winchester, a workaday village whose major point of interest is a plaque on one of the town's 19th-century brick buildings, which marks the birthplace of Major General Leonard Wood, born here in 1860. He was a hero of the Spanish-American War, and went on to serve as Governor of Cuba and Chief of Staff of the U.S. Army. The Town lattice **Coombs Bridge** (1837) is on Old Westport Road.

Side Trip

Before you turn left (east) onto Route 119, detour a few miles west on that road to this drive's most handsome covered bridge. The Town lattice **Winchester-Ashuelot Bridge,** built in 1864, has been described as "pure American Gothic architecture adapted to bridge building."

Head east on Route 119 through Richmond, where the Four Corner Store advertises free advice and good coffee.

Turn left onto Rhododendron Road and follow signs to the National Natural Landmark 494-acre **Rhododendron State Park,** where a wooded wildflower trail winds for a mile up Little Monadnock Mountain. The park is lovely at any time, but if you're here in mid-July, you're in for a special treat: that's prime blossom time for the 16 acres of *Rhododendron maximum,* the largest stand of wild rhododendrons north of the Allegheny Mountains and east of the Mississippi. Many of the shrubs grow as high as 20 feet.

Back on Route 119, continue into Fitzwilliam, a gracious 18th-century village with a lovely green lined with Federal-style houses, and a fair number of antique shops. The Historical Society's 1837 **Amos J. Blake House** on the Common was the home of a 19th-century attorney whose office remains here, intact. Next door is the 1796 Fitzwilliam Inn (closed as of this writing). The entrance to the town hall, built in 1817 as a Congregational church, is framed by a two-story pedimented portico supported at each end by Ionic columns resting on locally quarried granite blocks. The four-story steeple has a square clock tower, belfry, and a bell cast by Paul Revere.

At the intersection of routes 119 and 12, turn north on Route 12. On the outskirts of Troy, **turn right onto Gap Mountain Road** to 1,107-acre **Gap Mountain Reservation. Follow the road for 8/10 mile, bearing right at the first fork. At another 8/10 mile, take a sharp left.** The parking lot is about 2/10 mile on the left. The hike to the 1,862-foot summit is fairly easy, and if you're here early enough in blueberry season (July and/or August), you might be able to pick some. Numerous hiking trails crisscross the mountain, including the 160-mile **Metacomet-Monadnock Trail,** which begins in Meriden, Connecticut and ends at Grand Monadnock.

At the edge of downtown Troy, turn right off Route 12 onto Monadnock/Jaffrey Road.

Up ahead, the view of Mount Monadnock from the back lawn of **The Inn at East Hill Farm** is spectacular. **Continue to the junction of Route 124 and turn east (right) onto Route 124 toward Jaffrey.**

a solitary peak..

The toll road at **Monadnock State Park** (seasonal parking) once provided access to a series of hotels on the mountain. The earliest, the Grand Monadnock Hotel, was built on the summit in 1823. The last, the Halfway House, closed its doors in the 1960s. Several trailheads begin here.

Just past the toll road turn-off, turn left at the sign for the park entrance and hiking trails to the top of **Mount Monadnock** ("one that stands alone" in the local Algonquin tongue). Last year more than 130,000 people hiked America's most often-climbed mountain – as many as 6,000 on one day. Why the popularity? The peak is close to several large metropolitan areas, and it's a very "climbable" mountain. There are 36 trails of varying difficulty; the shortest and easiest is the four-mile White Dot Trail (we tackled it in full hiking gear one day alongside two six-year-old girls dancing along in black patent leather shoes).

The six-state view from the 3,165-foot summit is sublime. Ralph Waldo Emerson wrote of it,

> *Every morn I lift my head,*
> *See New England underspread*
> *South from St. Lawrence to the Sound,*
> *From Katskill east to the sea-bound.*

Only one mountain in the world is ascended by more climbers each year than Mount Monadnock – Japan's Mount Fuji.

Continue into Jaffrey. On the outskirts of town, in Jaffrey Center, is the town's original Meeting House, raised on the day of the Battle of Bunker Hill in 1775. In back of the church, in the Old Burying Ground, are interred former slave Amos Fortune (see below), and the novelist Willa Cather, who, in 1918, worked on *My Antonia* and the Pulitzer Prize-winning *One of Ours* here. An inscription from *My Antonia* is engraved on Cather's headstone, in the far southwest corner of the cemetery: "The truth and charity of her great spirit will live on in the work which is her enduring gift to her country and all its people."

Amos Fortune, who settled in Jaffrey in the late 18th century and became a wealthy tanner, made a generous bequest to the town's school. When the building was abandoned in 1927, townspeople voted to use the money for a public speaking contest. Since that year the Amos Fortune Forum *has presented a lecture series on subjects of public interest and importance to the community. Seven free lectures are presented Friday evenings in July and August at 8 p.m. in the Jaffrey Center Meeting House. On Mr. Fortune's tombstone is the inscription: "Lived reputably, died hopefully."*

The **Melville Academy Museum,** housed in an 1833 school, has historic exhibits and a period schoolroom.

Continue out of town on Route 124 past **Silver Ranch Airpark,** offering scenic flights beginning at $99 for up to three people. **Kimball Farm,** right next door, also transports customers to new heights, dishing up homemade ice cream since 1939. It's now an entertainment miniplex, with bumper boats, farm animals, live animal shows, a pitch & putt golf course, a country store, and a grill.

an open-air cathedral

Turn right onto Prescott Road and continue for several miles to **Cathedral of the Pines** in **Rindge.** The sanctuary, "where all people can come and worship, each in his own way … " is in a stand of pines overlooking Mount Monadnock. It's dedicated to the memory of Lieutenant Sanderson ("Sandy") Sloane, an American aviator shot down over Germany in 1944, who had planned to build his home here after the war. The cross is of New Hampshire granite; the Altar of Nations, containing stones from every state in the Union, and the Memorial Bell Tower, are dedicated to America's war dead. Check the Cathedral website (see "Attractions" below) for a schedule of services.

Head back onto Route 124, and continue east. Look for a plaque on the left side of the road marking the site where a tollgate stood between 1803-1822 to collect tariffs from drivers herding cattle along the third New Hampshire turnpike.

Continue through tiny Wilder Village; a marker indicates the site of Wilder's Chair Factory, which in the early 1800s manufactured more than 25,000 spindle-backed chairs in more than 40 designs. In 1869 a freshet washed out the mill dam; deprived of water power, the factory closed. Today the chairs are highly collectible antiques.

Turn left onto Nashua/West Road over Spofford Gap, and continue to the intersection with Route 45.

Side Trip

Head north on Route 123 to Sharon to visit the **Sharon Arts Center,** which exhibits the works of regional and nationally acclaimed artists in two galleries. The center also has galleries and an artists' resource center in Peterborough (see below).

Turn left (north) onto Route 45 into Temple, home of the state's first glassmaking factory, which opened here in 1780; and **Temple Band**, "America's First Town Band," which began playing in 1799. The ensemble performs at venues throughout the area. The Congregational Church facing the Town Common was built in 1842. The Old Burying Ground is dedicated to the "wives and mothers of 1776."

Little has changed at the circa 1800 National Register of Historic Places **Birchwood Inn** since Henry David Thoreau spent a night here. The dining room possesses a superb mural by Rufus Porter, an itinerant painter who worked throughout New England during the early 19th century.

Continue north on Route 45, past the Temple Mountain State Reservation. The state's newest preserve – a 352-acre swath of wilderness – had been one of the country's oldest downhill ski areas, in operation from 1938 until 2001. When it closed, a couple from Temple purchased the land. In 2007, after much hard work by a consortium of private citizens and public officials, the reservation became one of the largest state acquisitions in Southern New Hampshire in almost 30 years.

Turn west (left) onto Route 101 at the intersection.

Side Trip

At the junction of routes 101 and 45, cross over Route 101 and continue approximately 4 1/2 miles to the National Historic Register landmark **Frye's Measure Mill**. The company has been making colonial boxes, designed to give farmers, fishermen, and shopkeepers a standard unit to measure dry goods since 1858. In the late 1960s, at the request of Eldress Bertha Lindsay of the Canterbury, New Hampshire Shaker Community, the company also began making Shaker boxes using the sect's technique of shaping strips of maple around wooden forms, and fastening them with copper tacks. Today Frye's is one of the country's few remaining water-powered mills, and its only active measure mill. The gift shop sells folk art, and antique fire trucks and firefighting apparatus are on display. 1 1/2-hour tours are given Saturdays in season at 2 p.m. (reservations recommended).
Continue west on Route 101. At 489-acre **Miller State Park** (New Hampshire's first state park, opened in 1891), a 1 1/2-mile paved road winds steeply to the summit of 2,288-foot **Pack Monadnock**. On clear days, Manchester and the Boston skyline are visible. The 21-mile (one way) Wapack Trail, which follows the ridge of the Wapack Range from Watatic Mountain in Ashburnham, Massachusetts to the Pack Monadnocks, crosses here (as well as at Temple Mountain State Reservation).

the real "Grover's Corners" . . . .

Continue into **Peterborough** – "A Good Town to Live In" – immortalized in the 1930s by Thornton Wilder, who used it as the model for Grover's Corners in his play *Our Town*. The best way to see the town's many historic sites is with a copy of the Chamber of Commerce's "A Walking Tour of Peterborough" brochure. Among places of interest: the Bulfinch-designed, 1825 National Historic Register Unitarian Universalist Church; the **Historical Society Museum**; and the 1833 library, the first in the world to be supported by town funds. The **Peterborough Players**, a professional summer theater company since 1933, was the first to perform *Our Town*. The small **Mariposa Museum & World Culture Center** in the Baptist Church gives visitors the opportunity to explore different cultures through exhibits and hands-on activities.

Side Trip

Just south of Peterborough on Route 123, **Rosaly's Garden** is one of the state's largest certified organic gardens. Overlooking Mount Monadnock, it's a grand place to pick berries, and stock up on local produce, flowers, and herbs.

American composer Edward MacDowell (1861-1908) wrote more than 50 compositions, including "Woodland Sketches," "Keltic Sonatas," and "New England Idylls." One of the founders of the American Academy of Arts and Letters, he became in 1960 the second musician ever to be elected to the Hall of Fame for Great Americans. In 1896 MacDowell and his wife, pianist Marian Nevins MacDowell, purchased an estate in Peterborough and began to spend summers here. MacDowell planned to open his estate to other artists to provide them with a tranquil and inspiring place to work, but he became terminally ill before he could realize his dream. His wife started the MacDowell Colony in 1907; artists who have come to work here over the years have included Stephen Vincent Benet, Edwin Arlington Robinson, Thornton Wilder, Leonard Bernstein, and James Baldwin.

In 1937, a sign at the entrance announced "Visitors Most Welcome, Save on Sunday". Today, visitors are not welcome, save one day each year, usually in mid-August, when the Edward MacDowell Medal is awarded to an artist who has made an outstanding contribution to American culture. On that day, all are invited to tour the artists' studios, and attend the Medal presentation. The MacDowell Colony is on High Street.

Head west out of town on Route 101 to Dublin, home of *Yankee* magazine (parent of *The Old Farmer's Almanac,* the oldest continuously published periodical in the country). With the help of a flagpole in the center of town, Dublin has the highest village center in the state. Although it was first settled by Scotch-Irish families in 1753, the pioneers were defeated by dense woods and returned to Peterborough, leaving behind only the name. It would be another 18 years before settlers would finally stay long enough to incorporate. Gold was discovered on the eastern end of town in 1875, but the diggings closed down after a year.

Local business people, however, struck a mother lode far more lucrative than that thin yellow vein: tourists. By 1879, 10 houses had opened their doors to travelers who flocked here each summer. The challenging, nine-mile Pumpelly Trail to the summit of Mount Monadnock, cut by scientist and explorer Raphael Pumpelly, begins on Lake Street. Travelers with kids will want to stop at **Friendly Farm**, five acres of lawns, pastures and paddocks that are home to a whole menagerie of farm animals.

In the center of Dublin, turn off Route 101 onto New Harrisville/Dublin Road to the National Historic Landmark 19th-century industrial community of **Harrisville**, the state's best-preserved and most photographed village. Although the last mill shut down its looms in 1970, the buildings themselves are preserved in a park-like setting around a millpond perched above Goose Creek Ravine. One now houses **Harrisville Designs**, a small company selling products for weavers and knitters, and educational toys.

Return to Route 101 on Chesham Road, turn right, and continue west on Route 101 back to Keene.

information *All area codes are (603) unless otherwise indicated.*

Greater Keene Chamber of Commerce (352-1303), 48 Central Sq., Keene 03431. keenechamber.com

Greater Peterborough Chamber of Commerce (924-7234), jct. Rtes. 101 and 202, Peterborough 03456. greater-peterborough-chamber.com

Historic Harrisville (827-3722), P.O. Box 79, Harrisville 03450. historicharrisville.org

Jaffrey Chamber of Commerce (532-4549), 7 Main St., Jaffrey 03452. jaffreychamber.com

Monadnock Travel Council: monadnocktravel.com.

Rindge Chamber of Commerce (899-5051), P.O. Box 911, Rindge 03461. rindgechamber.org

lodging

Monadnock Lodging Association, P.O. Box 1088, Keene 03431. Links to inns, B&Bs and resorts: nhlodging.org

Apple Gate B & B (924-6543), 199 Upland Farm Rd., Peterborough 03458. 4 rooms with private baths in a white clapboard 1832 Colonial across from an apple orchard a few miles from town. applegatenh.com $-$$

Auk's Nest B&B (878-3443), 20 East Rd., Temple 03084. Children and pets are welcome at this 1770s cottage with 2 rooms and a 3-room suite. Adjacent to hiking/skiing trails. nhlodging.org/auksnest.html $

Benjamin Prescott Inn (532-6637), Rte.124E, Jaffrey 03452. 1850s Greek Revival farmhouse adjacent to a dairy farm has 10 spacious rooms and suites with private baths; some have private balconies. Breakfast included. benjaminprescottinn.com $$-$$$

The Birchwood Inn (878-3285), Rte. 45, Temple 03084. 3 rooms and 2 suites with private baths. Breakfast included; dinner in the London Tavern ($-$$), featuring English fare served Wed.-Sun. thebirchwoodinn.com $-$$

Colony House B&B (352-0215), 104 West St., Keene 03431. 4 beautifully appointed guest rooms in an 1819 National Historic Register Federal-style brick house in the historic district. colonyhouse104.com $$

Harrisville Inn (827-3163), 797 Chesham Rd., Harrisville 03450. 5 antiques-filled rooms with private baths in a classic, 2-story b&b close to town. Several overlook Mt. Monadnock. harrisvilleinn.com $-$$

The Inn at East Hill Farm (242-6495), 460 Monadnock St., Troy 03465. 150-acre 4-season resort/working farm offers cottages and inn rooms, and a full roster of resort amenities including indoor and outdoor pools, whirlpools, sauna, tennis, horseback riding, and children's programs. FAP. east-hill-farm.com $$$

Jack Daniels Motor Inn (924-7548), 80 Concord St. (Rte. 202), Peterborough 03458. 17 comfortable, nicely appointed rooms with all of the amenities. jackdanielsinn.com $$

Old Schoolhouse B&B (563-9240), 12 Oxbow Rd., Dublin 03444. Hike up Mt. Monadnock from the front door of this 1846 schoolhouse converted to a cozy inn. Breakfast served in your room or the dining room. $

Woodbound Inn & Resort (532-8341), 247 Woodbound Rd., Rindge 03461. Nestled on the shores of Lake Contoocook, the 4-season, full-service resort has rooms in the main building and 1-2 bedroom lakeside cabins with fireplaces. Amenities include a private beach, 12 miles of hiking trails, a 9-hole, par 3 golf course, and a tennis court. woodbound.com $$-$$$

off the drive

The Hancock Inn (525-3318), 33 Main St., Hancock 03449. The state's oldest inn (1789) has 14 rooms with 4-poster or canopy beds and private baths; some gas wood stoves, and several with murals by Rufus Porter (if you're a real fan, you might want to stay in the Rufus Porter Room). Rate includes breakfast buffet. Costumed waitstaff in the candlelit restaurant (Tues.-Sat.), where Shaker cranberry pot roast is the signature dish. Sun. brunch in the Tavern. hancockinn.com $$-$$$

restaurants

Aylmer's Grille, Woodbound Inn & Resort (532-4949), 247 Woodbound Rd., Rindge. After running a restaurant in Jaffrey, chef Aylmer has moved here, continuing to prepare his imaginative take on American classics. Patrons can watch their meals being prepared in the open kitchen. L & D Tues.-Sat. $$-$$$

Blue Trout Grill (357-0087), 176 Main St., Keene. Creative American dishes include a lunch pastrami Reuben cured and smoked on the premises, and a dinner crispy calamari appetizer followed by hickory-smoked ribs. L & D. $$-$$$

The Café at Noone Falls (924-6818), 50 Jaffrey Rd. (Rte. 202), Peterborough. Simple breakfasts; lunch features homemade soups, sandwiches on homemade baguettes, and specials such as pad Thai noodles and quiche. Mon.-Sat. 8:30 a.m.-4 p.m. $-$$

Del Rossi's Trattoria (563-7195), Rte. 137, Dublin. Italian trattoria in Yankee country a few miles west of town; salads, homemade pastas, and seafood. Folk music and poetry Fri. and Sat. nights. L Tues.-Fri., D Tues.-Sun. $-$$

Elm City Restaurant & Brewery (355-3335), Colony Mill Marketplace, 222 West St., Keene. The ales and lagers are handcrafted; the menu, with walnut crusted pork loin, and chicken & cheese tortellini, goes far beyond standard pub fare. L & D. $-$$$

Kimball Farm (532-5765), Turnpike Rd. (Rte. 124), Jaffrey. L & D

Lilly's on the Pond (899-3322), 377 Rte. 202 (north of the junction with Rte. 119), Rindge. Creative but moderately priced continental fare in a renovated, 1790s sawmill overlooking a millpond. The menu is large, and the ambiance charming. L & D Tues.-Sun. $-$$

Luca's Mediterranean Café (358-3335), 10 Central Sq., Keene. The Italian-born chef prepares European dishes with a hint of North Africa and the Eastern Mediterranean. The results: treats such as pappardelle Bolognese, grilled French pork chops, and, for dessert, tiramisu. L Mon.-Fri., D nightly. $$-$$$

Pearl Restaurant & Oyster Bar (924-5225), 1 Jaffrey Rd., Peterborough. Creative Southeast Asian fare in a mall at the edge of town. The oysters are shucked to order, and dishes such as sweet glazed pork ribs, and sesame crusted rare ahi tuna, exceed expectations. D Mon.-Sat. $$-$$$

Peterborough Diner (924-6202), 10 Depot St., Peterborough. A 1950s Worcester lunch car with traditional diner fare, including great breakfasts (eat the Belly Buster by yourself and get it half price), and classic blue-plate specials. B, L & D. $

off the drive

Pickity Place (878-1151), 2 mi. off Rte. 31, Nutting Hill Rd., Mason. 1786 cottage used for "Grandmother's House" by Elizabeth Orton Jones, illustrator of "Little Red Riding Hood," serves herbal-themed, 5-course lunches. Seatings at 11:30 a.m. and 12:45 and 2 p.m.; reservations. $$

attractions

Cathedral of the Pines (899-3300), 10 Hale Hill Rd., Rindge. May-Oct. cathedralofthepines.org

Fitzwilliam Historical Society Amos J. Blake House Museum (585-7742), 66 Rte. 119W, Fitzwilliam. Exhibits include a period home and schoolroom, and a 1779 fire engine. Memorial Day weekend-Labor Day, Sat. p.m., Thurs. a.m.

Friendly Farm (563-8444), Rte. 101, Dublin. Late May-Labor Day; weekends through mid-Sept.

Frye's Measure Mill (654-6581), 12 Frye Rd., Wilton. Tues.-Sat., Sun. p.m. in summer; Thurs.-Sat., Sun. p.m. in winter.

Gap Mountain Reservation. For information: Monadnock State Park (see below).

Horatio Colony Museum (352-0460), 199 Main St., Keene. May-mid-Oct., Wed.-Sun. 450-acre Nature Preserve, off Daniels Road, is open dawn to dusk. Free.

Keene Historical Society (352-1895), 246 Main St., Keene. Mon-Fri.; Wed. until 9 p.m.; Sat. a.m. Free.

Mariposa Museum & World Culture Center (924-4555), 26 Main St., Peterborough. Daily in summer; Sept.-mid-June, Wed.-Sun.

Melville Academy Museum (532-7455), Thorndike Pond Rd., Jaffrey. 1833 Greek Revival schoolhouse. July & Aug., Sat. & Sun. p.m. Free.

Miller State Park (924-7433), Rte. 101, Peterborough. Mid-Apr.-mid-Nov.

Monadnock State Park (532-8862), Dublin Rd., Jaffrey Center.

Monadnock-Sunapee Greenway Trail (357-2115 or 225-7274), P.O. Box 164, Marlow, 03456.

Peterboro Basket Company Factory Outlet (924-3861), 130 Grove St., Peterborough. Outlet store for the family-owned company that has been making baskets since 1854. Also, pottery, candles, linens, and more.

Peterborough Historical Society Museum (924-3235), 19 Grove St., Peterborough. Tues.-Sat.

Rhododendron State Park (532-8862), Rte. 119W, Fitzwilliam. Mid-May-mid Nov.

Rosaly's Garden (924-3303), Rte. 123, Peterborough. Mid-May-Columbus Day.

1773 Meetinghouse (site of Amos Fortune Forum Series): contact Jaffrey Chamber of Commerce (see "Information" above.)

Sharon Arts Center (924-7256), 457 Rte. 123, Sharon. In Peterborough, the Fine Art Gallery is at 30 Grove St.; Gallery & Resource Center is at 20-40 Depot Sq.

Shieling State Forest (271-2214), Old Street Rd., Peterborough. 45 acres of woods and wildflower trails for hiking and walking the dog (on a leash).

Swanzey Historical Museum (352-4579), Rte. 10, W. Swanzey. Memorial Day-Columbus Day.

Temple Mountain State Reservation, Rte. 101, Temple. For information: Monadnock Conservancy (357-0600).

Thorne-Sagendorph Gallery at Keene State College (358-2720), Wyman Way, Keene. Collection includes 19th-century landscapes. Call for hrs.

Wapack National Wildlife Refuge (off Rte. 101 at Miller State Park). 1,672 acres on North Pack Monadnock.

Wyman Tavern Museum (357-3855), 339 Main St., Keene. June -Labor Day, Tues.-Sat.

activities

Contoocook Lake Beach, Quantum Road, Jaffrey. Sand beach.

Edward MacDowell Lake (924-3431), 75 Wilder St., Peterborough. Swimming, picnic area, barbecue grills, hiking trails, and fishing.

Jaffrey Bandstand. Many Wednesday evenings in summer: contact Chamber of Commerce (see "Information" above.)

Monadnock Berries (242-6417), 545 West Hill Rd., Troy. Pick your own berries.

Monadnock Music (924-7610). Free chamber music concerts throughout the region, and a ticketed series in the Peterborough Town House. Schedule: monadnockmusic.org

Peterborough Players (924-7585), Hadley Rd., Peterborough. Dramas, comedies, and musicals in an air-conditioned, 19th-century barn. Schedule: peterboroughplayers.org

Shire Town by Foot (352-1895), 246 Main St., Keene. Walking tours of the city.

Silver Ranch Airpark (532-8870), Rte. 124, Jaffrey.

Spokes & Slopes (924-9961), 109 Grove St., Peterborough. Mountain and road bike rentals.

Summers Back Country Outfitters (357-5107), 16 Ashuelot St., Keene. Kayak and canoe rentals and sales.

Temple Band (878-2829). Schedule: templeband.org

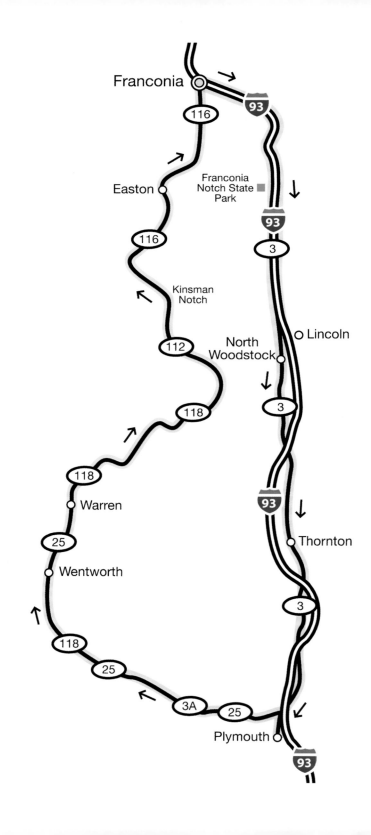

Drive **11**

Franconia Notch and the
Western White Mountains

112 miles

major**attractions**

- Kinsman Notch
- The Frost Place

- Franconia Notch State Park
- Lincoln

*T*his drive begins with a drive through the westernmost of the White Mountains' great notches, home of a late, great stone icon of New Hampshire. Continue south past several lively year-round resorts to the college town of Plymouth, then head back through rugged Kinsman Notch and finish with a visit to one of Robert Frost's rural homesteads.

Begin the drive at Exit #3 off I-93/Route 3, the gateway to the **White Mountain National Forest (WMNF). Franconia Notch State Park** –enveloping what is possibly the most spectacular stretch of interstate highway in the nation –

winds for eight miles between the peaks of the Kinsman and Franconia mountain ranges. From north to south, here are some of the highlights:

– **Echo Lake** at the foot of Cannon Mountain, with a sandy beach ($), fishing, and boating facilities.

– **Cannon Mountain Aerial Tramway**, the first lift of its type in North America, which has carried about 7,000,000 passengers to the top of the mountain since it made its maiden run in 1938. It's a five-minute ride to the 4,200-foot summit, where there are walking trails and an observation tower. The **New England Ski Museum,** at the base of the mountain, exhibits vintage ski films, memorabilia, and videos.

– Much of New Hampshire, New England (and dare we think the world?) went into mourning when **The Old Man of the Mountain**, a natural rock formation that towered 1,200 feet above Profile Lake, collapsed on May 3, 2003. It was one of the region's most beloved landmarks, immortalized on state license plates, and by writers including Daniel Webster, who said of the Great Stone Profile: "Men hang out their signs indicative of their respective trades: shoemakers hang out a gigantic shoe; jewelers, a monster watch... but up in the mountains of New Hampshire, God Almighty has hung out a sign to show that there He makes men."

Although there were early rumors that the state would try to recreate the Great Stone Face, it will be remembered instead in a roadside memorial at the base of the mountain. As of this writing, plans for the design are still being finalized.

– A short distance to the north, **Profile Lake**, the headwaters of the Pemigewasset River, attracts anglers fly-fishing for brook trout.

– At the southern entrance to the notch, at the **Flume Gorge & Visitor Center**, the **Flume** ($) is an 800-foot-deep gorge formed over the course of countless millennia by Flume Brook. The rock here is granite, riven by intrusions of molten lava hardened into basalt dikes. By constantly wearing away at the dike over which it flows on its way to the Pemigewasset River, Flume Brook carved this deep chasm between 70-foot-high granite walls. There's a walkway beside the stream, within the walls of the flume. A shuttle transports visitors from the center to the gorge entrance.

The Flume was discovered by 93-year-old "Aunt" Jess Guernsey while she was out fishing one day in 1803.

Between Echo Lake and the Flume, there's a nine-mile, paved recreational trail for biking, several covered bridges (Sentinel Pine Bridge at The Pool, and Flume Bridge), rocks to climb, birds to spot (look for peregrine falcons on Cannon's cliffs), moose for drivers to watch out for, and a network of fine hiking trails. In addition to the **Appalachian Trail** (the trailhead is near the Flume parking area), some of the most popular include a 1 ½ -mile loop to Bald Mountain and Artists Bluff (trail begins in the parking area on Route 18 across from Peabody Base Lodge); the 3-mile round-trip hike to Lonesome Lake, which begins at Lafayette Place; and the hike to Kinsman Falls, less than one mile round trip, which begins at the Basin. The Visitor Center has detailed maps and guides, including the excellent *Appalachian Mountain Club White Mountain Guide.*

The section of I-93 that winds through the notch represents a compromise that settled a fierce and complicated debate waged from the late 1960s to the early 1980s over how to connect the loose ends of this interstate highway at either end of the notch. Environmentalists wanted a two-lane highway; the government wanted to finish the four-lane interstate. The road you drive today is a hybrid – a mini-interstate unlike any other portion of the national system of superhighways.

The WMNF, comprising nearly 800,000 acres in New Hampshire and western Maine, was established in 1911 largely through the efforts of John Wingate Weeks (see Drive 12).

Note: Some parking areas in WMNF require a permit. The cost is $20 for an annual pass, $5 for a one to seven consecutive day pass; or $3 for a one-day pass. There are fee tubes at many of the area, or passes can be purchased at Visitor Centers (see "Information" below) or stores and campgrounds throughout Mount Washington Valley.

bears and beer

At **Parkway Exit #1, head south on Route 3** alongside the Pemigewasset River. If the kids have grown bored with the scenery, they're bound to perk up along the next stretch through one of the state's few remaining, old-time "tourist" areas: miles of old-fashioned cottage colonies, miniature golf courses, hot dog and ice cream stands, a water park, and other related businesses, all clustered like barnacles on the narrow strip wedged between I-93 and the WMNF.

Lincoln owes its recent spate of development to several factors: in addition to its proximity to the Notch – and to Cannon Mountain Ski Area –it's at the western terminus of the Kancamagus Highway (see Drive 12) and the Pemigewasset Wilderness, and just a mile east of **Loon Mountain** ski area and summer resort complex.

Clark's Trading Post, one of New Hampshire's oldest tourist draws, was founded in 1928 for the purpose of raising and exhibiting Eskimo sled dogs. A few years later Florence and Edward Clark brought in a few trained bears as an attraction for travelers. Today, a half-hour show starring North American black bears still draws the crowds. Descendants of the Clarks have added a host of other attractions, including the White Mountain Central Railroad, a standard-gauge wood burning locomotive which steams through a 1904 covered bridge and along the Pemigewasset; Segway rides; bumper boats; and antique cars, motorcycles, and a fire station.

In downtown Lincoln, hop aboard the **Hobo Railroad's** vintage cars for scenic excursion along the Pemigewasset. Ride the rails with a "hobo's lunch" – a sandwich, chips and a drink served on a souvenir 'hobo bindle stick." The state operates two information centers in town.

Although less developed than its neighbor to the north, **North Woodstock** is amply supplied with restaurants and lodgings. If you're in the mood for a tad more formal meal than the hobo's lunch, buy a ticket for the **Lafayette Dinner Train**, which serves a five-course dinner to passengers as it follows alongside the Pemigewasset.

Stop at the venerable **Fadden's General Store** for provisions, gifts, maple syrup, and a whiff of nostalgia. You can order up a pint of freshly brewed ale at the **Woodstock Inn, Station & Brewery**.

Side Trip

Just south of North Woodstock, turn left onto Route 175 and continue south to the left hand turn onto scenic Tripoli Road (closed in winter) which winds for nine miles, through Thornton Gap (where the challenging, 6 4/10-mile Mount Osceola Trail climbs to the summit of 4,340-foot-high Mount Osceola), past the trailheads for several other hiking trails, to where it merges with Route 49 (West Road). Continue south on Route 49 to the self-contained ski/summer resort village of **Waterville Valley**, centered at the Town Square, a huge clapboard structure housing restaurants, lodgings, and shops. Activities include paddleboats, golf, biking, and, of course, hiking. Follow Route 49 back to Route 3 south alongside the Mad River and resume the drive below, in West Campton.

On Route 3, watch on the left for Turkey Jim's Bridge; the original was built in 1883 to connect a turkey farm with the mainland. The present bridge, built in 1958, is one of three covered bridges in **West Campton**. The Campton-Blair Bridge is two miles north of Livermore Falls; the Campton-Bump Bridge is one mile east of Route175 at Campton Hollow.

college town in the foothills . . . .

Continue into Plymouth. Although once a thriving mill town and busy railroad junction, today the town's economy revolves around the 4,000 students who attend

Plymouth State College. The bustling downtown, with businesses like Louis Samaha Store, a Main Street fixture since 1917, and the 1946 **Main Street Station** (formerly the landmark Fracher's diner), seems to have made the transition quite comfortably. The college's **Silver Cultural Arts Center**, which hosts the New Hampshire Music Festival concert series, provides the community with a full plate of cultural events.

The British cannon in front of the restored 1889 Town Hall was captured by American troops in 1777. On the Common, there's a bronze sculpture by George Borst called "Kneeling Boy Scout," which has a fountain (perfect for animals to drink from) and a plaque honoring Nathaniel Hawthorne. The author used to stay at the Pemigewasset House. Hawthorne died in the hotel on May 18, 1864, and it burned in 1909. The 5 ½ -mile self-guided **Plymouth Heritage Trail** of 14 historically significant sights begins at the Plymouth Regional Senior Center (the former railroad depot) on Green Street.

Backtrack to Route 25/3A (Tenney Mountain Highway) and head west into the Baker River Valley along a portion of one of New Hampshire's Scenic & Cultural Byways.

The Baker River, which roughly parallels Route 25, was named for Lieutenant Thomas Baker, who, with a company of 34 rangers from Northampton, Massachusetts, destroyed a Pemigewasset Indian village while passing through in 1712. The Bay State rewarded the expedition with a scalp bounty of £40 and promoted Baker to the rank of captain.

Side Trip

Turn right off Route 25 onto Main Street (which becomes Stinson Lake Road) into tranquil, 19th-century **Rumney Village,** where Mary Baker Eddy, founder of the Christian Science movement, lived from 1860-1862. The home (open by appointment only) has been restored to appear as it did when she lived here with her husband, the town dentist. Continue on Stinson Lake Road to glacially formed, crystal-clear **Stinson Lake**, which has a reputation for fine trout fishing. There's also a beach and a hiking trail to the summit of Stinson Mountain and the Three Ponds area. Keep an eye out for moose occasionally spotted here.

On the way back through Rumney Village, turn left onto Quincy Road to visit 40-acre **Quincy Bog**, where more than 115 species of birds have been sighted. The bog plants bloom in May and June. Covered bridge #44 was built in 2001 to span the Baker River.

caves, cascades ... and Robert Frost

Continue west on Route 25 to **Polar Caves Park**. More than 50,000 years ago a continental glacier moved south over the mountains and valleys. As the ice sheet thawed, great blocks of granite cracked and loosened from Hawks Cliff and tumbled down, forming a series of caves and passages which are great fun to explore.

After Route 25 merges with Route 118, the road becomes Moosilauke Highway, named for the 4,802-foot mountain peak on the southwest edge of the WMNF.

Although **Wentworth**, one of New Hampshire's prettiest villages, was settled in 1774-75, many of the buildings were destroyed in a flood in 1856. Several, however, including the 1829 Congregational Church with its unusual tiered steeple, and the 1815 Thomas Whipple House, survived and are clustered around the handsome common.

On the outskirts of **Warren** watch on the right for the **Warren Fish Hatchery**, a state-of-the-art facility for salmon rearing and management of trout brood fish populations.

Warren just may possess the most unusual "downtown" centerpiece in the state: a 68-foot Redstone Missile. The eight-ton craft was moved here on a flatbed truck in 1971 by native son Henry "Ted" Asselin. A sign next to the missile points the way to the Jesse Bushaw Memorial Trail, which follows a defunct railroad bed past an old mica mine.

When Route 118 splits off from Route 25 just north of Warren, turn onto Route 118 (right), which winds back into the WMNF.

Ready for a swim? Park near the iron bridge by Moosilauke Carriage Road and take a dip in the Baker River, which runs alongside the road. Turn onto Ravine Lodge Road to Dartmouth College's 1930s **Moosilauke Ravine Lodge**, one of New England's largest log buildings. It's open to the public in season for lodging and meals, and is the trailhead for several paths that ascend the southeast side of 4,802-foot Mount Moosilauke.

At the intersection with Route 112, turn left onto Route 112 to head into the Lost River Region and **Kinsman Notch**, named for Asa Kinsman, an early pioneer who was on his way to claim a parcel of land in the town of Landaff when he discovered he'd taken a wrong turn. Rather than turn back, he and several companions used axes to hack their way nine miles through the wilderness to the other side.
If you wish instead to return to the North Woodstock/Lincoln area, bear right at the 118/112 fork onto Route 112.

The road between Mount Moosilauke and Kinsman Ridge is one of the most dramatic and least traveled sections of the WMNF. It winds past cascades, dramatic rock formations, and magnificent mountain vistas.

At **Lost River Gorge & Boulder Caves**, the river winds through glacially formed boulder caves and potholes – some as large as 25 feet wide and 60 feet deep – before emerging at Paradise Falls at the foot of the gorge. Visitors can take a self-guided tour along board-walks, across bridges, and up ladders; and explore a series of rocks and caves. More than 300 varieties of native flowers, ferns, and shrubs are on display in the Nature Garden.

Two excellent hiking trails begin just past the entrance to Lost River: the rigorous but rewarding **Beaver Brook Cascades**, a 2 2/10-mile hike almost straight up to the summit of Mount Moosilauke alongside a series of magnificent waterfalls; and the **Kinsman Ridge Trail**, a grueling 16 7/10 -mile segment of the Appalachian Trail which ends at the Old Man in the Mountain parking area in Franconia Notch.

At the intersection with Route 116, turn right onto Route 116 into the Easton Valley, past **Kinsman Lodge** and the **Franconia Inn**, and watch for the turn-off to **The Frost Place**. Poet Robert Frost moved into this 1859 farmhouse overlooking Franconia Valley when he was 40 years old, and lived here for five years. Today the simple white structure is preserved as a museum. Exhibits include a rare collection of Frost's Christmas card poems, personal letters, and first editions. Throughout the summer a poet-in-residence gives readings in the barn; and visitors can follow a short Nature Trail, lined with quotations from Frost's poetry, through the woods.

Continue on Route 116 into Franconia, gateway to Franconia Notch. Nathaniel Hawthorne, John Greenleaf Whittier, and Washington Irving were among the writers who vacationed here. The **Iron Furnace Interpretive Center** on Route 18 preserves the state's only remaining blast furnace, all that is left of the iron industry that thrived here from 1800 to 1865. Iron ore was carted from mines in Sugar Hill, and molded into everything from kettles to heating stoves.

The handsome wooden building that dominates the Franconia townscape was built in 1884, the gift of Moses Arnold Dow, a magazine publisher, who wanted to establish a model educational institution in his adopted town.

> Just specimens is all New
> Hampshire has,
> One each of everything
> As in a showcase,
> Which naturally she
> doesn't care to sell.
>
>   *-- Robert Frost,*
>   *"New Hampshire"*

Side Trip

Take Route 117 out of Franconia to **Sugar Hill**. It's hard to imagine that this upscale hill town – now known for its many fine inns – was a hotbed of religious fanaticism in the early 19th century. It was here that Baptist clergyman William Miller began to preach that the world would end on October 22, 1844. As related in the New Hampshire volume of the *American Guide Series*, "Many believed in him so firmly that they harvested no crops that year, and either sold their livestock or gave it away. They prepared themselves by six weeks of prayer and fasting and on the last day gathered either in the cemetery or at the church, clothed in white flowing robes and ready for their ascension. ... One man went out into the field to give a final exhortation to some 'unsaved' neighbors. Worn out with fasting and prayer, he sat down on a haystack and went to sleep. The recreants then removed most of the hay and touched a match to what was left. The Millerite awoke with a start, shouting, 'Hell – just as I expected.'"

The view of the Presidential, Franconia, and Kinsman Ranges from the **Sunset Hill House** is unparalleled.

You can pick up I-93 north and south at Franconia.

information *Area codes are (603) unless otherwise indicated.*

Appalachian Mountain Club (617-536-0636), 5 Joy St., Boston, MA 02108. outdoors.org

Baker Valley Chamber of Commerce (764-9380), P.O. Box 447, Rumney 03266. bakervalleychamber.org

Franconia Notch Chamber of Commerce (823-5661), Main St., Franconia 03580. franconianotch.org

Lincoln-Woodstock Chamber of Commerce (745-6621), Lincoln Village Shops, Lincoln 03251. lincolnwoodstock.com

Plymouth Chamber of Commerce (536-1001), P.O. Box 65, Plymouth 03264. plymouthnh.org

Waterville Valley Region Chamber of Commerce (726-3804), 12 Vintinner Rd., Campton 03223. watervillevalleyregion.com

White Mountain National Forest Headquarters (528-8721), 719 N. Main St., Laconia 03246. Visitor Centers: Gateway Visitor Center (745-3816), Exit 32 off I-93, Lincoln; Lincoln Woods (630-5190), Kancamagus Highway, Lincoln. fs.fed.us/r9/white

White Mountains Visitor Center (745-8720), Exit 32 off I-93, North Woodstock. visitwhitemountains.com

lodging

Campton Inn B&B (726-4449), 383 Owl St., Campton 03223. 5 rooms with shared or private baths in a rambling, 1836 village farmhouse. Children and well-behaved dogs ($) are welcome with advance approval. camptonbb.com $-$$

The Common Man Inn & Spa (536-2200), 231 Main St., Plymouth 03264. Rooms range from cozy to spacious, with decks, lofts and fireplaces. Indoor pool, Jacuzzi, sauna, and exercise room, and full service spa. Pets in some rooms. Foster's Boiler Room restaurant ($$-$$$) serves American fare nightly (from noon weekends). thecmaninn.com $$-$$$

Cozy Cabins (745-8713), Rte. 3, Lincoln 03251. Riverfront complex has 9 rustic 1-2 bedroom cabins with cable TV; some kitchens. Play area. May-Oct. cozycabins.com $-$$

Federal House Inn B&B (536-4644), 27 Rte. 25, Plymouth 03264. Elegant accommodations in an 1835 inn on 2 manicured acres just out of town. 5 antiques-filled rooms with queen beds, private baths, luxury linens, and a/c. There's a TV in the library, and an outdoor heated spa. 3-course dinner is served for 6 or more. federalhouseinnnh.com $$-$$$

The Franconia Inn (823-5542), Rte. 116, Franconia 03580. 1863, 3-story inn on 107 acres has 32 rooms and suites with private baths ranging in size from cozy to spacious. Tennis, outdoor pool and Jacuzzi, stables, bicycles, and lawn games. MAP, B&B or EP. The restaurant ($$-$$$) serves American dishes in a charming candlelit room overlooking the mountains. Rathskeller lounge. Closed Apr.-mid-May. franconiainn.com $$-$$$

Franconia Notch Motel (745-2229), Rte. 3, Lincoln 03251. 12 units with TV, a/c, and individual heat; and 6 2-room screen-porched cottages (summer) on the Pemigewasset River just ½ mi. south of the Notch. franconianotch.com $

Hilltop Acres (764-5896), 6 Buffalo Rd., Wentworth 03282. Classic farmhouse has rooms with private baths and cable TV in the main building, and 2 basic housekeeping cottages with kitchenettes, fireplace, and screened porches. Pets welcome in cottages. May-Nov. $-$$

The Homestead (823-5564), Rte. 117, Sugar Hill 03585. This 1802 inn – one of the oldest family-run inns in the country – was expanded in 1898 and has 20 rooms in the main house (shared baths) and annex. The inn has hand-hewn virgin timbers, wide pine boards, antiques, and loads of family heirlooms. Breakfast included. thehomestead1802.com $-$$

Indian Head Resort (745-8000), Rte. 3, Lincoln 03251. Resort complex has 98 rooms with lake or notch views, and cabins with fireplaces and screen porches. All units have 50-inch plasma TVs. Indoor and outdoor heated pools, tennis, paddleboats, spas, and a restaurant ($$-$$$). indianheadresort.com $$-$$$

Kinsman Lodge (823-5686), 215 Easton Rd., Rte. 116, Franconia 03580. As "comfortable as an old slipper," this 1880s country inn has 2nd-floor rooms with shared baths. Several cozy common rooms (one with TV). Children and pets welcome. Breakfast included. kinsmanlodge.com $

Lodge Resort (745-3441), Rte. 112, Lincoln 03251. Standard rooms, studios, and suites with kitchenettes and balconies in a riverfront resort hotel. Indoor and outdoor pools, Jacuzzi, sauna, tennis courts, game room, and picnic and barbecue area. lodgeresort.com $$-$$$

Moosilauke Ravine Lodge (May-Oct., 764-5858; off-season, 646-6543), Ravine Lodge Rd., Warren 03279 (mailing address: P.O. Box 65, Warren 03279). Rooms in the lodge and outlying bunkhouses sleep up to 12; showers and toilets are in the main building. Optional family-style breakfast and dinner. dartmouth.edu $

Sugar Hill Inn (823-5621), Rte. 117, Sugar Hill 03580. 10 guest rooms and 6 cottage suites in a beautifully restored inn with original wide pine and maple flooring, stenciled walls, antiques, and great views. Breakfast included. Restaurant (see "Restaurants" below), and spa services. MAP available. sugarhillinn.com $$-$$$

Sunset Hill House (823-5522), 231 Sunset Hill Rd., Sugar Hill 03586. Striking, 1882, 3-story inn overlooking the Presidential Range has 30 air-conditioned, antiques-filled rooms (some with Jacuzzis and fireplaces). Heated pool, 9-hole golf course (the state's oldest), restaurant (see "Restaurants" below), and tavern. Breakfast included. MAP available. sunsethillhouse.com $$-$$$$

Waterville Valley (Central Reservations: 800-468-2553). Lodging options include condominiums, the all-suite Golden Eagle Lodge; the Black Bear Lodge with 1-bedroom suites and full kitchens; and the 85-room Snowy Owl Inn. waterville.com $-$$$$

Wilderness Inn B&B (745-3890), Rte. 3/Courtney Rd., N. Woodstock 03262. 1912 shingled lumber mill owner's home near town has 7 antiques-filled rooms and suites with private baths, cable TV, and a/c. Also, a "honeymoon" cottage with a sleigh bed, fireplace, and deck overlooking Lost River. thewildernessinn.com $-$$

Woodstock Inn (745-3951), Main St., Rte. 3, N. Woodstock 03262. 33 rooms and suites in the inn and 4 nearby buildings range from small with shared bath, to grand suites with whirlpool tubs and gas fireplaces. Breakfast (included) is served in the Clement Room Grille, which also serves dinner; and there's entertainment in Woodstock Station & Brewery. Guests have use of Loon Mountain's spa. woodstockinnnh.com $-$$$

restaurants

Biederman's Deli (536-3354), 83 Main St., Plymouth. Under Chase Street Market. The popular pub (high-definition big-screen TVs) is a sandwich lover's paradise, with thousands of combinations of premium cold cuts and cheeses, and a fine assortment of boutique beers on tap. L & D daily; closed Sun. in summer. $

Café Lafayette Dinner Train (745-3500), Rte. 112, "Eagle's Nest", N. Woodstock. Reservations recommended. Schedule: nhdinnertrain.com $$$$

The Common Man (745-3463), Pollard Rd., Lincoln. This member of the popular (and ever growing) NH chain features prime rib, apple chicken, pot roast, and macaroni & cheese; Tues. special is twin Maine lobsters. Upstairs grill, with couches and a fireplace, serves lighter fare. D $$

Gypsy Café (745-4395), 117 Main St., Lincoln. Eclectic fare in a small, cozy, and cheerful setting. Enchiladas and chicken salad shares the menu with spicy sesame chicken wings and steak nachos. L & D Wed.-Sun. $-$$

Italian Farmhouse (536-4536), Rte. 3, Plymouth. This popular Common Man offshoot specializes in hearty Italian-American dishes, including pasta, pizza baked a wood-fired, brick oven, and a kids' menu. D Sun.-Fri. $-$$

Lucky Dog Tavern & Grill (536-2260), 53 S. Main St., Plymouth. The upstairs dining room serves pub-style fare, but this place is all about The Pound downstairs, where local bands rock the house. L Fri.-Sun.; D. $

Main Street Station (536-7577), 105 Main St., Plymouth. Hearty breakfast and luncheon classics in a beautifully preserved 1954 diner. B & L, Sun. until 1 p.m. $

Polly's Pancake Parlor (823-5575), Rte. 117, Sugar Hill. Pancakes rule at this ever-popular tourist spot, housed in an 1830s restored carriage shed. Also waffles, French toast, sandwiches and homemade desserts. May-late Oct. B & L. $

Sugar Hill Inn (823-5621), Rt. 17, Sugar Hill. Romantic, fireside 4-course prix-fixe dinners served Thurs.-Mon. (Thurs.-Tues. during foliage.) Appetizers might include whipped Brie; entrees such as crispy wild sockeye salmon and free range duck breast. $$$$

Sunset Hill House (823-5522), 231 Sunset Hill Rd., Sugar Hill. Choose from a la carte, table d'hote or a chef's table menu, featuring dishes such as maple-glazed salmon with caviar, and sauté of venison. Also a table d'hote menu ($$$$) for ages 6 and under (no a la carte children's menu). Less formal fare in the tavern. $$$-$$$$

Truant's Taverne (745-2239), Main St., N. Woodstock. A local landmark since 1978, this pub/restaurant serves up favorites including burgers and fajitas in a lively setting where the action often centers around the foosball table. L & D $

Woodstock Inn Station & Brewery (745-3951), Main St., Rte. 3, N. Woodstock. The menu at this converted train station includes everything from burritos to burgers to barbecued ribs. Beer is brewed at the Woodstock Inn brewery, which shares space. L &D $-$$

attractions

Cannon Aerial Tramway (823-8800), I-93, Franconia Notch. Late May-Oct.

Clark's Trading Post (745-8913), Rte. 3, Lincoln. Open daily; bear shows Memorial Day weekend-fall. General admission includes all rides and attractions.

Fadden's General Store & Sugar House (745-2406), 109 Main St., Rte. 3, N. Woodstock.

Franconia Notch State Park (823-8800), Franconia. Flume Gorge Visitor Center (745-8391). No fee to drive through. Fee: Flume Gorge (daily mid-May-mid-Oct.) and Echo Lake State Beach.

The Frost Place (823-5510), Ridge Rd., Franconia. Memorial Day-July 5, Sat. and Sun. p.m.; July 5-Columbus Day Weekend, daily p.m. except Tues.

Harman's Cheese & Country Store (823-8000), Rte. 117, Sugar Hill. The "World's Greatest Cheddar Cheese," along with maple syrup and maple products, preserves, gift baskets, and local crafts.

Hobo Railroad (745-2135), 64 Railroad St., Lincoln. Late June-Oct.; late May-late-June, weekends. Schedule: hoborr.com

Loon Mountain (745-8111), 60 Loon Mt. Rd. (Rte. 112), Lincoln. 4-season resort has horseback and pony rides, mountain bike trails and rentals, and gondola to the mountaintop, where local artisans produce crafts.

Lost River Gorge & Boulder Caves (745-8031), 1712 Lost River Rd. (Rte. 112), Kinsman Notch, N. Woodstock. Early May-late Oct.

Mary Baker Eddy House (786-9943), 58 Stinson Lake Rd., Rumney. By appointment.

Mt. Washington Valley Children's Museum (356-2992), 2396 White Mt. Hwy., N. Conway. Exhibits at this small museum geared to the younger set encourage exploration and touch. Wed.-Sun. in summer.

Mountain Wanderer Map and Book Store (745-2594), 57 Main St., Lincoln. Maps of all sorts for every outdoor activity, and travel books.

New England Ski Museum (823-7177), Cannon Mountain, Franconia Notch. Memorial Day-Mar. Free.

New Hampshire Homecraft Cooperative (726-8626), Rte. 3, Campton. Crafts for sale in an 1878 one-room schoolhouse. Mid-June-mid-Oct.

Plymouth Heritage Trail (536-1001), Plymouth.

Polar Caves Park (536-1888), 705 Rte. 25, Rumney. Early May-Oct.

Sugar Hill Historical Museum (823-5336), Main St., Sugar Hill. Exhibits include the development of region's iron and tourism industries. Early June-mid-Oct., Fri. & Sat.

Warren Fish Hatchery (764-8593), Rte. 25, Warren. Interactive exhibits, tour, and nature trails. Hatchery open year-round; visitor center May-Oct. Free.

activities

Note: for a round-up of arts, cultural and heritage events throughout the North Country, log onto: aannh.org

Alpine Adventures Outdoor Recreation (888-745-9911), 41 Main St., Lincoln. Canopy tours with 13 zip lines on 300 acres.

Adventure Center (236-4666), Town Square, Waterville Valley Resort. Mountain and tandem bike, and tag-along rentals.

Corcoran's Pond (236-4666), Waterville Valley Resort. Paddleboat, canoe and sunfish rentals; sandy beach.

Hobo Hills Adventure Golf (745-2125), Main St., Lincoln. Miniature golf. June-Labor Day, daily; spring and fall, weekends.

Hobo Railroad (745-2135), Rt. 112, Lincoln. Weekends late May-early June; daily late June-foliage season. Schedule: hoborr.com

Jack O'Lantern Resort Golf Course (877-321-3636), Rte. 3, Woodstock. 18-hole, par 70 course in the mountains.

North Woodstock Concerts on the Common (745-8752). Free concerts some summer Sat. evenings.

Pemi-Baker River Adventures (536-5652), 33 Sanborn Rd., Plymouth. Kayak, tube, rafting and canoe rentals and shuttle service; tours on Baker and Pemigewasset rivers. Memorial Day-Labor Day, daily.

Plymouth Ski & Sports (536-2338), 103 Main St., Plymouth. Canoe and kayak (single or double) excursions ranging from 45 minutes to 9-½ hrs. Shuttle service.

Rhino Bike Works (536-3919), 1 Foster St. (next to The Common Man Inn), Plymouth. Road and mountain bike rentals, group rides.

Silver Center for the Arts (535-2787), 17 High St., Plymouth State College. New Hampshire summer music festival, professional and student stage productions, children's theater. Schedule: plymouth.edu/silver/

Ski Fanatics (726-4327), 23 Vintinner Rd., Campton Plaza, Campton. Paddle the Pemi shuttles; kayak, canoe and mountain bike rentals.

Whale's Tale Water Park (745-8810), Rte. 3, Lincoln 03251. 11 waterslides, a wave pool, a ¼- mi. long lazy river, and kids' play area. Free tubes. Memorial Day-late June, weekends; summer daily.

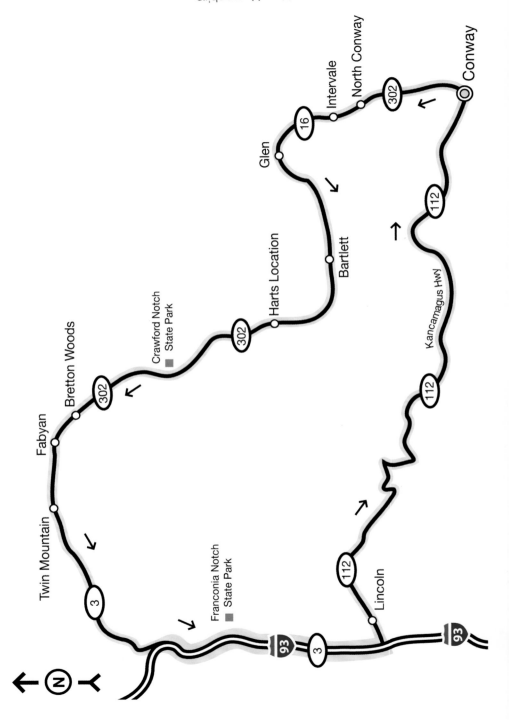

Drive 12

From the Kancamagus to Crawford Notch

82 miles

major **attractions**

- Crawford Notch
- Kancamagus Highway
- Conway outlet stores
- Conway Scenic Railroad

- White Mountain National Forest
- Mount Washington Hotel and Resort
- Mount Washington Cog Railway

$\mathcal{F}$ollow a spectacularly scenic road carved through the heart of the White Mountain National Forest, then head into North Conway to cruise the outlet stores. The route threads back into the mountains and continues through Crawford Notch, centermost of northern New Hampshire's three great passes. Just beyond are two of the region's most famous landmarks – an Edwardian confection of a hotel, and a most unusual railway.

In 1867 the state of New Hampshire sold most of the land in the White Mountains to lumber companies for $26,000, launching a period of slash-cut wood lands, forest fires, and over-harvesting of timber. In 1901, in opposition to this destruction, the Society for the Preservation of New Hampshire Forests (SPNHF) was organized. At the Society's urging, Congress passed the Weeks Act, creating the **White Mountain National Forest** (WMNF), in 1911. Named in honor of John Wingate Weeks, who was instrumental in moving the legislation through Congress, the Act authorized the federal government to purchase 1,000,000 acres of land for $6 million.

Today, the WMNF covers 774,496 acres in New Hampshire and Maine, and includes five designated wilderness areas, hundreds of miles of hiking trails, four downhill ski resorts partly or entirely on Forestland, lakes, ponds, waterfalls, and 23 roadside campgrounds. Small portions are still harvested for timber.

Note: Some WMNF parking areas require a permit. The cost is $20 for an annual pass, $5 for a day pass good for one to seven consecutive days; or $3 for a one-day pass. There are fee tubes at many of the areas, or passes can be purchased at Visitor Centers (see "Information" below) or stores and campgrounds throughout Mount. Washington Valley.

through the heart of the forest . . . .

Begin in Lincoln (for information on Lincoln, see Drive 11), the western terminus of the Kancamagus Highway (Route 112). The "Kanc", New England's first National Scenic Byway, lies almost entirely within the borders of the WMNF, winding for nearly 35 miles alongside the Pemigewasset and Swift rivers and climbing to almost 3,000 feet as it crosses the flank of Mount Kancamagus before dropping down to the Saco River at Conway. Along the way there are picnic areas, swimming holes, panoramic views, and hiking trails. The paved road is open all year. (Note: More than 750,000 vehicles travel the highway each year, and traffic can be very heavy in summer and during fall foliage. The best time to drive the Kanc in these seasons is early in the morning. There are no motorists' services along the road.)

Kancamagus (Kan-kuh-mog-us, "the fearless one") was the grandson of Passaconaway, a peace-loving chief who united some 17 tribes into the Pennacook Confederacy and ruled as their first "Sagamon" until he died in 1669. Kancamagus followed his father, Wonalancet, as third and final Sagamon, trying to keep peace between his people and an increasing number of white pioneers who came to this region. Finally, in defeat, he and his followers moved north to Quebec. Years later, he returned to lead an Indian raid on Dover (see Drive 16).

Side Trip
Turn off to **Loon Mountain,** a ski resort that in the summer offers a sky ride to the summit, trail bike rides and tours, horseback riding, a skate park, and a climbing wall.

Continue out of Lincoln on Route 112. A few highlights along the Kanc, in the order you'll pass them traveling west to east:

– Lincoln Woods, where a suspension footbridge crosses the river to a swimming area.

– Kancamagus Pass, the highest point on the highway.

– Sabbaday Falls, where an easy 4/10- mile trail follows a brook to a series of cascades in a narrow flume.

– Passaconaway Historic Site, where the early 1800s Russell-Colbath Historic Homestead offers a glimpse into the lives of the region's earliest settlers. The 1/2-mile Rail 'n River Forest Trail which begins here is perfect for families with young kids, and is stroller accessible.

Ruth, the daughter of Amzi Russell, who helped his father build the Russell-Colbath Historic Homestead, married a carpenter named Thomas Alden Colbath and lived there with him until one night in 1891 when he left the house, saying he'd be back in a little while. Each night, for the next 39 years, Ruth put a lamp in the window to help her husband find his way home. He finally did, in 1933 – three years after Ruth's death. When asked where he'd been, he'd reply only vaguely that he'd been in California, Cuba, and Panama.

– Bear Notch Road: this 9 3/10-mile road (closed in winter) winds through the 3,000-acre Bartlett Experimental Forest, a field laboratory for research on the ecology and management of northern hardwoods and associated ecosystems. The road ends in Bartlett on Route 302. Along the way there are terrific views of the 75,000-acre Pemigewasset Wilderness (nicknamed the "Pemi"), one of the largest roadless tracks in the east.

– Rocky Gorge Scenic Area, where the Swift River has worn a narrow passage through solid rock, forming a series of ponds perfect for cooling off on a summer's day (swim only in designated areas). There's a footbridge to Falls Pond, where a trail circles the water.

Many of the region's finest hiking trails begin along the Kanc. A few of the more popular include:

– Lincoln Woods Trail (2 8/10 miles, easy): this footpath crosses a 160-foot-long suspension bridge and follows an abandoned railroad grade to the beginning of the Wilderness Trail into the Pemi. A 4/10- mile turnoff from the trail goes to Franconia Falls, a massive granite ledge with a water chute.

Timber baron J.E. Henry logged the area surrounding the Lincoln Woods Trail – and much of the Kanc – in the late 1800s and early 1900s. In 1917 the Parker-Young Company bought Henry's land and continued logging. In the 1930s the firm sold the parcel to the Federal Government, with the stipulation that they be allowed to harvest timber. The sale added some 100,000 acres to the National Forest, and the company ceased operations in 1946. But today visitors can still see the remains of cutting along old logging roads (called "dugway roads" because they're dug into mountain slopes), bridge abutments, and abandoned rail beds.

– Greeley Ponds Scenic Area and Greeley Ponds Trail (roughly 5 miles, moderately difficult) goes to Upper Greeley Pond, surrounded by old-growth timber and towering cliffs; and the shallow Lower Greeley Pond: both are good for trout fishing.

– Champney Falls Trail (6 miles, easy), named for the 19th-century landscape artist Benjamin Champney.

– Boulder Loop Hike (2 8/10 miles, easy-moderate): offers great views of Mount Chocorua and the Swift River Valley en route.

Side Trip

Moat Mountain is a popular spot for rock hounds to collect quartz crystals. To try your hand, head north on West Side Road and turn onto Passaconaway Road, then left onto High Road and follow the signs. At the parking lot at the end of the road, hike 3/4 mile to the Moat Mountain Site. For information, contact the WMNF.

Turn north off Route 112 onto Route 16 and continue into Conway, tucked in an intervale between the Saco and Swift rivers. Mount Chocorua and the Sandwich Range are to the southwest, and Mount Washington looms to the north. Conway and North Conway owe their growth to two principal factors: art and tourism.

Alternate Route

In Conway, just before the junction of routes 112 and 16, turn north (left) at the traffic light onto West Side Road to bypass the towns of Conway and North Conway and the many shopping outlets that lie between them. This country byway paralleling busy Route 16 passes by two covered bridges (the 1890 **Conway-Saco River Bridge,** and the 1869 **Conway-Swift River Bridge**), **Echo Lake State Park,** and 54-acre **Dahl Sanctuary** on the Saco River before it joins Route 302 just west of Glen. (If you choose this route, turn west (left) onto Route 302 at the **Covered Bridge House B&B** to resume the drive.)

skiing, shopping, and a scenic railway . . . .

By the middle of the 19th century the area was an important center for artists associated with the White Mountain School. The most famous of them, Benjamin Champney, worked here about 1850. Landscape master George Innes and the Hudson River School pioneer Thomas Cole also helped spread word of the region's beauty, which by the late 1800s was attracting an increasing number of tourists whose interests were recreational rather than artistic.

The biggest thing ever to hit the Conways was downhill skiing. In 1936, North Conway businessman Carroll Reed established the country's first open-enrollment ski school at the **Eastern Slope Inn,** and hired Hannes Schneider, an Austrian émigré who had taught the Tyrolean ski troops in the army of his native country. From then on, skiers flocked to New Hampshire to sample the hell-for-leather backcountry delights of Tuckerman Ravine (see Drive 13), and later to patronize growing commercial areas such as Mount Cranmore, Black Mountain, Wildcat, Attitash, Cannon, and Bretton Woods.

The latest chapter in the area's tourism story was written in the 1980s, when the five-mile stretch of Route 16 between Conway and North Conway was transformed into a shopper's paradise and a sprawl opponent's nightmare. It's lined with more than 200 outlet stores, including L.L. Bean, Eddie Bauer, Banana Republic, and April Cornell. (Remember: there's no sales tax in New Hampshire.)

The centerpiece of the bustling town of **North Conway** is the 1874, mansard-roofed depot that marked the end of the line for the "snow trains" that brought skiers into town until 1961. Now the northern terminus for **Conway Scenic Railroad**, the yellow wooden building has its original telegraph and phone equipment and furnishings. The railroad operates seasonal excursions to Conway and Bartlett, using antique coaches and parlor cars. If you're a true railroad buff, you might want to spring for First Class seating aboard the beautifully-restored, 1898 Pullman Parlor-Observation Car *Gertrude Emma*, in service on the Conway line. The train to Bartlett crosses the Frankenstein Trestle in Crawford Notch. Lunch and dinner are served aboard the 1929 dining car Chocorua. (Tables seat four.)

Has Fido always pined for a train ride? He's welcome aboard the Conway Scenic Railroad as long as he's leashed.

Side Trip

Just past the Eastern Slope Inn, turn left onto River Road, continue for two miles, and watch for a dirt road on the left. It's an easy ½- mile walk to Diana's Baths, a series of cascading falls that plummet to potholes alongside Lucy Brook (no swimming: the brook goes into a public water supply). Continue to West Side Road and follow signs to **Echo Lake State Park**, where there's a fine swimming beach and picnic area, and a road that winds for a mile to the top of Cathedral Ledge, a 700-foot vertical wall famous among technical climbers. From here you can see hawks, falcons, and much of the Saco Valley.

Continue north on Route 16 through Intervale. Just north of the village Route 16A, which parallels Route 16 for several miles before rejoining the highway just south of **Glen**, is lined with motels and condominiums.

For more than 20 years, Roger and Nelly Hartmann traveled the world collecting model railroad items. Their collection is on display at the **Hartmann Model Railroad & Toy Museum** – more than 16,000 square feet of space that includes Lionel and American Flyers, HO modular layouts, and handmade train and car displays.

At the intersection of routes 16 and 302, head west on Route 302 into the Saco River Valley. There's a good swimming hole ahead: a few miles down Route 302, turn right onto Jericho Road and continue 4 4/10 miles to the Rocky Branch trailhead. Walk alongside the river back toward the highway for about 50 yards to Rocky Branch Brook, a delightful spot to cool off. For details, see the *White Mountain Guide*, published by the Appalachian Mountain Club.

Note: If you took the West Side Road bypass from Conway, resume the drive below.

The restored, 1850 **Bartlett Covered Bridge** next to the **Covered Bridge House B&B** now houses the Covered Bridge Gift Shoppe.

At **Attitash**, hop aboard the chairlift to the summit and plummet down the 3/4-mile alpine slide on your own wheeled sled, and then cool off on a waterslide. With the **Grand Summit Hotel and Conference Center,** a driving range, mountain bike and hiking trails, horseback riding, and a variety of other activities, the ski area is now a year round resort.

In Bartlett, Bear Notch Road connects with the Kancamagus Highway.

Continue on Route 302. About 3 1/2 miles west, watch for the Nancy Pond trailhead. They're named for the first woman to pass through Crawford Notch. Nancy – her last name is lost to history – had been working in Jefferson in the late 1700s for Colonel Joseph Whipple when she fell in love with one of his servants. The man promised to take her with him to Portsmouth, and he entrusted him with her savings while she went to her nearby home to prepare for the journey. Upon her return, she learned that her lover had fled. Ignoring warnings about traveling alone in the approaching winter, she tried to catch up with him. Trekking through deep snow, she made it through Crawford

Notch, but was found dead – her soaked clothes frozen to her body – alongside the brook later named for her.

The trail goes **to Nancy Brook Virgin Spruce Forest and Scenic Area**, a National Natural Landmark with a 1,600-acre stand of virgin spruce, and then continues to the Pemi Wilderness.

Continue west on Route 302 through Hart's Location, home to the elegant, granite **Notchland Inn**, built in 1862 by Boston photographer Samuel Bemis. The inn is on the site of Abel Crawford's Mount Crawford House (see below), and the restaurant was that hostelry's tavern. Hart's Location has the smallest population in the state – 42, at last count.

Crawford Notch, between Bartlett and Twin Mountain, was accidentally discovered by moose hunter Timothy Nash in 1771. He immediately reported his find to Governor John Wentworth, who was interested in developing roads into the state's interior. The governor agreed to give Nash a tract of land at the northern end of the notch if the backwoodsman could bring a horse south to Portsmouth along the route he had described. Nash and a friend rode, pushed and cajoled a farm horse through Crawford Notch, sometimes using a rope sling to lower the animal over ledges and down steep banks. Nash and his friend got their land grant, and New Hampshire had a wilderness pass through the White Mountains to the upper Connecticut Valley.

The Notch got its name from the family of Abel and Hannah Crawford, who settled on the notch road in 1792 and raised nine children. Crawford, a hunting guide for "gentlemen strangers," must have felt that his home still needed a few more people: he opened it to travelers as the Mount Crawford House in 1852. This was the first hostelry in the notch, and, in its day, one of the most famous in New England.

Just ahead, in 6,000-acre **Crawford Notch State Park**, Route 302 winds for six miles past some of the most magnificent scenery in New England.

Watch on the left for the Arethusa Falls Trail (2 6/10 mile, easy-moderate) to the highest falls in the state, which plummets more than 200 feet. This trail connects with the Ripley Falls Trail, which continues for another 2 1/10 miles to 100-foot-high Ripley Falls.

Just past the trailhead is the **Willey House Historic Site**. It was here, in the fall of 1825, that Samuel Willey, Jr., his family, and two workmen were caught in a violent storm.

Abel Crawford was working near the Willey home when a half-mile portion of the mountain behind the house roared down. He described the event in his *History of the White*

Mountains: "While there they [the Willeys] saw on the west side of the road a small movement of rocks and earth coming down the hill, and it took all before it. They saw, likewise, whole trees coming down, standing upright, for ten rods together, before they would tip over – the whole still moving slowly on, making its way until it had crossed the road, and then on a level surface some distance before it stopped. This grand and awful sight frightened the timid family very much."

The Willeys ran to a nearby shelter. The landslide split just above their house, surged past, and reunited below it. The Willeys were killed, but their house survived intact.

Several trailheads begin here, including the easy, 1/2 -mile Pond Loop Trail.

To the left is Frankenstein Cliff, named for Godfrey Frankenstein, a Cincinnati artist who often painted in this area. Across from the Dry River Campground, the 500-foot-long Frankenstein Trestle, built in 1905 by the Maine Central Railroad to replace the original in 1875, soars 80 feet above Frankenstein Gulf.

Saco Lake, the source of the Saco River, is near the parking lot for the Mount Willard and Avalon trails. Numerous cascades in the notch feed into the Saco, including the Beecher, Pearl, Flume, and Silver: several are visible from the road.

Ahead on the left is **Highland Center at Crawford Notch**, the Appalachian Mountain Club's newest four-season lodge and outdoor education center. The facility offers a wide range of lodgings, hearty meals, and loads of outdoor activities. A number of trails start here.

At the northern end of the notch, there are panoramic views of the Presidential Range from Eisenhower Memorial Wayside Park.

> *The 2 9/10-mile section of the Crawford Path between Route 302 at Crawford Notch and Mount Pierce is believed to be the country's oldest continuously maintained footpath.*

The White Mountain Hiker Shuttle between AMC lodgings and trailheads runs daily from early June through mid-September, and weekends and holidays from mid-September through mid-October. A fare of $16 for AMC members and $18 for nonmembers is charged for a ride of any length. For route information, call 466-2727 or check the AMC website: outdoors.org

grande dame of the mountains.................

Bretton Woods, in a glacial plain at the base of Mount Washington, is home to one of the grandest hotels in the northeast, the **Mount Washington Hotel and Resort**. It's one of two survivors of the White Mountain resort hotels built in the days when wealthy clients arrived by rail – with steamer trunks and servants in tow – to spend the summer. The other, the **Mountain View Grand Hotel & Resort**, is in nearby Whitefield.

The Mount Washington was the creation of railroad speculator Joseph Stickney, who bought the Old Mount Pleasant House and a 10,000-acre tract and, in 1902, opened his spare-no-expense hotel. Built by Italian artisans and laborers who boarded on site throughout the two years of construction, the palatial new resort incorporated steel framework, the latest in plumbing, heating, and electricity, and its own telephone exchange. Mr. Stickney oversaw the triumphant grand opening (as did Ethan Allen Crawford III) and the first two seasons of operation before he died in 1903. The granite, Episcopal Joseph Stickney Memorial Church of the Transfiguration, **on Route 302 just beyond the hotel**, was dedicated to the entrepreneur a few years afterward.

In 1944 the entire hotel was reserved by the U.S. government for the World Monetary Fund Conference, at which representatives of 44 nations shaped the economic framework of the postwar world. The summer-long deliberations resulted in the fixing of the gold standard, the adoption of the U.S. dollar as the benchmark against which other national currencies were valued, and the creation of the World Bank.

Today the 4-season hotel offers activities including golf, tennis, a spa, hiking, and a canopy tour ride that whisks riders high above the trees and slopes. The adjacent 1896 **Bretton Arms Country Inn** provides a more intimate lodging environment. **Bretton Woods Ski Area** is down the road.

Turn right off Route 302 onto Base Road at Fabyan's Station Restaurant and continue for six miles to the **Mount Washington Cog Railway**, an improbable piece of Victorian technology whose locomotives push cars – clanking and wheezing – three miles to the summit of Mount Washington (see Drive 14). The world's "first mountain-climbing cog rail" was invented in 1869 by inventor Sylvester Marsh, who built his railway for $39,500. Dubbed Old Peppersass (because it resembled an old-fashioned peppersauce cruet), the first locomotive was shipped to Littleton and then hauled the last 25 miles piecemeal by oxen. The base station has a visitor center, museum, restaurant, and gift shop.

> *When Sylvester Marsh was granted his state charter to build the Mount Washington Cog Railroad in 1858, one New Hampshire legislator snidely remarked that he should also be permitted to lay tracks to the moon.*

Continue on Route 302 out of Crawford Notch, as the road veers west alongside the Ammonoosuc River, to **Twin Mountain**, a tourist center with numerous budget-priced motels and tourist cabins. **At the intersection of routes 302 and 3, turn north on Route 3 to begin Drive 11, or south on Route 3 to return to I-93.**

information *Area codes are (603) unless otherwise indicated.*

Appalachian Mountain Club (AMC) (617-523-0636), 5 Joy St., Boston, MA 02108. For hut reservations: 466-2727. outdoors.org.

Conway Village Area Chamber of Commerce (447-2639), Rte. 16, Conway 03818. conwaychamber.com

Mt. Washington Valley Chamber of Commerce & Visitors Bureau (356-3171), Village Sq., Rte. 16, N. Conway 03860. mtwashingtonvalley.org

Twin Mountain Chamber of Commerce (846-5408), Box 194, Twin Mountain 03595. twinmountain.org

White Mountain Attractions (800-346-3687), 200 Kancamagus Hwy., N. Woodstock 03262. visitwhitemountains.com

White Mountain National Forest Headquarters (528-8721), 719 N. Main St., Laconia 03246. Visitor Centers: Gateway Visitors Center (745-8720), Exit 32 off I-93, Lincoln; Lincoln Woods (630-5190), Kancamagus Highway, Lincoln. Saco Ranger District (447-5448), Kancamagus Highway, Conway. Open daily in summer. fs.fed.us/r9/white.

lodging

AMC's Highland Center at Crawford Notch (466-2727), Rte. 302, Bretton Woods 03574. 15 lodge rooms with private baths; 19 lodge bunkrooms with shared baths; and a 16-person bunkhouse. Free use of L.L. Bean gear. outdoors.org $-$$

Attitash Grand Summit Hotel and Conference Center (374-1900), Rte. 302, Bartlett 03812. 143 deluxe and condominium-style rooms; health club, heated outdoor pool, spa, fitness center, nursery (by reservation), and restaurants. attitash.com $$-$$$

The Bartlett Inn (374-2353), Rte. 302, Bartlett 03812. Informal family complex surrounded by the WMNF range from cozy rooms (with private baths) in the inn to romantic whirlpool rooms with wood burning fireplaces to family-size housekeeping cottages. Pets ($) in cottages with prior notice. Outdoor hot tub, heated in-ground pool. Breakfast included. bartlettinn.com $$-$$$

Bretton Arms Inn (278-3000), Rte. 302, Bretton Woods. 34 spacious and elegantly furnished rooms in a handsomely restored inn on the grounds of the Mount Washington Hotel. The intimate dining room serves dinner and a complimentary breakfast. mountwashingtonresort.com $$$-$$$$

The Buttonwood Inn (356-2625), Mt. Surprise Rd., N. Conway 03860. 1820s farmhouse on 5 secluded acres has 10 cozy guest rooms with Shaker furnishings and private baths: two have gas fireplaces. Outdoor heated pool and gardens. Breakfast included. buttonwoodinn.com $$-$$$

Carlson's Lodge (846-5501), Rte. 302, Twin Mountain 03598. Spacious motel rooms with all the modern conveniences. Amenities include an outdoor pool, game room (pool and ping pong), sitting room with woodstove and kids' play area. Continental breakfast included. carlsonlodge.com $-$$

Covered Bridge House B&B (383-9109), Rte. 302, Glen 03838. 5 guest rooms (4 with private bath) in a lovely Colonial Revival house overlooking the Saco River. Outdoor hot tub. coveredbridgehouse.com $-$$

Cranmore Inn (356-5502), 80 Kearsarge St., N. Conway 03860. The valley's oldest continuously operated inn (since 1863) has 16 antiques-filled rooms on the 2nd and 3rd floors in the main building, and 1- and 2-bedroom housekeeping units in The Stables. Some have shared baths; all have a/c. Fireplaced common room, heated pool, and 7-person hot tub. Breakfast included. cranmoreinn.com $-$$

Cranmore Mountain Lodge (356-2044), 859 Kearsarge Rd., N. Conway 03860. The one-time home of Babe Ruth is a mix of country inn, farm, and resort, with 20 units (including 4 suites; 2 with kitchenettes), all with private baths, and all but 1 with TV. Pool, Jacuzzi, tennis, mountain bike and hiking trails. Breakfast included. cranmoremountainlodge.com $$-$$$

The Darby Field Inn & Restaurant (447-2181), 185 Chase Hill Rd., Albany 03818. 1826 farmhouse 6 miles from N. Conway has 9 spacious, handsomely furnished rooms and suites (including several with fireplaces), and fine candlelight dining. Breakfast included; MAP available. darbyfield.com $$-$$$

Eastern Slope Resort (356-8621), 2760 Main St., Rte. 16, N. Conway. National Register of Historic Places complex has a variety of accommodations, including inn rooms, townhouses, suites, 2- and 3-bedroom units, and cottages. Indoor pool, outdoor hot tub, game and exercise rooms, clay tennis courts, and spa. easternslopeinn.com $$-$$$$

Hostelling International White Mountains (447-1001), 36 Washington St., Conway 03818. Classic hostel accommodations in a renovated farmhouse include 5 dorm rooms with 6 bunks in each room, and 4 rooms that sleep up to 5. Shared baths. Linens provided; fully-equipped kitchen. conwayhostel.com $

The Mount Washington Hotel and Resort (278-1000), Rte. 302, Bretton Woods 03575. Accommodations range from basic rooms to tower suites in the main building; motel-style accommodations in The Lodge; and 1-5 bedroom townhouses. Guests have access to a recreation facility with an indoor pool, Jacuzzi, and racquetball courts. Restaurants; MAP available. mountwashington.com $$$-$$$$

Northlander Motel (846-5520), Rte. 3, Twin Mountain 03595. Standard rooms, suites, efficiencies, and cottages. Heated pool, playground. Pets welcome. northlandermotel.com $

The Notchland Inn (374-6131), Rte. 302, Harts Location 03812. Historic mansion on 100 acres has 12 rooms and suites with wood-burning fireplaces, and 3 cottages (pets welcome in cottages). Breakfast (included) and dinner (see "Restaurants" below) is served in the elegant dining room. MAP available. notchland.com $$$-$$$$

Perry's Motel & Cottages (356-2214), Rte. 16A, Intervale. An old-fashioned, kid-friendly complex with basic housekeeping and non-housekeeping cottages, motel rooms; heated pool, huge playground, picnic tables, and grills. perrysmotel.com $$

Stonehurst Manor (356-3113), Rte. 16, N. Conway 03860. Circa 1900 mansion on 33 secluded acres has 24 elegant rooms (7 with fireplaces), fully equipped housekeeping condos, an outdoor pool, and a restaurant ($$-$$$) featuring wood-fired pizzas and pit-smoked prime rib. Pet friendly ($). MAP available. stonehurstmanor.com $$-$$$

The White Mountain Hotel and Resort (356-7100), West Side Rd., N. Conway 03860. Cathedral and White Horse Ledges form the backdrop for this full-service resort with 80 luxurious rooms and suites. Restaurant (see "Restaurants" below) and English-style pub, championship golf course, tennis, and health club. whitemountainhotel.com $$-$$$

off the drive

Mountain View Grand Resort & Spa (866-484-3843), 120 Mountain View Rd., Whitefield 03598. Built in 1865, one of the White Mountains' last grand hotels has undergone an extensive restoration. Rooms range from small to spectacular; amenities include a spa, 9-hole golf course, and several restaurants. mountainviewgrand.com $$$-$$$$

restaurants

AMC Highland Center at Crawford Notch (278-4453), Rte. 302, Bretton Woods. Breakfast and lunch buffets; family style dinner Sat.-Thurs.; buffet Fri. Beer and wine available. $

The Bernerhof (383-39132), Rte. 302, Glen. European-style inn with comfortable, antiques-furnished guest rooms ($$) has long been well known for contemporary and middle European cuisine. Specialties include *delice de Gruyere* (cheese croquettes), *raclette*, and Wiener schnitzel. Taste of the Mountains Cooking School classes here. bernerhofinn.com $$$

Conway Scenic Railroad (Reservations: 356-5251 or online), N. Conway. Lunch is served on the 11:30 a.m. and 1:30 p.m. departures. Dinner is served on "sunset" trips. Meals are provided by Crawford's Pub & Grill. conwayscenic.com

Crawford's Pub & Grill, Attitash Grand Summit Hotel (374-1900), Rte. 302, Bartlett. Casual dining with pub-style fare, pizza, and entrees such as pork osso buco, wild mushroom ravioli, and rotisserie chicken. $$

Delaney's Hole in the Wall (356-7776), 2966 White Mt. Hwy., N. Conway. Family-friendly spot serves up terrific baby back ribs and chicken wings alongside a large selection of freshly made sushi. Live music Wed. nights. $-$$

Elvio's Pizzeria and Restaurant (356-3307), Main St., N. Conway. Popular for pizza, subs, pasta, and daily specials. L & D. $

Fabyan's Station Restaurant (278-2222), Rte. 302, Bretton Woods. American fare and pub snacks, including broiled fish, burgers, and wings, in a beautifully restored former railroad station. L & D. $-$$

Ledges Dining Room at White Mountain Hotel and Resort (356-7100), 2560 West Side Rd., N. Conway. Well-prepared and beautifully presented dishes are served up alongside magnificent views in this handsome room. But highlights of the week are the Fri. night seafood buffet ($$$$), and Sun. brunch. B, L & D. $$$

May Kelly's Cottage Restaurant and Pub (356-7005), 3002 White Mt. Hwy. (Rte. 16), N. Conway. The menu at this Irish bar and restaurant looking out on Whitehorse Ledge includes meatloaf, mixed grill, and shepherd's pie. Music Fri. from 8 p.m., and Sun. from 3 p.m. $$

Moat Mountain Smokehouse & Brewing Co. (356-6381), 3378 White Mt. Hwy., N. Conway. Award-winning ales and lagers brewed on site, along with an extensive menu that includes BBQ ribs, burgers, pizza, and quesadillas. L & D daily. $-$$

The Notchland Inn (374-6131), Rte. 302, Hart's Location. A 5-course candlelight dinner is served Wed.-Sun. most of the year, and Tues.-Sun. during foliage. The seasonal menu might include an appetizer of spinach pine nut ravioli, seared duck breast, and caramel pecan tart. $$$$

Peach's (356-5860), 2506 White Mt. Hwy. (Rte. 302), N. Conway. Hearty breakfast might include banana cream or apple butterscotch pancakes; lunch offerings such as tahini salad, and bacon & pesto paninis (or breakfast, which is served all day). 7 a.m.-2:30 p.m. $

Red Parka Pub (383-4344), Rte. 302, Glen. For more than 30 years, this family-oriented spot has been popular for steaks, ribs, and poultry, and a huge salad bar. The tavern (opens at 3:30 p.m. weekdays, 3 p.m. on weekends), which serves the full restaurant menu, has live entertainment. D nightly. $-$$

Scottish Lion Inn and Restaurant (356-6381), Rte. 16, N. Conway. Scottish, American and European specialties include prime rib, steak and mushroom pie, and finnan haddie. Also, 8 tastefully decorated rooms with private baths and a/c. ($$). L & D, & Sun. brunch. $$-$$$

The 1785 Inn (356-9025), Rte. 16, Intervale. Award-winning dining in an historic inn overlooking the Saco River. The extensive appetizer menu includes a tableside Caesar salad and crab imperial; entrees such as roast duck and rack of lamb. B& D. $$$

A Taste of Thai (356-7624), 1561 White Mt. Hwy (Rte. 16), Conway. Ably prepared and nicely presented dishes in an unassuming spot tucked between the outlet stores. The chefs make food as mild or spicy as patrons wish. $$

attractions

Dahl Sanctuary (New Hampshire Audubon Society: 224-9909). Rte. 16, Conway. A 54-acre property with 1,800 ft. of unspoiled shoreline on the Saco River, and a gentle, 1-mi. trail.

Conway Historical Society (447-5551), Eastman-Lord House Museum, 100 Main St., Conway. 12 period rooms from 1820 to 1945; and a walking tour brochure of Conway Village. Memorial Day-Labor Day Wed.-Sat. Call for hrs.

Conway Scenic Railroad (356-5251), Rte. 16, N. Conway. 1- to 5-hr. excursions to Conway, Bartlett, or through Crawford Notch; lunch and dinner excursions. Apr.-Dec. Schedule: conwayscenic.com

Echo Lake State Park (356-2672), off Rte. 302, Conway. No pets.

Hartmann Model Railroad & Toy Museum (356-9922), Rtes. 16/302, Glen. July & Aug.; June, Sept. & Oct., Wed.-Mon.; Nov.-May Fri.-Mon.

Mt. Washington Cog Railway (846-5404), Base Rd. off Rte. 302, Bretton Woods. Mid-June-Oct,: advance reservations recommended. Round trip takes 3 hrs., including a 20-minute stop at the summit. In summer, trains leave on the hour. Schedule: thecog.com

Weather Discovery Center (356-2137), 2779 Main St. (Rte. 16), N. Conway. Learn about the Mt. Washington Observatory before heading up the mountain at this interactive learning center. Late May-early Sept. Free.

activities

Attitash Alpine Slide, Waterslides & Scenic Sky Ride (374-2368), Rte. 302, Bartlett. Mid-June-Labor Day; weekends May-mid-June & Labor Day-early Oct.

Bretton Woods Canopy Tour (278-4947), Mt. Washington Resort, Rte. 302, Bretton Woods.

Farm by the River B&B and Stables (Stables: 356-6640; inn: 356-2694), 2555 West Side Rd., N. Conway. Horse drawn carriage, wagon, horseback, and pony rides (the last by appointment for ages 2-8). Ride & stay packages at the b&b, with 9 comfortable rooms in a farmhouse on 70 acres. ($$-$$$)

International Mountain Climbing School (356-7064), 2733 Main St., N. Conway. Rock and ice climbing, family climbs; Mt. Washington ascents.

League of New Hampshire Craftsmen (356-2441), Rte. 16, N. Conway. Handcrafts by some of the state's finest artisans.

Loon Mountain Resort (745-8111), 60 Loon Mt. Rd., Lincoln.

Mount Washington Valley Theater Company (356-5776), Eastern Slope Inn Playhouse, Main St., N. Conway. Live Broadway musicals presented by professionals at an historic, 1887 playhouse. Schedule: mwvtheatre.org

North Country Angler (356-6000), Rte. 16, N. Conway. Fly fishing equipment, guide, and advice. Up-to-the-minute information on where and what they're biting.

Northern Extremes (356-4718), 1946 White Mt. Hwy. (Rte. 16), N. Conway. Canoe and kayak rental, shuttle, and white water instruction on the Saco River.

Pemi Valley Excursions (745-2744), Main St., Lincoln. 2 ½ - 3 hr. moose and wildlife tours.

Peter Limmer and Sons (356-5378), Rte. 16A, Intervale. Superbly crafted – some customers say the best in the world – custom and stock hiking boots. Allow 1 hr. for a fitting.

Pirate's Cove Adventure Golf (356-8807), Rte. 16, N. Conway. 18 creative holes of miniature golf. May-mid-Oct.

Ragged Mountain Equipment (356-3042), Rte. 16 & 302, Intervale. Factory store with outdoor equipment clothing and fabric, including their own "Made in Intervale" line.

Zeb's General Store (356-9294), 2675 Main St., North Conway. Everything from honey to hot sauce to penny candy to hammocks, and a whole lot of "mooseabilia".

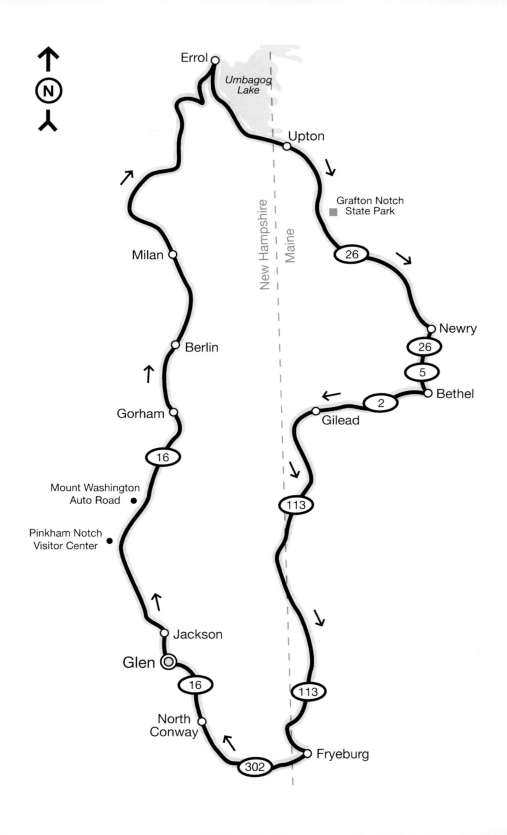

Pinkham Notch, Mount Washington, and Northern Woods and Waters

146 miles

major attractions

- Pinkham Notch
- Mount Washington Auto Road
- Lake Umbagog National Wildlife Refuge
- Mount Washington State Park
- Evans Notch
- Grafton Notch State Park
- Bethel

*D*rive north in the shadow of the Presidential Range, heading into Pinkham Notch as it threads past towering Mount Washington, New England's loftiest peak, and the exhilarating auto route to the summit. The route continues into New Hampshire's North Woods, once the seat of a logging empire, and follows the wild Androscoggin River past the Lake Umbagog National Wildlife Refuge and into Maine's Grafton Notch State Park. South beyond the handsome town of Bethel the route passes through scenic Evans Notch before returning to New Hampshire.

Note: Vehicles parked on White Mountain National Forest land are required to display a parking pass, unless the parking area is a designated free parking zone. Passes are available at area businesses and National Forest Ranger Stations.

Head north out of Glen on Route 16 into the heart of the **White Mountain National Forest**, with the Presidential Range to the west, and Wildcat and Carter ridges to the east. The road through **Pinkham Notch** (named for Joseph Pinkham who settled here in 1790), winds alongside the eastern flank of 6,288-foot Mount Washington, highest point in New England, called "Agiochook"(the dwelling place of the Great Spirit) by Native Americans. It passes by campgrounds, trailheads, and the glacially scoured Great Gulf Wilderness, framed by some of the highest of the Presidentials.

> *If you're traveling with small kids and in a hurry to hit the road, you might want to create a diversion at the junction of Rtes. 302 and 26 in Glen.* Story Land, *a small but engaging theme park, is right here and hard to miss.*

Turn right onto Rte. 16A through the 1876 covered Honeymoon Bridge to **Jackson**, a classic New England settlement built around a green at the foot of the Wildcat Brook rapids. The town is home to an 18-hole golf course as well as the non-profit **Jackson Ski Touring Foundation**, a cross-country skiing center with 95 miles of finely groomed trails, which connect many of the area's inns and shops. **The Wentworth Inn**, a small "grand" hotel in the village center, has been one of the area's premier lodgings for more than 150 years.

North on Route 16, at the **Glen Ellis Falls Scenic Area**, a short trail passes through a tunnel under the highway and down a stone walkway and stairs, built in the 1930s by the Civilian Conservation Corps (CCC), to a 66-foot waterfall. A steep, 3 2/10-mile hike up the Glen Boulder Trail goes to the base of the huge glacial erratic – a boulder left by the retreating ice sheet – visible from the highway.

> *According to legend, the daughter of a local Indian chief promised her hand in marriage to one man even though she had fallen in love with another. To set things right, the chief proclaimed that his daughter would go to the man who could shoot an arrow closest to the center of a target. When her lover lost the contest, the couple fled. Unable to escape, they held hands and jumped into Glen Ellis Falls. Today, some say that when the conditions are right they see the star-crossed lovers, still holding hands, in the mist.*

Continue to Pinkham Notch Visitor Center and the AMC Pinkham Notch Camp.

> *A group of Bostonians interested in hiking, climbing and the natural history of the mountains at their northern doorstep founded the AMC in 1876. (Despite the orga-*

nization's name, its prime focus always has been the White Mountains.) In 1888 the Club built the first of its huts at Madison Spring, in a col, or saddle, above the walls of Madison Gulf between Mount Madison and Mount Adams. Madison Spring, replaced after a fire in 1941, remains the northernmost in what became a string of eight AMC huts, not counting the base camp and North Country headquarters of the Club at Pinkham Notch. The others, completed between 1904 and 1964, are: Carter Notch, east of Pinkham between Wildcat Mountain and Carter Dome; Lakes of the Clouds, at the 5,000 ft. level on Mount Washington; Greenleaf, on the shoulder of Mount Lafayette; Mizpah Spring, on Mount Clinton; Zealand Falls and Galehead, on the northern fringes of the Pemigewasset Wilderness; and Lonesome Lake, in Franconia Notch. The huts are between three and six miles apart –approximately a day's mountain hiking – and all offer meals and bunk space. The club also maintains the Highland Center at Crawford Notch (see Drive 12), Cold River Camp (see Evans Notch below), as well as several lodgings in Maine.

THE AMC quite naturally found itself involved in maintaining the network of trails that links the huts; over the years the Club has evolved an informal yet deeply rooted position of co-stewardship with the Forest Service in the White Mountains. It is involved in environmental research and occasional lobbying, in the training of volunteers, and in instructional programs ranging from rock climbing to telemark skiing to whitewater canoeing. The AMC maintains a search-and-rescue staff of trained volunteers: the core of this group is the "notchwatchers" on 24-hour duty at Pinkham.

Parking at Pinkham Notch Visitor Center is free, and several trails begin here, including a ¾-mile hike from the parking lot to **Crystal Cascade**, a lovely mountain waterfall (follow the Tuckerman Ravine Trail until you see steps on the right leading to the Cascade overlook); and the moderately difficult, 4 8/10-mile **Tuckerman Ravine Trail** to Hermit Lake at the mouth of Tuckerman Ravine. Every year the large, glacial cirque, famous for its spectacular scenery, collects an average of 55 feet of snow which blows off the Presidential Range, making it a prime destination from late March through May for backcountry skiers who come to challenge themselves at "Tucks," with its 40-foot freefall drop over the headwall. The trail is one of the most heavily traveled in the White Mountains: up to 3,000 people may visit the ravine on a spring day. The number of memorial markers along the trail is a testament to the difficulty of the ravine and the sometimes-treacherous weather conditions (avalanches are common in spring). Be sure to check conditions before hiking or skiing here. Inquire at the lodge about overnight accommodations.

Just to the north is **Wildcat Mountain Ski Area,** whose gondola whisks sightseers to the top of the mountain from late May through mid-October. On the area's new ZipRider thrill ride, riders soar above the mountains at 45 miles per hour seated in harnesses clipped to a cable.

to the rooftop of New England . . . .

Continue a few miles to the turnoff for the Mount Washington Auto Road, the world's first mountain toll road. It was completed in 1861 after seven years of off-and-on labor involving horses, oxen, and human muscle. The eight-mile route to the top was originally traversed by stout Concord coaches, pulled by eight horses each, which left from the **Glen House**, across from the entrance (now, hired vans leave from here in spring, summer and fall; in winter, sightseeing tours leave from the nearby **Great Glen Trails Outdoor Center**). Private auto travel began in 1908, and in 1912 the company operating the road began using gasoline-powered coaches to carry passengers disinclined to trust their own driving skills, and hotel guests who had left their Pierce-Arrows at home. Today the Auto Road (toll), safe and smoothly graded, is open between mid- May and October (weather permitting).

> *In 1998, Canadian Frank Sprongl set the current record of 6 minutes, 41.99 seconds, base to summit, in the Mount Washington Hill climb Auto Race. His ride was an Audi S2.*

The oft-repeated cliché is that 6,288-foot Mount Washington has the "worst weather in the world," and in terms of sheer dramatic changeability this probably is true. The South Pole just stays consistently miserable; nobody freezes there because they dressed for a lark in 70° weather and got caught in an ice storm. Yet this is what can and does happen on Mount Washington.

If there is a single instance that has contributed more than any other to the mountain's reputation for climatic extremes, it is the one that occurred on Thursday, April 12, 1934: instruments at the summit observatory recorded a wind speed of 231 mph, the greatest ever documented on the planet. Although the wind speed since then has never recorded higher than 200 mph, the mountain's reputation is safely entrenched.

> *Among workers at the Mount Washington Observatory, there's an informal "Century Club." The qualifications? Venture outside when summit winds exceed 100 miles per hour.*

P.T. Barnum called the view from the top "the second greatest show on earth." If you're fortunate enough to be at the summit on a clear day, you'll be able to see sunlight glint off the Atlantic at Portland Harbor, 75 miles to the east; looking in the other direction, you should be able to make out Mount Mansfield in Vermont, and Whiteface and Mount Marcy in the Adirondacks (Marcy is 139 miles away).

The Observatory is in the contemporary Sherman Adams State Park Building, part of

Mount Washington State Park. In addition to a snack bar and gift shop, the building also houses the **Summit Museum,** with exhibits on the natural and human history of the mountain. Be sure to visit the restored **Tip Top House,** the oldest building on the mountain, which opened in 1853 as a hotel (it is now a state historic site).

The Four Thousand Footer Club

Want to become a member one of New Hampshire's most exclusive –and least formal – clubs? All you have to do is climb to the top of each of the state's 48 mountains which are 4,000 feet or higher. Then send your name to the Appalachian Mountain Club (see "Information" below), and they'll send you a certificate.

Several hiking trails begin at the **Dolly Copp Campground,** one of the largest campgrounds in the National Forest System. The "Imp Profile" of Imp Mountain, one of the peaks of the Carter Range to the east, is visible from here.

An Independent Woman

The campground is on the site of a farm owned by early pioneers Dolly and Hayes Copp, who came here as newlyweds in 1831. Dolly was known throughout the region for the fine linen and woolen articles she produced, many of which she sold to tourists staying at the nearby Glen House. On the day of the couple's Golden Jubilee, she proclaimed, "Hayes is well enough. But fifty years is long enough for any woman to live with a man." That day, the two divided their possessions and she moved to Auburn, Maine, where she remained until her death.

How the White Mountains got their names

Ernest Poole, in The Great White Hills of New Hampshire, *relates how the Presidentials were named: "Ethan Allan [Crawford] was to become our first great climber, trail builder and mountain guide ... Ethan and his father blazed the famous Crawford Path [to provide hikers with an easier access to the summit of Mount Washington] and, as the climbers then increased, with them went Ethan Allan as guide. In 1820 ... Crawford, 'loaded equal to a pack horse' with heavy wraps and food supplies, including 'a plenty of what some call Black Betts or O-b-Joyful,' took up a big party of seven. On reaching the summit of Washington, they named the neighboring peaks Madison, Adams, Jefferson, Monroe, Franklin and Pleasant, toasting and cheering each one. Louder and louder grew the cheers till at last, with a two-hundred-pound drunk leaning heavy on their loaded guide, they made the long descent to camp by nine o'clock that night."*

Gorham, in a valley at the confluence of the Androscoggin and Peabody Rivers, and at the junction of routes 16 and 2, has been a base for those planning to explore the northern White Mountains since 1851, when the St. Lawrence & Atlantic Railroad first delivered tourists here. This history is chronicled in the **Gorham Historical Society & Railroad Museum.** Moderately priced motels and fast-food restaurants line Main Street.

The Gorham Mountaineer, *August 25, 1882: "What girls' lives were like 60 years before: ... They learned to eat green apples and green cucumbers, dried salt pork, boiled potatoes. They ran barefoot, often times until old enough to earn a pair of calfskin shoes. Their clothing was thin, but they had an abundance of exercise. They climbed about the barn after hen's eggs, up an apple tree after fruit like squirrels, and over fences like dogs ... They paddled about in the neighboring brook and never thought of catching cold ... They learned to spin and weave. They attended school, but usually did not learn much for it was thought that they did not need to know much to become wise mothers. ..."*

Continue north out of Gorham on Route 16. Just north of the Gorham city limits is **Nansen Ski Jump.** Erected in 1936, and once the largest in the eastern U.S., it has a 170-foot steel frame and is 260 feet long. It was closed in 1988. Nansen Ski Club and Touring Center, the country's oldest ski club, has trails at **Milan Hill State Park.**

Tiny Milan (pronounced MY-lan) is the headquarters for **North Woods Rafting,** which offers "a variety of rafting programs for the young, old, brave, and timid. ..." throughout the region. And indeed, patrons can opt for adventures ranging from a Class III whitewater rafting trip down the Androscoggin River to a pontoon boat tour on Lake Umbagog (see below).

shades of logging days

Continue north to Berlin (pronounced BER-lin), "The City That Trees Built," at the confluence of the Dead and Androscoggin Rivers. The trees in that epithet were the ones cut down to feed the region's pulp mills, but the local paper industry has all but disappeared. In the industry's heyday, the immigrants who came from around the world to work here built some wonderful buildings, including the onion-domed, Eastern Orthodox Church of the Holy Resurrection (on the National Register of Historic Places) at 20 Petrograd Street; the Stick-style Congregational Church of Christ on Main Street; and St. Anne's Church at 58 Church Street. **Northern Forest Heritage Park,** "celebrating the working forest," encompasses the Historic Brown Company House, an operating blacksmith shop, visitor center, and riverside amphitheater for concerts, ethnic festivals, and logging competitions. The park also offers historic boat tours of the Androscoggin River.

As you continue north out of town watch for boom piers in the river: a series of them – chains of logs linked end to end, from pier to pier – permitted log drivers to divide the logs and channel them to paper companies in Berlin.

The road hugs the west bank of the Androscoggin as you continue north. From Dummer, it follows alongside a portion of the **Northern Forest Canoe Trail**, a 740-mile route (including 55 miles of portages) that connects the major watersheds across the Adirondacks and northern New England. It stretches from Old Forge, New York, through Vermont, Quebec, and New Hampshire, to Fort Kent, Maine.

Thirteen Mile Wood Scenic Area, designated a "Watchable Wildlife corridor" by the state of New Hampshire, offers some of the state's finest trout fishing and whitewater canoeing. **Androscoggin Wayside Park**, on a bluff overlooking the river, is a delightful spot for a picnic.

Errol, on the Androscoggin River in the Upper Androscoggin Valley, is in the heart of the Northern Forest – a vast swath of hardwood trees such as maple and beech, and the boreal conifers spruce and pine. The tiny lumbering and farming village has a few lodgings and restaurants (plan to eat dinner early), and an airplane sightseeing service.

Errol's major tourist attraction is the 13,000-acre **Lake Umbagog National Wildlife Refuge**, dedicated to conserving the area's wetlands and protecting migratory birds. The refuge encompasses the 8,700-acre lake, and is home to bald eagles, as well as a wide variety of other birds, including ospreys, loons, and 25 species of warblers, kingfishers, and blue herons. Mink, otter, and moose are just a few of the refuge's year-round residents. **Saco Bound** has an outpost here, and runs several programs, including a Class II and III rafting trip on the Pontook Rapids, a half-day adventure camp, and a paddle down the Androscoggin River. **Northern Waters Outfitters** offers kayak tours on the Androscoggin, pontoon boat tours, rafting, and canoeing in the wildlife refuge.

Side Trip

Detour north 5 1/2 miles past Errol to visit Refuge headquarters, open most weekdays and some summer weekends. The 1/3-mile-long, handicapped-accessible **Magalloway River Trail** is about a mile north of the headquarters.

Umbagog, which laps across the border into Maine, is named for an Abenaki word meaning "clear lake or water." One of its most unusual features is Floating Island, a mass of vegetation, which moves according to wind direction. The lake, at the head of the Androscoggin River, was once the collecting point for logs floated down river from the North Woods. When the melting snows raised the water levels, the timber would be herded down the river by men with caulked boots using the long, jam-breaking peaveys or "cant dogs."

The Legend of Chief Metallak

Metallak, the last chief of the Coosuc people and himself the son of a chief, moved with his bride and his tribe to the shores of the Androscoggin. Although he built a reputation for fearlessness, his people sickened and died off and his children moved away. When his wife died he took her by canoe down the Androscoggin (then "Ameroscoggin"), through rapids and whirlpools, to an island, and there buried her and stayed by her grave until years later, when hunters found him very ill and took him to Stewartstown. Metallak Island in Lake Umbagog is named in his honor.

. . . .

Jigger Johnson, a logger's logger and northern New Hampshire legend, "went into the woods" at the age of 12. Just 5 feet 6 inches tall, he fought his way up to the position of boss and threatened to kill anyone who didn't do his job right. In his book The Great White Hills of New Hampshire, Ernest Poole describes him:

"When stripped, his whole body showed the scars left by scores of calked boots; but men left his head alone, for his bite was swift and his teeth were strong. He is said to have bitten off a man's ear and spit it out when the fight was done. When once with his crew he went into Berlin and got thoroughly soused, some of his men laid for him on the dark road back to camp and 'calked' him well and, with both his arms and legs broken, left him for dead. But Jigger managed to wriggle and roll to a neighboring pigsty, rolled into manure to keep warm and so slept off his drunk, was found by a forest ranger and taken to a hospital whence a month later he emerged limping a bit but still going strong."

on into Maine . . . .

As the Androscoggin flows out of Errol it heads into Maine to join the Kennebec River on its way to the Atlantic Ocean. This drive, too, heads into Maine: **at the junction of routes 16 and 26 turn southeast onto Route 26**. Two miles past the turn watch for a scenic overlook, which offers magnificent mountain views.

Route 26 passes a huge swath of the wildlife refuge, continues through the rustic town of Upton, and passes **Paradise Point Cottages** before descending into the magnificent **Grafton Notch State Park**, a 3,192-acre realm of waterfalls, hiking trails, and scenic vistas. Several of the attractions, such as Screw Auger Falls and Mother Walker Falls, require little or no walking. But from the top of the viewing platform at the pinnacle of Old Speck Mountain (8-mile round trip hike), hikers will be rewarded with vistas of Maine's Mahoosuc Range to the south and east, and the White Mountains to the west. The hike to Table Rock (2 1/2 mile loop) also offers spectacular views.

About ½ mile after leaving Grafton Notch, watch on the left for a large white farmhouse and a parking area for the 24-acre **Wight Brook Nature Preserve,** home to Step Falls, one of the state's highest waterfalls. A short and easy path leads to its base; but for a truly magnificent view, take the longer and steeper trail to the top. The natural pools that have formed here are terrific places to cool off. The Maine Nature Conservancy stewards the property.

At the intersection with routes 2/5/26, stay on Route 26 toward Bethel.

Side Trip

About three miles after the intersection, turn right toward **Sunday River Ski Area** and continue approximately four miles, bearing right at the fork onto Sunday River Road to visit the much-photographed **Artist's Covered Bridge.** Built in 1872, the 87-foot Paddleford truss bridge spans the Sunday River.

Back on Route 26, continue into Bethel, one of the state's prettiest and most historic villages. **The Bethel Historical Society's Regional History Center** on Broad Street is a good place to begin a visit: it provides information on the area's rich history as well as the 38 structures (many private residences) in the **National Historic District.** Built between 1774 and the 1920s, they range from the stately 1813 Federal-style Dr. Moses Mason House, which serves as the Society's headquarters, to the 1912-13 **Bethel Inn,** one of the area's premier lodgings.

Bethel's proximity to Sunday River Ski Area and several mountain ranges have helped to establish it as a premier resort destination. But equally important to the town's development was the founding, in 1947, of the NTL Institute, an internationally renowned center for programs in personal interaction and group dynamics. The Institute, along with Gould Academy, founded in 1836, help give Bethel a cosmopolitan flair (and an excellent selection of restaurants and lodgings) unusual in a town of its size (approximately 2,600).

Head west out of Bethel on Route 2 to the left-hand turn in Gilead onto Route 113, a Maine Scenic Byway through **Evans Notch**. The most scenic time of year here is foliage season, when boughs of gold form a canopy over the narrow road as it winds its way along the Wild River, through mountain passes, alongside waterfalls, and past roaring streams. But this tiny Maine portion of the White Mountain National Forest is a gem at any time of the year, and a particular favorite of snow shoers in winter, when the road is closed. For those who want to prolong their visit, the AMC maintains **Cold River Camp**, a compound of 25 cabins that sleep one to six people, complete with kerosene lamps, fireplaces, and bathhouses.

Ready for a swim? Just a short distance after turning off onto Route 113, watch for a suspension bridge in Hastings. There's a nice sandy beach, but no lifeguard.

At the intersection with Route 302, in Fryeburg, turn west (right) back into New Hampshire and then continue on Route 302, which merges with Route 16 north through North Conway back to Glen (see Drive 14 for Conway and North Conway).

For more than 150 years the Fryeburg Fair has been one of the preeminent country fairs in New England, and it shows no signs of slowing down. For one week (late September-early October) locals and tourists pack in for activities such as ox pulls, sheep judging, harness racing, and flower shows. For information: fryeburgfair.org

information

Androscoggin Valley Chamber of Commerce (603-752-6060), 961 Main St., Berlin, NH 03570. androscogginvalleychamber.com

Appalachian Mountain Club (AMC) and Pinkham Notch Visitor Center: (603-466-2727). outdoors.org

Bethel Area Chamber of Commerce (207-824-2282), 8 Station Place, Bethel, ME 04217. bethelmaine.com

Evans Notch Visitor Information, White Mountain National Forest (207-824-2134), 16 Mayville Rd. (Rte. 2), Bethel, ME 04217. fs.fed.us/r9/forests/white_mountain/contact/info_centers.php

Grafton Notch: Maine State Parks (207-287-3821); maine.gov/doc/parks

Jackson Area Chamber of Commerce. (603-383-9356), P.O. Box 304, Jackson, NH 03846. jacksonnh.com

Maine Nature Conservancy (207-729-5181), 14 Maine St., Brunswick, ME 04011. nature.org

Mt. Washington Valley Visitors Bureau (603-356-3171), Box 2300, N. Conway, NH 03860. mtwashingtonvalley.org

Northern Forest Canoe Trail (802-496-2285), P.O. Box 565, Waitsfield, VT 05673. northernforestcanoetrail.org

Umbagog Area Chamber of Commerce (603-482-3906). visitlakeumbagog.com

White Mountain National Forest Information Center (603-466-2713), 300 Glen Rd., Rte. 16, Gorham, NH 03581. fs.fed.us/r9/forests/white_mountain

lodging

Akers Pond Inn, Hotel & Cabin Rental (603-482-3471), 820 Colebrook Rd. (Rte. 26), Errol, NH 03579. Simple, comfortable lodgings geared to outdoor enthusiasts. Guests have use of paddleboats and canoes on the 300-acre pond. Continental breakfast. akerspondinn.com $

Cold River Camp: (see AMC Information above)

Bethel Hill B&B (207-824-2461), 66 Broad St., Bethel, ME 04217. 3 spacious suites in an antiques-filled home in the Historic District. All have sitting areas, private baths, whirlpool tubs, and wi-fi. Full country breakfast. bethelhill.com $$-$$$

Bethel Inn Resort (207-824-2175), on the Common, Bethel, ME 04217. A classic New England resort on 200 acres in the heart of town. Amenities include a golf course, outdoor heated pool, spa, and fitness center. bethelinn.com $$$-$$$$

Eagle Mountain House (603-383-9111), 179 Carter Notch Rd., Jackson, NH 03846. National Register of Historic Places hotel has 96 rooms and suites, a 9-hole golf course, tennis courts, heated pool, and a wraparound verandah overlooking Wildcat River and Carter Notch. B&B, MAP, and packages. Dining room serves classic New England fare. eaglemt.com $$-$$$

Errol Motel and Efficiencies (603-482-3256), Main St. (Rte. 26), Errol, NH 03579. Clean, comfortable, and simple; kitchenettes available. errol-motel.com $

Inn at Jackson (603-383-4321), Thorn Hill Rd., Jackson, NH 03846. Landmark b&b designed by architect Stanford White and built in 1902 by the Baldwin piano family has 14 spacious rooms with bath (5 with fireplaces), and a hot tub/Jacuzzi. Breakfast included. innatjackson.com $$-$$$

Inn at Thorn Hill (603-383-4242), Thorn Hill Rd., Jackson, NH 03846. Romantic, 1895 Victorian inn, also designed by Stanford White, overlooking the village has 16 rooms in the main inn, and 6 rooms in 3 cottages and a carriage house. The dining room specializes in New England fusion cuisine and has an excellent wine list. B&B or MAP. innatthornhill.com $$$

Paradise Point Cottages on Lake Umbagog (603-482-3834), Rte. 26, Errol, NH 03579. 1- and 2-bedroom year-round waterfront cottages 7 miles east of Errol; kitchens, docking facilities, pets welcome. No credit cards. Note: linens are not provided. paradisepointcottages.com $$

Sudbury Inn (207-824-2174), 151 Main St., Bethel, ME 04217. All 18 rooms have private baths, cable TV and wi-fi; pets welcome. Breakfast included. sudburyinn.com $$

The Wentworth Inn (603-383-9700), 1 Carter Notch Rd., Jackson, NH 03846. 62 rooms and suites (some with fireplace and/or Jacuzzi), golf course, tennis courts, and heated outdoor pool. B&B or MAP. Also 2-3 bedroom condo rentals. thewentworth.com $$-$$$

off the drive

The Balsams (877-225-7267), 1000 Cold Spring Rd., Dixville Notch, NH 03576. One of the North Country's destination landmarks, this grand resort hotel sits in the midst of 15,000 mountain acres. Activities include golf, fishing, swimming, and hiking. thebalsams.com $$$-$$$$

restaurants

BBQ Bob's Real Pit BBQ (207-824-4744), Orange trailer at the Good Food Store, Rte. 2, Bethel, ME. "You don't need teeth to eat our beef." L&D in season. $

Bethel Inn and Country Club (207-824-2175), Common, Bethel, ME. Elegance is the watchword at this classic inn, which serves traditional fare by candlelight in a formal dining room overlooking the golf course. B; D Fri. & Sat. $$-$$$

Café di Cocoa & DiCocoa's Market (207-824-5282), 119 and 125 Main St., Bethel, ME. Fresh baked scones, bagels, and other tasty treats served from 7 a.m. Lunch and dinner feature extremely creative vegan and vegetarian dishes. $

Gideon Hastings House (207-824-3496), 22 Broad St., Bethel, ME. Authentic Italian cuisine elegantly prepared and served by a transplanted New Yorker in the dining room of an 1848 Greek Revival home overlooking the Common. Among house specialties: osso buco, braised lamb shank, and monkfish scaloppini. Also a 4-bedroom b&b. D Thurs-Sun. $$-$$$

La Bottega Saladino (207-466-2520), 152 Main St., Gorham, NH. Homemade pastas, paninis, and other Italian specialties, as well as a market for stocking up on picnic goodies. L & D (closed Sun. & Mon.) $

Northland Restaurant & Dairy Bar (603-752-6210), Rte. 16N, Berlin NH. Just a mile north of town, this informal spot serves up fried seafood plates, turkey dinners, and homemade pie. $

Red Fox Bar & Grille (603-383-6659), Rte. 16A, Jackson Village, NH. Hearty appetizers, sandwiches, and entrees. Sports bar, microbrews, and a Sun. jazz breakfast buffet 7:30 a.m.-1 p.m. L Sat. and Sun., D. Playroom for toddlers and a movie room for the older set. $-$$

Sunday River Brewing Company (207-824-4253), 29 Sunday River Rd., Bethel, ME. The microbrews are made on site, at the entrance to the mountain access road. The smokehouse barbecue, outdoor seating, and casual atmosphere make this a great spot to kick back and soak in the scenery. L & D. $-$$

Wildcat Inn and Tavern (603-383-6502), Rte. 16A, Jackson, NH. One of the area's liveliest night spots hosts live music Tues. and weekends, and serves dishes such as black bean quesadilla and chicken pot pie from 4 p.m. Tues.-Sat. The more formal dining room serves creative country cuisine: D Wed., Fri. and Sat. Also, family-friendly rooms and cottages. $$-$$$

attractions

Berlin City Heritage Tour (603-752-6060). Driving tour includes National Register of Historic Places churches and sites relevant to the city's rich history. androscogginvalleychamber.com

Gorham Historical Society & Model Railroad (603-466-5338), Railroad St., Gorham, NH. Memorial weekend-Columbus Day.

Lake Umbagog National Wildlife Refuge (603-482-3415), 2756 Dam Rd., Errol, NH. fws.gov/northeast/lakeumbagog

Mt. Washington Auto Road (603-466-3988), Rte. 16, Great Glen, NH. Guided van, from 8:30 a.m.-5 p.m., takes approximately 1 1/2 hrs., with 1/2 hour at summit. Tours leaving before 9:30 a.m. include an hour stay at the summit. Or, drive up yourself (just make sure your brakes are in good shape). Mid-May-late Oct., weather permitting.

Mt. Washington State Park (603-466-3347), Gorham, NH. Seasonal.

Mt. Washington Summit Museum (603-356-8345), P.O. Box 2310, N. Conway, NH 03860. Seasonal.

Northern Forest Heritage Park (603-752-7202), 961 Main St., Berlin, NH. Museum Mon.-Sat. Boats tours June-Oct., Wed.-Sat. Boats depart from the dock – rain or shine – at 5 p.m.

Pinkham Notch Visitor Center and Lodge (603-466-2727), Rte. 16, Gorham, NH 03581.

Wight Brook Nature Preserve (also known as Step Falls Preserve) (207-729-5181), Route 26, Newry, ME. The Nature Conservancy's first Maine property.

activities

Bethel Outdoor Adventure & Campground (207-824-4224), 121 Mayville Rd. (Rte. 2), Bethel, ME. Canoe, kayak and bike rentals, shuttle and guide service.

Great Glen Trails Outdoor Center (603-466-2333), Rte. 16, Pinkham Notch, NH. Year-round recreation includes mountain biking, canoeing, kayaking, fly-fishing, x-c skiing, snowshoeing, snow tubing, and sighting tours up the Mt. Washington Auto Road.

Jackson Ski Touring Foundation (603-383-9355), Rte. 16A, Jackson, NH.

Moose Tours (603-466-3103), Gorham Information Center, Main St., Gorham, NH. Three-hour guided bus tours offered from late May to early Oct at dusk. Reservations recommended.

Northern Waters Outfitters, (603-482-3817) Umbagog Wildlife Refuge, Errol, NH.

North Woods Rafting (603-528-0136), 49 Butternut Lane, Conway, NH. A host of guided adventures including rafting, moose tours, bicycling, backpacking, and pontoon rides.

Saco Bound (603-447-2177), Main St., Center Conway, NH 03813.

Saint Kieran Community Center for the Arts (603-852-1028), 155 Emery St., Berlin, NH. Exhibits and performances in a late nineteenth century baroque style church with an 1898 pipe organ.

Story Land (603-383-4293), 850 Rte. 16, Glen, NH. Young kids will enjoy this low-key, well-organized theme park. Admission includes unlimited rides and all shows.

Wildcat Mountain Ski Area (603-466-3326), Rte. 16, Pinkham Notch, NH. Gondola rides and ZipRider. Late May-early June, weekends; mid-June-mid-Oct. daily.

off the drive

Sunday River Ski Area (207-824-3000), 15 South Ridge Rd., Newry. 4-season resort offers gondola rides (Fri.-Sun. spring-fall), an award-winning, 18-hole golf course, mountain biking, hiking, and a spa service. Lodging options include condominiums, the Grand Summit Resort Hotel, and Jordan Grand Resort Hotel (see "Lodgings" above.)

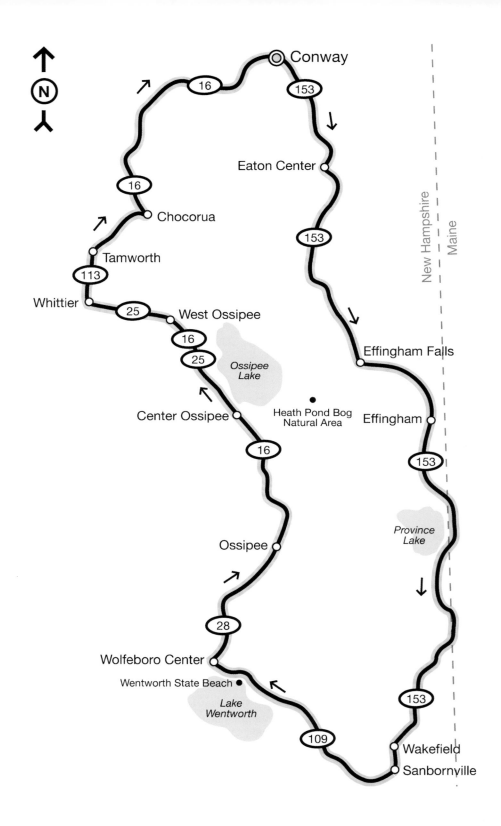

Along New Hampshire's Eastern Border

146 miles

major **attractions**

- White Lake State Park
- Hoyt Wildlife Sanctuary
- Wentworth State Beach
- Remick Country Doctor Museum and Farm
- Mount Chocorua

This drive meanders along the Maine border, threading together a skein of tidy small towns set amidst rolling countryside and amply supplied with comfortable inns and resorts. The route loops around lovely Lake Ossipee, then skirts the eastern slopes of Mount Chocorua, a scenic southern outrider of the White Mountains.

Begin the drive by heading south out of Conway on Route 153, following the Saco River Valley to Crystal Lake.

Side Trip

At Crystal Lake, turn left on Brownfield Road to reach Snowville, a tiny village settled in the early 1800s by Joseph Snow. He left his Maine home at age 24 to find a suitable homestead, and ended his search at the base of Foss Mountain. Here he found a brook that provided waterpower for a sleigh factory. Homes built by Snow and his relatives still stand along the road. Turn onto Stewart Road and follow the sign to **Snowvillage Inn**, overlooking Mount Washington and the Presidential Range. The inn's executive chef, Matthew Taylor, holds weekend cooking schools. Continue past the inn to the summit for spectacular views.

Helen Keller often stayed at the nearby summer home of her editor, Nella Henney. Mrs. Henney tied a rope from her front door to a tree so the blind woman could enjoy walking alone. "Sunshine bewitches the weariness out of us ... rains give me the fairy thrill of dripping like the wildflowers at my feet. This is a nest of peace, twice blessed," she wrote.

Continue on Route 153 to tiny **Eaton Center** and its 1884 Greek Revival **Inn at Crystal Lake**. Just past the inn, the much - photographed, 1879 Little White Church on the lakeshore is a popular spot for weddings.

Side Trip

The area's newest arts center, **Stone Mountain**, which has hosted talents such as Marty Stuart, The Capitol Steps, Rosanne Cash, and Shawn Colvin, is just a few miles from here in Brownfield, Maine. Both daytime and evening events are scheduled throughout the year at the 200-seat timber frame music hall in the foothills of the White Mountains. Dinner is served on performance nights; lunch is served at the Rooster Revue, a variety show held every third Tuesday of the month.

Just ahead on Purity Lake is 1,000-acre **Purity Spring Resort**, which has been catering to families for more than 100 years. Among the resort's activities are boating, canoeing, fishing, water skiing, an indoor pool and fitness complex, and tennis courts. King Pine Ski Area is affiliated with the resort.

Just past the resort, **turn left onto Horseleg Hill Road** to New Hampshire Audubon Society's 140-acre **Hoyt Wildlife Sanctuary**, a hardwood forest with a kettle-hole bog, frequented by great blue heron, pileated woodpeckers, black-throated blue warblers, and beaver. Look for pitcher plants and delicate rose pogonias in the lower bog, and white pine and rattlesnake plantain orchids on the highest eskers (elongated hills made up of gravel and other material left behind by a receding glacier).

Side Trip

To visit **Freedom,** turn left off Route 153 onto Freedom Village Road. This quintessential New England village with handsome homes, a white clapboard town hall, and an 1867 First Congregational Church got its name when it split away from Effingham. Victorian period rooms in the **Freedom Historical Society and Museum** depict middle class life of 150 years ago.

Route 153 intersects with Route 25 at **Effingham Falls.** The first of the Effinghams – on the Ossipee River – grew to be a thriving mill town about 1820 when Joseph Huckins harnessed the water from the falls to power saw and gristmills. In later years, bedsteads and woolen goods were manufactured here. Today the tidy homes in the Effinghams are testament to the booming, 19th-century economy.

Side Trip

The views of the Presidential Range and – on a clear day – the Atlantic Ocean from the top of the 50-foot fire tower at the summit of 1,907-foot **Green Mountain** are well worth the moderately steep 2 8/10-mile hike. At the intersection of routes 153 and 25, turn west (right) onto Route 25; drive 2/10 mile, then turn left onto Green Mountain Road. Turn left onto High Watch Road, then left again after 2/10 mile, at the T-junction. The trailhead is 1 2/10 mile farther on the right.

center of New England . . . .

Continue south on Route 153, which follows the same course as Route 25 for a short distance before that road veers into Maine. **Approximately a mile after the road splits (bear right and stay on Route 153) watch on the left** for the Audubon Society's 380-acre **Charles Henry & Mabel Lamborn Watts Wildlife Sanctuary,** where a trail wanders through forest and swamp alongside the Ossipee River. Watch for otter and waterfowl. There are usually maps in the mailbox.

A roadside plaque in Effingham tells of the Union Academy, the state's first state teachers' college, once located on the second floor of the huge building on the hill. The privately owned, three-story Squire Lord's Mansion, with its second-floor Palladian window and octagonal domed cupola, was built by Isaac Lord in 1822. The 1798 Effingham Meetinghouse was used for village gatherings for almost a century.

Several large stone hearths on the western shore of Province Lake are proof that Native Americans camped here long ago. Today's visitors are just as likely to find golf balls – evidence of the 18-hole **Province Lake Golf Club** (open to the public), which is actually in Maine.

Continue south to **Wakefield,** the "center of New England." More than 200 years ago this was the intersection of two stagecoach routes, and the village that grew up around it has changed little over the years. Twenty-six of the 18th- and 19th-century buildings in Wakefield Corner National Historic Area are listed in the National Register of Historic Places. The **Wakefield Inn**, built as a private residence in 1803 and then opened as a stagecoach stop in 1890, still retains many of its original features, including windows with Indian shutters and a three-sided fireplace in the common room.

a governor's retreat

Continue on Routes 153/16 a short distance and turn north (right) onto Route 109. Ahead is the turnoff for the **Governor John Wentworth State Historic Site.** A stone foundation is all that remains of the grand retreat the colonial governor built in 1768 on his 6,000-acre estate overlooking Lake Wentworth.

The two-story mansion, set amidst stables, barns, and coach houses, was 100 feet long, 40 feet wide, and had six-foot-high windows. Furnishings were hauled by horse-drawn wagons from Portsmouth to Lake Winnipesaukee, and then transported to a landing on Lake Wentworth. No public official or private citizen had ever selected a summer home site so far out in the wilderness at that early date, and the logistics of the manor's construction and supply made it all the more impressive.

The governor had a 45-mile road constructed to link Portsmouth with his retreat. His wife, Lady Frances, described her travels in a letter she wrote on October 4, 1780: "You may easily think I dread the journey, from the roughness of the carriage, as the roads are so bad and I, as great a coward as ever existed. ... The Governor would attempt, and effect if possible, to ride over the tops of the trees on Moose Mountain, while I even tremble at passing through a road cut at the foot of it. ... The roads are so precarious in the winter that it is impossible. ... I hope the roads will be better next year."

Governor Wentworth and his wife didn't have many years in which to enjoy their back-country Versailles. In 1775, before construction was completed, they were forced into exile by the onset of the American Revolution. Wentworth was later appointed governor of Nova Scotia; he built the magnificent Province House in Halifax, which still serves as the official residence of the lieutenant governor. His New Hampshire retreat burnt to the ground in 1820, the year of his death.

Just past the site is **Wentworth State Beach**, on six-mile-long Lake Wentworth.

In Wolfeboro Center, at the intersection of routes 109 and 28, turn north (right) onto Route 28. Duncan Lake in Ossipee, at the junction of routes 28 and 16, was a favorite fishing spot of President Grover Cleveland. He named his fishing camp Acorn Lodge, and hauled in many a fine bass. Today the lake is stocked with rainbow and brook trout.

Continue north on Route 16 to Center Ossipee and the intersection with Route 25. **Turn east (right) onto Route 25** to reach **Ossipee Lake Natural Area** and **Heath Pond Bog**, whose acidic environment supports classic bog vegetation including magnificent bog orchids. There's a short loop trail here.

Although there's no public beach on six-mile-long Lake Ossipee, it's a fine spot to fish for brook and rainbow trout. There's a boat launch at Deer Cove, on the western shore.

In the January, 1962 issue of Yankee, W. A. Swanburg related a curious incident that took place in 1914 on the south shore of Lake Ossipee, where a man named Frederick J. Small had moved with his wife. Mr. Swanburg described him: "gray haired, fiftyish, undersized, he walked with a limp and looked mean enough to bite." A self-described inventor who tinkered with electrical energy, Mr. Small insured his wife for $20,000, then proceed to rig a device that would burn down the house with her in it and leave behind no evidence. The house burned, but Mrs. Small didn't. She fell into lake water that had flooded the basement, where the sheriff found her "bludgeoned, strangled, and shot." The sheriff credited Lake Ossipee with the arrest of Mr. Small, who was hung in Concord Prison on January 15, 1918.

Backtrack to the junction of Routes 16/25 and turn right to continue north. As you approach West Ossipee, bear left to stay on Route 25.

Side Trip

Instead of following Route 25 as it breaks off from Route 16 at West Ossipee, continue into town on Route 16 and bear right at Route 41 north. Continue past Lily Pond. Turn right at a dirt road to reach the Nature Conservancy's **West Branch Pine Barrens** (pine barrens are woodlands that depend upon wildfires to hinder growth and maintain the status quo). When a massive wildfire swept across eastern New Hampshire in 1947, the Ossipee Pine Barrens, a 3,000-acre wilderness of extremely rare pitch pine/scrub oak barrens, thrived.

Today the state's last intact pine barrens, one of North America's finest "northern variant" pitch pine/scrub oak barrens, is home to a wide variety of birds and insects, including common nighthawks, rufous-sided towhees, brown thrashers, and 12 species of rare moths and butterflies (five are found nowhere else in the state). A network of trails threads through this rare ecosystem.

Side Trip

At West Ossipee, head north a few miles on Route 16 to **White Lake State Park,** at the edge of the White Mountain National Forest. A two-mile footpath loops through the Black Spruce Ponds preserve to a 72-acre stand of mature, native pitch pines designated a National Natural Landmark. There are views of the Sandwich Range, including Mount Chocorua, from the sandy beach.

Just after bearing west onto Route 25 from Route 16/25, look on the right for the 132 foot 7 inch Paddleford truss Whittier covered bridge, built in the 1870s across the Bearcamp River. The was added later.

Continue west on Route 25 to Whittier, named for poet John Greenleaf Whittier, who spent many summers here. Just to the south is Mount Whittier, at the northern end of the Ossipee Range.

At the intersection of routes 16 and 113, turn right onto Route 113. Continue past several "pick your own apple" farms to **Tamworth,** where President Grover Cleveland spent many summers. The **Barnstormers Summer Playhouse** was founded by his son, Francis, in a converted feed store in 1931, and is now the country's oldest Actors Equity house. Dinner-theater packages are available with the 1833 **Victorian Tamworth Inn,** on the banks of the Swift River.

Other Tamworth landmarks include Remick's Grocery Market, a town institution since 1865; the 1792 church; and the cemetery, where many of the town founders are interred.

Two generations of Remicks served as physicians here from 1894 to 1993. Dr. Edwin C. Remick has preserved a slice of history at the **Remick Country Doctor Museum and Farm.** Exhibits include the family's home, with antique period furnishings and a turn-of-the-century doctor's office, and displays interpreting early farm life. Visitors to this living history museum are invited to participate in a variety of hands-on activities, and kids will enjoy learning about farm life a century ago.

Side Trip

Detour north out of Tamworth on Route 113A to the **Hemenway State Forest,** where there's a short, self-guided nature trail as well as a path to the Great Hill fire tower, which offers views of the Mount Chocorua Scenic Area and White Mountain National Forest just to the north. Several trails, including the Big Rock Cave Trail to a boulder cave, begin a bit farther north on Route 113A.

a legendary peak . . . .

Head east out of town on Route 113 to the junction of Route 16 and the village of Chocorua, in the shadow of Mount Chocorua.

Rugged, 3,475-foot Mount Chocorua, at the eastern end of the Sandwich Range, is extremely popular with hikers. Trails start at various points in the area and merge just below the treeless summit (the Piper and Brook Trails go to the top). Consult the Appalachian Mountain Club's *White Mountain Guide* for a description of the trails and locations of the trailheads.

> *Like Mount Chocorua, Mount Passaconaway is part of the Sandwich Range. It's named after a 17th-century Penacook chief who, legend has it, did not die but was carried to the top of Mount Washington in a sled pulled by 24 wolves. From there, he ascended into the heavens in a cloud of fire.*

Side Trip

Detour north of Chocorua Village, past **Riverbend Inn,** to lovely – and mostly undeveloped – Lake Chocorua, on the southern side of Mount Chocorua. There's a pleasant beach and boat launch on the northern edge of the lake.

The Legend of Mt. Chocorua

After many years of hostilities between the Indians and the early English settlers, Chocorua, chief of the Pequawket Indians, a 'silent haughty warrior with brooding passion in his eyes," befriended a man named Cornelius Campbell, leader of a group of Englishmen who had settled in the Conway region. One day when Chocorua left his son in the care of Campbell and his wife, the boy ate some maple syrup laced with fox poison and died. Chocorua didn't believe that the incident was an accident and, when Campbell was away, slaughtered the Englishman's family.

As Ernest Poole relates the story in The Great White Hills of New Hampshire, "Campbell tracked the chief at sunrise up the mountain which bears his name and, when he reached the pinnacle, shouted to him to throw himself down. To that the Indian replied: 'The Great Spirit gave life to Chocorua and Chocorua will not throw it away at the command of a white man!'

'Then hear the Great Spirit speak in White Man's Thunder!' Campbell roared. He fired his musket. Chocorua fell, then raised himself on one arm and made the famous curtain speech, repeated later in thousands of cabins:

'A curse upon you white men! May the Great Spirit curse you when he speaks in the clouds and his words are fire! Lightning blast your crops! Wind and fire destroy your homes! The Evil One breathe death on your cattle! Panthers howl and wolves fatten on your bones.'

The curse long rested on the spot. Often raided by wolves and bears and their cattle dying of plagues, the settlers left the valley. And even though later the cattle plague was proved to be due to muriate of lime in the water which they drank, the story was still widely told."

Continue east of Chocorua on Deer Hill Road, past several apple orchards, to Silver Lake, in **Madison**. There's a boat launch to the south on Route 41, and there's good fishing for rainbow, lake and brook trout, large and smallmouth bass, and pickerel.

At the intersection with Route 113, turn north and watch on the left for the turnoff to **Madison Boulder**. During the Ice Age, more than 25,000 years ago, the glacier retreated from this area, leaving behind the largest known glacial erratic (boulder) in North America, and one of the largest in the world. The National Natural Landmark measures 87 feet long by 37 feet high by 23 feet wide, and is estimated to weigh 4,662 tons. Although it has become a target for spray-painted graffiti, this boulder in the middle of a forest in the middle of nowhere is still an awesome sight.

Continue north on Route 113 back to Conway.

information *Area codes are (603) unless otherwise indicated.*

Greater Ossipee Area Chamber of Commerce (539-6201), Rte. 28, Ossipee 03864. ossipeevalley.org.

Greater Wakefield Chamber of Commerce (522-6106), P.O. Box 111, Wakefield 03872. wakefieldnh.org

Mount Washington Valley Chamber of Commerce (356-5701), Main St., N. Conway 03860. mtwashingtonvalley.org.

lodging

Gilman Tavern Inn (323-9123), 74 Main St., Tamworth 03886. 4 lovely rooms with private baths and a/c in a c. 1820 village colonial home. Breakfast included. gilmantaverninn.com $

Inn at Tamworth (323-7721), Main St., Tamworth 03886. Each of the 16 rooms at this 1833 village hostelry has a private bath, fine linens, and down comforters. Breakfast included. Outdoor pool, restaurant (see "Restaurants" below), and pub. innattamworth.com $$-$$$$

The Inn at Crystal Lake (447-2120), Rte.153, Eaton Center 03832. 1884 Greek Revival inn over-looking the lake has 11 rooms with private baths, cable TV, a/c, and phones. Restaurant (see below) and pub (the bar was originally in Boston's Ritz-Carlton). innatcrystallake.com $$-$$$

Mount Whittier Motel (539-4951), Rte. 16, Ctr. Ossipee 03814. Pleasant, family-friendly motel has 19 standard units, as well as loft rooms that sleep 5. All have a/c and cable TV. Outdoor pool. 2 pet friendly rooms ($). May-Nov. mountwhittiermotel.biz $

Purity Spring Resort (367-8896), Rte. 153, E. Madison 03849. Accommodations at this 4-sea-son resort include rooms in the 1800s lodge, hillside cottages, and a renovated farmhouse. FAP in summer includes the Fri. smorgasbord. purityspring.com $$-$$$

Riverbend Inn B&B (323-7440), Rte.16, Chocorua 03817. Secluded romantic retreat has 10 guest rooms decorated with antiques and original art; sitting rooms with fireplaces, and a library; and decks and a patio. Breakfast included; weekend dinner by reservation. riverbendinn.com $-$$

Snowvillage Inn (447-2818), Snowville 03849. 18 rooms with private baths on 10 scenic acres. Options include 2nd floor rooms in the main inn; rooms with fireplaced living rooms in the Chimney House; and the pet friendly Lodge with 2-story living rooms. MAP available (see "Restaurants" below). snowvillageinn.com $$-$$$

Wabanaki Lodge (323-8536), Rte. 16, W. Ossipee 03890. 5 rustic cottages at a KOA camp-ground on the secluded shore of Moore's Pond. All have cold running water, kerosene lan-terns, and outhouses; all but 1 have a fireplace or woodstove. Private beach, recreation hall, and fishing. chocoruacamping.com $

Wakefield Inn B & B (522-8272), 2723 Wakefield Rd., Wakefield 03872. This 1804, 3-story inn has one of the tallest 'flying' staircases in New Hampshire. 7 rooms with private baths have an eclectic assortment of early American furnishings. Breakfast included. Dinner served Fri. and Sat. by reservation. wakefieldinn.com $$-$$$

Wind Song Motor Inn (539-4536), Rte. 16, W. Ossipee 03890. Classic motel rooms with phones, TV, refrigerators, and microwaves. Continental breakfast; pets in some rooms. wind-songmotorinn.com $

restaurants

The Inn at Tamworth (323-7721), Main St., Tamworth. The diverse menu at The Garden's Res-taurant includes shrimp scampi and penne Alfredo. Bobby's Pub ($) serves more casual fare, and there's homemade pizza. $$-$$$

Palmer House Pub, Inn at Crystal Lake ((447-2120), Rte. 153, Eaton Center. Entrees such as rack of lamb and pan seared sea scallops, along with a pub menu ($). Tues. is Mexican night. D Tues.-Sun. $$$

Rosie's Restaurant (323-8611), Rte.16, Tamworth. The hottest spot in town for hearty down home fare – including outstanding breakfasts – in a casual, friendly environment. B & L; D Thurs.-Sat. $-$$

Sleigh Mill Grille at Snowvillage Inn (447-2818), Snowville. Award-winning cuisine features dishes with an American flair, with entrees such as Cajun red snapper, porcini mushroom pouch, and grilled rack of lamb. $$$-$$$$

Whittier House Restaurant & Tavern (539-4513), Rte. 16, W. Ossipee. Extensive menu includes everything from burgers to Greek salads to schnitzel and seafood linguini in a casual, family friendly setting. L, D, & Sun. brunch buffet. $$

Wakefield Inn & Restaurant (522-8272), 2723 Wakefield Rd., Wakefield. It's no surprise that the innkeepers host culinary retreats and cooking classes: the elegantly prepared dishes, featuring traditional French cuisine, include appetizers such as rustic tart with roasted cherry tomatoes and fennel, and entrees such as flank steak stuffed with smoked gouda and roast red peppers. D Fri. and Sat. $$$$

The Yankee Smokehouse (539-RIBS), Rtes. 16/25, W. Ossipee. Authentic open pit barbecue includes baby back ribs, smokehouse fries, baked beans, and corn chowder. Save room for dessert. $

attractions

Barnstormers Summer Playhouse (323-8500), 100 Main St., Tamworth. Plays and musicals. Schedule: barnstormerstheatre.org

Freedom Historical Society and Museum (539-6526 or 539-3665), Maple St., Freedom. Memorial Day-Labor Day, Sat. a.m. Donation.

Hoyt Wildlife Sanctuary (224-9909), Rte. 153, E. Madison.

Madison Boulder Natural Area (323-2087), off Rte. 133, Madison.

Remick Country Doctor Museum and Farm (323-8382), 58 Cleveland Hill Rd., Tamworth. July-Oct., Mon.-Sat.; off season, Mon.-Fri. Wagon rides ($) at 11:30 a.m.

Farmers' and crafts market, Wakefield Marketplace, routes 153 & 16, Sanbornville. Sat. Memorial Day-Columbus Day weekend.

Wentworth State Beach (569-3699), Rte. 109, Wolfeboro. Beach, picnic area, bathhouse, grills.

West Branch Pine Barrens. For information: The Nature Conservancy (224-5853), 22 Bridge St., Concord 03301.

White Lake State Park (323-7350), Rte. 16, Tamworth. Swimming, camping, hiking.

activities

Canoe King (323-7442), Rte. 16, W. Ossipee. Canoe and kayak rentals; shuttle service to Bearcamp River.

Concerts by the River; behind the Other Store, Tamworth Village. Folk, bluegrass, children's shows, and whatever. Sundays 3-5 p.m. Donation.

Lakefront Landing (539-4245), 85 Pequawket Trail, Center Ossipee. Half and full day rentals of 18 ft. and 20 ft. pontoon boats, and 18 ft. Larson bowrider ski boat. 12 ft. aluminum fishing rowboats with 6 hp outboards available for full day only.

Ossipee Lake Marina (539-8456), 65 Marina Rd., Freedom. Rentals of ski boats, pontoon boats, Yamaha Waverunners, and fishing boats.

Province Lake Golf Club (207-793-4040), Rte. 153, Parsonsfield, ME.

off the drive

Stone Mountain Arts Center (866-227-6523), 695 Dug Way Rd., Brownfield, Maine. Schedule: stonemountainartscenter.com

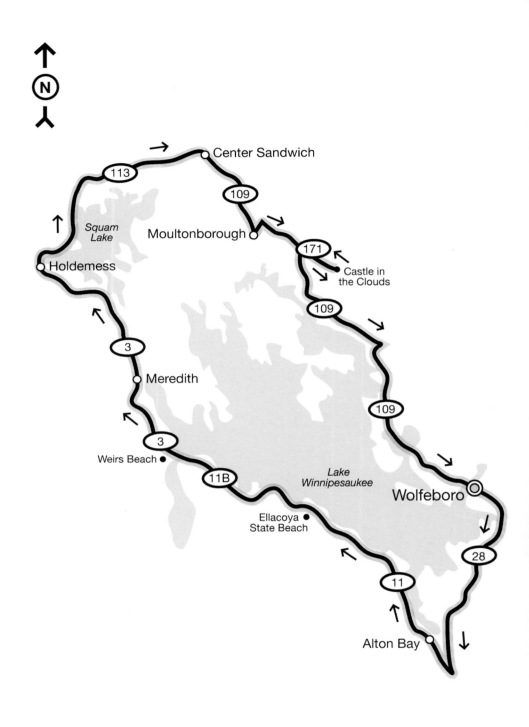

Around Lake Winnipesaukee

78 miles

major attractions

- Wolfeboro
- M/S Mount Washington
- Ellacoya State Beach
- League of New Hampshire Craftsmen

- Weirs Beach
- Castle in the Clouds
- Libby Museum
- Loon Center and Markus Audubon Wildlife Sanctuary

Lake Winnipesaukee, America's largest freshwater lake contained entirely within one state, is New Hampshire's favorite freshwater playground. But the lively towns and rolling countryside along its 283-mile shoreline are as great an attraction as the big lake itself. This drive circles Winnipesaukee, and takes in places as diverse as a center for New Hampshire craftsmanship, a neighboring lake famous for its movie role, and an industrialist's dream castle.

Note: if you have limited time, we recommend that you take the portion of this drive that goes between Holderness and Wolfeboro. It is more scenic, has less traffic, and has some of the major attractions, including the not-to-be-missed Castle in the Clouds.

Begin at Wolfeboro, the largest town directly on the lake. Wolfeboro calls itself "America's oldest summer resort" because of its popularity with a single discriminating vacationer: It was here, on a smaller nearby lake later named after him, that Colonial Governor John Wentworth created his 6,000-acre country estate in 1769 (see Drive 14).

Today, Wolfeboro is a popular resort town, and its Main Street is lined with boutiques and restaurants. Private yachts and sightseeing boats (including the **M/S** *Mount Washington*; see below) bustle in and out of the harbor, jockeying for space with windsurfers and water skiers. A good way to sightsee (particularly in summer, when traffic can be extremely frustrating) is aboard **Molly the Trolley.** Among Wolfeboro's places of interest are **Hampshire Pewter Company,** where you can watch craftsmen create fine pewter pieces and tour the factory; Brewster Free Academy (52 South Main Street), built to educate students "of good moral character"; the Romanesque Municipal Building, with its handsome clock tower; **Wolfeboro Historical Society's** museum complex, which includes a 19th-century schoolhouse, a replica of an early firehouse, and an 18th-century farmhouse; the natural history **Libby Museum**; and the **Wright Museum,** showcasing the enterprising spirit of Home Front America during World War II with a huge collection of memorabilia, vehicles, films and artifacts. The **New Hampshire Boat Museum** traces the history of pleasure boating in the Lakes Region.

Mount Washington Cruises operates three ships that offer day, evening, charter and island mail delivery cruises on Lake Winnipesaukee. The flagship 230-foot M/S Mount Washington, *which offers cruises from late May through late October, has ports of call in Wolfeboro, Alton Bay, and Weirs Beach (home port). The 85-foot M/V* Doris E, *with ports in Weirs Beach and Meredith, provides scenic one-hour tours of the smaller islands adjacent to Weirs Bay. The 85-foot M/V* Sophie C, *the oldest floating post office in the country, sails from Weirs Beach and delivers mail to residents of five islands.*

Head south out of town on Route 28 along the eastern shore of the lake to **Alton Bay.** The first M/S *Mt. Washington* was built here in 1872. That huge building overlooking the bay is Bay View Pavilion. It first opened for business in 1921 as a roller skating rink and dance hall, but soon provided a venue for big name entertainers including Louis Armstrong, The Dorsey Brothers, and Harry James. The original building burnt in 1928, but was quickly rebuilt and now hosts a variety of entertainment. Free summer concerts are presented at the town's bandstand.

Head west out of town on Route 11 along the shores of Alton Bay. After approximately 4 1/2 miles, watch for signs for Mount Major. The 3-mile hike to the summit follows an old logging road for some distance before getting steeper and traversing several ledges. At the 1,780-foot summit there's a stone shelter and terrific views.

As you continue along the southwest shore, the Ossipee and Sandwich Mountains loom across the lake. **Ellacoya State Beach**, the lake's only state swimming area, has a sandy beach, bathhouse, refreshment stand, and picnic area.

Lake Winnipesaukee takes its name from an Indian word roughly translated as "smile of the Great Spirit." The story goes that centuries ago Ellacoya, daughter of Chief Ahanton of the Penacook Tribe which lived along the northern shores of the lake, was courted by Kona, the chief of a hostile tribe to the south. Ahanton was at first enraged to find Ellacoya in love with his sworn enemy, but Ellacoya begged her father not to kill him. Impressed as much by Kona's bravery as by his daughter's Pocahontas-style entreaties, Ahanton gave the couple his blessing. After the wedding feast, Kona and Ellacoya set out under starry skies for his village, and at the moment their canoe reached the middle of the lake the clouds parted and the sun emerged to sparkle on the waters.

Legend aside, recent archaeological excavations have documented that Native Americans camped on Winnipesaukee's shores as early as 8,000 B.C. The Penacook encampment along the stream that connects Paugus Bay to the lake proper is believed to have been one of New England's largest seasonal Indian communities. Discoveries of artifacts and gravesites verify the site's importance.

Modern-day anglers are drawn to the big lake for much the same reason as those early inhabitants: Winnipesaukee continues to offer some of New Hampshire's best salmon and trout fishing.

a lively little resort

Turn off **Route 11** onto **Route 11B** to **Weirs Beach**. Native Americans used a basket-woven trap called a "weir" to catch shad passing through the channel as the fish migrated from Lake Winnipesaukee to the Merrimack River.

Weirs Beach is the gaudiest – and in summer, the busiest – of the lake's shoreside communities. It's been a major tourist destination since the second half of the 19th century when the Boston, Concord, and Montreal Railroad first pulled into town; by 1900, four express trains arrived daily from Boston.

Today's Weirs Beach is a hodgepodge of video arcades, bowling alleys, water slides, and boat rentals. It's also the mid-point for the **Winnipesaukee Railroad**, and homeport of the M/S *Mount Washington*. Although it's primarily a family resort, the atmosphere at Weirs Beach changes every June during Laconia Motorcycle Week (see side trip below).

> Motorcycle enthusiasts have gathered annually along Lake Winnipesaukee's southern shores since 1923.

When the old M/S Mount Washington *burned, owner Captain Leander Lavallee had two options: he could buy a new boat at a cost upwards of $250,000, or a used vessel. Captain Lavallee purchased the 203-foot iron-hulled steamship* Chateaugay, *an 1888 Lake Champlain passenger ship that had been converted to an automobile ferry in 1925. He paid $20,000, then had the superstructure removed and the hull cut into 20 sections for rail shipment from Burlington, Vermont to Lakeport, on Paugus Bay. Once reassembled, the hull was fitted with a new superstructure and two triple-expansion steam engines. Rechristened* Mount Washington II, *the boat was launched in August 1940. Captain Lavallee's company went bankrupt and, after World War II, new owners refitted the old steamship with twin diesel engines. She emerged as the M/S* Mount Washington, *which cruises the lake today.*

In 1652, Governor John Endicott of the Massachusetts Bay Colony sent an expedition up the Merrimack River. Members discovered Lake Winnipesaukee, and carved their initials on the appropriately named Endicott Rock in Weirs Beach to mark the colony's northern boundary. Today the rock is a State Historic Site, and stands – with the initials still visible – in **Endicott Rock Park** in the center of town.

Side Trip

Rent a boat and head to **Stonedam Island Wildlife Preserve** for a delightful day on the lake's largest undeveloped island. There's an historic log cabin, a beach, and a self-guided nature tour. **The Lakes Region Conservation Trust,** which administers the island, can provide information.

Side Trip

Head south on Route 3 and bear right onto Business Route 3 into **Laconia**. Throughout its history as an industrial center, the city has been home to companies manufacturing everything from nails to knitting machines to railroad cars. The country's oldest original brick textile mill, the National Register **Belknap Mill**, now serves as the Lake Region's year round art and history center, and houses the country's only industrial knitting museum. But most people associate the town with New Hampshire International Speedway's annual Laconia Motorcycle Week, a June event that draws more than 100,000 motorcyclists and racing fans. Although the track is actually 10 miles away, Laconia is the major service area for the throngs.

Head out of Weirs Beach on Route 3, past a raft of antique stores, restaurants, motels, and the **Funspot**, an arcade with a terrific selection of vintage, as well as high-tech, games. About a half mile past Funspot, watch for **Kellerhaus**, the home of the sundae smorgasbord. On the way into **Meredith**, the self-proclaimed "latchkey to the White Mountains", there's a **League of New Hampshire Craftsmen** store, an offshoot of the main store that we'll be visiting in Center Sandwich.

Before I-93 was built through the Pemigewasset Valley to the west, the "latchkey" metaphor meant a good deal more; but in any event, Meredith is still a good staging ground for further exploration of the shores of Winnipesaukee and smaller nearby lakes.

At the intersection of routes 3 and 25, a section of **The Inns & Spa at Mills Falls** (partly shown on our cover) is housed in an old linen mill straddling water running from an underground canal connecting Lake Waukewan in the hills above to Winnipesaukee below. The inn's Waterfall Café is a delightful spot for breakfast or a light lunch. **Turn left here** to go into downtown Meredith.

Side Trip

Turn right onto Route 25 into **Center Harbor**. Once crowded with small summer hotels, today this is a quiet community of private homes and an historic inn. The Tudor-style **Kona Mansion**, built in 1900 by one of the partners in Boston's Jordan Marsh department store, has a 9-hole, par-3 golf course, private beach, and a boat dock. The Town Band plays at the bandstand on Friday nights through the summer.

Take Route 25B back toward Route 25. Turn right onto College Road to the 157-acre **Chamberlain-Reynolds Memorial Forest**, administered by the **Squam Lakes Association**. There are several beaches along the mile-long waterfront and a boardwalk through a swamp, where a sharp eye can spot great blue herons, ducks, belted kingfishers and nesting loons. In late August and September, watch for migrating warblers. Take the 3 4/10-mile hike up Red Hill for spectacular views of Winnipesaukee and Squam Lake. Continue on Route 25B back to the intersection of Route 3/25 and turn right.

the real "Golden Pond" . . . .

Continue north out of Meredith on Route 3/25 to **Squam Lake**, the second largest of New Hampshire's more than 1,300 glacially shaped lakes and ponds. Along with Katharine Hepburn and Henry Fonda, Squam starred in the 1981 movie *On Golden Pond* – but you'd never know the lake had been discovered by Hollywood when you drive into its main village, sleepy **Holderness**. With the exception of one stretch of back road that connects Center Sandwich with Center Harbor, hardly any of the routes that circle the lake come anywhere near its shores.

Development is tightly controlled by the Squam Lakes Association, and it's not hard to imagine that, nearly 30 years later, Norman Thayer of *Golden Pond* fame would still be entirely at home in one of the lake's tasteful cottages, set well back from the shore. **Turn right onto Route 113 to reach** Squam Lakes Natural Science Center, a 200-acre nature center with native wildlife in a woodland setting, nature trails, interactive exhibits, and animal programs. Hop aboard one of the center's pontoon boats for a loon cruise, or take their *Golden Pond* Tour, and then have lunch at the café overlooking three-acre Kirkwood Gardens.

When the production crew for On Golden Pond *was ready to shoot the loon scenes, they had a problem: there were no loons on Squam Lake. They contacted Herb Cilley, a retired University of New Hampshire maintenance man and self-taught ornithologist from nearby Bow Lake. Mr. Cilley brought some loons up from his lake so they could get their shot.*

Ready to enjoy a secluded picnic or take a dip? Rent a canoe, kayak, or sailboat at the Squam Lakes Association Resource Center (Route 3) and head to Moon or Bowman Island. Both allow primitive camping with advance reservations.

Route 113 winds through some of the state's prettiest countryside, past horse farms, lakes, and old cemeteries (there's a particularly interesting one just after you enter Sandwich).

Side Trip

If you're up for a short, somewhat steep, but very rewarding hike, turn right onto Pinehurst Road about 4 9/10 miles past the Science Center, and continue for 9/10 mile (bear left at the fork) to West Rattlesnake Mountain Natural Area parking area. Follow signs to the Pasture Trail – it begins on the left by an old sugarhouse. The trail leads to the peak of 1,260- foot-high West Rattlesnake Mountain, where there are terrific views of the lakes, islands, and surrounding mountains.

a crafty town . . . .

At the intersection of routes 113 and 109 is the lovely village of **Center Sandwich,** surrounded by the Ossipee Mountains, Red Hill, and the Squam and Sandwich ranges. The village is famous as the place where **the League of New Hampshire Craftsmen** got its start. Its predecessor, Sandwich Home Industries, was the 1926 creation of Mrs. J. Randolph Coolidge, a wealthy Massachusetts native who encouraged the preservation, practice and teaching of traditional home artisanry, and helped set up a shop where New Hampshire natives could sell their handicrafts.

In 1931 the state government got behind the idea, and the League of Arts and Crafts – later the League of New Hampshire Craftsmen – began to establish stores throughout the state. The descendant of the original shop is still here, selling everything from pottery to handcrafted toys to homemade jams. Across the street, the 1849 **Corner House Inn** is a fine place for lunch or dinner.

The **Sandwich Historical Society Museum** operates the 1850 Elisha Marston House, a handsome, antiques- and art-filled Cape Cod structure with subtle Greek Revival decoration. The Methodist Meetinghouse, with its unusual freestanding brick chimney, is one of the most photographed buildings in the state. The fairgrounds, on the outskirts of town, comes to life each Columbus Day weekend with the Sandwich Fair, a local institution since the 1880s.

Take Route 109 south out of town toward Sandwich.

Side Trip

Since 1987 the people of Sandwich and Tamworth have been working to protect more than 3,000 acres of undeveloped land in the Bearcamp Valley, home to the pristine Bearcamp River immortalized by John Greenleaf Whittier (who summered in Tamworth) in his poem "Sunset on the Bearcamp." Today, the **Bearcamp River Trail** offers several hiking options ranging from a one-mile walks to a 12-mile hike from Sandwich Notch in the White Mountain National Forest to Hell's Gate, a rocky gorge in South Tamworth. For a brochure, send a self-addressed stamped envelope and a request for a Bearcamp River Trail Guide to the Sandwich Town Hall, Center Sandwich 03227.

The **Old Country Store** at the intersection of routes 25 and 109 in **Moultonborough** was built as a stagecoach stop in 1781, and is one of the oldest continually operating stores in America. Among the exhibits in the upstairs museum is the Concord Coach that passed through town in the mid-1800s. The store is a trove of New Hampshire-made products and groceries, including a terrific aged cheddar, and barrel cured pickles.

Turn right onto Route 25, and then left onto Blake Road at Moultonborough Central School (watch for the Loon Center sign), and after one mile turn right onto Lee's Mill Road to the 193-acre **Loon Center and Markus Audubon Wildlife Sanctuary,** headquarters for the Loon Preservation Committee. Remember those loons in On Golden Pond? Some were really decoys, one of which is on exhibit in the center, which is devoted to loon education and preservation. You can press a button to hear the harrowing cry and idiot laugh of the bird whose population is decreasing in New England as humans intrude upon their breeding grounds. Trails pass through woodlands, upland forests, marshes, streams, and a mile of shoreline, where, if you're lucky, you'll hear the real McCoy.

Loon nesting sites are always close to the water, as the birds' ability to get around on land is in no way equal to their skill at swimming and diving.

a millionaire's dream home . . . .

Back on Route 25, turn right onto Route 109, and then right onto Route 171 to Castle in the Clouds, the wonderfully eccentric centerpiece of a 5,500-acre estate that shoe industrialist Thomas G. Plant designed as a retirement home for himself in 1913. The mansion, built of granite quarried on site and overlooking the Ossipee Mountains, is filled with household conveniences that Mr. Plant created, including a centralized intercom system, a central vacuuming system with its own incinerator, and a self-cleaning oven. His favorite room, the library, had a secret private reading room that only he had access to.

Mr. Plant moved here in 1914 with his bride, Olive, who was 24 years younger and a foot taller than him. The couple lived here until he died –
destitute – in 1941. A combination of factors contributed to his bankruptcy, including a devastating fire at his Boston shoe plant (said to be the largest single fire in Boston's history); and investment in Russian bonds just before the October Revolution. But when offered money in return for permission to harvest his land, Mr. Plant refused: he didn't want to damage his property. At the time of his death he was in debt for approximately $500,000. His friends took up a collection for his burial.

In addition to numerous activities throughout the summer, the castle hosts a Thursday Jazz at Sunset series.

Backtrack to Route 109 and continue through Melvin Village, on Tuftonborough Bay. Just past the village, watch on the left for Abenaki Tower. A 6/10-mile trail goes to the tower, where there are rewarding views of Lake Winnipesaukee and the Ossipee Mountains.

On the outskirts of Wolfeboro, overlooking Winter Harbor, dentist Henry Libby built the **Libby Museum** in 1912 to house his extensive collection of mounted specimens and artifacts. Among the objects displayed are Abenaki maps and drawings, and a 350-year-old dugout canoe. A plaque next to the museum commemorates the 67-mile road that Governor Wentworth built to travel to Dartmouth College for the 1771 Dartmouth College commencement.

information *Area codes are (603) unless otherwise indicated.*

General Lake Winnipesaukee Information: thelaker.com

For a Weirs Beach vacation-planning guidebook: weirsbeach.com

Lakes Region Association Information Center (744-8664), New Hampton 03256. lakesregion.org

Lakes Region Chamber of Commerce (524-5531), 383 S. Main St., Laconia 03246. laconia-weirs.org

Meredith Area Chamber of Commerce (279-6121), 272 DW Hwy., Rte. 3, Meredith 03253. meredithcc.org

Squam Lakes Area Chamber of Commerce (968-4494), P.O. Box 665, Ashland 03217. squamlakeschamber.com

Squam Lakes Association (968-7336), Rte. 3, P.O. Box 204, Holderness 03245. squamlakes.org

Wolfeboro Chamber of Commerce (569-2200), 32 Central Ave., Wolfeboro 03894. wolfeborochamber.com

lodging

Center Harbor Inn (253-4347), 294 Whittier Hwy., Rte. 25, Center Harbor 03226. This 4-story waterfront motel has pleasant motel-style rooms with 2 queen beds, small refrigerators, cable TV, and private balconies. Also, efficiency units. Private sandy beach. centerharborinn.com $$

Glynn House (968-3775), 59 Highland St., Ashland 03217. 13 rooms and suites in an 1896 Victorian b&b close to Squam Lake and the village. All rooms have private baths, some have fireplaces, and a few are pet friendly. The inn can arrange tours of the lake. glynnhouse.com $$$

Inns & Spa at Mill Falls (800-622-6455 or 279-7006), Rtes. 3/25, Meredith. The lakefront complex includes 4 luxuriously appointed inns (many rooms with in-room fireplaces), shops, 7 restaurants, and a full service spa. millfalls.com $$-$$$

Jonathan Beede House B&B (284-7413), 711 Mt. Israel Rd., Center Sandwich 03227. A handsomely restored 1787 home adjacent to the National Forest and close to Squam Lake has 4 antiques-filled guest rooms. jonathanbeedehouse.com $-$$

Kona Mansion (253-4900) P.O. Box 458, Center Harbor 03226. 10 guest rooms; 4 1- and 2-bedroom housekeeping cottages, and 2 3-bedroom chalets. Breakfast and dinner in the ornate Victorian dining room. MAP available. $-$$$

The Manor on Golden Pond (968-3348), Rte. 3, Holderness. Historic estate overlooking Squam Lake has 17 well-appointed guest rooms, and 6 suites, and cottages. Most have wood burning fireplaces and views, some have 2-person whirlpools. The restaurant (see "Restaurants" below) has a fine reputation. manorongoldenpond.com $$-$$$

The Nutmeg Inn (279-8811), 80 Pease Rd., Meredith. Beautifully restored 1763 inn with original floorboards, secret passages, and fireplaces has 8 rooms with private baths. Outdoor pool. bbhost.com/nutmeginn/ $$

Olde Orchard Inn (476-5004), 108 Lee Rd., Moultonborough 03254. A picture-perfect 1790 Federal home on 12 acres just a mile from the lake has 9 guest rooms of varying sizes with private baths; some have fireplaces. Rate includes candlelit breakfast. oldeorchardinn.com $$-$$$

Sandy Point Beach Resort (875-6000), 190 Mount Major Hwy., Alton Bay 03810. Winnipesaukee's largest family resort has moderately priced standard motel units, beach efficiencies, and cottages (weekly in summer), many with scenic views and patios. Paddleboat and canoe rental; game room; private beach, and restaurant. sandypointbeachresort.com $-$$

Shalimar Resort by the Lake (524-1984), 650 Laconia Rd., Rte. 3, Winnisquam 03289. 2-story motel on Lake Winnisquam has rooms ranging from cozy singles to lakefront kings. Restaurant; free use of paddle and rowboats, and canoes; indoor pool, Jacuzzi, whirlpool, and sauna. Karaoke in the pub Fri. and Sat. nights. shalimar-resort.com $$-$$$

Squam Lake Inn (968-4417), Rte. 3 & Shepard Hill Rd., Holderness 03245. 1890 Victorian farmhouse has 8 classic b&b rooms on the 1st and 2nd floors with private baths and queen or king beds. squamlakeinn.com $$-$$$

Three Mile Island (466-2727). Volunteer-managed, family-oriented AMC property with 47 cabins on a 43-acre wooded island. Education programs, sailing, swimming. Rate includes 3 meals. June-Sept. by reservation. 3mile.org

The Wolfeboro Inn (800-451-2389 or 569-3016), 90 N. Main St., Wolfeboro. Lakefront resort offers a variety of accommodations in a restored, 1812 inn with a modern addition. All 44 rooms and suites have baths, TV, and a/c; some have water views and decks. Restaurant and tavern. wolfeboroinn.com $$$

restaurants

Bailey's Bubble (569-3612), Railroad Ave., Wolfeboro. Stroll on over for a fabulously thick frappe, a cookie sandwich sundae, or an Almond Joy ice cream cone with jimmies. $

Corner House Inn (284-6219), 22 Main St., Center Sandwich. Specialties such as lobster and mushroom bisque, pan-seared duck breast, and shellfish sauté. Special events include storytelling dinners and live music in the pub. D & Sun. brunch; L June-Oct. $$-$$$

The Crazy Gringo (366-4411), 306 Lakeside Ave., Weirs Beach. A large selection of classic Tex-Mex dishes, huge margaritas, and a kid's menu in a lively spot near the beach. $-$$

Garwoods Restaurant & Pub (569-7788), 6 N. Main St. Wolfeboro. Fish and chips and haddock Newbury are especially tasty when you sit at a table on the deck overlooking the bay. The indoor dining room, however, is cozy and inviting. L & D. $$

Hart's Turkey Farm Restaurant (279-6212), Rtes. 3/104, Meredith. The menu at this restaurant owned by the Hart family since 1954 features turkey in all its permutations (turkey livers, turkey meatloaf, turkey croquettes), but pasta, fish, seafood and beef dishes are also well represented. Homemade pastries and ice cream. L & D daily. $-$$

J T's Bar-B-Q and Seafood (366-7322), Rte. 3, Weirs Beach. Family-friendly spot serves up popular favorites including ribs, chicken, lobster pie, and prime rib. Can't decide? Order the Round Up Platter. $-$$

Kellerhaus (366-4466), 29 Endicott St. N., Weirs Beach. Is there anything more perfect than an ice cream buffet? Patrons build their own sundaes, and then, as if things weren't sweet enough, browse through the gift store, which has a huge selection of homemade candy. Waffle breakfast. $

The Manor on Golden Pond (968-3348), Rte. 3, Holderness. Award-winning dining in elegant, fireplaced surroundings might include an appetizer of Maine lobster and white fish paté, and an entrée of prosciutto-wrapped Chatham Bay cod. The wine list is superb. The less formal bistro menu includes tapas. $$$$

Mise En Place (569-5788), 96 Lehner St., Wolfeboro. Creative continental dishes such as Mediterranean ravioli with sun dried tomatoes, and prosciutto-wrapped grilled shrimp, served in a small, softly lit room with linen tablecloths. L Mon.-Fri, D Mon.-Sat. $$$

Shibley's at the Pier (875-3636), Rte. 11, Alton Bay. The location is perfect, the lobster rolls and burgers tasty, and the outdoor patio a wonderful place to enjoy a meal. L & D $-$$

The Woodshed (476-2311), Rte. 109, Lees Mill Rd., Moultonborough. Popular for more than 20 years, this restaurant in an authentic 1860s barn and farmhouse serves American fare including prime rib, seafood, and steaks; raw bar. D & Sun. brunch. $$$-$$$$

Yum Yum Shop (569-1919), 16 N. Main St., Wolfeboro. Everything is baked here and, of course, yummy. Try the blueberry pie bar and gingerbread cookies.

attractions

Annalee Doll Gift Shop (279-3333), 44 Reservoir Rd., Meredith. Home base and gift shop for the dolls created by Annalee Thorndike.

Belknap Mill (524-8813), 25 Beacon St., The Mill Plaza, Laconia. Mon.-Fri. year round.

Castle in the Clouds (476-5900), Rte. 171, Moultonborough. Mid-May-late Oct., daily; weekends in May. Schedule: castleintheclouds.org

Chamberlain-Reynolds Memorial Forest, College Rd., Center Harbor. For information: Squam Lakes Association (968-7336), P.O. Box 204, Holderness 03245. squamlakes.org

Clark House Museum Complex, Wolfeboro Historical Society (569-4471), 233 S. Main St., Wolfeboro. Call for hrs.

Ellacoya State Beach (293-7821), Rte. 11, Gilford. Weekends from mid-May; daily mid-June – Labor Day. Camping early May – mid-Oct.

Keepsake Quilting (253-4026), Senter's Marketplace, Rte. 25B, Center Harbor. "America's largest quilt shop" has more than 8,000 bolts of cotton fabric and quilts.

League of NH Craftsmen (284- 6831), 32 Main St., Center Sandwich. Mid-May-mid-Oct. Also, Rte. 3, Meredith (279-7920); and 15 N. Main St., Wolfeboro (569-3309).

The Libby Museum (569-1035), Rte. 109, Wolfeboro. June-mid-Sept., closed Mon.

The Loon Center and Markus Wildlife Sanctuary (476-5666), 183 Lees Mills Rd., Moultonborough. July 1-Columbus Day; closed Sun. off-season. Free.

New Hampshire Boat Museum (569-4554), 397 Center St., Rte. 28, Wolfeboro. Memorial Day-mid-Oct.

Old Country Store and Museum (476-5750), 1011 Whittier Hwy., Moultonborough.

Sandwich Historical Society Museums (284-6269), 4 Maple St., Center Sandwich. Late June-Aug., Tues.-Sat.; Sept.-early Oct., Wed.-Sat.

Squam Lakes Natural Science Center (968-7194), 23 Science Center Rd., Holderness. May-Nov.

Stonedam Island Wildlife Preserve (253-3301), Lakes Region Conservation Trust, P.O. Box 766, Center Harbor 03226 (see "Information" above). lrct.org

Wright Museum (569-1212), 77 Center St., Rte. 28, Wolfeboro. May-Oct.; Feb.-Apr., Sun. p.m. only.

off the drive

New Hampshire Motor Speedway (783-4931), 1122 Rte. 106N, Loudon. Schedule: nhms.com

activities

Anchor Marine Corporation (366-4311), Winnipesaukee Pier, Weirs Beach. Ski and deck boat, and pontoon boat rentals.

Dive Winnipesaukee (569-8080), 4 N. Main St., Wolfeboro. All levels of training, and lake charters. Certified divers can visit wrecks aboard the "Lady Go Diva", which sails Fri.-Sun. Also, special adventure series dives.

Curt Golder's Angling Adventures (569-6426), 79 Middleton Rd., Wolfeboro. Fishing guide service.

Great Waters Music Festival (569-7710), 58 N. Main St., Wolfeboro. Summer concerts in the weather proof pavilion range from classical to pop to folk to country. Schedule: greatwaters.org

Gunstock Mountain Resort (293-4341), 719 Cherry Valley Rd., Gilford. One hr. trail rides depart from Cobble Mountain Stables. Also, scenic chair lift rides during special events.

Hampshire Pewter (569-4944), 43 Mill St., Wolfeboro. Closed Sun. Tours Mon.-Fri.10 and 11 a.m., & 1, 2 and 3 p.m.

Meredith Marina (279-7921), 2 Bayshore Drive, Meredith. Rentals of cruising, fishing, and ski boats, canoes, boogie boards and tubes.

Millie B Antique Boat Ride (569-1080), Wolfeboro Town Dock, Wolfeboro. Half-hr. antique speedboat rides.

Molly the Trolley (569-1080). Wolfeboro. 45-minute narrated tours on an antique trolley. Late June-Labor Day; call 569-2200 for spring and fall schedule.

Mount Washington Cruises (366-531), Weirs Beach. Daytime and evening dinner/dance cruises. May-Oct. Schedule: cruisenh.com

Nordic Skier Sports (569-3151), 47 N. Main St., Wolfeboro. Bicycle rentals.

Old Country Store (476-5750), Rtes. 25/109, Moultonborough.

Riveredge Marina (800-675-4435 or 968-4411), 81 River St., Ashland. Boat, fishing, and pontoon rentals on Squam Lake.

Squam Boat Livery (968-7721), Rte. 3 at the Bridge, Holderness. Canoe, kayak, sunfish rentals.

Squam Lakes Association (968-7444), Rte. 3, Holderness. Canoe, kayak and sailboat rentals by half day or full day. Memorial Day-Labor Day; Mid-May-Memorial Day and Labor Day-Columbus Day, weekends; Reservations only for full day rentals.

Squam Lake Tours (968-7577), P.O. Box 185, Holderness 03245. Tour includes a motor past Thayer Cottage immortalized in the movie *On Golden Pond*.

Thurston's Marina (366-4811), Rte. 3, Weirs Beach. Ski and pontoon boat, and Tigershark watercraft rentals.

Trexier's Marina (253-7315), 15 Long Island Rd., Moultonboro. Rentals range from kayaks to 17-ft. runabouts with 75 hp motors to 21-ft. deck boats with 190 hp motors.

Weirs Drive-In Theater. The state's largest drive-in has 4 screens. It's near the Weirs Beach Water Slide: Schedule: weirsbeach.net/drivein.html

Wet Wolfe Rentals (569-1503), 17 Bay St., Wolfeboro. Jet skis, fishing and pleasure boat rentals.

Wild Meadow Canoes & Kayaks (80 253-7536), Rte. 25, Center Harbor. Canoe and kayak instruction and rental.

Winnipesaukee Scenic Railroad (279-5253), 154 Main St., Meredith, and 211 Lakeside Ave., Weirs Beach. Cruises alongside the lake weekends in preseason and daily in summer. In fall, there's a dinner train as well.

Winnipesaukee Playhouse (366-7377), 36 Endicott St., Laconia. Professional off-Broadway style theatre. Schedule: winniplayhouse.com

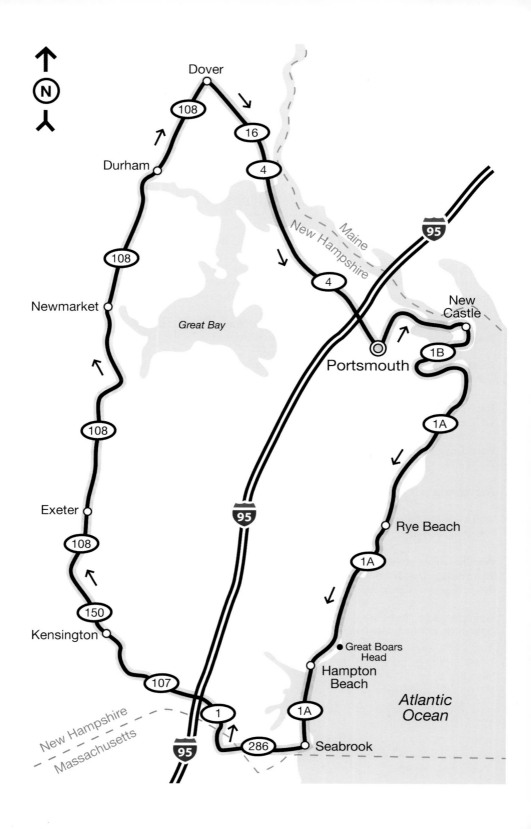

The New Hampshire Seacoast

55 miles

major **attractions**

• Portsmouth	• Hampton Beach	• Odiorne Point State Park
• New Castle	• Exeter	

New Hampshire's seacoast is the shortest in the United States – a mere 18 miles – but it packs in a wealth of scenic, historic, and architectural splendor. Starting at the old colonial capital of Portsmouth, this drive follows the shoreline south, then turns inland toward a vast salt-water estuary and a picturesque prep school town. Return to Portsmouth by way of Durham, seat of the University of New Hampshire, and Dover, home to the state's largest children's museum.

Begin at Portsmouth, where an English skipper first dropped anchor in the waters of what would become New Hampshire. The year was 1603 and the visitor was Captain Martin Pring, master of the vessels *Speedwell* and *Discover*, who made an unsuccessful visit to shore looking for sassafras. Pring didn't linger at the mouth of the Piscataqua, and neither did Samuel de Champlain, who stopped by in 1605 while exploring the coastline south of his Nova Scotia base of operations.

The first party of colonists to establish a settlement in the vicinity of Portsmouth was led by David Thompson, who arrived just south of the Piscataqua at Odiorne Point (see below) in 1623. Within a year, there was a small community on the south shore of the river's ample and well- protected harbor. These settlers, who had come to the New Hampshire coast under the auspices of Britain's royally chartered Council for New England, were joined in 1631 by a group of Massachusetts planters who secured a charter for a community they called Piscataqua, but soon rechristened Strawbery Banke. ("Portsmouth" wasn't adopted until 1653.)

It wasn't long before Portsmouth became an important shipbuilding center. Merchant and fishing vessels came first, but in 1690 the first man o' war slid down the ways into the mouth of the Piscataqua. During Portsmouth's halcyon years of shipbuilding, however, it was the merchants who made the city's economy and gave it the character it has so carefully burnished and preserved. During the mid-1700s, Portsmouth's yards were averaging 25 ships per year; a hundred years later, 10 new vessels were built annually -- but they were larger and faster ships, including more than 30 of the peerless Yankee clippers.

Portsmouth Highlights

Although New Hampshire's state capital has long since been removed to Concord, and the state's largest city is Manchester, Portsmouth retains the genteel aura of its days as the headquarters of colonial government and one of pre-Revolutionary America's most important seaports. Its outsized role was made possible by the fine natural harbor at the mouth of the Piscataqua River – a feature underscored by the continuing presence of one of the United States' oldest military installations, the Portsmouth Naval Shipyard, which actually is located across the harbor in Kittery, Maine.

The U.S.S. Albacore sits high and dry – and open to visitors – at Albacore Park, just off I-95's exit #7 on the way to downtown Portsmouth. The Albacore was the first blimp-shaped submarine, and was once the fastest in the world. It was launched in Portsmouth in 1953, and decommissioned and returned here in 1985.

Strawbery Banke preserves Portsmouth's old name in its 17th-century spelling – and also preserves a restored town-within-a-town, a 10-acre living history museum that tells the story of the evolution of the city's oldest neighborhood from 1650 to

1950. Today's visitors can enter 10 furnished houses, ranging from gracious Georgian mansions to the modest homes of small tradesmen. There are also artisans' shops, where colonial-era crafts are demonstrated; period gardens; and a Pisca-taqua Gundalow, a flat-bottomed boat used from the mid-1600s to the mid-1800s to transport goods upriver from Portsmouth.

The Governor John Langdon House, a Georgian mansion built in 1784, was proclaimed by 1789 visitor George Washington to be the "handsomest house in Portsmouth."

The Moffatt-Ladd House was built at a cost of $12,000 by sea captain turned ship owner John Moffatt as a wedding present for his son, Samuel. Although the elder Moffatt had also given Samuel a Harvard education, the young man didn't inherit his father's business sense. Within five years, he had to flee to the West Indies to escape his creditors. John Moffatt moved in, and lived in the house for the remainder of his 94 years. On the lawn of the National Historic Landmark is a horse chestnut tree planted by William Whipple after he returned from signing the Declaration of Independence in 1776.

The Wentworth Gardner House, built as a gift from Madame Mark Hunking Went-worth to her son Thomas in 1760, is considered one of the finest examples of Georgian architecture in New England. New York's Metropolitan Museum of Art once owned the house and had plans to move it to Central Park.

Among the other "must see" sights in Portsmouth: the 1758 National Historic Landmark John Paul Jones House; the 1807 Rundlet-May House; the state's oldest standing structure, the 1664 Jackson House; the 1716 Warner House; and the 1807 St. John's Church, which displays one of the oldest organs in the country, and a "Vinegar Bible" (so called because of a misprint of the word "vineyard"), one of only four in existence in the United States. The 1803 Athenaeum, across from the 1731 North Church, is one of the country's oldest subscription libraries. On the waterfront, the magnificently landscaped Prescott Park, the oldest and largest outdoor venue in New England, presents free events throughout the summer.

Many of the city's restaurants and shops are clustered on Ceres and Market streets.

Side Trip

"A heap of bare and splintery crags,
Tumbled about by lightning and frost,
With rifts and chasms, and storm-bleached jags,
That wait and growl for a ship to be lost."

This is how James Russell Lowell described the cluster of rocky and virtually treeless islands nine miles off the New Hampshire coast that is now known as the Isles of Shoals. They were "discovered" by Captain John Smith in 1614, but it is likely that Spanish, Portuguese and Basque fishermen were using them as cod-drying stations even before his arrival. Fishermen named the islands because of the way fish "shoaled" or schooled here.

In 1839, Thomas Laighton came to the islands to serve as a lighthouse keeper. Later he opened a hotel on Appledore Island to cater to the summer tourist trade. His daughter Celia Laighton Thaxter (1835-1894) returned to Appledore each summer throughout her adult life. Here she held her famous literary salons, and cultivated the exquisite flower garden captured on canvas by the American Impressionist painter Childe Hassam. Today, the island is home to Cornell University's Shoals Marine Laboratory.

The Oceanic Hotel, on Star Island survives as the center for a program of summer conferences held under the auspices of the Star Island Corporation, affiliated with the Unitarian Universalist Church. Overnight guests are welcome to stay in one of the rustic guest rooms (and set their own schedule), during the summer conference season, which runs from mid-June through mid-September.

Several companies in Portsmouth, including the Isles of Shoals Steamship Company, offer narrated boat tours of the Isles, Celia Thaxter's garden, and Star Island, where day visitors are welcome.

history, and historic lodgings.........................

Follow Route 1B along the coast to New Castle, a one-square-mile island connected to the mainland by bridges. This is where New Hampshiremen staged their famous raid on Fort William and Mary in December 1774, presaging the revolutionary battles of the following spring. Rebuilt in 1808 and renamed **Fort Constitution**, the old garrison still stands. Many of the saltbox-style fishermen's houses along New Castle's winding lanes predate the fort, and look as they'll survive another century or two. Great Island Common, overlooking the ocean, is a delightful spot to picnic.

Continue on Route 1B past the grandest structure on the island, the **Wentworth by the Sea**, a vast Victorian ark built in 1874. It was here, in 1905, that delegates gathered for a peace conference that ended the Russo-Japanese War. Today the magnificently renovated grand hotel offers deluxe lodgings, an 18-hole golf course, a spa, and a marina.

President Theodore Roosevelt was awarded the Nobel Peace Prize for his role in bringing Russian and Japanese delegates to the negotiating table at the Wentworth.

At the intersection of routes 1B and 1A turn north on Route 1A and then turn right onto Little Harbor Road to the **Wentworth-Coolidge Mansion**, home to Benning Wentworth, the Royal Governor of New Hampshire from 1741-67.

Henry Wadsworth Longfellow wrote of the 40-room mansion in his poem "Lady Wentworth":

> It was a pleasant mansion, an abode
> Near and yet hidden from the great highroad,
> Sequestered among trees, a noble pile,
> Baronial and colonial in its style.
>
> Gables and dormer windows everywhere,
> And stacks of chimneys rising high in air,
> Pandaran pipes, on which all winds that blew
> Made mournful music the whole winter through.

During the late 1800s, the mansion was the summer home of historian Francis Parkman. It now belongs to the state, which offers tours. The **Coolidge Center for the Arts**, on the grounds, mounts several exhibits throughout the summer.

a short and scenic coast

Continue south on Route 1A. **Odiorne Point State Park** encompasses the largest undeveloped stretch of shore on New Hampshire's coast. Here is where Champlain and John Smith first spied land, and where David Thompson and his party built their trading post. Today, the site is dotted with the remnants of Fort Dearborn, a collection of World War II observation bunkers and gun turrets. There are also miles of trails, tidal pools and salt marshes teeming with bird, plant, and sea life. **Seacoast Science Center**, on the grounds of the park (separate admission fee), is managed by the New Hampshire Audubon Society and features exhibits relating to the area's rich history.

South of here, Route 1A dips and turns alongside the rocky cliffs, past Wallis Sands State Park (swimming and bath house), Rye Harbor State Park (fishing, picnic area) and Jenness Beach State Park (swimming, bath house). **Island Cruises** travels from Rye Harbor to Star Island several times a day.

It was next to the present site of the Rye Beach Motel that the Atlantic Cable, "The Voice Beneath the Sea," was laid in 1874. The telegraph cable stretched 2,500 miles to the Irish coast.

In North Hampton, turn onto Chapel Road to **Fuller Gardens**, built in the 1920s for Massachusetts Governor Alvin T. Fuller. More than 1,700 rose bushes, a Japanese garden, a conservatory with tropical and desert plants, and a formal English perennial border are among the highlights. Across the way is the 1877 Union Chapel, built to resemble an English country church. Inside, there is an elegant vaulted ceiling, and an altar and altar window designed by Tiffany.

Side Trip

Fans of poet-humorist Ogden Nash (the wit who gave us "Candy/is dandy/But liquor/is Quicker") can make a pilgrimage to his burial place in his family plot at Little River Cemetery. Head west on Route 111, through North Hampton Center to the corner of Woodland Road and Atlantic Avenue. Look for his grave at the rear, near the stone wall.

Continuing south on Route 1A. Stately mansions overlook the sea at Little Boar's Head (one is the governor's official summer residence). North Hampton State Beach offers excellent swimming and a two-mile path, lined with beach rose bushes, which winds along the rocky ridge to the Rye Beach Club.

> At Great Boars Head, look for John Greenleaf Whittier's "Grisley Head of the Boar... [which] tosses the foam from tusks of stone ... as it juts into the ocean." (from his poem "The Tent on the Beach.")

The character of this seaside drive quickly changes **to the south along Route 1A** at **Hampton Beach**, a throwback to an earlier species of oceanside resort. There's nothing the slightest bit chic about it: on one side of Route 1A is a long boardwalk, with steps leading down to the broad strand of Hampton Beach State Park. On the other side is a Smithsonian-quality slice of honky-tonk, amusement arcade, beachfront Americana. **Hampton Beach Casino** hosts a summer-long series of top entertainment, often causing major traffic jams. Activities include free concerts and fireworks throughout the summer. (Note: there's talk of a redevelopment plan, so if you're a fan of this fading resort genre, don't delay your visit here.)

Eunice Cole, a 17th-century resident of Hampton, was a self-proclaimed witch. One day a group of young people sailing down the Hampton River on a fishing ship passed by her shack. A girl climbed up on the ship's shrouds and shouted, "Fie on the witch." According to legend, Cole replied, "You are very brave today, but I hear the little waves laugh and tell me that your broth that awaits you at home will be very, very cold." Unfortunately, her prediction proved true: the ship sank in a storm off the Isles of Shoals later that day, and all were lost at sea. Several years later she was tried before the Quarter Sessions, which found "noe full proof" of witchcraft. But in deference to popular opinion, they decided to punish her anyway, taking her to jail and at-

taching a heavy shackle to her leg for several days. When she died a short time later, her neighbors dug a hole outside her hut, drove a stake into her corpse, and buried her with no marker for her grave.

Turn right off Route 1A onto Route 286, past **Brown's Seafood Lobster Pound,** and through Salisbury, and South Seabrook, and **turn north (right) onto Route 1.** Turn left onto Route 107 and continue past **Master McGrath's** (great ribs) and Seabrook Greyhound Racing Park. **Turn right at the stop sign onto Route 150,** which winds through the countryside and the charming village of Kensington, a cluster of 19th-century white buildings at a bend in the road. **At the junction of Route 108, turn right to Exeter.**

prep school town . . . .

Exeter, one of New Hampshire's earliest settlements (only Portsmouth and Dover are older), was first settled by the Reverend John Wheelwright, a dissenter from the Puritan orthodoxy of Boston. He came here in 1638 and negotiated a deed for the surrounding territory from the sagamore (chief) of the Squamscott tribe. He was joined by only a handful of co-religionists at first, but by 1642 the town had grown sufficiently large to assume equal footing with its two predecessors.

Over the course of the 17th and 18th centuries, Exeter grew in political importance. Throughout most of the American Revolution it was the state's capital; on July 21, 1774, the first Provincial Congress met here, and on January 5, 1776 adopted a written constitution that effectively proclaimed New Hampshire's independence – seven months before a messenger rode into town with the more famous declaration written by Thomas Jefferson and adopted in Philadelphia. The **American Independence Museum,** in the Ladd-Gilman House that served as the State's Treasury from 1775 to 1789 and the governor's mansion for 14 years, offers a glimpse of America's – and Exeter's – experience during the Revolutionary War. The museum's circa 1775 Folsom Tavern on Water Street is undergoing extensive restoration.

Throughout the late 18th century Exeter grew in prosperity, with much of the area's industry dependent upon the power provided by Squamscott Falls. By 1800, its mills turned out everything from paper to snuff to chocolate to sailing ships: some of the country's finest frigates were also built here.

Exeter's past two centuries have seen the water-powered mills fall silent, and a much more famous enterprise rise to prominence. The town is home to Phillips Exeter Academy, founded in 1783 by John Phillips, a successful Exeter merchant who had five years earlier established the other Phillips Academy in his native Andover, Massachusetts.

Today Phillips Exeter, in the Front Street Historic District, is one of America's most prestigious college preparatory schools. Among its alumni are Robert Todd Lincoln, whose father, President Abraham Lincoln, visited him here; and Daniel Webster, remembered by his classmates as a "shy boy who could not make a declamation."

Exeter natives include Amos Tuck, founder of the American Republican Party, who in 1853 named all splinter groups opposed to slavery "Republicans."

Head north out of Exeter on Route 108.

an estuarial treasure

Turn right onto Route 33 (Portsmouth Avenue) and follow the brown and white New Hampshire Fish and Game Department signs to Depot Road. **Great Bay Estuary and Reserve** – the largest inland body of salt water in New England – covers 4,471 acres of tidal waters and mud flats, 48 acres of shoreline, and 800 acres of salt marshes, tidal creeks, woodlands, and open fields. Fed by numerous rivers and creeks, the reserve provides a fertile environment for a wide variety of birds (including nesting bald eagles in winter), other wildlife, and plant species, including many that are threatened or endangered. At **Great Bay Discovery Center**, the Reserve's main headquarters for educational programs and exhibits, gentle trails lead to viewing areas, and, at low tide, into the mud flats.

The center offers four-hour interpretive kayak trips for persons 18 years and older; experience is not necessary and instruction is provided, but advance reservations are highly recommended.

Back on Route 108, continue to Newmarket, a well-preserved, 19th-century mill town at the falls of the Lamprey River. The water below the falls was deep enough at high tide to float large vessels, making it easy to bring heavy equipment and supplies to town. This, and its natural source of waterpower, contributed to the town's growth as an industrial center. Although it now exists primarily as a bedroom community for Portsmouth and Durham, Newmarket's early mill days are preserved in the National Historic District, which includes the 1840 Rivermore Mill on Main Street, now home to **Riverworks Restaurant and Tavern** and several shops.

Side Trip

Turn right onto Bay Road (which becomes Durham Point Road) for about four miles, and then right onto Adams Point Road to **Adams Point Wildlife Management Area** and the trailhead for the Adams Point Trail, an easy 45-minute walk (1 4/10 mile) around the peninsula separating Little Bay from Great Bay. The Jackson Estuarine Laboratory, a University of New Hampshire estuarine research facility, is located here.

Continue on Route 108, alongside the Oyster River, into **Durham.** The town's first colonists came from Dover, sailing into the Oyster River via the Piscataqua and the upper reaches of Great Bay (or Little Bay, as its narrow northern arm is called). They found the elbowroom they were looking for, but paid for it with vulnerability to Indian attacks. A raid here in 1675 marked the opening of hostilities in King Philip's War, while the 1694 sacking and burning of the town ranked as one of the worst atrocities of the era of French-English hostility. The attack was carried out by Indians, but planned in Quebec and led by a French soldier. More than 100 residents were killed or taken captive, and most of the town was reduced to ashes.

Like Exeter, Durham was a hotbed of activity during the Revolution. It was Durham men who stole more than 100 barrels of gunpowder, cannon, and guns from the British at Fort William and Mary in New Castle (see above) and for two days chopped ice in the Oyster River so they could float the material downstream and hide it in town.

Today, Durham is home of the **University of New Hampshire** (UNH), the state's principal public institution of higher learning. The university started life as a state agricultural college in Hanover, but moved here in 1893 when a rich farmer's legacy became available on condition that the school be transplanted to the site of his Durham farm. Modern-day UNH, though, is more devoted to the liberal arts than to agriculture. That said, be sure to visit the Jesse Hepler Lilac Arboretum at Nesmith Hall.

Continue north on Route 108 to Dover, a former mill town, has reinvented itself as a service center for UNH and as a bedroom community for Portsmouth. A self-guided walking tour brochure (available at the Chamber of Commerce) provides an overview of the town's history. One of Dover's major attractions today is the **Children's Museum of New Hampshire,** the state's largest museum for kids. It's a low-tech, high-energy, hands-on kind of place, geared for youngsters who enjoy using their imagination.

Dover's other major attraction is the quirky and fascinating **Woodman Institute,** whose main building houses several floors of "stuff" – collections of war-related uniforms and guns, period furniture, family treasures, and old documents. Also on the grounds are the 1813 three-story brick Hale House, home of abolitionist U.S. Senator J.P. Hale; and the 1675 Damm Garrison, New Hampshire's oldest intact garrison house.

Head back to Portsmouth on routes 16 (toll road) and 4 (collectively known as the Spaulding Turnpike). On the way, stop at the **Red Hook Brewery,** (on the grounds of the former Pease Air Force Base), one of the country's largest craft brewers, for lunch and a tour.

information *All area codes are (603) unless otherwise indicated.*

Exeter Chamber of Commerce (772-2411), 24 Front St., Exeter 03833. exeterarea.org

Greater Dover Chamber of Commerce (742-2218), 299 Central Ave., Dover 03820. dovernh.org

Greater Portsmouth Chamber of Commerce (436-3988), 500 Market St., Portsmouth 03802. portsmouthchamber.org

Hampton Chamber of Commerce (926-8717), 22 C St., Hampton Beach 03842. hamptonbeach.org

New Hampshire State Beaches (271-3556): Parking fee at ocean facilities: $15/day between May 1-Oct. 1. Areas with parking meters enforced May 1-Oct. 1. Entrance fee at non-ocean state parks/beaches: $4 adults; $2 children. nhstateparks.com

Star Island Corporation (430-6272), 30 Middle St., Portsmouth 03801. starisland.org

lodging – Portsmouth

Ale House Inn (431-7760), 121 Bow St., 03801. Newly renovated boutique inn in a former brick brewery overlooking the river has bright, airy rooms and suites with private baths, coffee makers, fridge/freezers, and flat-screen HDTV. alehouseinn.com $$-$$$

The Governor's House (427-5140), 32 Miller Ave., 03801. This 1917 Georgian Colonial, home to Gov. Charles Dale from 1930-64, has 4 handsomely furnished rooms with Frette linens, and all modern amenities. Touring bikes available for guests' use. Continental breakfast included. governors-house.com $$$

Hilton Garden Inn (431-1499), 100 High St. 03801. Rooms at the city's newest downtown hotel have all the modern amenities. Indoor pool, fitness center, and restaurant. portsmouth-downtown.stayhgi.com $$$-$$$$

Sheraton Harborside (431-2300), 250 Market St., 03801. In-town hotel/convention center has 203 rooms and condominium suites. Indoor pool, sauna and exercise room. sheratonportsmouth.com $$-$$$

Sise Inn (433-1200), 40 Court St., 03801. In-town 19th-century Queen Anne b&b has 34 rooms and suites with period furnishings and full baths in the original section, and deluxe accommodations in a restored carriage house. siseinn.com $$-$$$

lodging – along the drive

Ashworth by the Sea (926-6762), 295 Ocean Blvd., Rte. 1A, Hampton Beach, 03842. Landmark, full service oceanfront hotel has 105 air-conditioned, oceanfront room and suites (many with balconies). There are an indoor pool, several restaurants, and live entertainment Wed. & Thurs. ashworthhotel.com $$-$$$

Blue Jay Motel (926-3711), 186 Ashworth Ave., Hampton Beach 03842. Classic, clean motel rooms with knotty pine walls and wall-mounted TVs range from standard doubles to studios with kitchenettes. bluejaymotelnh.com $-$$

DW's Oceanside Inn (926-3542), 365 Ocean Blvd., Hampton Beach 03842. Rooms in this oceanfront, elegantly furnished 1900s beach house have period furnishings; some have canopy beds. The deck is a lovely spot to sit and watch the tide come in. Memorial Day weekend-Columbus Day. oceansideinn.com $$$-$$$$

The Exeter Inn (772-5901), 90 Front St., Exeter 03833. Phillips Academy's 1932 Georgian-style brick inn has 46 well-appointed rooms and suites furnished with antiques and period pieces (7 have fireplaces); restaurant (see "Restaurants" below). theexeterinn.com $$$

Hickory Pond Inn (659-2227), One Stagecoach Rd., Durham 03824. 18 rooms in a pet friendly complex with a c. 1783 farmhouse and outbuildings. Rooms range from small and dark to spacious and cheery: 11 have TV and a/c. hickorypondinn.com $$-$$$

Highland Farm B & B (743-3399), 148 County Farm Rd., Dover 03820. Spacious, antiques-filled guest accommodations in large brick Victorian farmhouse on 75 acres with river frontage. Breakfast served in the formal dining room. Mid-June-mid-Oct. $$

The Inn by the Bandstand (772-6352), 6 Front St., Exeter 03833. 1809 home in town has 9 elegantly furnished rooms with twin and queen beds, private baths, phones, a/c, and TV; some have fireplaces. innbythebandstand.com $$-$$$

New England Conference Center and Hotel (862-2712), UNH Campus, 15 Strafford Ave., Durham 03824. Conference/hotel complex has a total of 115 well-equipped guest rooms. Acorns Restaurant serves Sun. jazz brunch. newenglandcenter.com $$

Silver Fountain Inn (750-4200), 103 Silver St., Dover 03820. 9 elegantly furnished rooms with private baths in a late 1800s beautifully restored, 3-story Victorian home. Breakfast included. silverfountain.com $$-$$$

Three Chimneys Inn (868-7800), 17 Newmarket Rd., Durham 03824. 1649 National Register inn has 23 handsome rooms with private baths in the inn and a 1795 carriage house: some have fireplaces and 4 poster canopy beds. Several restaurants include the ffrost Sawyer Tavern (see "Restaurants" below). threechimneysinn.com $$$

Wentworth by the Sea (422-7322), 588 Wentworth Rd., New Castle 03854. wentworth.com $$$-$$$$

restaurants – Portsmouth

The Friendly Toast (430-2154), 121 Congress St. The ambiance is over the top, and the breakfasts, with house specialties such as almond joy pancakes, and smoked salmon Benedict, are fabulous. Sandwiches—from chorizo burritos to Portobello melts – are equally creative. Kids half price. B, L, & D Mon.-Thurs.; around the clock from 7 a.m. Fri. until 9 p.m. Sun. $-$$

Jumpin' Jay's Fish Café (766-3474), 150 Congress St. The kitchen does wonders with flopping fresh fish: among the specialties – steamed mussels, haddock piccata, Cuban fisherman's stew, and an outstanding raw bar with more than 2 dozen kinds of oysters. D $$

The Library Restaurant (431-5202), 401 State St., Portsmouth. Casual but elegant surroundings at this upscale steak house whose menu features Kobe steaks and 24 oz. steaks. L, D & Sun. brunch. $$$-$$$$

Muddy River Smokehouse (430-9582), 21 Congress St., Portsmouth. BBQ, chili, 2 dozen beers on tap and a blues club downstairs. L & D $

The Portsmouth Brewery (431-1115), 56 Market St., Portsmouth. New Hampshire's original brewery serves an extended menu of pub grub, including a ploughman's platter, ½-lb. burgers, and spicy curried mussels. L & D. $-$$

restaurants on the drive

Brown's Lobster Pound (474-3331), Rte. 286, Seabrook Beach. For more than 50 years this classic lobster pound has been serving lobster in all its permutations, as well as seafood combination plates. L & D mid-Apr.-mid-Nov., Fri.-Sun. rest of year.

Epoch Restaurant and Bar (772-5901), The Exeter Inn, 90 Front St., Exeter. The sophisticated menu includes fennel-seared sea bass and pepper crusted Angus strip steak. Sun. brunch, with a "build your own" bloody Mary buffet, is a tradition. B &L Mon.-Sat., D nightly; Sun. brunch. $$$-$$$$

ffrost Sawyer Tavern, Three Chimneys Inn, 17 Newmarket Dr., Durham. Handsome surroundings and elegant fare, with appetizers such as butternut squash ravioli; and entrées including bouillabaisse, and Jefferson chicken. For the kids: burgers and fries (homemade, of course). D. $$$-$$$$

Little Jack's Seafood Restaurant (926-8053), 539 Ocean Blvd., Hampton Beach. Baked, broiled, steamed and fried seafood and shore dinners – including outstanding fried clams – in a casual eatery overlooking the ocean. L & D in season. $-$$

Loaf and Ladle (778-8955), 9 Water St., Exeter. For more than 2 decades a favorite destination for homemade soups, terrific sandwiches, creative salads, and daily specials such as sweet & sour pork. B, L & D. $

Master McGrath's (474-3540), Rte. 107, Seabrook. BBQ ribs, an all you can eat salad bar, chicken pot pie ... The menu is extensive, the ambiance pleasant, and everything is moderately priced. Breakfast, featuring dishes such as apple stuffed French toast and banana pancakes, is served until 2 p.m. weekends. L & D; weekend brunch. $-$$

Newick's Lobster House and Restaurant (742-3205), Dover Point Rd., Dover. Large portions of fresh seafood served in an informal atmosphere overlooking Great Bay. L & D. $$

Petey's Summertime Seafood and Bar (433-1937), Rte. 1A, Rye. Classic beachfront platters include fried clams, lobster, and fish and chips, on a deck overlooking the sea. L & D. $-$$

The Redhook Ale Brewery (430-8600), 35 Corporate Dr., Pease International Tradeport, Portsmouth. Tours daily ($). L & D. $-$$

Riverworks Restaurant and Tavern (659-6119), 164 Main St., Newmarket. The eclectic menu in the second floor dining room includes Thai lo mein, broccoli Alfredo, and beef stroganoff.

The tavern serves full and late night menus. L & D. $$

Saunders at Rye Harbor (964-6466), off Rte. 1A, Rye Harbor. Harborfront landmark serves fine lobster, fresh seafood, poultry, and prime beef. Live music weekends. L & D. $$-$$$

attractions – Portsmouth

Albacore Park (436-3680), 600 Market St. Memorial Day-Columbus Day; Columbus Day-Memorial Day, Thurs.-Mon.

Historic New England (617-227-3956): oversees the 1664 Jackson House, the Langdon House, and the Rundlet-May House, in Portsmouth; and the Gilman Garrison House in Exeter. For information: 436-3205. historicnewengland.org

Moffatt-Ladd House & Garden (436-8221), 154 Market St. Mid-June-fall. Tour includes the newly restored Moffatt-Ladd Warehouse.

Portsmouth Athenaeum (431-2538), 9 Market Sq. Tues., Thurs. and Sat. Tours Thurs. p.m. Free.

St. John's Episcopal Church (436-6902), Chapel St.

Strawbery Banke Museum (433-1106), 64 Marcy St. Mid-April - Oct.

Wentworth-Gardner House, 50 Mechanic St., and the c. 1740 Georgian Tobias Lear House, Hunking St. Open mid-June-mid-Oct. Thurs.-Sun. For information: 436-4406.

attractions on the drive

American Independence Museum (772-0861), One Governors Lane, Exeter. Mid-May-late Oct.; guided tours on hr. Wed.-Sat.

Children's Museum of New Hampshire 742-2002), 6 Washington St., Dover. Daily in summer; Tues.-Sat. (and Mon. holidays) rest of year.

Durham Historic Association (868-5436), Main St./Newmarket Rd., Durham. June-Aug., Wed. p.m.

Fort Constitution and Fort Stark State Historic Sites (436-1552), off Rte. 1B, New Castle. Free.

Fuller Gardens (964-5414), 10 Willow Ave., North Hampton. Mid-May-mid-Oct.

Gilman Garrison House (436-3205), 12 Water St., Exeter. June-mid-Oct., Tues., Thurs., Sat. and Sun. p.m. $

Great Bay National Estuarine Research Reserve (868-1095), 37 Concord Rd., Durham.

Great Bay Discovery Center (778-0015), 89 Depot Rd., Greenland. May-Sept., Wed.-Sun.; Oct., Sat. and Sun.; grounds open year round.

New Market Historical Society & Museum (659-7420), Granite St., Newmarket. Thurs. p.m. in summer.

Seacoast Science Center (436-8043), Rte. 1A, Rye. Apr.-Oct.; Nov.-March, Sat.-Mon.

Wentworth-Coolidge Mansion (436-6607), 375 Little Harbor Rd., Portsmouth. Mid-June-Labor Day, Wed.-Sun; weekends mid-Sept.-mid-Oct. Coolidge Center for the Arts mid-May-late Sept., Wed.-Sat., Sun. p.m.

Woodman Institute (742-1038), 182 Central Ave., Dover. Apr.-Nov., Wed.-Sun.; Dec.-Jan., weekends.

activities – Portsmouth

Isles of Shoals Steamship Co. (431-5500), 315 Market St. Whale watches; lighthouse, harbor island and Isles of Shoals cruises; Star Island picnics and explorations.

The Music Hall (436-2400), 28 Chestnut St. 1878 hall hosts music, theater, dance, and movies. Schedule: themusichall.org

Pontine Theatre (436-6660), 959 Islington St. Cutting-edge productions presented in an intimate performance space. Schedule: pontine.org

Portsmouth Harbor Cruises (436-8084), Ceres St. Dock. Narrated tours of the harbor, Isles of Shoals, Great Bay, and the Cocheco River. Luncheon cruises and guided tours of Celia Thaxter's garden on Appledore Island.

Prescott Park Arts Festival (436-2848), Prescott Park. Schedule: cityofportsmouth.com

Portsmouth Harbour Trail (610-5510), Greater Portsmouth Chamber of Commerce, 500 Market St. Guided walking tours of the city.

The Press Room (431-5186), 77 Daniel St. The city's long-running destination for live jazz, folk, and blues.

Seacoast Repertory Theater (433-4793), 125 Bow St. Live theater throughout the year. Schedule: seacoastrep.org

Water Country (427-1111), 2300 Lafayette Rd., Rte. 1 S, Portsmouth. New England's largest water park has more than 20 acres of fun.

activities on the drive

Atlantic Fishing and Whale Watch (964-5220), Rye Harbor State Marina, Rte. 1A, Rye Harbor. ½ day and full day fishing and whale watches.

Al Gauron Deep Sea Fishing and Whale Watching (926-2469), State Pier, Hampton Beach. ½ day, full day, and night fishing trips and marathons; whale watches July and Aug.

Emery Farm (742-8495), Rte. 4, Durham. Pick your own berries or buy them ready-picked, along with peaches, local crafts, home-baked bread, and pottery at this family farm, established in 1655.

Hampton Beach Casino (929-4100), 169 Ocean Blvd., Hampton. Schedule: casinoballroom.com.

Island Cruises (964-6446), Rye Harbor State Marina, Rte. 1A, Rye. Ferry to Star Island; lobster and Isles of Shoals tours spring-fall.

Salmon Falls Stoneware (749-1467), Oak St., Dover. Traditional American salt-glaze pottery.

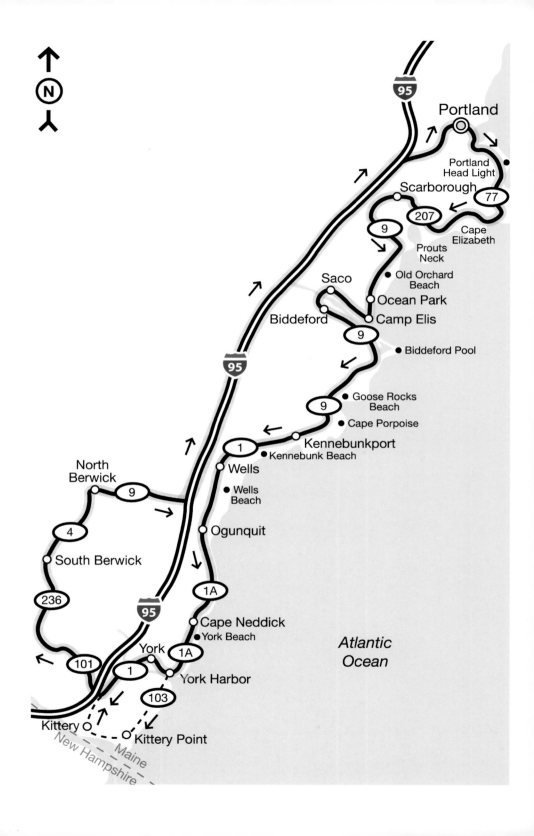

The Southern Maine Coast

136 miles

major **attractions**

- Ocean Park
- Ogunquit
- Historic Lighthouses
- Old Orchard Beach
- Kennebunkport
- Historic York
- Kittery Outlets

*H*ug the rugged Maine coast south of Portland by following byways that lead past picturesque lighthouses, the haunts of a famous artist and a U.S. president, and an old-fashioned seaside amusement park. In this most densely populated corner of the state, there are still miles of inviting beaches, and sanctuaries that preserve pristine dunelands, salt marshes, and bird habitats.

Note: This route passes through some of Maine's most scenic—and most congested—areas. If your time (or patience) is limited, we suggest hopping onto I-95 S after visiting Cape Elizabeth (Route. 207) and resuming the drive from the Kennebunk exit (#25, Route 9A back to Route 1 S).

Note: I-95 and the Maine Turnpike (toll) are the same road. I-295 parallels I-95 from Portland (exit 44 off I-95) to Gardiner (exit 103).

Head out of downtown Portland (see Drive 18) on Commercial Street over the Casco Bay Bridge (Route 77) to Cape Elizabeth, **and continue straight onto Broadway. Follow signs for Portland Head Light: turn right onto Cottage Road (which turns into Shore Road) at Red's Dairy Freeze.** The entrance to **Fort Williams Park** and **Portland Head Light** is about 2.7 miles after you cross the bridge.

One of the oldest and most photographed lighthouses in Maine has been warning sailors of rocky shores on the approach into Portland Harbor since 1791. It was immortalized in the famous poem "The Lighthouse" by Henry Wadsworth Longfellow, who was a frequent visitor here. Unfortunately, the warning didn't prove sufficient to the vessel *Bohemian*, out of Liverpool, which sank here in 1864. Following this disaster, officials raised the height of the lighthouse from 72 to 92 feet. The museum in the former keeper's house documents the history of the light and Fort Williams. (The tower is not open to the public). The park, originally intended to serve as an auxiliary outpost for a nearby fort, is a wonderful place to stroll. Some of the structures built to shore up harbor defenses during World Wars I and II are still in place.

When you leave the park, **turn left out of the parking lot and continue straight to Route 77 south.** The turn off to the entrance to **Two Lights State Park** will be on the left, across from The Good Table Restaurant. The park, with 41 acres of rocky headlands, provides majestic views of Casco Bay and the ocean as well as twin lighthouses built in 1828: the active eastern light, 17 miles out at sea, and the decommissioned western light, now a private residence. There are also remains of several World War II structures. Continue past the park entrance on Two Lights Road to the water and **The Lobster Shack Restaurant.**

Back on Route 77, continue south, past the Inn by the Sea, to 243-acre **Crescent Beach State Park,** with a mile-long, sandy beach, dunes, picnic areas, and – for Maine – moderately warm water. Next up is **Higgins Beach,** highly regarded for surfing and striped bass fishing. There's a small parking lot, which is usually full.

Side Trip

When Route 77 ends at the junction with Route 207, turn left onto Route 207 (Black Point Road) to reach the popular **Scarborough Beach State Park,** which has an excellent sand beach, dunes, hiking trails, and a lifeguard in season. Parking here is easier, but spaces are limited and tend to fill up early on weekends. Continue south to the very private **Prouts Neck,** immortalized in the paintings of onetime resident Winslow Homer. At the very end of Route 207 is Winslow Homer Road, posted with signs reading: "positively no passing," "private way," "no motor bikes," "no buses," and "for residents and their guests only." As you might guess, parking opportunities are minimal here. The **Prouts Neck Bird Sanctuary** is also on private land, and has no public parking. However, visitors who dine at the elegant—and well-situated – **Black Point Inn** can take a postprandial stroll through the sanctuary, which passes by the studio of Mr. Homer (acquired by the Portland Museum of Art in 2006, the studio is slated eventually to be open to the public). Be sure to include the Cliff Path (ask at the inn for directions).

In the fall of 1884, Winslow Homer left Prouts Neck on an extended trip to the tropics … to avoid jury duty in his adopted state of Maine.

Back at the junction of routes 77 and 207, head north on Route 207 through Scarborough, to the junction of Route 1/9, and turn left (south) onto Route 1/9. Continue to where Route 9 branches off to the left. Follow Route 9 W (yes, you're really traveling east here, but the sign will say 9W) for approximately 8/10 mile to the entrance for Scarborough Marsh Audubon Center, an awesome 3,100 acre swath of salt marsh, salt creeks, freshwater marsh and uplands that is home to a diverse number of birds. Facilities include a nature center; naturalist-led programs; and canoe and kayak rentals for trips along the Dunstan River.

an old-time resort

Continue on Route 9, across **Pine Point**, to **Old Orchard Beach**. The high-rise apartment complexes that ring the beach are a harbinger of gentrification, so if you're looking for a nostalgic journey back to days when a trip to the shore included a merry-go-round ride, a round of miniature golf, cotton candy, and a stroll on the pier, don't put off a visit. The seven-mile-long beach has an amusement park, Thursday night fireworks, and a general carnival atmosphere.

Long popular with French Canadians, Old Orchard Beach is sometimes called the "Quebec Riviera." The Grand Trunk Railroad first brought summer sojourners from Montreal in 1853.

The large number of motels keeps prices moderate, so this is a good place to look for reasonably priced oceanfront lodgings. Visitors with a taste for history might want to check out the 1730s, National Register of Historic Places Old Orchard Beach Inn: Maine's first hotel opened its doors as Ye Old Staples Inn in the 1830s, charging guests $1.50 a night.

Continue south on Route 9 alongside the Saco Bay for a few miles to historic **Ocean Park**, one of the country's few remaining "assembly centers," which were established around the country in the late 19th century for summer camp meetings. Known as the "Eastern New England Chatauqua," the community founded by Free Will Baptists in 1881 now has several gift shops, public tennis courts, and an old-fashioned ice cream parlor; and is a center for interdenominational religious, cultural, educational, and recreational activities. Many of the buildings are on the National Register of Historic Places. Programs include lectures, and, during the summer, a weekend Music Festival featuring opera, jazz, ragtime piano, and classical music in the 19th-century, octagonal 850-seat Temple.

All of Ocean Park is a State of Maine Game Preserve, and there are several walking trails through stands of majestic cathedral pines. A portion of the **Rachel Carson National Wildlife Refuge** is adjacent. It's one of 10 parcels of land between Kittery Point and Cape Elizabeth set aside for wildlife protection.

Just to the south, 117-acre **Ferry Beach State Park** has a sand beach, lifeguards, a picnic area, changing rooms, and several nature trails through marshes and dunes.

Farther south at **Camp Ellis**, the 128-mile-long Saco River, which originates in New Hampshire, empties into the Gulf of Maine. Take a stroll along, or drop a fishing line off, the nearly mile-long jetty. The beach is open to the public, and Saco Bay Sailing rents kayaks and offers scenic boat cruises.

> *Thomas Orcutt, a retired sea captain, served at Wood Island Light, at the mouth of the Saco River, for 19 years. Legend has it that the island is haunted by the ghost of a local police officer murdered by a squatter in 1896.*

Continue on Route 9 as it ducks inland into **Saco**, once home to the area's wealthy mill owners, and now home to one of Maine's oldest, quirkiest, and most interesting museums. The **Saco Museum** is a treasure trove of more than 10,000 historic artifacts, including local furniture, period costumes, decorative arts, paintings, and other *objets d'art*. Among the collections: a 19th-century, 850-foot-long panorama of *Pilgrim's Progress*; the country's first daguerreotype portrait camera; a recreated Colonial Revival kitchen; and an Empire-period bed chamber.

During the mid-1800s, Saco was home to one of the country's largest cotton milling complexes, and the buildings that line Main Street reflect the town's wealthy past. Some of the mills in the Factory Island Mill District, which were closed down in 1958, have been renovated for offices and residences.

Continue south out of Saco on Route 9 (be careful here: Route 1 splits off from Route 9. In Biddeford, turn east off Route 9 onto Route 208 south toward **Biddeford Pool**.

Side Trip

If you're a birder, a trip to Biddeford Pool is a must, particularly if you can time your visit with the falling tide. Where routes 9 and 208 split, stay on Route 208. After 6/10 mile turn left at the T intersection, and then bear right through two forks to Lester B. Orcutt Boulevard to the Maine Audubon Society's **East Point Sanctuary.** With its views of Wood Island Light and booming surf, the secluded, 30-acre preserve is spectacular at any time. In spring and fall, however, it's one of the best places in the state to observe bird migrations. Watch for gannets, sea ducks, terns, and harbor seals, and poison ivy.

Back on Route 9, continue south past the turn-off for Fortunes Rocks Beach. Turn left on Rocks Road to visit **Goose Rocks Beach,** just east of Cape Porpoise. The three-mile-long beach, with fine silver white sand, was named for a barrier reef rock formation known as "Goose Rocks", which is visible at low tide. Beach grass provides ideal nesting spots for piping plovers and lesser terns. Look for sand dollars as you walk along the beach. [Note: parking along this beach is extremely limited, and a permit, available at the Kennebunkport Police Station, is required: you might want to wait to do your beach-combing, or stay at the **Tides~by~the Sea.**

Continue on Route 9. Turn left at Atlantic Hall onto Pier Road to scenic **Cape Porpoise** – actually a group of islands – named by Captain John Smith who landed here in the 1600s. The area's first settlement is today a working harbor with a cluster of shops, art galleries, and restaurants. Just off shore, Goat Island Light, the state's last manned lighthouse, was automated in 1990.

Backtrack to Route 9 and continue south. Just out of town, turn left onto Wildes District Road, then left again just past the Wildwood Fire Department onto Turbats Creek Road. This road turns into Ocean Avenue when it reaches the water, passing Walker Point (summer home of President George H. W. Bush), St. Anne's Church, Spouting Rock and Blowing Cave (rock formations best observed between low and hide tides), and the historic Colony Hotel, before funneling into **Kennebunkport.**

One of Maine's most popular (and crowded) tourist destinations, Kennebunkport was originally a shipbuilding center: more than 1,000 oceangoing vessels were built here in the 1800s, and the handsome homes, churches, and public buildings around town stand as testament to the wealth amassed by its merchants, ship builders, and sea captains. Stop at the **Kennebunkport Historical Society** for a brochure detailing several walking tours of the village. The Society maintains several properties in town, including the 1853 Greek Revival Nott House, preserving the lifestyle of four generations from the late 1700s through the middle 1900s. If you'd rather have someone else do the driving (a wise idea on a crowded summer's day), opt for a narrated tour aboard the **Intown Trolley.**

> *Russian President Vladimir Putin caught a striped bass off Walker's Point while fishing with his American counterpart, George W. Bush.*

Side Trip

From Dock Square, turn left onto North Street (which changes its name to Log Cabin Road along the way) for 3 2/10 mile to the **Seashore Trolley Museum.** The world's oldest and largest museum of mass transit vehicles exhibits more than 225 refurbished cars, and visitors can hop aboard an antique electric trolley car for a 3-½ mile ride.

Side Trip

Just south of Kennebunkport, take Route 9A west to **Kennebunk,** a handsome town with a National Register Historic District of more than 24 sites including Colonial, Federal, Queen Anne, Greek Revival, and Italianate buildings. The **Brick Store Museum,** a four-building complex with extensive exhibits of local history and art, offers architectural walking tours ($). Be sure to drive by the Wedding Cake House (private) at 104 Summer Street (Route 35), a yellow and white Gothic Revival confection built by a shipbuilder for his wife in 1826.

Side Trip

From Kennebunk, take Route 99W to **Kennebunk Plains**, a 135-acre preserve amidst a 2,000-acre swath of protected land. The preserve, a habitat comprising grasslands, woods and ponds, is home to several rare and endangered species of vegetation and wildlife. Ninety percent of the world's northern blazing star population grows here, and when it blooms in early August, the landscape is a sea of purple. In July, the wild blueberries are ripe for picking. Watch for rare grassland and nesting birds such as grasshopper sparrows. The Plains is monitored by the **Maine Nature Conservancy**.

Head out of town on Route 9. At the traffic light just over the bridge, turn left onto Beach Avenue and follow signs for **Kennebunk Beach** (parking permit required in season, available at Kennebunk Town Hall). On the left, hidden by hedges, is **St. Anthony's Franciscan Monastery**, headquartered in a magnificent Tudor-style mansion. Visitors are welcome to stroll the sweeping grounds and visit the chapel and shrine. The monks operate a retreat and a guesthouse for those who want to linger a while.

refuge and reserve

Continue along the beach and back onto Route 9, past a section of the **Rachel Carson National Wildlife Refuge**. More than 250 species of birds have been spotted along the one-mile, protected coastal salt marsh nature trail.

Just past the refuge, turn left onto Skinner Mill Road to Laudholm Farm Road and the

1,600-acre **Wells National Estuarine Research Reserve.** Established in 1986 as a research, education and public recreation facility devoted to protecting the coastal environment, this wonderful property has seven miles of trails that wind through fields, woods, orchards, salt meadows, and along the water. Be sure to see the exhibits in the restored, 19th-century farmhouse. In fall, watch for migrating hawks, ospreys, and falcons.

Exit the Reserve onto Route 1 and head south through **Wells,** past several excellent used book stores, antique centers, and the **Wells Auto Museum,** which displays more than 80 classic cars as well as vintage arcade games and nickelodeon machines (and yes, they work). Numerous roads dart off Route 1 to the ocean. Turn left at the traffic light by the USA Inn onto Mile Road to Wells Beach.

Route 1 continues south into **Ogunquit.** The town has been known as an art colony since 1890, when artist Charles Woodbury first dubbed it an "artist's paradise."

> *Park your car at any municipal or private parking lot and hop aboard the Molly Trolley, which operates between July 1st and Labor Day. Among the stops are Perkins Cove and Ogunquit Beach.*

Today, galleries and small businesses line the streets of this paradise, and Narrow Cove, where Mr. Woodbury and other artists, including Edward Hopper, often set up their easels, is now home to **the Ogunquit Museum of Art,** hailed as "the most beautiful small museum in the world." The grounds, open daily free of charge, are graced with works by renowned sculptors including Bernard Langlais and William Zorach. To visit the museum, turn left off Route 1 in the center of town onto Shore Road toward **Perkins Cove,** and continue along Shore Road.

Perkins Cove, a scenic amalgam of fishing boats, boutiques, and restaurants, is a terminus for **Marginal Way,** a mile-long path that winds alongside the ocean through stands of pine and past profusions of wild roses. Note: parking places here fill up early: the best time to come is early morning, or park at one of the paid lots close by.

With 3 ½ miles of soft white sand and warm water, **Ogunquit Beach,** backing on the Ogunquit River, is considered one of the best beaches in the country. There is a public parking lot here.

> *The Ogunquit Playhouse, just south of town on Route 1, has been attracting big-name stars to perform in its comedies and musicals since 1933.*

From the cove, backtrack and turn left onto Shore Road and head south, past the turnoff for the Cliff House, across the Cape Neddick River to **York Beach.** In town, press your nose against the glass at The Goldenrod and watch as the folks make "goldenrod kisses," also known as saltwater taffy. They've been doing it for more than 100 years, and pump out more than nine million pieces a year. The luncheonette serves sandwiches, burgers, blueberry strudel, and more than 135 flavors of homemade ice cream.

From the beach follow Ocean Avenue/Nubble Road to the tip of the peninsula and Sohier Park, home to the much-photographed **Nubble Light** (also known as Cape Neddick Light), built in 1879 near the entrance to the York River. The lighthouse is on an island, and inaccessible, but the Welcome Center at the park has information.

Loop back on Nubble Road to Route 1A south and follow alongside beautiful – and often crowded – Long Sands Beach (metered parking). In **York Harbor**, the beautifully preserved 1718 **Sayward-Wheeler House**, once the home of a wealthy local merchant, is open for tours on weekends (see Historic New England under "Attractions" below). Across the road (on Route 103) hike over the Wiggley Bridge, which divides the York River and Mill Pond, into **Steedman Woods** (a property of the Old York Historical Society) preserve. A 1-mile loop trail provides great scenery and bird watching.

On Route 1A, follow signs into **York Village**. The **Old York Historical Society** maintains seven historic museum buildings, including the Old Gaol, a School House, and the society's headquarters at Jefferds' Tavern. Costumed volunteers do a fine job of bringing the area's rich history to life, and guided and self-guided tours are available. Ask about the society's many special events, including "Ghostly Tours," which offers a unique perspective on the town's history: a 45-minute evening walking tour by candlelight includes a trip through an old cemetery.

In 1710 the ship Nottingham Galley ran aground on the island that is now home to Boon Light. Six miles from shore, and with no way to get to get off the island, the survivors resorted to cannibalism. For many years after, local fishermen left provisions in case of more shipwrecks.

Option: if you want to skip the historic Kittery portion of this tour and head straight for the shopping outlets, continue on Route 1A to the intersection with Route 1, and head south into Kittery (turn right at the intersection to visit **Stonewall Kitchen Café**, a short distance to the north on Route 1).

history ... and shopping

Kittery, " Gateway to Maine," is home to one of New England's major discount outlet centers. More than 125 retail outlets line both sides of Route 1 for more than a mile. Don't miss the Kittery Trading Post, a local institution since 1926.

Kittery is also one of Maine's first settlements. **Backtrack on Route 1A from York Village to the beginning of Route 103 and turn right (south)** toward **Kittery Point** on the Piscataqua River. If you're ready for a swim, and don't mind steep parking fees and crowds, turn left onto Gerrish Island Lane and follow signs to **Fort Foster**, a municipal beach with an 1800s fort overlooking Portsmouth Harbor.

Further up on Route 103 is the well-preserved **Fort McClary Historic Site**, with an 1846 blockhouse. (That's the Portsmouth Naval Shipyard across the way). The 50-feet-high, granite **Whaleback Lighthouse** visible from shore was built in 1872 to guard the entrance to the Piscataqua River.

After a sharp bend in the road, watch on the right for the 1760 Lady Pepperell House (closed to the public), a two-story Georgian with a hip roof and four large chimneys. It was the home of Lady Pepperell, wife of the "richest man in the Massachusetts Bay Colony" until her death in 1789. Opposite the house is the 1730 First Congregational Church, remodeled in 1874. Behind the church, in the Old Burial Ground, the tomb of Levi Lincoln Thaxter, husband of the poet Celia Thaxter, who kept a famous literary and artists' salon on the nearby Isles of Shoals, bears an epitaph written by Robert Browning. Another reads:

> 'A powerful God doth as he please.
> I lost my wife in the raging seas.
> The Kittery friends, they did appear
> And my remains they buried here.'

When Route 103 intersects with Route 236, follow Route 236 back to Kittery; when it merges with Route 1 at the rotary, head north on Route 1 a short distance to the **Kittery Historical and Naval Museum**, on the right. The museum has a rich collection of ship models, paintings, scrimshaw, and other nautical gear. Nearby, the **John Paul Jones Memorial** (across from **Warren's Lobster House**) honors the man whose sloop *Ranger* was built and launched from nearby Badger's Island in 1877.

Head north on Route 1 a short distance to the left hand turn onto Route 101 to the intersection of Route 236. Note: if not visiting the **Historical and Naval Museum**, you can stay on Route 236 to South Berwick, but Route 101 is a more scenic road.

Continue on Route 236 toward **South Berwick, and turn left just after the intersection** to visit **Vaughn Woods State Park**, along the Salmon Falls River, which "shall forever be left in the natural wild state, and forever be kept as a sanctuary for wild beasts and birds."

Nearby is the 18th-century, Georgian-style **Hamilton House** (see Historic New England under "Attractions"), a magnificently preserved Georgian mansion often visited by Admiral John Paul Jones. Now a National Historic Landmark, the home was the setting for local author Sarah Orne Jewett's book, *The Tory Lover*, and is filled with Chippendale, Hepplewhite and Sheraton pieces.

South Berwick, on the Salmon Falls River, is a town of "firsts." It was first in Maine to be settled; the first cows landed at Cow's Cove; and Berwick Academy, founded in 1791, is the state's oldest secondary school. And it was here the first American attempt was made to grow grapes commercially.

It was also the birthplace of Sarah Orne Jewett (born in 1849, she died here in 1909, and is buried in the Portland Street Cemetery on Agamenticus Road), and today the **Sarah Orne Jewett Homestead**, built in 1780 and purchased by her grandfather, is open for tours under the auspices of Historic New England (see "Attractions" below). If you have time, take a stroll through Old Fields Burying Ground; some of the stones date back to the 17th century.

Return to Kittery and take I-95 north back to Portland.

information *All area codes are (207) unless otherwise indicated.*

Biddeford-Saco Chamber of Commerce (282-1567), 138 Main St., Suite 101, Saco 04072. biddefordsacochamber.org.

Cape Elizabeth: capeelizabeth.com

Greater Somersworth Chamber of Commerce (South Berwick) (603-692-7175), 58 High St., P.O. Box 615, Somersworth, NH 03878.

Greater York Region Chamber of Commerce (York and Kittery) (439-7545), 1 Stonewall Lane, York 03909. gatewaytomaine.org

Kennebunk-Kennebunkport Chamber of Commerce (967-0857), 17 Western Ave, Kennebunk 04043. visitthekennebunks.com

Maine Beaches: mainebeachesassociation.com

Maine Nature Conservancy, (792-5181), 14 Maine St., Brunswick 04011. nature.org

New Hampshire Beaches: nhstateparks.com/beaches.html

Ocean Park (934-9068), 14 Temple Ave., Ocean Park 04063. oceanpark.org

Ogunquit Welcome Center (646-2939), Rte. 1, Box 2289, Ogunquit 03907. ogunquit.org.

Old Orchard Beach Chamber of Commerce (934-2500), P.O. Box 600, Old Orchard Beach 04064. oldorchardbeachmaine.com

Southern Maine Coast Tourism Association (800-639-2442). southernmainecoast.com

Wells Chamber of Commerce (646-2451), Rte. 1, P.O. Box 356, Wells 04090. wellschamber.org.

lodging

Academy Street Inn B&B (384-5633), 15 Academy St., South Berwick 03908. 1903 Grand Colonial-style Victorian has 5 elegantly furnished, antiques-filled rooms with private baths. Full breakfast; children over 10. virtualcities.com $$

Black Point Inn (883-2500), 510 Black Point Rd., Scarborough 04074. A landmark since 1878, this inn with an 18-hole golf course is surrounded on three sides by water. Some say that the quality and service have slipped since the old days; others say it's close to paradise. The 25 rooms offer ocean or bay views; some private decks. MAP. (Note: an 18% guest service charge is added to the room rate.) blackpointinn.com $$$$

Cabot Cove Cottages (967-5424), 7 South Maine St., Kennebunkport 04046. 15 1- and 2-bedroom cottages on spacious grounds overlooking a tidal cove. Rowboats and canoes; children and pets. cabotcovecottages.com $$

Captain Lord Mansion (967-3141), 6 Pleasant St., Kennebunkport 04046. Intimate, historic inn has large, elegantly furnished rooms with 4-poster canopy beds and working fireplaces. captainlord.com $$-$$$$

Cliff House (361-1000), Shore Rd., Ogunquit. 160 guest rooms on 70 acres overlooking the ocean. Fitness room, tennis courts, indoor and outdoor pools. One restaurant specializes in seafood, the other in California cuisine. Sun. champagne brunch buffet, with harp music, ($$$$) is a standout. cliffhousemaine.com $$$

The Colony Hotel (967-3331), 140 Ocean Ave., Kennebunkport 04046. The port's oceanfront "grand hotel has 123 comfortable rooms, a heated saltwater pool, and a private sandy beach. Lobster is a specialty at the restaurant, which serves traditional regional fare. Pets ($). May-Oct. thecolonyhotel.com/maine $$-$$$$

Franciscan Guest House, Franciscan Monastery (967-4865), 26 Beach Ave., Kennebunk Beach 04043. Simple, somewhat dated, but inexpensive lodging; all units have private baths, a/c, and cable TV; outdoor saltwater pool. $-$$

Inn by the Sea (799-3134), 40 Bowery Beach Road, Crescent Beach, Cape Elizabeth 04107. 57 luxury accommodations at the edge of the ocean range from 1-bedroom units in the main lodge to 2-level, waterfront cottages with fireplaces. Not only is the inn pet friendly, it even provides Bowser with a beach towel (a massage for you and/or your pet is optional). The Sea Glass Restaurant serves 3 meals and offers *al fresco* dining. innbythesea.com $$$-$$$$

Kennebunkport Motor Lodge (967-2338), 22 Wildes District Rd., Kennebunkport 04046. Pleasant standard motel units just minutes from town. Beach passes available. All rooms have refrigerators and a/c. Outdoor heated pool. kennebunkportmotorlodge.com $$

Lafayette Oceanfront Resort (646-2831), Wells Beach 04090. Large, oceanfront complex includes several motels with a variety of accommodations; indoor pool and whirlpool. Open year round. wellsbeachmaine.com $$-$$$

Lodge at Turbat's Creek (877-594-5634), 7 Turbat's Creek Rd., Kennebunkport 04046. 26 recently remodeled motel-style rooms set in a wooded grove a few miles from town. Heated outdoor saltwater pool, free touring bicycles, and continental breakfast. lodgeatturbatscreek.com $$-$$$

Cape Arundel Inn (967-2125), 208 Ocean Ave., Kennebunkport 04046. "The closest to a bed on the ocean", this oceanfront inn and dining room is actually three properties: the 1895 main inn; a more traditional-style motel; and the second-floor 1895 Carriage House. The menu includes entrees such as oven roasted native haddock and sautéed Maine lobster ($$$). capearundelinn.com $$-$$$$

Long Beach Motor Inn (363-5481), 271 Long Beach Ave. York Beach 03910. Motel and efficiency units on 3 acres overlooking the beach. Pool, lawn games. longbeachmotorinn.com $$-$$$

Old Orchard Beach Inn (934-5834), Six Portland Ave., Old Orchard Beach 04064. A block from the ocean, this grand old hotel offers classic and premier rooms, and 2-bedroom housekeeping suites. oldorchardbeachinn.com $$

Rhumb Line Resort (967-5457), 41 Turbat's Creek Rd., Kennebunkport 04046. Spacious, nicely-furnished units in a family-friendly resort with a full range of amenities, including indoor and outdoor heated pools, hot tubs, a spa, and a fitness center. rhumblinemaine.com $$-$$$

Saco Motel (284-6952), 473 Main St., Rte. 1, Saco 04072. A classic 1950s-style motel with clean rooms and reasonable rates. sacomotel.com $

Sleepytown Motel & Resort (646-5545), Rte. 1, Wells 04090. Perfect for families, the property has 42 motel units and 38 1- and 2-bedroom housekeeping cottages with screen porches on a 12-acre compound. Heated pool, playground, restaurant. Open May-Oct. sleepytown.com $-$$

Sparhawk Resort (646-5562), 85 Shore Rd., Ogunquit 03907. Within walking distance of town, the immaculate resort has 51 nicely furnished oceanfront units with private balconies, plus suites in nearby buildings. Minimum stays in summer months. Mid-April-late Oct. thesparhawk.com $$-$$$

Stage Neck Inn (363-3850), Rte. 1A, York Harbor 03911. Small, European-style oceanfront resort with 58 deluxe guest rooms, an 18-hole golf course, tennis courts, beach, indoor and outdoor pools, a restaurant ($$-$$$), and a casual grill. stageneck.com $$-$$$

Tides Inn By~the~Sea (967-3757), 252 Kings Highway, Goose Rocks Beach, Kennebunkport 04046. "The Grand Yellow Lady" overlooking the sea has 22 cozy rooms without TV or phones to intrude. Continental breakfast. 2-bedroom beachfront condo-style units available by the week. tidesinnbythesea.com $$$-$$$$

Union Bluff Hotel (363-1381), 8 Beach St., P.O. Box 1860, Short Sands Beach, York Beach 03910. Handsomely restored oceanfront hotel offers rooms (some water views) with private decks, fireplaces and balconies. The dinner menu ($$) includes steamers, chowder, lobster, prime rib, and the house specialty, "haddock in a brown bag". Pub menu. unionbluff.com. $$-$$$

The White Barn Inn (967-2321), Beach Ave., Kennebunkport 04046. One of the region's premier properties, a member of Relais & Chateaux, has 24 rooms and suites with fireplaces and whirlpool baths. The restaurant (see below) is one of the area's most highly acclaimed. whitebarninn.com $$$-$$$$

restaurants

Arrows (361-1100), 41 Berwick Rd., Ogunquit. One of Maine's (and the country's) most highly regarded restaurants, in an elegantly refurbished 18th-century farmhouse, serves innovative American cuisine. 6- and 10- course tasting menus are options. Dinner July-Labor Day, Tues.-Sun.; call for off-season hrs. Fri. in spring and fall is Bistro Night. $$$-$$$$

Bob's Clam Hut (439-4233), 315 Rte. 1, Kittery. Another contender for "everybody's favorite fried clams", this self-serve spot has been making customers happy since 1956. L & D. $ -$$

Cape Neddick Lobster Pound- Harborside Restaurant (363-5471), 60 Shore Rd., Cape Neddick. For more than 50 years a favorite for lobster, seafood, steak, and sandwiches; outdoor deck overlooks the river. Save room for homemade desserts. L & D. $-$$$

Cape Pier Chowder House (967-0123), Town Pier, Cape Porpoise. Lobsters, steamers, and blueberry pie. The spectacular view isn't extra. Memorial Day-Labor Day; spring and fall Fri.-Mon. $-$$

Chauncey Creek Lobster Pier (439-1030), Chauncey Creek Rd., Kittery Point. Lobsters, steamers, chowder, chicken, and pizza at picnic tables on the pier or indoors; raw bar. L & D in summer; weekends in fall. $-$$

The Clam Shack (967-2560), at the Bridge, Kennebunkport. Many consider this take-out-only landmark one of the top seafood shacks in the region. $

Clay Hill Farm (361-2272), Clay Hill Rd., Cape Neddick. New American cuisine in gracious surroundings on a 30-acre wildlife and bird sanctuary. Among specialties: lobster bisque, seafood scampi, and prime rib. 3-course dinners with wine are offered Wed. & Sun. D. Get directions when making a reservation. $$$

The Goldenrod (363-2621), 2 Railroad Ave., York Beach. Memorial Day-Labor Day. Visitors have been watching salt water taffy being made here since 1896. B, L, & D served in the rustic dining room or at the marble soda fountain. Usually on the menu: broiled sea scallops, prime rib, and fried clams. Children's menu. $-$$

The Good Table (799-4663), 527 Ocean House Rd. (Rte. 77), Cape Elizabeth. The Kostopoulos family has been serving classic comfort food and Greek specialties since 1986. *Gyros* and spanakopita share the menu with lobster rolls, fish and chips, and chowders. B Sat., L & D Tues.-Sat; Sun. 8 a.m.-3 p.m. $-$$

Hattie's (282-3435), 109 Mile Stretch Rd., Biddeford Pool. The spot for a hearty breakfast, homemade chowder, pie, and fabulous views. B, L & D. $-$$

Joseph's by the Sea (934-5044), 55 W. Grand Ave., Old Orchard. A great view and American/French fare are specialties. Try the lobster potato cake, seared scallops, and finish with strawberry Pavlova. April- Dec. B Sat. & Sun., D Thurs.-Sat. $$

Lobster Shack (799-1677), 225 Two Light Rd., Cape Elizabeth. A landmark since the 1920s, the oceanfront restaurant overlooking Portland Harbor serves traditional seafood favorites and classic "turf" choices. Outdoors picnic tables or indoor dining. End of March-end Oct. Warning: don't stand right under the foghorn. $-$$

Lord's Harborside Restaurant (646-2651), Harbor Rd., Wells Harbor. This waterfront lobster pound/restaurant has been a local favorite since 1969, with dishes such as lobster stew (made with butter and cream) and pick-your-own lobsters. L & D Wed.-Mon. $$

Maine Diner (646-4441), 2265 Post Road, Rte. 1, Wells. The long-standing local favorite serves up fine lobster pie, award-winning chowder, and breakfast all day. B, L & D. $

MC (646-6263), Perkins Cove. Arrows owners run this lower cost option, which serves dinner Wed.-Mon. Specials include Wed. date night (3 courses with wine) and Sun. jazz brunch (11 a.m.-2:30 p.m.). House specialties include lobster "mac and cheese" with lobster, and sesame-crusted, deep fried rainbow trout. $$-$$$

Merriland Farm (646-5040), 545 Coles Hill Rd., Wells. Baked blueberry French toast, cheddar roasted haddock, and berry-filled crepe with fresh whipped cream are just a few treats at this 200+-year-old berry farm. B & L; D Fri. and Sat.

Pepperland Café (384-5535), 279 Main St., S. Berwick. A small café with a big reputation. The menu, which includes many pub items, changes with the seasons, but offerings are consistently good. $-$$

Pier 77 (967-8500), 77 Pier Rd., Cape Porpoise. For those who want ambiance along with a superb view. Steamed mussels and lobster are staples, along with penne Bolognese and grilled lamb sirloin. L & D Wed.-Mon. Music weekends. $$-$$$

Spurwink Country Kitchen (799-1177), 50 Spurwink Rd., (Rte. 77), Scarborough. Cellophane-wrapped crackers and creamy cheese spread set the tone for this unpretentious, family-friendly spot where roast turkey, liver and onions, and pot roast are always on the menu. $-$$

Stonewall Kitchen Café (351-2712), 2 Stonewall Lane, York. It's easy to fill up on the store's free samples, but the informal café serves up wraps and sandwiches, including a lobster BLT. $

Tasty Thai (439-9988), 182 State Rd., Kittery Traffic Circle, Kittery. Authentic cuisine in a warm, welcoming spot. Specials include Tamarind duck, ginger fish, and Pad Thai. L & D Wed.-Mon. $-$$

When Pigs Fly (363-0612), 447 Rte. 1, Kittery. The name of the bakery may be your first reaction when you see the prices, but these outstanding handcrafted artisan breads are worth every penny. The chocolate bread and Hog Heaven are among the favorites.

The White Barn Inn (967-2321), Beach Ave., Kennebunkport. 4-course, fixed price dinners at this Relais & Chateaux inn, whose elegant, candlelit restaurant, in 2 restored 1820s barns, features contemporary cuisine with a European flair. Dinner might begin with pan seared quail breast and *fois gras*; entrees have included beef tenderloin glazed in a Roquefort cheese crust, and halibut with wild leek bulbs. A tasting menu is also offered. D. $$$$

Wormwood's (282-9679), Camp Ellis Beach, Saco. Large (and small) portions of fresh seafood, Cajun-style steak, pasta, chicken, and steak in a family-friendly dining room. B, L, & D. $-$$.

attractions

Barn Gallery (646-8400), 1 Bournes Lane, Ogunquit. Exhibits the works of members of the Ogunquit Art Association; special events include a chamber music festival, and an art auction. Late May-late Sept.

The Brick Store Museum (985-4802), 117 Main St., Kennebunk. Closed Mon.

Douglas N. Harding Rare Books (646-87850, 2152 Post Rd., Wells. A must for used-book lovers, a rambling red building jam -packed with books, prints, and maps.

East Point Sanctuary (781-2339), Lester B. Orcutt Boulevard, Biddeford Pool. Contact: Maine Audubon Society (781-2330), 20 Gilsland Farm Rd., P.O. Box 6009, Falmouth 04105.

Fort Foster (439-2182), Pocahontas Rd., Kittery Point. Sandy beach, lifeguards, playground, fishing pier, walking paths, remains of 1872 Fort Foster.

Franciscan Monastery (967-2011), Beach Rd., Kennebunkport.

Kennebunkport Historical Society (967-2751), 125 North St., Kennebunkport. Call for hrs.

Kennebunk Plains: see Maine Nature Conservancy in "Information" above.

Kittery Historical & Naval Museum (439-3080), Rte. 1, Kittery. Items and artifacts reflect the city's historical and maritime past. June-Columbus Day, closed Sun. & Mon.

Kittery Trading Post (888-KTP-MAINE), Rte. 1, Kittery. 3 floors of outdoor gear and clothing. The place to find most everything.

Ogunquit Museum of American Art (646-4909), Shore Rd., July-Oct.

Old Berwick Historical Society/Counting House (384-5162), Main and Liberty St., S. Berwick. Exhibits in a c.1830 cotton mill. July & Aug. Sat. & Sun. p.m.; fall, Sat. p.m.

Old York Historical Society (363-4974), 207 York St., York Village. June-Columbus Day, Tues.-Sat., and Sun. p.m.; call for off-season hrs. $

Portland Head Light and Fort Williams Park, 1000 Shore Rd., Cape Elizabeth. Admission to lighthouse.

Rachel Carson National Wildlife Refuge (646-9226), Rte. 9, Wells. Dawn to dusk; headquarters open Mon.-Fri.

Saco Museum (283-3861), 371 Main St., Saco. Summer: Tues.- Fri. p.m. (free Fri. after 4 p.m.); call for off-season hrs.

Scarborough Marsh Audubon Center (883-5100), Rte. 9, Pine Point Rd., Scarborough. Canoe rental and naturalist-led tours June-Labor Day; Sat. & Sun. Memorial Day-June and Sept.

Seashore Trolley Museum (967-2800), 195 Log Cabin Rd., Kennebunkport. Memorial Day-Columbus Day; May and late Oct., Sat. & Sun.

South Berwick: Historic New England oversees the Hamilton House (384-2454), 40 Vaughan's Lane; and the Sarah Orne Jewett House (384-2454), 5 Portland St. June-mid-Oct., tours on hr. beginning at 11 a.m.

Sohier Park Welcome Center, Nubble Light (363-7608), Nubble Rd., Cape Neddick. Memorial Day weekend-mid-Oct.

Sayward-Wheeler House (384-2454), 79 Barrell Lane Extension, York Harbor. June-mid-Oct., 2nd and 4th Sat. of the month, tours on hr. beginning at 11 a.m.

Vaughn's Island Preserve, Kennebunkport. The 96-acre island, separated from mainland by two tidal creeks (Turbats Creek and Porpoise Cove), is accessible by foot 3 hours before and after low tide.

Vaughan Woods State Park (490-4079), 28 Oldsfields Rd., S. Berwick. 250 acres include picnic facilities and hiking along the Salmon Falls River.

Wells Auto Museum (646-9064), Rte. 1, Wells. Mid-June-mid-Sept.; Memorial Day and Columbus Day weekends.

Wells National Estuarine Research Reserve (646-1555), 342 Laudholm Farm Rd., Wells. Grounds year round; visitor center Memorial Day weekend-Columbus Day; mid-Jan. to mid-Dec., Mon.-Fri. Lectures, nature walks and programs. Fee Memorial Day weekend-Columbus Day.

The Wright Gallery (967-5053), Pier Rd., Cape Porpoise. 2 floors overlooking the harbor display exhibit traditional New England art by more than 40 artists.

activities

Arundel Barn Playhouse (985-5552), 53 Old Post Rd., Arundel. Professional summer theatre in a renovated 1800 barn.

Balloons over New England (800-788-5562), Kennebunk. Hot air balloon rides launch from different sites: call ahead.

Bay View Beach, Bay View Road, Saco. Sandy beach, free parking.

Booth Theater Co. (646-8142), Betty Doon Motor Hotel, 5 Beach St., Ogunquit. Community theater performs musicals, dramas, and children's performances. Schedule: boothproductions.com

Cape-Able Bike Shop (967-4382), 83 Arundel Rd., Kennebunkport. Bike rentals.

Captain Satch & Sons (337-0800), Wells Harbor Town Dock. In and off shore sports fishing trips. Mid-May-Oct.

Chick's Marina (967-2782), Kennebunkport. Fishing/sightseeing cruises, boat and canoe rentals. $

Cinemagic Stadium Theaters and IMAX (282-6234), 779 Portland Rd., Saco.

Coastal Watercrafts (967-8840), 4 Western Ave., Kennebunkport. Jet ski, boat and canoe rentals. Deborah Ann Cruises (361-9501), Perkins Cove, Ogunquit. Whale watches.

Eldredge Bros. Fly Shop (363-9269), 1480 Rt. 1, Cape Neddick. Fresh and saltwater fishing trips and equipment rental; kayak rental.

Finestkind Scenic Cruises (646-5227), Barnacle Billy's Dock, Perkins Cove, Ogunquit. Scenic and cocktail cruises.

First Chance Whale Watch (967-5507), Kennebunkport Bridge behind Mobile Station, Kennebunkport. Lobster tours and whale watches.

Funtown/Splashtown USA (284-5139), Rte. 1, Saco. Amusement and water park. Free parking; unlimited ride pass.

Gone with the Wind (283-8446), 524 Pool Rd., Biddeford. Guided ocean kayak trips; kayak rentals.

Ghostly Tours (363-3000), 250 York St., Rte. 1A, York. Late June-Labor Day, Tues.-Sat. at 8 p.m.; Sept.-Oct. Fri. and Sat. at 7 p.m.

Hackmatack Playhouse (698-1807), 538 Rte. 9, Berwick. Professional summer stock theater; children's shows. Schedule: hackmatack.org

Intown Trolley Co. (967-3686), Kennebunkport.

Kayak Rentals and tours: York Parks and Recreation (363-1040), 186 York St., York. Also, guided tour along Long Sands Beach.

Ogunquit Playhouse (646-5511), Rte. 1, P.O. Box 915, Ogunquit 03907. Late June-Labor Day. Schedule: ogunquitplayhouse.org

Saco Bay Sailing (283-1624), 14 Beach Ave., Saco. Recreational and sailing excursions from Camp Ellis.

Scenic Eco-Cruise aboard The Atlantic Explorer (967-4050 for reservations; 967-4784 for information). At the Nonantum Resort, Ocean Ave., Kennebunkport.

Schooner Eleanor (967-8809), Arundel Wharf Restaurant, Kennebunkport. 2 hr. sailing trips aboard gaff rigged 50 ft. schooner.

Seafari Charters (439-5068), 7 Island Ave., Kittery. Deep-sea fishing, scuba diving, whale-watching charters.

Shoreline Explorer (324-5762), mid-June-early Sept. Park your car and board a series of trollies/buses that travel along the coast from Kennebunk to York. shorelineexplorer.com

Trina Lyn Fishing Charter (283-2352), Camp Ellis. Private sport fishing charters.

York's Wild Kingdom (363-4911), Rte. 1, York. Maine's largest zoo/ amusement park; animals, live demonstrations, petting zoo, picnic area.

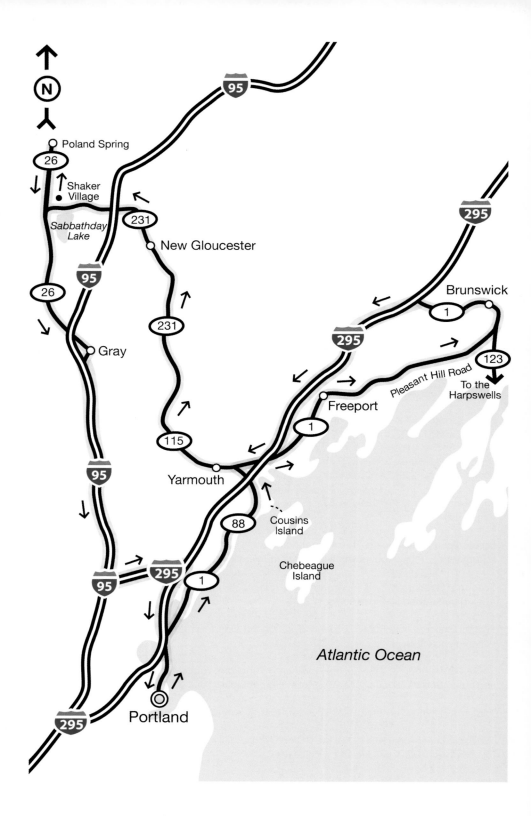

Portland to Poland Spring – with a Stop to Shop

100 miles

major attractions

- Portland
- Freeport Outlets
- Bowdoin College Museums
- Pineland Farms
- Sabbathday Lake Shaker Village
- Poland Spring

*B*egin this drive in Portland, the historic seaport on Casco Bay, and head north along a coast which contrasts a bucolic nature preserve with New England's busiest outlet shopping center. After visiting a classic college town with its impressive museums, venture inland to discover a model farm, the well-preserved vestiges of an all-but-vanished religious community, and an old-time spa resort.

Head north out Portland on Route 1.

Just before the intersection of routes 1 and 88, turn left onto Gilsland Farm Road to the Gilsland Farm Audubon Center, on the Presumpscot River. The Maine Audubon Society's headquarters, on 65 acres of wetlands, meadows woods, and salt marsh, has a state-of-the-art, "green" solar-heated visitor and education center, 2 1/2 miles of trails, and a well-stocked store.

If you're visiting in late June, look for wild poppies in the meadows and fields. They're a legacy of the property's first owner, David Moulton, who planted more than 400 varieties when he was creating his "gentleman's farm" here. Most were dug up after he died, but some continue to flourish. (Moulton named his farm for a character in Sir Walter Scott's novel, *The Talisman*.)

Turn off Route 1 onto Route 88 and continue north.

Portland highlights

Although it's still New England's busiest seaport in terms of tonnage, Portland has become a regional economic hub as well as the seacoast's most important arts center north of Boston. Downtown Portland – especially the compact, brick-and-granite "Old Port" neighborhood – has shed its workaday image and now boasts shops, galleries, microbreweries, and what's said to be the highest per capita concentration of restaurants in America. (Note: Unless provided here, practical information for the places listed below can be found under "Attractions" or "Activities" at the end of this drive.)

The Portland Museum of Art has a fine collection of European and American paintings, sculpture, and decorative works, with special strength in American artists such as Winslow Homer, Andrew Wyeth, and Rockwell Kent.

The Children's Museum & Theatre of Maine has hands-on lobster boat, car repair, fire truck, diner, and shipyard play areas, along with many more opportunities for kids to use their imagination in realistic settings. There's also a dress-up and puppet theatre, and a full schedule of special exhibits.

The Portland Observatory Museum is the place to go for sweeping panoramas of Casco Bay and the Calendar Islands, and even New Hampshire's Mount Washington. The former maritime signal tower, dating to 1807, is the last structure of its kind in the U.S.

Victoria Mansion is a beautifully preserved masterpiece of mid-19th century Italianate architecture – and its wildly ornate interior is a testament to the era's love of the lavish.

A century older than Victoria Mansion, the 1755 Tate House is a riverside gem that showcases the far more reserved neoclassical tastes of the late colonial era.

The Longfellow House, headquarters of the Maine Historical Society, is maintained as it was when Henry Wadsworth Longfellow spent his boyhood here in the early 1800s.

The Portland Harbor Museum focuses on the city's long and fascinating maritime history.

Harbor Cruises are offered by Bay View Cruises and Casco Bay Lines. The latter is a ferry service connecting downtown Portland with five of the inhabited Calendar Islands in Casco Bay. Eagle Island, now a state park, was once the home of Arctic explorer Admiral Robert Peary. For a much longer voyage, hop aboard the Bay Ferries Limited CAT for the 5 ½-hour trip to Yarmouth, Nova Scotia (be sure to bring a passport, enhanced Driver's License, or other approved document for your return to the U.S.!)

Portland is renowned for its lovely parks. Deering Oaks on Forest Avenue features a lovely rose garden and a Saturday farmers' market, while Eastern Promenade in the city's East End offers splendid bay and lighthouse views.

Side Trip

Chebeague Island (pronounced "sheh-BIG"), at approximately three miles wide and five miles long, is the largest of the more than 300 Calendar Islands (so named because it was once thought that there were approximately 365) in Casco Bay. To visit the island, turn right onto Gilman Road, and follow signs to Cousins Island. After crossing the bridge, turn left onto Wharf Road to the parking lot ($20/day) to hop aboard the Chebeague Transportation Company's passenger ferry. Bring along a bicycle to explore the island (or take a chance that Mac "The Bikeman" Passano, close to the ferry on South Road, has one that you can borrow; call ahead). Several inns will meet the ferry by arrangement. Note: the parking lot fills up early in the summer, but there's a satellite parking lot on Route 1 in Cumberland with bus service to the ferry; check the website (see "Activities" below for the ferry schedule and The Bikeman's number).

Eartha and the outlets

Route 88 merges with Route 1 in Yarmouth. Just after you get on Route 1, watch on the right for the **Delorme Map Store**, home to "Eartha," the world's largest and most detailed rotating globe. The **Maine Information Center**, on the left, is extremely well equipped with brochures for the whole state.

Continue north on Route 1 into **Freeport**. It's a bit difficult to understand Freeport's decision to turn itself into a giant shopping mall, but with almost 200 outlet stores, there's no disputing the success of its mission. It's easy to understand why the shops were attracted here, however. At the center of town is **L.L. Bean**, the retailing and mail-order phenomenon that first put the town on the map when Leon Leonwood Bean started marketing his Maine Hunting Shoe in 1912. Today Bean's stays open around the clock to accommodate the more than 3 1/2 million people who shop here each year, and malls like the recently opened **Freeport Village Station**, with more than 27 retailers, continue to thrive.

But look beyond the outlets, to a town with a fascinating history. In the 1800s South Freeport was a shipbuilding center and port for wooden vessels that set sail from the Harraseeket River laden with goods, including barrels of locally-harvested mackerel. In 1820, papers were signed at the **Jameson Tavern** (see "Restaurants" below) making Maine a separate state from Massachusetts. Freeport has two historic districts: the 6,000-acre Harraseeket Historic District, and the Main Street district. The **Freeport Historical Society**, which oversees the 1830 **Harrington House Museum,** distributes a self-guided walking tour brochure. The Society also operates the **Pettengill Farm**, a 140-acre saltwater farm with an 1810 saltbox home on Harraseeket Estuary.

Side Trip

Three miles south of town in South Freeport, **Atlantic Seal Cruises** sets sail from the town wharf for narrated trips around Casco Bay and Eagle Island, as well as a six-hour Thursday cruise **to Seguin Island Lighthouse** in July and August (departs at 10 a.m., returns at 4 p.m.).

Just across from L.L. Bean on Main Street, **turn onto Bow Street and continue for a mile** to Upper Mast Landing Road to visit the Maine Audubon Society's **Mast Landing Sanctuary. Continue on Bow Street to Wolf Neck Road** to **Wolf Neck Woods State Park.**

art and the Arctic at Bowdoin

To get to historic **Brunswick** (without taking Route 1 North), **turn off Bow Street onto Pleasant Hill Road. Continue straight until the end, and then turn left on Maine Street** (Maine's widest main street) into town, past **Bowdoin College**. Founded in 1794, it was named for James Bowdoin, governor of Massachusetts (Maine was part of Massachusetts at that time) in 1785-1786, and a founder of the American Academy of Arts and Sciences, whose family contributed both land and money to the fledgling school. The governor's son, James, contributed his collection of paintings by Dutch and Italian masters, which is now the foundation of the college's superb holdings in European and American works on exhibit at the **Bowdoin College Museum of Art** in the copper-domed Walker Art Building designed by Charles F. McKim.

Bowdoin alumni include Nathaniel Hawthorne, Henry Wadsworth Longfellow, Franklin Pierce, Hannibal Hamlin (Lincoln's first vice president), and explorers Robert Edwin Peary (class of 1877) and Donald Baxter MacMillan (class of 1898), leaders of the first expedition to reach the North Pole. The **Peary-MacMillan Arctic Museum** is filled with artifacts – and stuffed animals – relating to the explorers' journeys.

> An often unsung hero of Robert Peary's expeditions was his longtime colleague Matthew Henson, arguably America's greatest African-American explorer.

One of the holdings of the **Pejepscot Historical Society** is devoted to another Bowdoin luminary. The **Joshua L. Chamberlain Museum** is housed in the home of the former college president, Maine governor (four terms), and Civil War hero. The Society also oversees two properties standing side by side in a 19th-century Italianate house: the **Skolfield-Whittier House**, the unchanged home of three generations of sea captains and physicians, including Dr. Frank Whittier, whose forensic work is the focus of an exhibit at the **Pejepscot Museum**.

General Chamberlain and his bride were among the first to take their vows in the elegant, neo-Gothic **First Parish Church**, designed in the mid-1840s by Richard Upjohn, architect of Bowdoin's College Chapel, as well as New York City's Trinity Church. The interior is notable for its exuberant wooden arches.

Established in Brunswick in 1717, First Parish Church has long been an integral part of the social fabric of the town. The Abolitionist Movement attracted many prominent supporters: according to lore, here, in pew 23, Harriet Beecher Stowe had a vision of the death of Uncle Tom, and went home to pen her novel Uncle Tom's Cabin. Bowdoin graduate (class of 1825) Henry Wadsworth Longfellow delivered his Morituri Salutamus (Salute to Death) here in 1875. Ralph Waldo Emerson, Eleanor Roosevelt, and Dr. Martin Luther King, Jr. are among the luminaries who have spoken here.

Brunswick is also home to Naval Air Station Brunswick, commissioned in 1943 to train Royal Canadian Air Force pilots. It's scheduled to be decommissioned in 2011.

Side Trip

The Harpswells – three peninsulas "down east" of Brunswick – are dotted with classic seaside villages, comfortable lodgings, and terrific restaurants. Head out of Brunswick on Route 123 to Route 24 to visit one tiny outpost, **Bailey Island**, accessible by a unique cribstone bridge from Orrs Island. A statue at Land's End commemorates Maine's fishermen. **Casco Bay Lines** departs daily at noon from Cook's Wharf for a one-and-three-quarter-hour nature cruise.

Return to Route 1, head south, and follow signs onto I-295. Stay on I-295 south to exit 17 back onto Route 1 and into Yarmouth (on Route 115 – Main Street). This hand-

some town on the Royal River, first settled in 1636, was a major shipbuilding center in the 1800s. Today, the major event is the very popular Clam Festival held during the third weekend in July.

The scroll borders and winged death heads on many 18th-century tombstones were usually carved by local cabinetmakers. The grave of Indian scout Joseph Weare (1737-74), buried in Pioneer Cemetery on Gilman Street, is typical of the times.

a model farm

Continue through town on Route 115 to the intersection of Route 231, and head north on 231 along a lovely country road to **Pineland Farms**, a privately owned, 5,000-acre working farm open to the public. On the former grounds of a "school for the feeble-minded," the farm is funded by the Libra Foundation, a non-profit organization established by philanthropist Elizabeth B. Noyce.

A section of the property is devoted to mixed use, but the major portion is home to an experimental farm, complete with a creamery, barnyard animals, and a dairy. The highlight, however, is the farm's Equestrian Center, a state-of-the-art facility that breeds, promotes and trains Dutch Warmblood sporthorses, and offers riding lessons. Begin a visit at the Welcome Center/Market, where you can opt for a self-guided farm tour ($), or take a two-hour trolley tour ($). Guesthouses on the property offer overnight accommodations.

Elizabeth Bottomley Noyce, the daughter of a factory worker from Auburn, Massachusetts, had the very good fortune to marry a co-inventor of the microchip. When he left her for another woman in 1975, Mrs. Noyce received half his assets, including a large chunk of Intel Corporation stock and a 50-acre estate in Maine, where the couple had summered. She became a year-round resident, and pioneered a program she labeled "catalytic philanthropy" – investments to bolster the state's economy. By the time she died in 1996 she had bequeathed approximately $75 million, including funding for a project to rehabilitate Portland's decaying downtown (credited with attracting L.L. Bean to the area), and for Pineland Farms.

Side Trip

Continue north on Route 202 to **Hodgman's Frozen Custard Stand**, a local landmark since the 1940s, for rich, creamy homemade custard (vanilla, chocolate, and a special of the day), along with sundaes, floats, and custard pies.

last of the Shakers

Continue north on Route 231 a short distance to where it ends at a blinking light at the junction of Route 202. Go straight across Route 202 onto Bald Hill Road, and then bear left onto Sabbathday Lake Road (which will turn into Shaker Road, and then Chandler Hill Road). Turn right onto Outlet Road at the sign to the Outlet Beach Snack Bar. Continue past **Outlet Beach** (which should be renamed "no" beach; it seems to have more rules than frontage) on **Sabbathday Lake** to the left turn (just before Route 26) for **Sabbathday Lake Shaker Village**. The world's only remaining active Shaker Community is also a National Historic Landmark.

Members of the *United Society of Believers in Christ's Second Appearing*, a religious movement founded in 1747 in Manchester, England, were nicknamed "Shaking Quakers" because of the agitated way in which members' bodies moved when they prayed. Ann Lee, a young English woman attracted to the movement, became their leader after experiencing religious visions.

Always interested in innovation despite their austere lifestyle, the Shakers pioneered the practice of selling seeds in paper packets, and likely invented the flat broom and other practical devices.

In 1774 "Mother Ann" and eight disciples landed in New York City and founded a community in Albany that they called Niskayuna. According to records, "Eight remained faithful." By 1787 the Church, now led by American converts, had founded 18 communities in 10 states, including the community here, established in 1783. According to the village's website, it was referred as "the least of Mother's children in the east ... one of the numerically smallest and poorest of the eastern Shaker Communities."

Today, the 1,800-acre village encompasses 18 buildings. Six that are open to the public document the movement's history. The museum houses approximately 13,000 artifacts, including furniture, "fancy" sales goods, and Shaker crafts, with an emphasis on the four communities that once thrived in Maine. The store sells Shaker-made goods, local handicrafts, and culinary herbs and medicinal teas. Guided 75-minute tours depart from the reception center.

Sunday Meeting, held at 10:00 a.m. at the Meeting House during the summer months, and in the Chapel at the Dwelling House the rest of the year, is the only service open to the public.

Turn right onto Route 26 to **Poland Spring Preservation Park**, on the grounds of **Poland Spring Resort**.

Wentworth Ricker purchased land at Poland Spring from the Sabbathday Lake Shakers in 1797, intending to build a home here. Within a few years, he opened an inn called the Mansion House. Legend has it that his son, Hiram, sold the first glass of "health-giving" water for 15¢ in 1860, after the family ox put on weight from drinking at the nearby spring. For the next 100 years, the resort was a premier vacation destination.

By the 1970s, however, several buildings were vacant and others were leased to organizations such as the Women's Job Corps to make ends meet. In 1971, most of the resort was leased to the Yogi Mahareshi and 1,000 of his followers for a transcendental meditation center. Mel Robbins was sent by his development company to investigate the feasibility of tearing down existing buildings to construct luxury condominiums around an 18-hole, Donald Ross-designed golf course, but the land was judged unsuitable. Robbins, however, bought the resort and began renovations.

The resort now encompasses several historic lodgings, the golf course, and Preservation Park, whose handsomely restored 1895 Spring House and Bottling Plant houses exhibits and a gift shop. The Maine State Building used at the 1893 Chicago World's Fair and moved here by freight train a year later is now a library and art museum. A summer concert series is presented at the elegant, stone 1912 All Souls Chapel.

Accommodations at the resort range from "subcompact: when you smile your cheeks touch the walls" to a two-bedroom suite in the Roosevelt House (with TV), or a lakefront cottage a mile from the main inn.

Moose, lynx, mountain lions and black bears are just a few of the diverse species living at the **Maine Wildlife Park, to the south on Route 26**. Most of the residents have one thing in common, however: they've been injured, orphaned or become human-dependent. Visitors can feed many of them, and there are special presentations on Saturdays from mid-May through August.

To return to Portland, continue south on Route 26 to I-95 to I-295.

information *All area codes are (207) unless otherwise indicated.*

Freeport Merchants Association (865-1212), Hose Tower, 23 Depot St., Freeport 04032. freeportusa.com

Maine Information Center (846-0833), 1100 Rte. 1, Yarmouth. visitmaine.com

Portland Convention & Visitors Bureau (772-5800), 94 Commercial St., #300, Portland 04101. visitportland.com

Southern Mid-Coast Maine Chamber of Commerce (877-725-8797), 2 Main St., Topsham 04086. Bath-Brunswick area. midcoastmaine.com

Yarmouth Chamber of Commerce (846-3984), 162 Main St., Yarmouth 04096. yarmouthmaine.org

lodging – Portland

The Eastland Park Hotel (775-5411), 157 High St., 04101. The city's historic, downtown hotel has had a major facelift, and offers pleasantly furnished rooms, and, from the rooftop lounge, fabulous views. Pets welcome. eastlandparkhotel.com $$-$$$

Holiday Inn by the Bay (775-2311), 88 Spring St., 04101. Overlooking the harbor and within walking distance of the Old Port, the hotel has 239 rooms, an indoor pool, fitness center, and free parking. innbythebay.com $$-$$$

The Inn at St. John (773-6481). 939 Congress St., 04102. This venerable landmark offers 39 clean, comfortable, and pet friendly lodging on 3 floors. Rooms range from luxury to value (shared baths), which are on upper floors with no elevator. innatstjohn.com $-$$

Morrill Mansion B&B (774-6900), 249 Vaughan St., 04102. Classic lodgings in an 1800s era townhouse restored to its original Italianate elegance. 7 rooms on the 2nd and 3rd floors, all with private bath; ¾ mi. from downtown. morrillmansion.com $$-$$$

Portland Harbor Hotel (775-9090), 468 Fore St., 04101. One of the city's newest luxury hotels – in the heart of the Old Port – offers well-appointed accommodations overlooking their garden or the city. portlandharborhotel.com $$-$$$$

lodgings – along the drive

Brookside Motel (846-5512), Rte. 1, Yarmouth 04096. Classic, clean, and comfortable rooms. $-$$

Brunswick Inn on Park Row (729-4914), 165 Park Row, Brunswick 04011. 15 handsomely furnished rooms with private baths or showers in the historic inn and carriage house. Some have TV; all come with full breakfast. The wine bar (with martinis, too) is open Wed.-Sat. brunswickbnb.com $$-$$$

Chebeague Island Inn (846-5155), 61 South Rd., Chebeague Island 04017. 21 cozy rooms in a classic oceanfront hotel. All have queen size beds, private baths, harbor or garden views, , and include breakfast and use of bicycles. No phones or TV. The dining room serves 3 meals daily in season. Late May-Columbus Day. chebeagueinn.com $$$-$$$$

Chebeague Orchard Inn B&B (846-9488) 66 North Rd., Chebeague Island 04017. 5 rooms (3 with private baths) in a handsome home on 22 acres. chebeagueorchardinn.com $$-$$$

Freeport Inn (865-3106), 335 Rte. 1, Freeport 04032. Hilltop motel a few miles south of town has 86 nicely furnished units. Restaurant, pool; canoe rental. Pets welcome. freeportinn.com $$-$$$

Harraseeket Inn (865-9377), 162 Main St., Freeport 04032. One of the town's most elegant lodgings encompasses buildings from 1798 to 1997. Period furnishings in the 84 rooms and 6 suites include canopy beds. Breakfast included. Indoor pool; 2 restaurants (see "Restaurants" below). Pet friendly. harraseeketinn.com $$-$$$$

The Isaac Randall House (865-9295), 51 Independence Drive, Freeport 04032. Freeport's first b&b, an unfussy but antiques-filled farmhouse close to town, has 12 air-conditioned bedrooms (2 with fireplaces), and welcomes kids and pets. isaacrandall.com $$-$$$

Little Island Motel (833-2392), 44 Little Island Rd., Orrs Island 04066. The only thing better than being near the water is being over it, and that's where the 9 simple rooms at this small resort are; bicycles and boats are available for guests. Breakfast included. littleislandmotel.com $$-$$$

Log Cabin (833-5546), Bailey Island 04003. All 9 rooms at this spacious inn have spectacular ocean views; 4 have kitchens. Dinner ($$$-$$$$) is served to guests from 6-6:30 p.m. logcabin-maine.com $$$-$$$$

Maine Idyll Motor Court (865-4201), 1411 Rte. 1, Freeport 04032. 20 old-fashioned, comfortable housekeeping cottages 2 mi. north of town have been owned by the same family since they opened in the 1930s. Cottages sleep 2-6, have TVs, and modern baths; some have fireplaces. Breakfast included. Pets welcome. Mid-Apr.-mid Nov. maineidyll.com $-$$

Parkwood Inn (725-5251), 71 Gurnet Rd., Brunswick 04011. Pleasant, motel-style lodgings with a/c, microwaves, refrigerators, and TVs. Fitness center, indoor heated pool, exercise room, and laundry. Breakfast included. parkwoodinn.com $$-$$$

Pineland Farms (688-4604), 16 Pineland Drive, New Gloucester 04260. pinelandfarms.org

Poland Spring Resort (998-4351), 543 Maine St., Poland Spring 04274. Spartan but comfortable lodgings in 3 inns and 11 cottages. Rates include meals and are a bargain, but guests must bring their own soap, towels, and drinking glasses (and TVs), and add a 17% service charge. polandspringresort.com

Sea Escape Cottages (833-5531), 23 Sea Escape Lane, Bailey Island 04003. Waterfront suites and well-appointed housekeeping cottages rent by the day or week. seaescapecottages.com $$

Wolf Cove Inn on Tripp Lake (998-4976), 5 Jordan Shore Rd., Poland 04274. 7 second-floor lakefront rooms, and 3 suites with whirlpool baths and gas fireplaces on a sprawling lakeside estate. wolfcoveinn.com $-$$$

restaurants – Portland

Duck Fat (774-8080), 43 Middle St. Our grandmothers knew…and so do the owners of this downtown hot spot: food tastes better when it's fried in duck fat. The house specialty is Belgian fries, with a choice of dipping sauces (truffle ketchup, garlic aioli…). Put them along with a cup of white bean & apple smoked bacon soup, and a duck confit panini, and you've got a meal. L & D daily. $

Five Fifty-Five (761-0555) 555 Congress St. Standouts at this small, chic, and candlelit spot include truffled lobster "mac & cheese", hanger steak, a superb cheese plate, and for dessert, house-made ricotta. D nightly; Sun. brunch. $$$-$$$$

Fore Street (775-2717), 288 Fore St. The menu changes daily, but the quality remains consistently high, with tasty treats such as wood-oven roasted mussels, grilled marinated hanger steak, and succulent hand-harvested scallops. D nightly. $$-$$$

Green Elephant Vegetarian Bistro (347-3111), 608 Congress St. Asian-influenced cuisine served in cozy but elegant surroundings. Even confirmed carnivores will love dishes such as vegan peanut curry, and veggie citrus spare ribs. L & D Tues.-Sat. $-$$

restaurants – along the drive

Beale Street BBQ & Grill, Bath (also in South Portland and Augusta). The roadside stand that was born in Freeport has blossomed into one of the area's most popular barbecue chains, with specialties such as pulled pork, smoked ribs, and jambalaya. No reservations. $-$$

Bombay Mahal (729-5260), 99 Maine St., Brunswick. Genuine Indian food includes tandoori and lamb specialties, as well as a large selection of vegetarian dishes, curries, hot breads, and Indian beer. Buffet Sat. and Sun. 11:30 a.m.-3 p.m. L & D. $-$$

Calder's Clam Shack (846-5046), 108 North Rd., Chebeague Island. Greek specialties share the menu with seafood platters, sandwiches, and pizza at this take-out spot with a few outdoor picnic tables. $

Clayton's (846-1117), 447 Rte. 1, Yarmouth. Gourmet sandwiches, soups, salads, and fresh baked desserts. Try the chicken salad sandwich with Danish bleu cheese, mayo and red grapes. Mon.-Fri. 7 a.m.-7p.m.; Sat. 8:30 a.m.-5 p.m. $

Cook's Lobster House (833-2818), Rte. 24, Bailey Island. Spectacular views and off-the-boat-fresh seafood have made this waterfront "in the rough" spot popular since 1955. $-$$

Day's (846-5871), Rte. 1, Yarmouth. Lobster dinners and rolls, fish and chips, steamers, and homemade crab cakes; eat at picnic tables in back or take out. Summer: Mon.-Sat. 8 a.m.-6 p.m., Sun. 8 a.m.-3 p.m. $-$$

Fat Boy Drive In, 111 Bath Rd., Brunswick. A vintage diner, with classic diner food, fabulous frappes, and yes – curbside service. L &D. $

The Freeport Café (865-3106), Freeport Inn, 31 Rte. 1, Freeport. The all-day breakfast, with tasty treats such as homemade muffins, eggs Benedict, and blueberry pancakes, is the draw here. Sunday, there's a breakfast buffet. B, L & D. $

The Great Impasta (729-5858), 42 Maine St., Brunswick. Homemade Italian favorites in a small, casual, and family-friendly place, which has been satisfying diners for more than 20 years. L & D Mon.-Sat. $-$$

Harraseeket Inn (865-9377), 162 Main St., Freeport. Elegant and creative dining, with specialties such as tableside chateaubriand for two. The tavern ($-$$) has a wood-fired oven and grill and a lighter menu, and serves a daily lunch buffet. Sun. brunch is a standout. $$$

Harraseeket Lunch & Lobster Co. (865-4888), Main St., So. Freeport. Popular indoor/outdoor waterfront dining, featuring fresh seafood to stay or go. No credit cards. L & D. $-$$

Hodgman's Frozen Custard (926-3553), 1108 Lewiston Rd., New Gloucester. Mother's Day-Labor Day 11:30 a.m.-9:30 p.m.

Jameson Tavern (865-4196), 115 Main St., Freeport. 1779 tavern serves fresh seafood, poultry and meat specialties in several small, elegant rooms. Lighter menu in the tavern. Outdoor patio. L & D. $$

Morrison's Chowder House (865-3404), 4 Mechanic St., Freeport (also Portland). Many think that this tiny spot tucked away on a side street has the town's best lobster rolls; also chowders and whoopee pie. $

Muddy Rudder (846-3082), Rte. 1, Yarmouth. Since 1976 the "Rudder" has been serving seafood, meat and poultry dishes in a casual, nautically themed spot overlooking the river. The extensive menu includes more than 125 items. L & D. $-$$$

Pineland Farms Market Café (688-4531), 15 Farm View Dr., New Gloucester. Specialty sandwiches and salads, along with assorted dessert treats. L daily. $

Thai Garden Restaurant (865-6005), 491 Rte. 1, Freeport. L & D Mon-Sat.; Sun. D. When you're ready for something other than lobster. $-$$

attractions – Portland

Children's Museum & Theatre of Maine (828-1234), 142 Free St. 3 floors of exhibits for all ages. Daily in summer; Tues.-Sun. off season.

Longfellow House and Maine Historical Society (774-1822), 489 Congress St. May-Oct.

The Portland Harbor Museum (773-3800), 510 Congress St. Late May-mid-Oct.

Portland Museum of Art (775-6148), 7 Congress Sq. Maine's largest art museum, designed by the firm of I.M. Pei, houses a superb collection of American and European art. Daily in summer; Tues.-Sun. off season.

Portland Observatory Museum (774-5561), 138 Congress St. Daily late May-Columbus Day. Guided tours on the half hr.

Tate House (774-6177), 1267 Westbrook St. Early June-mid-Oct., Tues-Sat.

Victoria Mansion (772-4841), 109 Danforth St. 45-minute guided tours at quarter after and quarter to the hr. May-Oct.

attractions – along the drive

Bowdoin College, Brunswick: Peary-MacMillan Arctic Museum (725-3416), Museum of Art (725-3275); both closed Mon. Free.

Desert of Maine (865-6962), 95 Desert Rd., Freeport. The family that farmed here in the late 1700's, discovered the results of failing to rotate crops, massive land clearing, and overgrazing: soil erosion uncovered a natural desert. Narrated tours, and a museum in a 200+-year-old barn. Early May-mid-Oct.

First Parish Church (729-7331), 9 Cleaveland St., Brunswick. Tues. noontime organ concerts beginning in mid-July are played on the 1883 Hutchings, Plaisted & Company pipe organ.

Freeport Historical Society (865-3170), 45 Main St., Freeport. Walking tours. Harrington House & Gardens open in summer Mon., Thurs., Fri., & Sat. Pettengill Farm farmhouse open by appointment; grounds open year round.

Gilsland Farm Audubon Center (781-2330), 20 Gilsland Farm Rd., Falmouth.

Maine Wildlife Park (27-657-4977), 56 Game Farm Rd., Gray. Mid-Apr.-Veteran's Day.

Mast Landing Sanctuary (781-2330), Upper Mast Landing Rd., Freeport.

Pejepscot Historical Society (729-6606): Pejepscot Museum, 159 Park Row, closed Sun., free; Skolfield-Whittier House Museum ($), 161 Park Row, late May-mid-Oct., Thurs.-Sat., tours at 11 a.m. and 2 p.m.; Joshua Chamberlain Museum ($), 226 Maine St., late May-mid Oct., Tues.-Sat., tours twice an hour.

Pineland Farms (688-4539), 15 Farm View Dr., New Gloucester.

Poland Spring Preservation Park (998-7143), 115 Preservation Way, Poland Spring. May-Oct.

Range Pond State Park (998-4104), Empire Rd., Poland. 750-acre park includes a beach, nature trails, playground, and changing facility.

Sabbathday Lake Shaker Museum (926-4597), 707 Shaker Rd., New Gloucester. Memorial Day-Columbus Day, closed Sun. Tours at 10:30 and 11:30 a.m., and 12:30, 1:30, 2:30 and 3:15 p.m.

Wolfe's Neck Woods State Park (865-4465), 426 Wolfe's Neck Rd., Freeport. 233 acres of pine and hemlock forests, a salt marsh estuary, and shore along the Harraseeket River and Casco Bay. April-Oct.

activities – Portland

Bay View Cruises (761-0496), 184 Commercial St., Portland. 117-passenger boat offers cruises of the bay.

Casco Bay Lines (774-7871), Ferry Terminal, Commercial St. Cruises on Casco Bay and daily ferry service to 5 Casco Bay Islands.

Mainely Tours (774-0808). Narrated trolley tours around Portland and to Portland Head Light.

Old Port Mariner Fleet (775-0727), Long Wharf, Commercial St. Scenic cruises, whale watches, deep-sea fishing.

Portland Discovery Land & Sea Tours (774-0808), Long Wharf. By land, by sea, or both: trolley tours, lighthouse cruises, and boat trips to Eagle Island.

Portland Schooner Company (874-9300). Vintage daily and overnight schooner sails on Casco Bay.

Bay Ferries Limited *CAT* (888-249-SAIL; catferry.com) takes passengers and vehicles on the 5 ½ hr. trip (one way) to Yarmouth, Nova Scotia. Although this is a convenient way to cross, the *CAT* has limited outside seating and does not make for a very exciting day trip.

activities – along the drive

Atlantic Seal Cruises (865-6112), 25 Main St., So. Freeport. Memorial Day weekend-late Oct. Reservations recommended.

Bowdoin International Music Festival (725-3322). July-early Aug.

Casco Bay Lines (774-7871), Cook's Landing, Rt. 24, Bailey Island. A 1 hr. 45 min. cruise sails daily at noon, late June-Labor Day.

Chebeague Transportation Co. (846-3700), Chebeague Island. Ferries begin operation at 7 a.m. from Yarmouth and 6:40 a.m. from Chebeague. Roundtrip fare is $10 (passengers only; no cars), and reservations are not necessary. If you wish to leave from Yarmouth, park in town ($20/day) at Cumberland Municipal Center and hop aboard one of the free shuttle buses that leave a half hr. before each ferry.

Cold River Vodka (865-4628), 437 Rte. 1, Freeport. Only Maine potatoes are used to make this distinctive vodka; the distillery and gift shop are open for tours and shopping Tues.-Sat. p.m.

Freeport Performing Arts Center, 30 Holbrook St., Freeport. Schedule: freeportpac.org

L.L. Bean Outdoor Discovery Schools (888-552-3261, pre-registration required). Weekend activities range from fly-fishing to kayaking to wingshooting. Walk-on adventures (no pre-registration required; 877-755-2326) include all equipment.

L.L. Bean's free Summer Concert Series in Discovery Park features nationally acclaimed artists Sat. evening late June-early Sept. at 7:30 p.m.

Mac "The Bikeman" Passano (846-7829), 168 South Rd., Chebeague Island.

Maine State Music Theatre (725-8769), Picard Theater. Also home to Bowdoin Summer Music Festival at Bowdoin College. Schedule: msmt.org

Marie L (846-9488), Chebeague Island. Trips to Eagle Island; sunset cruises; water taxi to and from Cousins Island; kayak trip support.

Outlet Beach on Sabbathday Lake (926-3388), Outlet Rd., New Gloucester. Public beach; canoe, kayak, and paddleboat rental; snack bar. Memorial Day-Labor Day.

Ring's Marine Service (865-6143), 22 Smelt Brook Rd., So. Freeport. Canoe and sea kayak rental.

Sea Escape Cottages & Charters (841-9124), Sea Escape Lane, Bailey Island. Private fishing, sightseeing charters, and cruises.

Thompson's Orchards (926-4738), 276 Gloucester Hill Rd., New Gloucester. Pick your own apples; donuts, apple cider, pies, and crafts. Seasonal weekend entertainment and hayrides. Labor Day-Christmas.

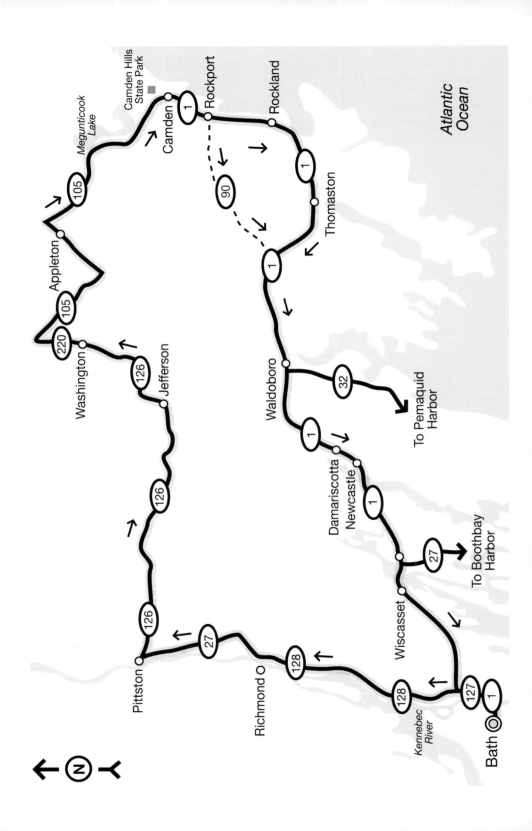

The Lower Kennebec Valley and the Coast from Camden to Bath

150 miles

major **attractions**

- Maine Maritime Museum
- Historic Homes
- Windjammer Cruises

- Farnsworth Art Museum
- Pemaquid Peninsula
- Boothbay Harbor

Beginning at one of America's most important shipbuilding centers, this drive takes in the scenery and historic architecture of the Kennebec River valley before turning east towards the rugged Maine coast. Following the shoreline, and often veering away from busy Route 1, the route links handsomely preserved village streets, the home ports of working windjammers, a surprisingly sophisticated art museum, a side trip to lively Boothbay Harbor, and a lighthouse that may be as familiar as the change in your pocket.

This drive begins in Bath, where more than 5,000 vessels have "gone down the ways" since the first full-rigged ship was launched here in 1762. In the mid-1800s it was America's fifth-largest seaport, with more than 200 shipyards: almost half of the wooden vessels built between 1862 and 1902 first took to the sea from "Maine's City of Ships."

This city on the western shore of the Kennebec River continues to thrive as a shipbuilding center. **Bath Iron Works**, a division of the defense contractor General Dynamics, employs approximately 9,000 people, and proudly proclaims at its entrance, "Through these gates pass the world's best shipbuilders." The shipyard has been awarded Navy contracts since 1893, and began building commercial vessels the following year.

A one-hour trolley tour of the Iron Works departs from the **Maine Maritime Museum**, a sprawling riverfront complex that focuses on the state's shipbuilding and seafaring heritage. Among the highlights at the museum: the Percy & Small Shipyard, the country's only surviving wooden shipbuilding yard; and the Maritime History Building, packed with artifacts, ship lore, and plenty of hands-on activities. The museum offers a variety of boat cruises, including a two-mile trip to tour the **Seguin Island Lighthouse**, which stands atop dramatic 180-foot cliffs. Built in 1795, the lighthouse is Maine's highest and second oldest.

Bath's historic district, with its many handsome brick buildings and 18th- and 19th-century mansions, has been preserved largely through the efforts of **Sagadahoc Preservation Inc**. SPI distributes several excellent walking and driving tour brochures (also available as podcasts), and offers guided walking tours in the summer (see "Activities" below).

Head north out of Bath on Route 1, turn left (north) onto Route 127 just over the bridge, then turn left (north) onto Route 128 (River Road) and continue as the road hugs the east shore of the Kennebec River, passing by sweeping lawns and magnificent homes reminiscent of the antebellum South, northern style.

After a few miles, a sign welcomes visitors to **Dresden Farmlands**, a fertile 10-mile stretch along the Kennebec that is home to some of the state's most productive vegetable and berry farms. Several roadside stands sell burst-in-your mouth-fresh berries in season.

Side Trips

Turn left onto Route 197 and cross over the river into **Richmond,** at the heart of the historic Tidewater Kennebec Region. From 1835 to 1857 the town was a thriving shipbuilding center, and the boat builders, sea captains, and merchants who lived here built one of the country's finest collections of Greek Revival homes, now a National Historic Register District.

Passenger ferries leave regularly from the Maine Department of Inland Fisheries & Wildlife's town landing for **Swan Island**, a National Historic Site. Teeming with nesting bald eagles, white-tailed deer, turkey, and other wildlife, the four-mile-long 1,755-acre wildlife management area was a town in the 18th and 19th centuries. The Department offers interpretive tours and environmental programs. Adirondack shelters are available for a maximum stay of two nights, and visitors can bring their bikes to the island. Advance reservations are mandatory (see "Attractions" below).

history and antiques

Back on Route 128, visitors who stumble upon the 1761 **Pownalborough Courthouse** – Maine's oldest court building – may feel they've stepped back in time to pre-Revolutionary days. The imposing, three-story edifice on the shores of the Kennebec has over the years served as a tavern, courtroom, judge's living quarters, post office, and dancing school. It's now owned by the Lincoln County Historical Society, which does a fine job of preserving this magnificent edifice and recalling its rich past. *Tip: Save your Courthouse admission stub – it's also good for admission to the 1811 Lincoln County Jail in Wiscasset (see below).*

When Route 128 ends, turn left onto Route 27 and continue north. Watch on the left for the **Major Reuben Colburn House**, built just four years after the Pownalborough Courthouse. In September 1775, a still-loyal Benedict Arnold and his force of 1,100 soldiers landed here on their way to engage the British at Quebec City during the rebel colonists' abortive effort to seize Canada. At the behest of George Washington, Major Colburn had 200 newly built "bateaux" waiting to carry the Arnold Expedition north. The boats were made of green wood, so the major and 20 volunteer carpenters tagged along, repairing leaks as they sailed. Drive a short distance past the house to view the one-room Colburn School and 1818 Riverside Cemetery (filled with lots of Colburns).

TutHill, just up Route 27, is a testament to one man's vision and a son's tenacity. It's a 55-acre village that looks strangely out of place in rural Maine – almost as if it was beamed down from another location. And in a way, some of it was: back in the 1980s Kenneth E. Tuttle moved several of the village's 24 18th- and 19th-century buildings here to save them from the wrecking ball. Others, such as the 1840 Greek Revival home of his son, Nathan, and the 1820 Episcopal Church where Nathan has one of his shops (there's another across the road), underwent extensive restoration. Today **Kenneth E. Tuthill Antiques** is one of Maine's premier dealers in high-end pieces, and the gleaming white village is a perfect setting for the treasures it displays.

In the January 5, 2009 issue of the Kennebec Journal, *reporter Mechele Cooper related the following story: Back in the 1980s a woman in a very cheap dress and carrying a plastic handbag walked in to Mr. Tuthill's shop, introduced herself as "Miss Moffitt," tossed $50,000 down on the counter, and told the dealer it was a down payment for his entire inventory.*

"If I die before I get to Texas to wire you the money, this is for your trouble," she told him. She didn't die: she wired the balance, sent a tractor trailer to pack everything up, and left him with an empty shop and almost $1 million.

In Pittston, turn right onto Route 126 and continue east, over the Sheepscot River and past Clary Lake. As you come into **Jefferson**, watch on the right for a circle of stones: the **Jefferson Cattle Pound**, 30 feet in diameter and 8 feet high, was built in 1828 to pen stray cattle until their owners bailed them out.

At the intersection, by the Jefferson Town House, continue east (left) on Route 126 through Jefferson. The northern end of Damariscotta Lake is to the right. The Damariscotta Condominiums -- newly converted tourist cabins -- are typical of a housing trend sweeping the state. Continue past the handsome 1808 First Baptist Church.

When Route 126 intersects with Route 32, continue a short distance on Route 32 to **Damariscotta Lake State Park**, a lovely little spot with a fine sandy beach and playground.

Back on Route 126, head out of town, past the **Jefferson House B&B**, and through the rolling countryside. **When Route 126 ends, turn left onto Route 220 toward Washington.**

Just out of town, visitors can pick berries, buy a freshly baked cookie, have a meal, get an ice cream cone, or just enjoy the view at **Sweet Season Farm.** Just past the farm is **Medomak Family Camp and Retreat Center**, and, a short distance past the camp entrance, a cemetery whose inscribed headstones all face the lake, giving it an empty, eerie look from the road.

After Washington, bear sharply to the right (east) onto Route 105. The drive continues through Appleton alongside a portion of the 50-mile **Georges River Scenic Byway.** Stay on Route 105 as it zigs and zags through the countryside before it follows along the shore of Lake Megunticook into Camden.

Penobscot Bay's Jewel

Even Hollywood has paid homage to tiny **Camden**, "The Jewel of the Maine Coast" on Penobscot Bay. Scenes for *In the Bedroom, Thinner,* and *Man Without a Face* were shot here. The handsome brick downtown with its scenic harbor, quaint neighborhoods, and outlying turn-of-the-19th-century shingle "cottages" built by wealthy summer residents have made the former shipbuilding center/mill town a popular tourist destination.

The harbor has been home port to a fleet of wooden schooners since 1936, and several offer windjammer cruises of varying duration. There are also lobster and harbor cruises, as well as sails around Curtis Island Lighthouse. Mae West and Lillian Gish are just a few of the actors who have performed at the elegantly restored 1894 Victorian **Camden Opera House.** Stop at the **Camden-Rockport-Lincolnville Chamber of Commerce** at the Public Landing for information, or check out the **Maine Windjammer Association** (see "Information" below).

One of the area's biggest attractions is visible from town. The 5,475-acre **Camden Hills State Park** encompasses two mountains: Mount Megunticook and Mount Battie. Edna St. Vincent Millay was so moved by the view from atop 800-foot-high Mount Battie that she immortalized it in her poem, "Renascence":

> All I could see from where I stood
> Was three long mountains and a wood
> I turned and looked the other way
> and saw three islands in the bay.

A plaque at the summit honors the poet, who summered in Camden. Visitors can hike to the top of Mt. Battie via several trails or drive up the paved toll road. The park entrance is off Route 1 a few miles north of town.

The 2 1/4-mile (round trip), rather steep Maiden's Cliff Trail up Mount Megunticook, whose trailhead begins off Route 52, 2 9/10 miles off Route 1, offers panoramic views of Lake Megunticook. The 600-foot-high white cross on a bluff at the summit memorializes 11-year-old Elenora French, who fell to her death from here in 1862.

Side Trips

As you head north out of Camden on Route 1, watch on the left for **Norumbega,** a Queen Anne fieldstone estate with a three-story turret, balconies, leaded glass windows, and a porte-cochere. Joseph B. Stearns, the inventor of duplex telegraphy, which revolution-ized the telegraph, used his millions to build the mansion in 1886. Today, it's an inn.

In **Lincolnville Beach,** the landmark **Lobster Pound Restaurant** is a popular stop for lobster. There's a take-out next door.

The **Maine State Ferry** sails three miles from Lincolnville Beach to **Isleboro** (20 minutes one way), a 14-mile-long island with many grand "cottages." Day trippers can take their bicycles and explore the narrow and winding roads, stopping at the now-automated Grindle Point lighthouse, whose keeper's cottage has been made into a **Sailors' Memorial Museum;** and Up Island Church, with its wall stencils and adjacent cemetery. For a grounding in local history, visit the Islesboro Historical Society in the old town hall.

Take Route 1 (also known as the Atlantic Highway) south out of Camden.

Turn left off Route 1 onto West St. to Pascal Avenue into **Rockport**, a handsome village overlooking Penobscot Bay. At the center of town, the 1891 **Rockport Opera House,** next to Mary Lea Park, and the **Center for Maine Contemporary Art** serve as the town's cultural hubs.

Continue of Route 1 south to Rockland. Portions of Route 1 have, in our opinion, become horribly built up, and traffic has kept pace. Some of the worst sprawl begins north of Rockland and continues to the Thomaston line. If you're not planning to visit Rockland or Thomaston, or taking a side trip to Port Clyde, there's a nifty alternate road: Route 90, just past the turnoff for Rockport, comes out, after 10 miles, just north of Waldoboro.

fine art ... and fine lobster

When Lucy Farnsworth inherited her family's 1854 Greek Revival home in **Rockland** in 1910, she drew the shades and lived as a recluse until her death at the age of 96. Her will, found in a cupboard, stipulated that the home and surrounding land be used to build an art gallery. A stash of $1.3 million in cash assured that her wishes would be carried out. We believe Lucy would be proud: one of New England's jewels, the **Farnsworth Art Museum**, is dedicated to showcasing works of American artists, particularly those who had some connection to Maine. The collection includes works by luminaries such as Thomas Cole, Louise Nevelson, and George Bellows, as well as more contemporary artists. Maine's first family of art is also highlighted: in addition to a superb exhibit of canvases by Andrew Wyeth, works by his father, N.C., and son, Jamie, are displayed at the museum's **Wyeth Center.** Lucy's home, the **Farnsworth Homestead**, is perfectly preserved as it appeared in the 1850s.

Edna St. Vincent Millay, the first woman to receive the Pulitzer Prize of Poetry, was born in Rockland. Louise Nevelson settled here with her parents in the early 1900s when they were one of only 30 Jewish families in town.

The backdrop for many of Andrew Wyeth's paintings, including *Christina's World,* was the **Olson House,** just 12 miles from Rockland. Administered by the Farnsworth, the house is on the National Register of Historic Places. Ask at the museum for directions.

Many artists exhibited at the Farnsworth drew inspiration from the natural beauty of the area, as well as from Rockland's rich history as a seafaring and commercial fishing hub. The city bills itself as the "lobster capital of the world," and each summer a festival pays homage to the *homard.* Rockland's harbor is homeport to one of New England's largest fleet of windjammers (see *"Information"* below), as well as a port of call for several cruise ships.

> *Soft-shell, or "shedder" lobsters, come on the market around mid-July. They're sweet and easy to eat, but have less meat in the claws. If you like claw meat, look for hard-shell lobsters.*

America's lighthouses, lifesaving service, and the U.S. Coast Guard are the focus at **The Maine Lighthouse Museum,** which houses the country's largest collection of lighthouse artifacts and mementos. Visitors can stroll along the 4,300-foot granite breakwater to Breakwater Lighthouse.

The **Maine State Ferry** terminal in Rockland provides service to three islands: **North Haven** (70 minutes one way), the most conducive to a day trip; nearby **Vinalhaven** (75 minutes one way), a quiet spot shared by summer residents and local fishermen; and the most remote and very scenic **Matinicus** (2 ¼ hours one way). Taking a car over requires some tricky and time-consuming advance planning.

Side Trip

Owls Head Transportation Museum, tucked away on the coast 3 ½ miles from Rockland, houses one of the world's finest collections of pioneer-era aircraft and automobiles. Demonstrations (and sometimes rides) are held on many summer weekends. From downtown, follow Route 73 for approximately three miles to Museum Street on the left. If you are continuing on to Port Clyde, after leaving the museum stay south on Route 73 to Route 131 south.

Continue south on Route 1 to Montpelier, on the outskirts of Thomaston. This Federal-style, two-story home on the hill, built between 1929-1931, is a faithful replica of the home of Revolutionary War hero and first U.S. secretary of war Major General Henry Knox. The 18 rooms are furnished with colonial and Federal period pieces, many of which belonged to the Knox family.

Side Trip

From Montpelier (corner of Route 1), head south on Route 131, along the St. George River, through Tenants Harbor, to **Port Clyde** at the tip of the St. George Peninsula. This tiny fishing village is home port for **Monhegan Boat Line,** whose 65-foot *Laura B* has been delivering freight and passengers to **Monhegan** – an island 10 miles out to sea – for more than 50 years**.** *(Note: be sure to make advance reservations for overnight stays on Monhegan.)* The company also operates various sightseeing cruises, including one which takes in **Marshall Point Light,** immortalized in the movie *Forrest Gump*; and Southern Island, owned by artist Jamie Wyeth.

Landlubbers can hike (or drive) a mile from the boat dock to **Marshall Point Light** (and

Museum), and visit the **Herring Gut Learning Center**, a marine science education center with a touch tank and aquaponic greenhouse.

Return on Route 131 to Route 1 and head a short distance south to Thomaston.

It's somewhat jarring, after wading through the traffic and sprawl on Route 1, to emerge on the main street of **Thomaston**. This charming seafaring town's historic district is lined with homes built between 1790 and the late 1800s. The area's rich history is narrated in **The Museum in the Streets**, a unique outdoor display of 25 plaques bearing historic photographs and legends.

On the way out of Thomaston, watch on the left for the **Maine State Prison Showroom**. It's the legacy of a jail that was located here from 1923 to 2002, when it was moved to Warren. For several days after the prison's closing, the public was invited to view the "dark and comfortless abode of guilt and wretchedness." The shop sells souvenirs, furniture and other products made by prisoners, who receive a share in the profits.

schooners and sauerkraut

Detour a short distance off Route 1 to Waldoboro, "home of the five-masted schooner," on the Medomak River. The town was settled by German emigrants brought to the New World in 1742 on the ship *Lydia* by General Samuel Waldo, a Boston merchant who owned half a million acres of land in the Penobscot region. Continue on Route 32 to see the beautifully preserved, circa 1772 **Old German Meeting House**. The inscription in the nearby cemetery stands as a testament to General Waldo's method of populating his land:

"This town was settled in 1748 by Germans who immigrated to this place with the promise and expectation of finding a prosperous city, instead of which they found nothing but wilderness."

In the 19th and 20th centuries Waldoboro was a renowned shipbuilding center: the first five-masted schooner, the *Governor Ames,* was built here in 1888 (her masts collapsed on her first voyage). At one time this was the country's sixth-busiest port.

Today, the town's major tourist draws are: the 1930s **Moody's Diner**, which has become an institution, complete with chicken croquettes, cream pie, and souvenir T-shirts; one of the country's oldest 5 & 10s; the 1936 Art Deco **Waldo Theatre**; and the **Kraut House**, famous for homemade Morse's sauerkraut. The **Waldoborough Historical Society Museum** complex includes a one-room schoolhouse and several buildings stuffed with local treasures.

Continue south on Route 1.

Side Trip

Just south of Waldoboro turn onto Route 1B to the **Pemaquid Peninsula**, a relatively uncrowded and at times breathtakingly scenic area that is one of our favorite places to explore. It's hard to get too lost: there are only two main roads (follow Route 32 south, and return north on Route 130). But the fun here is poking down side roads to tiny fishing villages and spectacular views of the rocky coast. Among places to visit: **Colonial Pemaquid Restoration and Fort William Henry**, and the 1827 **Pemaquid Point Lighthouse and Fisherman's Museum** (the lighthouse is depicted on Maine's quarter). **Hardy Boat Cruises**, in the picturesque village of **New Harbor**, offers service to **Monhegan Island**, as well as scenic cruises.

As you head north back to Route 1, turn off Route 130 onto Old Harrington Road to view the 1772 **Harrington Meeting House.**

In the movie "Message in a Bottle", the diner where Kevin Costner's character, Garret, had breakfast each morning, was actually Shaw's Fish & Lobster Wharf Restaurant *in New Harbor.*

Although it's several miles from the sea, **Damariscotta,** at the head of the Damariscotta River and the junction of Route 1, has the feel of an old seafaring town. In fact, for much of the late 18th century, it was a thriving shipping and shipbuilding center. It was also known for brick making, a skill that came in quite handy after a fire in 1845 devastated most of the buildings in the village. Today the bustling Main Street is lined with small shops, and cozy pubs and restaurants. The 1754 National Register of Historic Places **Chapman-Hall House** is one of Maine's oldest homes.

South on Route 1, the pretty little town of **Newcastle**, on the opposite shore of the river, is home to the 1808 **St. Patrick's Church** (32 Pond Rd.), the oldest Catholic Church in New England; and the 1883 **St. Andrew's Episcopal Church** (11 Glidden St.), on the shore of the Damariscotta River.

Side Trip

Continue south on Route 1 to Route 27 south to **Boothbay Harbor,** a popular seaside resort since the 1800s. The rather unscenic, 12-mile ride down the peninsula between the Sheepscot and Damariscotta rivers is broken up at mile nine by the **Boothbay Railway Village**, where visitors can hop aboard a narrow-gauge, coal-fired steam train for a ride through a recreated classic mid-1800s New England village. There's also a first-rate exhibit of more than 60 antique vehicles.

Along with Camden and Rockland, Boothbay Harbor is one of Maine's premier spots for boat tours, but during the summer months it has far more of the feel of a tourist resort than the others. From clambakes to sea kayak rentals to whale watches to schooner rides—it's all here and easily accessible in the compact village.

The **Boothbay Information Center** on Route 27 just north of town is an excellent place to get your bearings. Park your car in one of the public lots and hop aboard the **Rocktide Inn Trolley** (free; mid-June-Labor Day), which makes a scenic in-town loop. Highlights of a visit include: a walk across the harbor footbridge; a sail to **Monhegan Island**, 12 miles out to sea; a stroll through **Maine Botanical Gardens**; the **Maine State Aquarium** in West Boothbay Harbor; and a **Burnt Island Lighthouse Tour** aboard the *Novelty;* and, of course, a moonlight sail. **Boothbay Region Land Trust**, which conserves more than 800 acres of land throughout the region, offers 30 miles of hiking trails at various holdings. Maps are available at its office or at the Information Center.

Side Trip

Southport Island, east on Route 27, is home to **Hendrick's Hill Museum**. Built in 1810 by fisherman John Cameron, his family lived here for 100 years, and the museum preserves life on the island from 1800 to 1950. There's a great view of the 1892 Cuckolds Lighthouse from the public landing at the tip of **Cape Newagen**. A loop of the island from Boothbay Harbor, down Route 27 and back on Route 238, is approximately 11 miles.

If you've taken the Boothbay/Southport Island side trips, return to Route 1 via Route 27 and continue south.

Side Trip

Fort Edgecomb, an octagonal blockhouse built to protect Wiscasset from the English during the Embargo Act of 1807, never saw much hostile action. But today the scenic, three-acre state historic site on the Sheepscot River is a delightful spot to picnic and watch for harbor seals. Reenactments are staged on some summer weekends. Turn left onto Eddy Road to Fort Road just before the Route 1 bridge to Wiscasset.

Head over the Sheepscot River to **Wiscasset**, billed by local boosters as "The Prettiest Village in Maine." Whether or not you agree, it is certainly *one* of the prettiest. In its earlier days it was a thriving maritime center, and the elegant homes along the tree-lined streets reflect its prosperous past. A large section of the downtown is on the National Register.

To get an idea of how Wiscasset's upper crust lived, take a tour of the National Historic Landmark, Federal-style **Nickels-Sortwell House**, built in 1807 by a ship owner. After the Embargo Act of 1807 and the War of 1812 destroyed the local economy, the house became a hotel until it was refurbished, and eventually came under the supervision of Historic New England, which also oversees the 1807, Federal-style **Castle Tucker**, just a short distance away.

Another mansion— built in 1852 as a two-family "double house" – preserves a different kind of history: the **Musical Wonder House** is the repository of Danilo Konvalinka's lifetime collection of more than 5,000 rare music boxes, dating from 1796 to 1910. Other antique mechanical instruments, including singing birds, player pianos, and talking machines, are also on display. And yes, visitors do get to hear many of them on their guided tour.

Some of the town's less fortunate citizens were housed in a humbler abode: the Lincoln County Jail, in use from 1811 until 1954. The original cells -- complete with some rather elaborate graffiti – are among the exhibits. The jail is a part of **The 1811 Lincoln County Museum & Old Jail**, and headquarters of the Lincoln County Historical Association.

Continue south on Route 1.

Side Trip

In **Woolrich,** just before taking the bridge over the Kennebec River to return to Bath, turn left (south) onto Route 127 for 9 1/10 miles to the Maine Audubon Society's 119-acre **Josephine Newman Wildlife Sanctuary.** A portion of the 2 ½ miles of mostly wooded hiking trails cross bluffs that loom 120 feet above ocean coves. At approximately 13 miles from the Route 1 turnoff is **Reid State Park,** Maine's first state-owned saltwater beach. And what a beach it is: long, wide, and sandy, with towering dunes and a rocky headland. Facilities include a snack bar, a picnic area, and a bathhouse.

Cross over the Kennebec River back to Bath.

Side Trip

Another of Maine's most popular beaches is 14 miles south of Bath on Route 209 at the tip of the Phippsburg Peninsula. **Popham Beach State Park** has three miles of sandy shore (and often a strong undertow).

information *All area codes are (207) unless otherwise indicated.*

Bath Chamber of Commerce (443-9751), 45 Front St., Bath 04530. midcoastmaine.com

Boothbay Harbor Region Chamber of Commerce (633-2353), Rte. 27, Boothbay Harbor 04538. boothbayharbor.com

Camden-Rockport-Lincolnville Chamber of Commerce (236-4404), Public Landing, Camden 04843. camdenme.org

Damariscotta Region Chamber of Commerce (563-8340), 15 Courtyard St., Damariscotta 04543. damariscottaregion.com

Friends of Seguin Island (443-4808), 72 Front St., Bath. Maine's second oldest lighthouse. Summer tours. seguinisland.org

Maine State Ferry: Lincolnville Beach: 789-5611; Rockland Terminal, 596-2202; state.me.us/mdot/opt/ferry/ferry.htm

Maine Windjammer Association (800-807-9463) for cruises throughout the state. sailmainecoast.com

Penobscot Bay Regional Chamber of Commerce (596-0376), One Park Drive, Rockland 04841; the realmaine.com

Southern Midcoast Maine Chamber (Includes Dresden) (877-725-8797), 2 Main St., Topsham 04086. midcoastmaine.com

lodging

Blue Skye Farm B&B (832-0300). 1708 Friendship Rd. (Rte. 220), Waldoboro 04572. Commanding home perched above the Medomak River has 5 spacious bedrooms (2 downstairs share a bath; 3 upstairs with private baths). Common rooms include a kitchen for guests' use evenings. blueskyefarm.com. $$

Boothbay Harbor Inn (633-6302), 31 Atlantic Ave., Boothbay Harbor 04538. Rooms at this 60-room motel range from spacious, with balcony or patio overlooking the water, to economy without view. Windows on the Harbor Restaurant serves dinner nightly. Continental breakfast. boothbayharborinn.com $$-$$$$

Brown's Wharf Restaurant/Motel/Marina (633-5440), 121 Atlantic Ave., Boothbay Harbor. 70 motel units as well as apartments and several cottages by the week at this harborfront motel. The restaurant specializes in seafood. brownswharfinn.com $$-$$$

Camden Harbour Inn (236-4200), 83 Bayview St., Camden 04843. On a hilltop overlooking the village and bay, the inn's 18 rooms and suites all have king size beds, private baths, and mini bars; some have decks, balconies, patios or fireplaces. Room service available from Natalie's (see *"Restaurants"* below). camdenharbourinn.com $$$-$$$$

Camden Maine Stay Inn (236-9636), 22 High St., Camden 04843. B&B lodgings in a classic 19th-century farmhouse in the historic district. 8 rooms with private baths and a/c; some have soaking tubs and/or gas fireplaces. $$-$$$$

Clary Lake B&B (549-5961), 777 Gardiner Rd., Jefferson 04348. Cozy rooms with private baths in a 150-year-old farmhouse overlooking the lake. Continental breakfast included (full breakfast, add $5). bbonline.com/me/clarylake/ $

Craignair Inn (594-7644), 5 Third St., Spruce Head 04859. Old fashioned, cheerful oceanfront inn, built in 1928 to house workers from nearby quarries, has a variety of rooms ranging from spacious with private baths and air conditioning, to shared with ceiling fans. Housekeeping apt. Restaurant ($$-$$$) specialties include lobster Newburg and seafood a la Grecque. Breakfast included. craignair.com $-$$$

The East Wind Inn (372-6366), 21 Mechanic St., Tenants Harbor 04860. A waterfront property with 22 rooms, suites and apartments; the dining room serves a full complimentary breakfast, and dinner. Rooms in the inn have shared or private baths. Pets welcome. eastwindinn.com $$-$$$

Galen C. Moses House B&B (442-8711), 1009 Washington St., Bath 04530. Rooms at this National Register of Historic Homes 1874 Victorian mansion are spacious and lavishly furnished; all but the Carriage Room (where pets are welcome) have air conditioning. Breakfast included. galenmoses.com $$-$$$$

The Hotel Pemaquid (677-2312), 3098 Bristol Rd. (Rte. 130), New Harbor 04554. Classic turn-of –the-19th-century summer hotel just 120 yards from Pemaquid Lighthouse has been elegantly restored, and offers a variety of rooms and suites with private or shared baths. Mid-May-mid-Oct. hotelpemaquid.com $-$$$$

The Inn at Bath (443-4294), 969 Washington St., Bath 04530. Mid-1800s Greek Revival in the Historic District has 8 antiques-filled guest rooms with private baths; some have wood stoves and private entrances. Breakfast is excellent. innatbath.com $$$

The Inn at Round Pond (529-2004), 1442 Rte. 32, Round Pond 04564. A seaside 1800s mansard home with three spacious guest rooms and a garden cottage, all with sitting areas and a private bath. theinnatroundpond.com $$-$$$

The Island Inn (596-0371), Monhegan Island 04852. Perched on a bluff overlooking the harbor, the inn has 32 rooms (some with shared baths) and suites. Views range from garden to direct ocean. Breakfast included; dinner offered in the summer. Late May-mid-Oct. islandinnmonhegan.com $$$-$$$$

Jefferson House B&B (549-5768), 95 Washington Rd., Jefferson 04348. Classic accommodations in a family-friendly 1835 farmhouse on 12 country acres. Breakfast is served on the deck overlooking the waterfall, and guests can borrow a canoe for a river jaunt. jeffersonhousebb.com $

Medomak Camp Family Camp and Retreat Center (845-6001), 178 Liberty Rd., Washington 04574. Very basic one-room cabins sleep up to four. Full roster of activities require a week stay or longer. medomakcamp.com $

Mid-Town Motel (633-2751), 96 McKown St., Boothbay Harbor 04538. A small, classic 1950s motel with modern amenities 5 minutes from the harbor. midtownmaine.com $

The Monhegan House (594-7983), Monhegan Island 04852. The island's oldest continuously operating inn, a sprawling, 4-story building built in the 1870s, has 28 rooms on 3 upper floors. Baths are shared; the single rooms on the fourth floor are the cheapest. monheganhouse.com $$-$$$

The Mooring B&B (371-2790), 132 Seguinland Rd., Harmon's Harbor, Georgetown. The original home of Walter Reid, who donated land for Reid State Park, has 5 rooms with private baths, a/c, and ocean views. A full breakfast is included. themooringb-b.com $$-$$$

Newagen Seaside Inn (633-5242), Rte. 27S, Cape Newagen 04576. A classic, 20-acre, oceanfront resort on Southport Island, with remodeled guest rooms, suites, and cottages. Amenities include tennis courts, a freshwater pool, bowling alley, and croquet. newagenseasideinn.com $$-$$$$

Norumbega (236-4646), 63 High St., Camden 04843. This landmark Victorian has 10 rooms and 2 suites (including the penthouse, with a private deck and living area). With its coffered ceilings, carved Gothic fireplaces, and antiques, this is partly an inn, and partly a museum. Breakfast included. norumbegainn.com $$$-$$$$

Ocean House Hotel (372-6691), Port Clyde Rd., Port Clyde 04855. Built in the 1830s as a rooming house for mariners, this beautifully restored b&b has 10 rooms with shared or private bath; most with an ocean or harbor view. oceanhousehotel.com $-$$

Rocktide Inn (633-4455), 35 Atlantic Ave., Boothbay Harbor 04538. Harborside motel right in the middle of all the action; 90 pleasant, air conditioned units. Breakfast buffet. Mid-June-mid-Oct. rocktideinn.com $$-$$$

Sebasco Harbor Resort (389-1161), 29 Kenyon Rd., (Rt. 217), Phippsburg. A full-service 550-acre resort on the shores of Casco Bay. Accommodations range from cozy rooms in the main lodge to 10-room cottages. Golf, water sports, spa, and a camp just for kids. sebasco.com $$$-$$$$

Seaside Inn (800-710-2817 or 372-0700), 5 Cold Storage Rd., Port Clyde 04855. An 1850s sea captain's home overlooking the village has 8 cozy guest rooms. seasideportclyde.com $-$$

Squire Tarbox Inn (882-7693), 1181 Main Rd., Wiscasset 04578. Although it has a Wiscasset mailing address, this National Register of Historic Places property is on Westport Island, 8 ½ mi. off Rte. 1. 11 rooms in the 1763 original house, an 1820 addition, and a remodeled 1820s barn. Dinner in the cozy dining room or on a screened-in deck overlooking the gardens. Breakfast included. squiretarboxinn.com $$-$$$

restaurants

Anchor Inn Restaurant (529-5584), Round Pond. Overlooking Muscongus Bay, fresh grilled seafood is the star here, along with homemade desserts. L & D. $-$$

Beale Street Barbeque (442-9514), 215 Water St., Bath. Memphis-style barbeque in classier-than-usual surroundings. Slow smoked ribs are a specialty, along with jambalaya, shrimp creole, and for the less spice-inclined customers, mac & cheese. L & D. $-$$

Conte's 1894 Restaurant, Commercial St., Rockland. Large portions of Italian and fresh seafood in a love-it-or-hate-it down-home ambiance. There's a chalkboard menu, fresh baked bread, terrific salad with homemade dressing, and lots of garlic in the food. No credit cards. D. $$

Five Island Lobster Co., (371-2990), 1447 Five Islands Rd., (Rte. 127), Georgetown. Watch lobstermen at work from one of the outdoor picnic tables overlooking the harbor while you feast on their catch, plus steamers and fried clams. L & D daily in summer; call for off-season hrs. $-$$

King Eider's Pub and Restaurant (563-6008), 2 Elm St., Damariscotta. Crab cakes and local oysters lead the bill at this cozy and welcoming pub housed in an historic building in the center of town. Sit downstairs or in the more spacious upstairs dining room. L & D. $$-$$$

Lobster Pound Restaurant (789-5550), Rte. 1, Lincolnville Beach. Lobster is king at this large, open dining room overlooking the ocean: it's served up in chowder, stew, baked stuffed, boiled, rolls ... landlubber options also available. L & D May-late Oct. $-$$$

Mae's Cafe and Bakery (442-8577), 160 Centre St., Bath. The extensive menu at this popular spot features creative omelettes, hearty sandwiches, and fresh baked treats (try the cinnamon buns). B, L & Sun. brunch. $

Morse's Kraut House (866-832-5569), 3856 Washington Rd. (Rte. 220), North Waldoboro. The shop sells the company's sauerkraut, coleslaw, pickled, beets, and sour mustard pickles. Or enjoy them all at the small restaurant. B & L daily. $

Natalie's (236-7008), Camden Harbor Inn, 83 Bayview St., Camden. Chef Lawrence Klang, classically trained at Le Cordon Bleu in London, offers an ever-changing, sophisticated menu, but the Grand Lobster Menu is among his specialties. The wine list includes more than 200 labels. D nightly. $$$-$$$$

Shaw's Fish & Lobster Wharf Restaurant (677-2200), Rte. 32, New Harbor. Dining "in the rough" doesn't get much better: lobster, onion rings, and beer overlooking the water. A bit touristy, but hey, you're a tourist. $$-$$$

Sweet Season Farm (845-3028), 77 Liberty Rd., Washington. Berries are the specialty at this u-pick farm, which also bakes them into delicious desserts. The menu features half-pound Maine Angus burgers; top it off with a cone from the nearby dairy. B & L; D Fri.-Sun. $-$$

Waterman's Beach Lobster (596-7819), Waterman Beach Rd., South Thomaston. A true lobster-in-the-rough gem, this tiny spot offers picnic-table seating and several kid-friendly items. L & D Thurs.-Sun. $-$$

attractions

Boothbay Railway Village (633-4727), Rte. 27, Boothbay. Daily in summer; call for off-season hours.

Breakwater Light (785-4609), Jameson Point, Rockland Harbor. Gift shop open summer weekends.

Camden Hills State Park, Rte. 1, Camden.

Castle Tucker (882-7169), 2 Lee St., Wiscasset. June-mid-Oct., Wed-Sun. Tours on the hour beginning at 11 a.m.

Center for Maine Contemporary Art (236-2875), 162 Russell Ave., Rockport. Memorial Day-Oct., Tues-Sat, Sun p.m. Winter, Thurs-Sat., Sun. p.m.

Chapman Hall House, Main St. at Church St., Damariscotta. July and Aug. Tues.-Sun. p.m.

Conway Homestead and Cramer Museum (236-2257), Conway Rd., Camden. Camden-Rockport Historical Society maintains this complex which includes a c. 1770 house; timbered-style, 18th-century barn; blacksmith shop; and sugar house. July and Aug., Tues-Fri.

Edgecomb Potters (882-9493), 727 Bothbay Rd., Rte. 27S, Edgecomb (also Portland and Free-port). Glass, jewelry, and metal sculpture are displayed at the 28-acre gallery and studio complex, but the stars here are the breathtakingly beautiful porcelains.

The 1811 Lincoln County Museum & Old Jail (882-6817), 133 Federal St., Wiscasset. July and Aug.; June & Sept., Sat. & Sun.

Farnsworth Art Museum (596-647), 16 Museum St., Rockland. Museum, Memorial Day-Columbus Day; Wyeth Center, mid-May-Columbus Day; Farnsworth Homestead, Memorial Day-Columbus Day; call for off-season hours.

Fort Edgecomb (882-7777), 66 Fort Rd., Edgecomb. Memorial Day-Labor Day.

Fort William Henry and Colonial Pemaquid State Historic Site (677-2423), off Rte. 130, Pemaquid Harbor. Reconstructed fort resemble one built here by the English in 1692 and demolished by the French in 1696. The Old Fort House displays artifacts dug up from a 17th-century village still being excavated. Memorial Day-Labor Day.

Harrington Meeting House. Mon., Wed. and Sat. 2-5 p.m. Donation.

Hendricks Hill Museum (633-1102), 419 Hendricks Hill Rd., Southport. July and Aug., Tues., Thurs., and Sat. 11 a.m.-3.p.m. Donation.

Herring Gut Learning Center (372-8677), Port Clyde. Marine education center overlooking the harbor.

Josephine Newman Wildlife Sanctuary (989-2591), Five Islands Rd., Georgetown Center.

Maine Botanical Gardens (633-4333), Barters Island Rd., Boothbay Harbor. New England's largest botanical garden.

The Maine Lighthouse Museum (594-3301), One Park Drive, Rockland. June-Columbus Day, daily; off-season Thurs.-Sat.

Maine Maritime Museum (443-1316), 243 Washington St., Bath. Museum open daily. Bath Iron Works trolley tours: late May-mid June, Tues., 12:30 p.m. & Sat. 10 a.m.; mid-June-mid-Oct., Mon.-Wed, Fri. 12:30 p.m., Sat. 10 a.m. Reservations suggested.

Maine State Aquarium (633-9559), 194 McKown Point Rd., West Boothbay Harbor. Daily in summer; call for off-season hrs.

Maine State Prison Showroom (354-9237), Rte. 1, Thomaston.

Major Colburn House, 33 Arnold Rd., Pittston. July and Aug., Sat. & Sun. p.m.

Marshall Point Lighthouse Museum. May, Sat. & Sun. pm; Memorial Day-Columbus Day, Sat., Sun.-Fri. pm.

Montpelier (354-8062), 28 High St., Thomaston. Memorial Day weekend-Columbus Day, guided tours Tues.-Sun.

Musical Wonder House (882-7163), 16-18 High St., Wiscasset. Memorial Day weekend-Halloween, Mon.-Sat., Sun. p.m.

Nickels-Sortwell House (882-7169), 121 Main St., Wiscasset. June-mid-Oct., Fri.-Sun.; hourly tours begin at 11 a.m.

North Country Wind Bells (677-2224), Rte. 32, Round Pond. Former lobsterman Jim Davidson and his wife, May, craft wind bells that echo the tones of coastal and harbor bells. Weekends in summer, or by chance.

Olson House (354-0102), 427 Hathorne Point Rd., Cushing. Tours Memorial Day-Columbus Day.

Owls Head Transportation Museum (594-4418), Rte. 73, Owls Head.

Pemaquid Craft Co-op (677-2077), Rte. 130, New Harbor. 15 rooms packed with Maine-made arts and crafts.

Pemaquid Lighthouse ($) & Fishermen's Museum (donation) (677-2494), Rte. 130, Pemaquid Point. May-Oct.

Popham Beach State Park (389-1335; tide and parking hotline, 389-9125), 10 Perkins Farm Lane, Phippsburg. Mid-Apr.-Oct.

Pownalborough Courthouse/Lincoln County Historical Society (882-6817), 23 Court House Rd., Rte. 128, Dresden. July & Aug., Tues.-Sat., Sun. p.m.; June & Sept., Sat. & Sun.

Reid State Park (371-2303), 375 Seguinland Rd., Georgetown.

Sailors' Memorial Museum, Isleboro. Seasonal; closed Mon.

Swan Island Steve Powell Management Area: Maine Dept. of Inland Fisheries and Wildlife, P.O. Box 221, Swan Island, Richmond 04357. Visitors for either day visits or overnight camping must make advance reservations. For a brochure (with a reservation form), call 547-5322. May-Labor Day.

Thomaston Historical Society Museum. June-Aug., Tues.-Thurs. p.m.

Waldoboro Historical Society Museum, 164 Main St., Waldoboro. July & Aug. p.m.

activities

Balmy Days II (633-2284). Pier 8, Boothbay Harbor. Departs at 9:30 a.m. in summer.

Boothbay Region Land Trust (633-4818), 137 Townsend Ave., Boothbay Harbor.

Burnt Island Living History Tour (633-2284), *Novelty*, Pier 8, Bar Harbor. Early July-early Sept. p.m.

Camden Opera House (236-7956), 29 Elm St., Camden. Schedule: camdenoperahouse.com

Center for Maine Contemporary Art (236-2875), 162 Russell Ave., Rockport. Memorial Day-Oct, Tues.-Sat., Sun p.m.; rest of year, Thurs.-Sat., Sun. p.m.

Chocolate Church Arts Center (442-8455), 798 Washington St., Bath. Schedule: chocolatechurcharts.org

Great Gadzooks Tidewater Fishing (720-0857), 132 Dummer St., Bath. Striper and blue fishing on the Kennebec River.

Hardy Boat Cruises (800-278-3346), New Harbor.

Long Reach Lighthouse Cruises (888-6786), 804 Washington St., Bath.

Monhegan Boat Line (372-8848), Port Clyde. Boats depart daily; also puffin, nature, lighthouse, and sunset cruises.

Port Clyde Kayaks (372-8100), Port Clyde, Maine. Sea kayak tours of approximately 2 ½ hrs. include harbor and full-moon tours. Longer tours available. $

Rockport Opera House (236-2514), Central St., Rockport. Schedule: rockport.me.us/operahouse/

Sagadahoc Preservation, Inc. (443-2174). Walking tours of historic Bath (more than 6 people needed, $). Or check their website for a self-guided walking or driving tour: sagadahocpreservation.org

The Waldo Theatre (832-6060), Waldoboro. Schedule: thewaldo.org

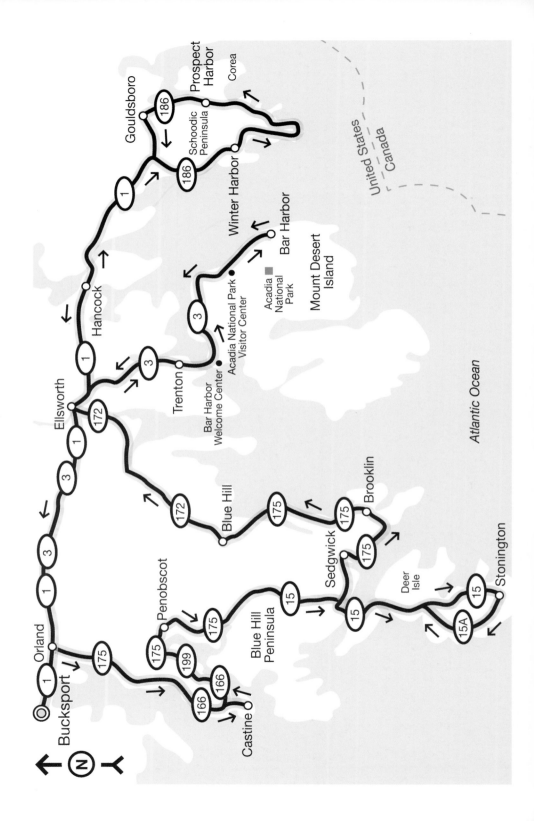

Drive 20

Buucksport to Blue Hill and Acadia

220 miles

major attractions

- Fort Knox
- Bar Harbor
- Acadia National Park
- Cadillac Mountain
- Schoodic Peninsula

*I*f Maine's famously jagged coastline were stretched out, it would extend for nearly 3,500 miles. Travelers along Route 1 enjoy seemingly endless opportunities for stretching out their own explorations by delving into dozens of sea-splashed peninsulas and coastal islands. Two of the loveliest and most fascinating are the Blue Hill Peninsula, where boatbuilding, seamanship, and fine crafts are honored traditions; and Mount Desert Island, largely the realm of Acadia, America's most-visited national park.

Who would guess that the world's tallest public bridge-observatory is in **Bucksport**? In just one minute visitors are whisked 42 stories up to the top of **Penobscot Narrows Bridge.** The **Observatory**, up two more levels, affords 360 degree views of the Penobscot River and the surrounding countryside, and is a great place to get oriented at the beginning of this drive.

The observatory also provides a birds-eye view of **Fort Knox** (not the one with the gold), named after Major General Henry Knox, the country's first secretary of war (see Drive #19). The fort was built to protect the Penobscot River from naval attack at a time when the U.S. and Great Britain disputed the location of Maine's northeast border. In 1869, 25 years after the project had drained $1 million from the Congressional coffers and the fort was not completed, construction ground to a halt. Today it is one of New England's best preserved fortifications.

Northeast Historic Film, in Bucksport's restored 1912 Alamo Theatre, is New England's only moving-image archive. A museum is open weekday business hours and weekends, when the theatre shows first-run films.

a Blue Hill ramble

Head north out of Bucksport on Route 1. Watch on the right for The Big Chicken Barn, one of Maine's largest bookstores/antique shops. In **Orland**, near the head of Penobscot Bay, **turn right on Route 175** onto the **Blue Hill Peninsula**, one of Maine's most scenic and most directionally-challenged destinations. Two-lane blacktops wind past farms, alongside coves, and through small villages, routes intersecting and often inexplicately changing numbers. Pay close attention to the driving directions below. Or, better yet, wander aimlessly: it may be the best way to soak in the charm of this scenic and still relatively undeveloped peninsula.

Side Trip
Continue a short distance on Route 1 past the turnoff for Route 175 to the blinking yellow light, and you're **H.O.M.E.** Homeworkers Organized for More Employment is spearheaded by the World Emmaus Movement, a Christian-based organization that came to Maine in 1970 to teach work skills to "those who suffer most." Today the cooperative community includes a free health clinic, soup kitchen, food bank, homeless shelter, and job and craft training, raising income at its craft shop and market.

Continue south Route 175 to Route 166 to Route 166 A, and follow Route 166 A into Castine. It's hard to imagine that this small, peaceful town, settled in 1604 at the confluence of the Penobscot and Bagaduce rivers, was for much of its history a hotly contested bit of real estate, variously claimed by the British, the Dutch, the French, and the United States. Fortunately, the U.S. eventually won out. The town's many handsome buildings in its Historic District are testament to its 19th-century status as one of the country's richest towns and major summer resorts. Castine suffered an economic downturn during the Depression, but received a major financial boost in 1941 when the **Maine Maritime Academy** began training merchant seamen here. Today more than 700 students live on the Academy's campus in the center of town. Their 500-foot-long training vessel, *the* T/S *State of Maine*, is open for 30-minute tours when in port.

Visitors can get a sense of Castine's rich history by taking a self-guided walking tour and visiting the Revolutionary War era, British-built **Fort George**. Begin at the **Castine Historical Society** for an overview. The **Wilson Museum**, housing the eclectic collections of anthropologist Dr. John Howard Wilson, encompasses the John Perkins House, the Blacksmith Shop, and the Hearse House.

Head north out of Castine on Route 166, bearing to the right when it joins Route 199 toward Penobscot. When Route 166 and Route 199 split, continue north on Route 199. After three miles, turn right onto Route 175 and head south. At approximately six miles, along the Bagaduce River, the **Reversing Falls** is created by the fast-flowing tides. In another six miles, pull over at the **Caterpillar Hill Rest Area** for stunning views of Deer Isle, Penobscot Bay, Camden Hills, and the Bay Islands.

Side Trip

It seems fitting that simple living advocates Helen and Scott Nearing, co-authors of *Living the Good Life*, built their last home in the woods on relatively remote **Cape Rosier**. The **Good Life Center at Forest Farm**, with an organic garden, greenhouse and yurt, is open for tours. While on the Cape, visit the 1,350-acre **Holbrook Island Sanctuary**, a secluded swath of upland forests and rocky shores on Penobscot Bay. Watch for great blue herons, peregrine falcons, and bald eagles, as well as deer, otter, and other marsh and forest creatures.

to the tip of Deer Isle . . . .

About a half mile past the rest area, Route 175 and Route 15 meet. When they split, stay on Route 15 and cross over the suspension bridge between Eggemoggin Reach and Penobscot Bay to Deer Isle, made up of a number of small villages. Granite, lobster, and tourism have sustained this prototypical Downeast community over the years. More recently, the internationally renowned **Haystack Mountain School of Crafts** has attracted many artists, and several have stayed to open up their own galleries. The school also maintains its own gallery at 22 Church Street. The nearby **Blue Heron Gallery** represents more than 100 artists, many of them affiliated with Haystack.

Continue south on Route 15. Although a few galleries and shops have begun to pop up in "downtown" **Stonington**, it still retains the simple charm of a working fishing village. The restored, 1912 National Register of Historic Places **Opera House** overlooks Commercial Pier, home port for a large fishing/lobstering fleet.

> *Roughly one in 30 million lobsters has an orange shell—but several turned up off the Maine coast within a few weeks in summer of 2009.*

Side Trip

In Stonington, hop aboard the mailboat (isleauhaut.com) to visit **Isle au Haut (pronounced** "eye-le-*ho*"), six miles out at sea. Nearly one-half of the island is an outpost of **Acadia National Park,** whose 18 miles of trails offer lots of opportunity to commune with nature without throngs of people nearby. The mailboat makes two stops: the town landing, and the park's Duck Harbor. The walk from the town landing to the park entrance is four miles, so be sure to debark at the right spot. There are only four miles of paved road and cycling is not allowed on hiking trails, so bikes are discouraged. However, there's a bike rental at the ferry landing.

Follow Route 15A out of Stonington back to where it meets Route 15 and head north back over the bridge to the intersection with Route 175. Turn right onto Route 175 towards Brooklin, on Eggemoggin Reach. The charming little village is home to the internationally renowned **WoodenBoat School**, which offers courses in boatbuilding, woodworking, and seamanship. *WoodenBoat* magazine is also published here.

Tiny Brooklin has been home to some big writing talents. E.B. White, author of beloved works including Charlotte's Web *and* Stuart Little, *and a frequent contributor to* The New Yorker, *lived here with his wife, Katherine, a founding editor of the magazine. They're buried in a local cemetery. Robert McCloskey, who wrote* Blueberries for Sal *and* One Morning in Maine, *was a part-time resident.*

The general store in the heart of town is the best place to get information on local happenings.

Continue north out of Brooklin on Route 175 along Blue Hill Bay (it merges with Route 172 in Blue Hill Falls). At the junction with Route 15, turn right onto Route 15 into Blue Hill, the largest town on the peninsula. A thriving shipbuilding center in the 18th century, today this classic New England village is a cultural mecca, with numerous art galleries, the **Kneisel Hall Chamber Music School** and festival, and several excellent inns and restaurants. Be sure to visit **Rackcliffe Pottery**, where dinner, bake, and serving ware is made from native clay.

Side Trip

Although a hike up **Blue Hill Mountain** is rewarding at any time of the year, it's a particular treat in late summer and early fall when bushes are lush with wild blueberries. Follow Pleasant Street (Route 15) to Mountain Road and the parking area: the Hayes Trail begins across the street; the Osgood Trail begins ¼ mile west of the parking lot.

The trails intersect at the summit. For information, contact the **Blue Hill Heritage Trust**.

gateway to Acadia . . . .

Head out of Blue Hill on Route 172, and continue north. When Route 172 ends at Routes 1/3, turn right and continue into Ellsworth **on Routes 1/3.** The "Gateway to Acadia National Park" has a small, rather quaint downtown along Route 1, and then, along Route 3 towards Mount Desert Island, a long string of shopping centers, fast food restaurants, fun parks, and motels. Ellsworth's major tourist attraction is **Woodlawn Museum: The Black House**, an 1828 Georgian mansion preserved as a time capsule. Visitors can stroll through the formal gardens, explore the manicured grounds and trails, and visit the barns filled with antique sleighs. The museum is on Route 172 at the intersection with Routes 1/3 just before the Union River Bridge.

Follow Route 3 toward Mount Desert Island. The **Mount Desert Island Chambers of Commerce and Acadia National Park Information Center**, just before the Thompson Island bridge, is well equipped with information and can help with last-minute lodging reservations.

Note: Mount Desert Island has far too many points of interest on far too many byways for us to map in this guide. We've given the highlights below, but be sure to pick up one of the many excellent brochures available for free at the Information Center. One of the most detailed is the 72-page **Bar Harbor & Acadia National Park Visitors' Guide.**

There's just one All American Road in New England – Mount Desert Island's **Acadia Byway**. The "All American" designation is the highest honor bestowed by the U.S. Department of Transportation, which selects the best from their 99 designated National Scenic Byways. To date just 27 roads have received this accolade.

From late June through mid-October the Island Explorer *bus provides free service along eight bus routes linking hotels, inns and campgrounds with several destinations in Acadia National Park, downtown Bar Harbor, Northeast Harbor, and Southwest Harbor.*

The Bar Harbor Ferry *provides daily passenger service between Bar Harbor and Winter Harbor from late June through August. The bus also meets the ferry at Winter Harbor and transports passengers to Schoodic Point, Birch Harbor, and Prospect Harbor.*

When French explorer Samuel de Champlain sailed into the Gulf of Maine in 1604 he named this land mass "Isles des Monts Desert," or "island of barren mountains." For the next 250 years farming and shipbuilding were the region's major industries. But beginning in the 1840s, Hudson River School painters Thomas Cole and Frederic Church visited the area and portrayed it so magnificently that they spawned a new industry – tourism.

Today, more than two million visitors visit Mount Desert Island's **Acadia National Park** each year, and, on summer weekends, it might feel like they're all in front of your car on the park's scenic, 20-mile Park Loop Road. But don't get discouraged: get out of the car and explore the beauty and, yes, solitude, of the park's more than 30,000 island acres. There are more than 125 miles of hiking trails; 45 miles of carriage roads accessible only by horse, horse-drawn-carriages, bikes, or on foot (see "Activities" below); secluded coves; and miles of the rocky coastline for which the area is most famous.

Highlights of Acadia National Park:

Begin a visit at the **Hulls Cove Visitor Center.**

The **Acadia Loop Road** winds through dense woodland and along a rocky shore to the top of 1,530-foot **Cadillac Mountain** (seven miles round trip off the Loop Road). There's a festive atmosphere when people gather to greet the sunrise at this highest point on the East Coast.

Popular stops along the Loop Road include:

Sand Beach. The water is seldom warmer than 55 degrees, but the setting is magnificent. The Ocean Path trail begins here and winds along the shore for two miles to Otter Cliff.

Jordan Pond House. Afternoon tea with popovers has been a tradition since the original restaurant opened in the late 1800s.

Nature Center at Sieur de Monts Spring. Exhibits of the park's natural world; walking trails; and the **Wild Gardens of Arcadia**, where more than 300 native species are identified along a series of thoughtfully designed garden paths.

Abbe Museum at Sieur de Monts Spring. Dedicated to preserving tribal history and artifacts of Native Americans. There's a branch of the museum in downtown Bar Harbor.

Champlain Mountain Overlook. Offers a magnificent panorama of the Gouldsboro Hills, Frenchman Bay and the tip of Schoodic Peninsula.

Thunder Hole. Just before high tide it really does sound like thunder when the huge waves push into a narrow opening in the rocks, forcing trapped air to compress.

Otter Cliff. The tidal pools that form here are best explored an hour before low tide. **Carriage Roads.** Financed and directed by John D. Rockefeller, Jr., and built between 1913 and 1940. There are several bike rentals in the area, and horse-drawn carriage rides are offered at **Wildwood Stables**.

Highlights outside of the park include:

Downtown Bar Harbor. In 1868 wealthy families such as the Astors, the Vanderbilts and the Rockefellers built elaborate summer "cottages" here (some with 50 rooms, servants' quarters, and stables), and the area became a plutocrats' playground. But in 1947 a fire raged across Mount Desert for 10 days, destroying many of the estates along Bar Harbor's "Millionaire's Road." Most of the wealthy summer "rusticators," their homes in ashes, left the area. A few of the cottages were spared, and several, such as **Ullikana** and **The Tides**, have been converted into opulent bed and breakfasts. Today's Bar Harbor is a thriving summer resort, with all of the activities and amenities of a first-class tourist destination.

Seal Harbor Beach. Public beach.

Northeast Harbor. Mooring for some of the area's grandest yachts, as well as home to several gardens maintained by the Mount Desert Land & Garden Preserve: **Asticou Azalea Garden**, a Japanese stroll garden designed and built by Charles K. Savage, owner of the **Asticou Inn;** and **Thuya Garden & Lodge**, the home of Joseph H. Curtis, whose elaborate gardens were also created by Mr. Savage.

Side Trip

Although there are five Cranberry Isles, only two cater to tourists: **Little Cranberry Island** (also known as Islesford); and, to a lesser extent, **Great Canberry Island**. On Little Cranberry, Acadia National Park's **Islesford Historical Museum** gives visitors an idea of island life. Several artists have galleries, and there's a restaurant, bed and breakfast, and kayak rental. Passenger-only ferries to both islands leave from Southwest Harbor and Manset; the Beal & Bunker mail boat sails out of Northeast Harbor. Two water taxis: *Delight* (244-5724), and *Cadillac* (244-0575 or boat cell: 801-1898) provide on-demand transportation.

Somes Sound. The only fjord on the east coast of the U.S. was formed by glacial action thousands of years ago.

The Quiet Side. Although it's not an official designation, folks on the west side of the horseshoe that makes up Mount Desert Island like to refer to their portion as the "quiet side." And after a busy day in Bar Harbor, you'll probably agree.
Quiet Side highlights:

Echo Lake. A delightful and popular freshwater beach.

Southwest Harbor. The quiet side's busiest village is home to the **Wendell**

Gilley Museum, which celebrates the life and work of the man who pioneered the field of decorative bird carving.

Bass Harbor. Although the 1858 lighthouse is closed to the public, the grounds are open, and provide magnificent ocean panoramas.

Side Trip

The Captain Henry Lee chugs six miles out to sea from Bass Harbor to **Swans Island**, a large island with a tiny year-round population of mostly fisherfolk, and not too much to do but kick back and relax. There's the Fine Sand Beach for swimming (brr!) and harbor seal watching, and a town center with a few lodgings and a general store. This can be a physically demanding day trip: the ferry docks four miles from the town center.

Seal Cove Auto Museum. This world-class collection of more than 100 antique cars and 35 vintage motorcycles includes a 1905 Pierce Arrow and a 1908 Stanley Steamer.

Acadia National Park's "secret" section

Return to the mainland, and turn east (right) on Route 1 toward Hancock and Sullivan. Hancock is home to the **Pierre Monteux School for Conductors and Orchestra Musicians**, which hosts a summer music series.
Taunton Bay rest area marks the beginning of the **Schoodic National Scenic Byway**, which continues for 27 miles to Inner Harbor on the Schoodic Peninsula. Along the way there's a reversing falls (Hancock Point), and sweeping views of Frenchman Bay, Mount Desert Island, Cadillac Mountain, and the sea.

But the true reward is **Acadia National Park's Schoodic Peninsula**, a vast, "secret," 2,300-acre swath of parkland with few crowds, pounding surf, and breathtaking ocean panoramas. **Turn off Route 1 onto Route 186 and head south for six miles, through bustling (for this area) Winter Harbor.** Follow signs to the right off Main Street to Big Moose

Road and the entrance to the park (no fee as of this writing). The 5 ½- mile road, one way except for a short section at the turnoff for Schoodic Point, circles the peninsula and offers splendid views of Mount Desert. Highlights along the way include Frazer Point, Schoodic Head (halfway between Frazer Point and Schoodic Point), and, of course the Point itself. A map at the entrance will help orient you.

Side Trip

At Inner Harbor, turn right onto Route 195 to **Corea,** a picture-perfect fishing village with a protected harbor.

Don't forget: the Bar Harbor Ferry provides transportation from Bar Harbor to Winter Harbor, and the Island Explorer bus provides free service from the terminal to the villages of Prospect Harbor, Winter Harbor, and the Schoodic section of Acadia National Park.

Return to Route 1 via Route 186.

---

information *All area codes are (207) unless otherwise indicated.*

Acadia National Park (288-3338), P.O. Box 177, Bar Harbor 04609. Open all year; Hulls Cove Visitor Center open mid-Apr.-Oct. Many roads, including the Park Loop Road, are closed from Dec.-mid-Apr. $ May-Oct. nps.gov/acad

Bar Harbor Area Chamber of Commerce (288-5103), 1201 Bar Harbor Rd., Trenton 04605. Also, Visitor Center at corner of Cottage and Main streets May-Sept. barharborinfo.com

Blue Hill Heritage Trust (374-5118): bluehillheritagetrust.org.

Blue Hill Peninsula Chamber of Commerce (374-3242), 107 Main St., Blue Hill 04614. bluehillpeninsula.org

Bucksport Chamber of Commerce (469-6818), 52 Main St., Bucksport 04416. bucksportbaychamber.com

Cranberry Isles: cranberryisles.com

Deer Isle-Stonington Chamber of Commerce (348-6124). Welcome Center open May-Oct. deerislemaine.com

Mount Desert Island Chamber of Commerce (276-5040), Northeast Harbor 04662. mountdesertchamber.com

Schoodic National Scenic Byway: schoodicbyway.org

Schoodic Area Chamber of Commerce (963-7658), P.O. Box 381, Winter Harbor 04693. Chamber prints an excellent informational brochure, available at stores in the area. acadia-schoodic.org

Southwest Harbor Information Center (244-9264), 20 Village Green Way, Southwest Harbor 04679.

Swans Island: swansisland.org

Trenton Chamber of Commerce (667-1259), 1007 Bar Harbor Rd., Trenton 04605. trentonmaine.com

lodging

Acadia View B&B (866-963-7457), 175 Rte. 1, Gouldsboro 04607. Perched on a bluff overlooking Frenchman Bay and Acadia National Park, the inn has 4 handsomely furnished, bright and and spacious guest rooms with private baths and decks. acadiaview.com $$-$$$

Asticou Inn (276-3344), 15 Peabody Dr., Northeast Harbor 04662. All the modern conveniences at this splendidly restored 1883 inn, and in several outbuildings which house cottages with kitchenettes. Amenities include a heated pool, clay tennis courts; live entertainment, and a well-regarded restaurant. asticou.com $$$$

Bar Harbor Grand Hotel (288-5226), 269 Main St., Bar Harbor 04609. A replica of the 1875 grand hotel that was destroyed in the 1947 fire. 70 rooms and 2-bedroom units have refrigerators, coffee makers, and high-speed internet; heated pool. barharborgrand.com $$-$$$

Bar Harbor Inn (288-3351), Newport Dr., Bar Harbor 04069. 8 acres in town overlooking Frenchman Bay. This landmark property has luxury rooms and suites in the main inn; an oceanfront lodge; and the Newport Building (no ocean views). Full service spa. The Terrace Grill hosts a popular lobster bake. barharborinn.com $$-$$$$

Black Duck Inn and Properties (963-2689), 36 Crowley Island Rd., Corea 04624. 4 rooms and 2 waterfront cottages on 12 acres overlooking the harbor. Breakfast included. blackduck.com $$-$$$

Blue Hill Farm Country Inn (374-5126), 578 Pleasant St., Blue Hill 04614. 7 classic b&b rooms with shared baths in the farmhouse, and 7 with private baths in the renovated barn. Breakfast included. Open year round. bluehillfarminn.com $-$$

The Blue Hill Inn (374-2844), 40 Union St., Blue Hill 04614. 11 elegantly furnished rooms and suites—including several with fireplaces—in a Federal-period inn in the center of the village. Breakfast included. bluehillinn.com $$-$$$$

The Brooklin Inn (359-2777), 22 Reach Rd., Brooklin 04616. 3 of the 5 cozy, second-floor rooms at this village inn have private baths. There's a popular restaurant (see "Restaurants") on the first floor, and a downstairs pub. The innkeepers organize sailing charters. brooklininn.com $$

The Castine Inn (326-4365), 33 Main St., Castine 04614. Built in 1898, this elegantly landscaped inn just a block from the harbor has 17 second- and third-floor rooms and suites with private baths. Rooms range from "quaint, Maine Island style to Simply Elegant." Many have views of the garden and/or harbor. Innkeeper Tom Gutow offers a 3-4 hr. cooking class. Continental breakfast. castineinn.com $$-$$$$

The Claremont (244-5036), Claremont Rd., Southwest Harbor 04679. Mt. Desert's oldest hotel opened its doors at the mouth of Somes Sound in 1884. The 6-acre shorefront resort has a variety of accommodations, including 24 hotel rooms, 6 rooms in the Phillips House, and 14 housekeeping cottages. Facilities include a restaurant, bar, rowboats, bicycles, and tennis and croquet courts. theclaremonthotel.com $$$-$$$$

Dragonflye Inn (359-8080), Brooklin 04616. An 1874 Victorian inn with 3 suites with queen-size beds, sitting rooms, microwaves, mini-fridges and private baths. Bicycles are available for guests, and the innkeepers offer 3-hr. sea kayak tours. $$-$$$

Harbor View Motel & Cottages (244-5031), 11 Ocean Way, Southwest Harbor 04679. 21 motel units include 3 efficiencies and 9 with decks overlooking the harbor. Also, a 3rd floor efficiency with deck, and 7 pet-friendly cottages with kitchens that rent by the week. Private beach. harborviewmotelandcottages.com $-$$

The Inn at Bay Ledge (288-4204), 150 Sand Point Rd., Bar Harbor. Perched on a cliff overlooking Frenchman Bay, 8 of the 9 rooms at the inn have water views; all have king or queen 4-poster or canopy beds. 3 cottages have rustic Maine furnishings. innatbayledge.com $$-$$$$

The Isleford House (244-0988), P.O. Box 12, Islesford 04646. Four cozy rooms in a village home. Breakfast included. cranberrysiles.com $

Main Stay Cottages, 66 Sargent St., Winter Harbor 04693. 5 newly renovated 1-4 bedroom waterfront cottages with kitchens, decks, and fireplaces next to the ferry landing. awa-web.com $-$$$$

Oakland House Seaside Resort (359-8521) , 435 Herrick Rd., Brooksville 04617. Accommodations at this 50-acre full-service, oceanfront resort include classic b&b rooms with shared or private baths, and 15 2- to 5-bedroom cottages and cabins with woodburning fireplaces. Cottages MAP in summer. oaklandhouse.com $$-$$$$

Oceanside Meadows inn (963-5557), P.O. Box 90, Prospect Harbor 04669. C. 1860 sea captain's home on a 200-acre nature preserve at the head of Sand Cove. 7 rooms in the house and 7 in an 1820s farmhouse all have private baths. A sandy beach is just a minute away. Full breakfast. oceaninn.com $$-$$$

Pentagoet Inn (326-8616), 26 Main St., Castine 04421. Three-story Queen Anne Victorian in the center of town has 16 antiques-filled rooms, most with king-size beds and some with clawfoot tubs and fireplaces. Bikes are free for guests, and rate includes breakfast. May-Oct. pentagoet.com $$-$$$$

Pilgrim's Inn & The Whale's Rib Tavern (348-6615), 20 Main St., Deer Isle 04627. Overlooking Northwest Harbor, this handsomely furnished 1793 post and beam home is on the National Register of Historic Places. Some of the 12 antiques-filled rooms and 3 cottages have gas stoves and sitting areas. pilgrimsinn.com $$-$$$

Taunton River B&B (422-2070), 19 Taunton Dr., Sullivan 04664. On the Schoodic Scenic By-way, this comfortable inn has 3 spacious roooms with shared or private baths. Rate includes breakfast. tauntonriverbnb.com $$

The Tides (288-4968), 119 West St., Bar Harbor 04609. National Register of Historic Places inn has 3 luxurious suites with sweeping views of Frenchman Bay. Built in 1887, the Greek Revival estate is close to town and the entrance to the park. Breakfast is served on the veranda. bar-harbortides.com $$$$

Twilite Motel (667-8165), 147 Bucksport Rd., Ellsworth 04605. 22 cozy, clean, and comfortable units with TV, a/c and phones on 5 acres just a mile from downtown. twilitemotel.com $-$$

Ullikana (288-9552), 16 The Field, Bar Harbor 04609. Secluded, yet just a minute from town, this 1885 English Tudor style mansion has 11 lovingly furnished, colorful, and spacious rooms, many with fireplaces or private terraces, and water views. The Yellow House, a sister inn, is close by. Breakfast included. ullikana.com $$-$$$$

restaurants

Ben and Bill's Chocolate Emporium (288-3281), 66 Main St., Bar Harbor. Lobster ice cream? Why not? It's Maine! There are also more than 60 flavors of hard-serve, a dozen of gelato, a variety of sundaes and frappes, and a huge selection of homemade chocolates. $

Black Dinah Café and Chocolatiers (335-5010), 1 Moore's Harbor Rd., Isle au Haut. Coffee, tea, and delicious pastries in a surprisingly urban setting, but the big draws are the homemade truffles and other chocolate goodies. July-Aug., Wed.-Sun.; Spring, Fri.-Sun. B & L. $

The Brooklin Inn (359-2777), Rte. 175, Brooklin. The organic menu features locally raised meat, poultry, and fish. The award winning wine list includes many inexpensive selections. The pub ($-$$) serves the regular menu as well as lighter fare. $$$-$$$$

Café This Way (288-4483), 14 1/2 Mt. Desert St., Bar Harbor. Worth a trip off the beaten path, this "comfy" and "quirky" spot serves eclectic fare such as Korean tuna tartare. Breakfast, too, is a culinary romp. B & D Mid-April-Oct. $$-$$$

Fisherman's Friend Restaurant (367-2442) & Harbor View Store (367-2530), School St., Stonington. Full service restaurant with terrific chowders, lobster rolls, and fried fish platters on one side (L & D daily in season), and a take-out deli/store/wine shop on the other. $-$$$

Fisherman's Inn Restaurant (963-5585), 7 Winter St., Winter Harbor. Seafood, Italian specialties, chowder, and homemade desserts. L & D. $-$$

Havana (288-2822), 318 Main St., Bar Harbor. American dishes with a Latin flair, with entreés such as *moqueca* (Brazilian stew with lobster, crab, shrimp and mussels), and butter-poached lobster, along with an award-winning wine list. D nightly. $$$-$$$$

Islesford Dock Restaurant (244-7494), Town Dock, Little Cranberry Island. Cherries and chicken livers, semolina gnocchi, and hand cut pasta? This is not your typical island snack bar. L Tues.-Sun., D nightly, Sun. brunch. $$-$$$$

Jordan Pond House (276-3316), Park Loop Rd., Acadia National Park, Bar Harbor. Serving lunch on the lawn or in the dining room, afternoon tea, and dinner daily from mid-May-late Oct. Dinner specialties include prime rib and crab cakes. L & D. $$-$$$

Pentagoet Inn (326-8616), 26 Main St., Castine. The charming, intimate dining room serves up treats such as lobster bouillabaisse, grilled anise dusted scallops, and lamb shanks, followed up by home-baked desserts. Start with a drink at the eccentric and charming pub. $$-$$$$

Reading Room Restaurant (288-3351), Bar Harbor Inn, Newport Drive, Bar Harbor. House specials lobster bisque and lobster pie share the menu with crispy duck, filet mignon, and a variety of fresh seafood. B & D. $$$$

Redbird Provisions (276-3006), 11 Sea St., Northeast Harbor. The talented chef combines local ingredients, Asian spices, and Italian flavors to create dishes such as truffled cauliflower soup, lamb seared with artichokes and summer wheat berries, and pan-seared arctic char with shitake mushrooms. Sunday supper is 4-course *prix fixe*. L & D Wed.-Sun. in season. $$$$

Red Sky (244-0476), 14 Clark Point Rd., Southwest Harbor. The freshest available New England ingredients are prepared with a Continental flair and served in a sophisticated ambiance. Among the standouts: pan-roasted duck breast, and magical lemon cake. D nightly in season. $$$-$$$$

Trenton Bridge Lobster Pound (667-2977), Rte. 3, Bar Harbor Rd., Trenton. You'll recognize this in-the-rough spot by the steam rising up from wood-fired cookers boiling lobsters in seawater. Lobster sandwiches, stew, and cocktails are also on the menu, along with steamed clams and blueberry pie. L & D Mon.-Sat. Memorial Day-Columbus Day. $-$$

attractions

Asticou Azalea Gardens (276-3727), Rte. 3/198, Southeast Harbor. May-Oct. Donation.

Abbe Museum (288-3519), 26 Mt. Desert St., Bar Harbor, and Abbe at Sieur de Monts, Acadia National Park. Daily in season; call for hrs.

Bar Harbor Historical Society (288-0000), 33 Ledgelawn Ave., Bar Harbor. Photos, paintings, and clothing from the Gilded Age. June-Oct., Mon.- Sat. p.m.

Bar Harbor Whale Museum (288-0288), 52 West St, Bar Harbor. The state's only museum dedicated to the study of whales. June-Oct.

Bartlett Estate Winery (546-2408, just off Rte. 1 on 175 Chicken Mill Pond Rd., Gouldsboro. One of Maine's premier wineries has been making fruit wines for more than 20 years. Tasting room open June-Oct.

Blue Heron Gallery (348-6051), 22 Morey Farm Dr., Deer Isle. Works of more than 100 artists, including many from the Haystack Mountain School of Crafts.

Blue Hill Historical Society, Holt House, Water St., Blue Hill. Summer: Tues. and Fri. p.m.

Castine Historical Society (326-4118); Abbott School. July-Labor Day Tues.- Sat.; Sun. p.m.

Fort Knox (469-6553), 711 Fort Knox Rd., Prospect. May-Oct.

George B. Dorr Museum of Naural History (288-5395), 105 Eden St., Bar Harbor. Students of the College of the Atlantic design displays depicting the state's natural world.

Good Life Center at Forest Farm (326-8211), 372 Harborside Rd., Harborside. Open year round, late June-early Sept. Thurs.-Mon. p.m. Call for off season hrs. Donation.

Haystack Mountain School of Crafts (348-2306), 89 Haystack School Dr., Deer isle. 1-hr. tours Wed. at 1 p.m. in summer. Gallery: 22 Church St., Deer Isle.

Holbrook Island Sanctuary (326-4012), 172 Indian Bar Rd., off Rte. 176, Brooksville.

Islesford Historical Museum (Acadia National Park); late June-Sept.

Mt. Desert Oceanarium & Lobster Hatchery (288-5005), Rte. 3, Bar Harbor, and Clark Point Rd., Southwest Harbor. Mid-May-mid-Oct., Mon.-Sat.

Mount Desert Island Biological Laboratory (288-3147), Maren Auditorium, 159 Old Bar Harbor Rd., Salisbury Cove. SPLASH is a hands-on, kid-friendly program where visitors learn about genetics and marine life. Mon. & Wed. late June-late Aug.

Penobscot Narrows Observatory (469-6553), Bucksport. May-Oct.; $ includes admission to Fort Knox.

Rackcliffe Pottery (374-2297), Ellsworth Rd., Rte. 172, Blue Hill.

Seal Cove Auto Museum (244-9242), 1414 Tremont Rd., across from Seal Cove Pond, Seal Cove. Memorial Day weekend-Columbus Day.

Sherman's Books and Stationary (288-3161), 56 Main St., Bar Harbor (also in Boothbay Harbor, Camden, and Freeport). Maine's oldest bookstore (since 1886) specializes in children's and adult books by and about Maine, gifts, and toys

Thuya Garden & Lodge (267-3727), Rte. 3, between Bar Harbor and Rte. 198. Late June-Sept. Donation.

T/S *State of Maine*, Maine Maritime Academy (800-464-6565 in Maine; 800-227-8465 out of state). Tours mid-July-late Aug., 10 a.m.-noon and 1-3 p.m.; mid-Sept.-late Apr., Sat. and Sun. 10 a.m.-noon, and 1-3 p.m. No tours the last week in Aug. or the first week in Sept.

Wendell Gilley Museum (244-7555), Rte. 102, Southwest Harbor. June-Oct., Tues.-Sun.; May, Nov. & Dec. Fri.- Sun.

The Wilson Museum (326-9247), Castine. Late May through Sept., p.m. Free except for the Perkins House.

WoodenBoat (359-4651), 41 WoodenBoat Lane, Brooklin. Books for boat builders, model kits, and hard-to-find tools.

Woodlawn Museum: The Black House (667-8671), Rte. 172, Ellsworth. June-Sept., Tues.-Sat., Sun. p.m. May & Oct., Tues.-Sun. p.m. Grounds open dawn to dusk.

activities

Acadia Bike (288-9605), 48 Cottage St., Bar Harbor. Bike rentals and group tours.

Acadia National Park Tours (288-0300). 2 ½-hr. tours of the park include a stop at the top of Cadillac Mountain.

Acadian Nature Cruise (288-2386), Bar Harbor Whale Watch Co., 1 West St., Bar Harbor. 2-hr. cruises narrated by professional naturalists. Sails at 10 a.m. and 1:15 p.m.; sunset cruises July & Aug. at 3:30 & 6 p.m.

Acadia Outfitters (288-8118), 106 Cottage St., Bar Harbor. Scooters, bicycles, and sea kayak rentals; guided sea kayak tours.

Aquaterra Adventures (877-386-4124), One West St, Bar Harbor. Kayak excursions, along with beginner's lessons.

Ardea EcoExpeditions (207-460-9731), 34 Hackmatack Rd., Gouldsboro. Activities include half and full day sea kayaking trips, hiking adventures, lobster bakes, and research expeditions.

Atlantic Climbing School (288-2521), 67 Maine St, Bar Harbor. Beginners are welcome to climb Acadia's cliffs; half and full day courses.

Bar Harbor Ferry Co. (288-2984). Ferry service between Bar Harbor and Winter Harbor; the *Island Explorer* meets the ferry and provides free transportation around the Schoodic Peninsula. downeastwindjammer.com

Bar Harbor Whale Watch Co. (288-2386), 1 West St., Bar Harbor. Whale spotting aboard a 112 ft. jet powered catamaran; island and lighthouse tours.

Beal & Bunker Mail Boat (244-3575), Northeast Harbor town pier.

The Cat (877-359-3760), Bar Harbor. High speed catamaran sails 3 hrs. to Yarmouth, Nova Scotia Mon., Tues. and Wed. in the a.m. and returns Mon. and Tues. in the p.m. A good way to get to Nova Scotia, a bad idea for a day cruise, as there's very little outside access while aboard. *Remember your passport or enhanced driver's license if heading to Canada.*

Cranberry Cove Boating Co. (460-1981 or 244-5882). Sails from Southwest Harbor and Manset. Service from May through Sept. Also bicycle rentals.

Finest Kind Kayak & Canoe Rental (348-7714), 70 Center District Crossroad, Deer Isle.

H.O.M.E. (469-7961), Upper Falls Rd., Orland.

Island Explorer (667-5796): exploreacadia.com

Isle au Haut Boat Services (367-5193), Seabreeze Ave., Stonington. Lobster fishing scenic tours, seasonal service to Acadia National Park landing at Duck Harbor; bicycle rentals on Isle au Haut.

The Joy of Kayaking (244-4309). Little Cranberry Isle. 1- and 2-person kayaks.

Kneisel Hall (374-2203), 54 Main St., Blue Hill. Faculty, guest, and students perform at the chamber music school's summer music festival. Schedule: kneisel.org

Maine State Sea Kayak (244-9500), 254 Main St., Southwest Harbor. ½ day and sunset sea kayak tours led by registered guides.

Maragaret Todd (288-2984), Bar Harbor Inn Pier. 2-hr. cruises aboard a 151 ft., 4-masted schooner. Also, windjammer and lobster sloop cruises, and fishing trips; ferry service to Cranberry Cove.

National Park Canoe and Kayak Rental (244-5854), Rte. 102, Somesville, Long Pond. Rentals; self-guided sunset tours.

National Park Tours (288-0300). 2 ½ hr. narrated bus tours. Boards in downtown Bar Harbor May-Oct.

Northeast Historic Film (800-639-1636), Alamo Theatre, 85 Main St., Bucksport. Mon.-Fri., and during scheduled movies and presentations Fri. and Sat. evenings and Sun at 2 p.m.

Oceanside Meadows Institute for the Arts and Sciences (963-5557) at Oceanside Meadows B&B, Prospect Harbor. The diverse schedule of summer events include performances by Opera Maine and lectures by astronomers and biologists. Schedule: oceaninn.com

Old Quarry Ocean Adventures (367-8977), 130 Settlement Rd., Stonington. Tours aboard a 38-ft. lobster boat; ferry service to Isle au Haut and other islands; bicycle, kayak, canoe, sailboat, and rowboat rentals.

Oli's Trolley (288-9899). Narrated trolley tours of Acadia National Park. Boards in downtown Bar Harbor May-Oct.

Pierre Monteaux School (422-3280), 13 Captain Bill Rd., Hancock. Schedule: monteuxschool.org

Quietside Cruises & Downeast Friendship Sloop Charters (266-5210), Dysart's Great Harbor Marina, Southwest Harbor.

Stonington Opera House (367-2788), School St., Stonington. Hosts a program of films and live performances. Schedule: operahousearts.org

Swans Island Ferry (244-3254). Summer: Mon.-Wed., Fri.-Sun. Schedule: maine.gov/mdot/opt/ferry/215-swan.php

Wildwood Stables (276-5271), Carriages of Acadia. Horse-pulled carriage tours along Acadia National Park's carriage roads.

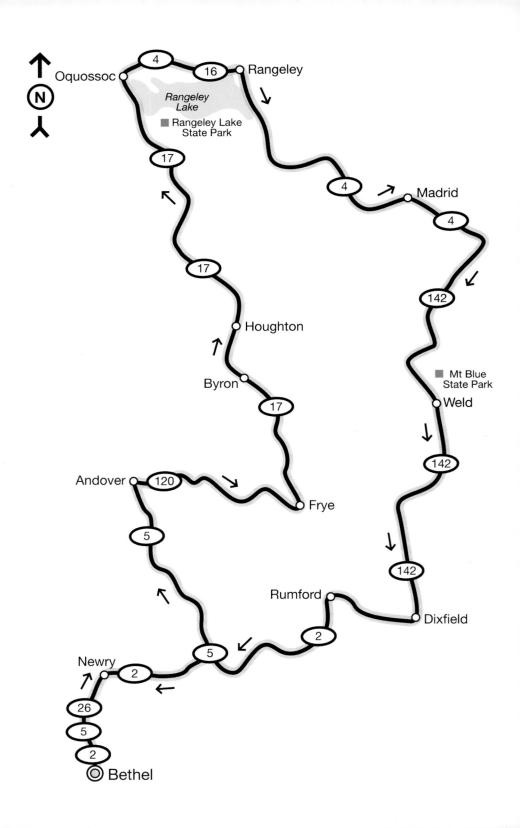

The Rangeley Lakes

140 miles

major **attractions**

- Coos Canyon
- Height of Land
- Wilhelm Reich Museum
- Sandy River & Rangeley Lakes
- Railroad
- Mount Blue State Park

Due to a printing error, the opening paragraph of Drive 20 was repeated at the beginning of Drive 21. Drive 21 (page 327) should begin with the following:

Winding roads in this scenic western corner of Maine thread through a maze of lakes and ponds, where the fishing is spectacular, moose sightings are frequent, and unspoiled wilderness vistas abound -- 35 miles of Route 17 between Houghton and Smalls Falls have been designated a National Scenic Byway. Along the way, pause for a boat cruise, a hike, or a ride on a narrow-gauge railroad.

Begin the drive by heading north out of Bethel (see Drive 14) on Route 5/26 to the junction of Route 2 in Newry. Turn right onto Route 2, and continue to the junction of Route 5. Turn left on Route 5 to Andover (settled by pioneers from Andover, Massachusetts). Take Route 120 east out of Andover for nine miles, through Roxbury Notch, and then turn left onto Frye Crossover Road into Frye. Turn left onto Route 17.

Feeling lucky? The country's first gold rush is said to have started in 1848 right here in **Byron**, where the Swift River has carved a gorge into bedrock, creating scenic **Coos Canyon**. Visitors can rent panning equipment at Coos Canyon Campground & Cabins or Coos Canyon Rock & Gift. Or test your luck another way: at the **rest area** the canyon's cliffs are popular with divers, who plummet into the deep, chilly river. The less intrepid can just enjoy a bracing swim.

Byron was named for poet George Gordon, Lord Byron (1788-1824).

Side Trip

In **Houghton**, turn left onto the dirt (and *very* rough) Houghton Road for about ¼ mile to a right turn onto Bemis Road. After 3 6/10 miles, bear left through gravel pit to a parking lot and hike a fairly easy ¾ mile (one way) to the quite spectacular 90-foot **Angel Falls**, one of the highest in New England.

Route 17 winds northward alongside the Swift River and around 2,365-foot Brimstone Mountain, until it reaches the left-hand pullover for **Height of Land**, one of the most magnificent vistas in New England. To the west is Elephant Mountain and New Hampshire's White Mountains. Mooselookmeguntic Lake, with its Toothaker and Students Islands, lies to the north.

more than 100 lakes . . . .

Up ahead on the right, the **Rangeley Scenic Overlook** also provides stunning views. Although nine-mile-long Rangeley Lake is the best known, there are actually 112 interconnected lakes and ponds in the lakes region, which encompasses more than 33,000 acres of conserved public access lands.

Turn right off Route 17 onto South Shore Drive to 869-acre **Rangeley Lake State Park**, a delightful spot to cool off on a hot day.

Toothaker and Students Islands are part of the Stephen Phillips Memorial Preserve, a huge swath of wilderness purchased more than 20 years ago by the forward-thinking Mr. Phillips. The preserve is open to the public; campsites at both mainland and island sites are available by reservation, and campers can rent canoes for a 24-hour period. To get to the headquarters, turn left onto Herbie Welch Road directly across from the Rangeley Lake State Park turnoff, and then bear left onto Stephens Road.

The Abenaki people who originally inhabited this region named the piece of land wedged between Rangeley and **Mooselookmeguntic** lakes **Oquossoc,** or "landing place". Today the small village that has since grown up here is still a popular boat launch: the *Oquossoc Lady,* a 28-foot, 1947 wooden launch, sails daily in season from **Saddleback Marina** for one hour cruises.

Mooselookmeguntic, another Abenaki word, translates as "portage to the moose feeding place" or "moose feeding among the trees," and this is still a prime spot to watch for the behemoths, particularly at dawn and dusk.

When Route 17 ends, turn right onto Route 4/16 toward Rangeley. The **Wilhelm Reich Museum,** also known as **Orgonon,** was the home, laboratory and research center of the Galician-born psychoanalyst whose controversial theories and experiments with sexual energy (orgonomy) ultimately landed him in jail, where he died of heart failure. He is buried here, amidst the 175 acres that he so loved. Visitors can visit the Orgone Energy Observatory, hike nature trails, and even stay in Dr. Reich's home (see *"Lodgings"* below).

Fans of the TV show *Northern Exposure* will feel instantly at home in **Rangeley.** The tranquil lakefront town (year round population 1,200), a destination for outdoor enthusiasts for more than 150 years, has one short main street anchored by the historic **Rangeley Inn,** shops and restaurants, and the lakefront **Chamber of Commerce** visitors' center. Tourists can choose from numerous sports camps and cottage complexes along the main roads or on remote shores.

> *In the early 1860s a fisherman hooked eight brook trout weighing a total of almost 52 pounds, launching Rangeley's reputation as a sports fishing paradise. Unfortunately, by the 1870s the area had became overfished. To insure tourists would keep coming, authorities introduced landlocked salmon to the lakes. In a classic "big fish eat little fish" scenario, the salmon ate the blueback trout who had been eaten by the brook trout, so today's brookies fail to reach the record size of days gone by.*

Head east out of town on Route 4. Stop at the pullover on the right for yet another fabulous view, and to read the informational plaques. One plaque tells of Cornelia "Fly Rod" Crosby, Maine's first official Maine Guide, and the first person to promote Rangeley as a sports fishing paradise. Another famous Rangleyite, milliner Carrie Stevens, become legendary for her hand-tied streamer flies, including the Gray Ghost pattern still used today.

Side Trip
Saddleback Mountain Ski Area is a 4-season destination. Several excellent hiking trails begin at the base lodge, and the legendary **Appalachian Trail** (a 2,175-mile footpath

from Maine to Georgia) runs across the ridge. A free moose tour departs from the Guest Service Center at 7:15 p.m. Mondays and Thursdays. To get there, turn left off Route 4 onto Dallas Hill Road for 2 ½ miles, and right onto Saddleback Ski Area Road for 2 ½ miles.

On Route 4 there's another turnoff on the right for **Rangeley Lake State Park**.

Turn left at the sign for **Cascade Stream Gorge Trail**, a steep 30-minute hike to a gorge and waterfall.

Approximately 12 miles from town, watch on the right for **Smalls Falls Picnic Area**, where a series of waterfalls cascade through a steep gorge into a pool perfect for swimming. A footbridge leads to several trails, including a short path to the top of the falls.

The road parallels Sandy River as it passes through Madrid. **At the intersection of Routes 4 and 142, turn right onto Route 142** into the Sandy River Valley as the road weaves through dense woods, past small farms and ponds.

Side Trip

Continue on Route 4 past the turnoff for Route 142 to **Phillips**, the birthplace of Cornelia "Flyrod" Crosby and home of the **Sandy River & Rangeley Lakes Railroad**, whose more than 120 miles of track was once the longest two-foot gauge railroad in the country. The *Rangeley Express* carried tourists from Farmington until the 1930s, when the automobile became a more popular mode of transportation. Today, on select days from June through October, visitors can hop aboard the railroad's restored train for a 50-minute ride.

5,021-acre **Mount Blue State Park** in **Weld** is divided into two sections: a sandy beach on Lake Webb; and the bulk of the park, a vast swath of woods and spectacular mountain views. To get to the beach, turn right off Route 142 onto West Road and continue for four miles. For the main section of the park, turn left onto Center Hill Road in the center of town.

The lakeside deck of the **Kawanhee Inn** is a delightful spot to enjoy a cocktail after 5 pm.

When Route 142 ends at the traffic light in Dixfield, turn right onto Route 2/17, and then turn left to cross the Androscoggin River and reach Route 108. Turn right onto Route 108 and continue until it intersects with Route 2, and continue west on Route 2 back to Newry. At Newry, turn left onto Route 5 to head back to Bethel (while this may sound convoluted, it's a good way to bypass Rumford traffic).

The American Guide Series volume Maine, A Guide Down East (revised edition, 1970), reports the following:

"Dixfield was named on a broken promise. When the township ... became the proper-
ty of Dr. Elijah Dix of Boston, he promised to donate a library if the place were named
for him. It was, when the town was incorporated in 1803. The townspeople received a
box of second-hand medical books and two German dictionaries."

information *All area codes are (207) unless indicated otherwise.*

Rangeley Lakes Region Chamber of Commerce (864-5364), P.O. Box 317, Main St., Rangeley
04970. rangeleymaine.com

lodging

Bald Mountain Camps (864-3671), P.O. Box 332, Oquossoc 04964. Established in the 1800s as
a sport fishing camp, the 15 log cabins have porches, fireplaces, spacious living room, and
full maid service. The rate – $135-$155 day/ person – includes 3 meals. Mid-May-mid-Sept.
baldmountaincamps.com

Coos Canyon Campground & Cabins (364-3880), Rte. 17, Byron. Cabins sleep up to 7 people;
all have full kitchens, telephones, TV and an outdoor barbecue. cooscanyoncabins.com $$

Country Club Inn (864-3831), P.O. Box 680, 56 Country Club Rd., Rangeley 04970. A small
resort with big views and few guests. The 20 simply furnished rooms all have private baths.
Amenities include the18-hole Mingo Springs Golf Course, and an outdoor pool. B&B or MAP.
countryclubinnrangeley.com $$

Kawanhee Inn and Restaurant (585-2000), 12 Ann's Way, Weld 04285. 10 lodge rooms (6 with
private bath), and Adirondack-style cabins with porches, kitchens, and fieldstone fireplaces.
Breakfast and use of canoes and kayaks included. MAP available. maineinn.net $$-$$$

Lakewood Camps (243-2959), P.O. Box 331, Andover 04216. 1,600- acre fishing camp on Lower Richardson Lake, established in 1853, can be reached only by boat (provided by the camp).
12 lakefront cabins sleep up to 6, and have generator-powered electricity and fireplaces. The
rate – $155 day/person – includes 3 meals. Mid-May-Oct. 1. lakewoodcamps.com

Lyons Lakeside Cabins (864-5899), P.O. Box 957, Rangeley 04970. 5 immaculate modernized
log cabins just a minute from town sleep 2-6; 3 are right on the lake. All have TV, fireplaces,
and kitchens. Year round. lyonslakeside.com $$-$$$

North Country Inn B&B (864-2440), Main St., Rangeley 04970. 4 spacious rooms with private
baths and cable TV; the lovely porch overlooks the lake and mountains. Year round. Children
6+. northcountrybb.com $-$$

Oquossoc's Own B&B (864-554), Rangeley Ave., Oquossoc 04964. Classic village lodging, with
5 cozy guest rooms (sleeps up to 14) on two floors; TV/VCR in living room. $

The Rangeley Inn & Motor Lodge (864-3341), 2443 Main St., Rangeley 04970. A classic lakefront inn meticulously restored, with 50 comfortably furnished rooms in the main building
and a separate motel in back. There's a handsome dining room, and a tavern for pub dining.
rangeleyinn.com $-$$

Town & Lake Motel and Cottages (864-3755), 2668 Main St., Rangeley 04970. Lakefront motel rooms and 2-bedroom cottages with fireplaces in the center of the village. Canoe and kayaks available; pets welcome. Open year round. rangeleytownandlake.com $$

restaurants

Bald Mountain Camps (864-3671), Oquossoc. Traditional New England fare; Friday night cook-out includes lobster, ribs, burgers and hot dogs. B, L & D early July-Fall. $$

BMC Diner (864-5844), 7 Richardson St., Rangeley. B & L Mon.-Sat., B Sun. $

Country Club Inn (864-3831), Rangeley Lake. International cuisine featuring dishes such as veal Gruyere and roast duck, along with spectacular lakefront views. B & D Wed.-Sun July-Fall. Reservations required. $$-$$$

The Gingerbread House (864-3602) Corner Rtes. 4/17, Oquossoc Village. Creative pizzas (the German is topped with sauerkraut, bacon, and onions), hearty breakfasts and lunches, and dinner entrees such as braised beef tortellacci, and barbecued ribs. B, L & D daily (closed Apr. and Nov.) $$-$$$

Kawanhee Inn (582-2000), Webb Lake, Weld. D Tues.-Sun. International fare might include Japanese-style fried calamari, provolone fritta, and buffalo meatloaf. Pub menu is served in the bar and on the lakefront deck. D. $$-$$$

Mooseley Bagels (864-5955), 2588 Main St., Rangeley. B & L Thurs.-Tues. $

Rangeley Inn (864-3341), 51 Main St., Rangeley. An old-fashioned and elegant room with international fare and a fine wine list. D Memorial Day-Columbus Day. The Fireside Pub opens at 4 p.m. year round. $$-$$$

Red Onion Restaurant (864-5022), 2511 Main St., Rangeley. The specialty is fresh dough pizza, but the hearty and diverse menu also includes chili, pot roast, fried liver and onions, and meat loaf. L & D daily. $-$$

attractions

Mt. Blue State Park (585-2347), 299 Center Hill Rd., Weld.

Rangeley Historical Society (864-2333), 2472 Main St., Rangeley.

Rangeley Lakes Region Logging Museum (864-3939), 221 Stratton Rd., Dallas Pit (1 mi. east of Rangeley Village). July & Aug., Sat. and Sun.

Rangeley Lake State Park (864-3858 summer; 624-6080 winter). 869 acres; the day use area has picnicking and swimming. May 15-Oct.

Saddleback Mountain Ski Area (866-918-2225), Rangeley.

Sandy River and Rangeley Railroad / Phillips Historical Society, Pleasant St., Phillips. Schedule: srll-rr.org

Stephen Phillips Memorial Preserve (864-2003), Oquossoc. May-mid-Sept. Call for campground reservations, or write: P.O. Box 21, Oquossoc 04964.

Wilhelm Reich Museum (864-3443), Dodge Pond Rd., Rangeley.
July and Aug., Wed.-Sun. p.m.; Sept., Sun. p.m.

activities

Note: There are numerous excellent fishing and hunting guides in the Rangeley area. Request a list from the Chamber of Commerce.

Bald Mountain Camp boat rental (864-3671), Oquossoc.

Bill Stevens, Registered Maine Guide (207-337-3052). Single- and multiple-day fly fishing trips along the Kennebago River, and on Kennebago and Little Kennebago lakes. Fly fishing instruction; guided fall hikes. kennebagoguide.com

Coos Canyon Campground & Cabins (364-388), Rte. 17, Byron. Gold panning, sightseeing tours, ATV and snowmobile tours, and guide service; canoe and kayak rental.

Coos Canyon Rock & Gift (364-4900), Rte. 17, Byron. Panning equipment, handmade jewelry, sandwiches.

Cupsuptic Campground (864-5249). Canoes, boats, kayaks, shuttle service.

Ecopelagicon Nature Store (864-2771). 7 Pond St., Rangeley. Kayak and paddleboat rental on Haley Pond, or delivery and pickup service. 4-hr. guided kayak tours include all gear. The store sells Maine outdoor and cookbooks, CDs, hand-made wooden toys, and games.

Haines Landing Marina (864-2393), Mooselookmeguntic Lake. Boat, canoe and kayak rental.

Lakeside Marina (864-9004), 2582 Main St., Rangeley. Pontoon and fishing boats, canoes, kayaks.

Oquossoc Cove Marina (864-3463), Rte. 4/17, Oquossoc. Pontoon, fishing, and ski boat rentals.

Seasonal Cycles Bike Shop (864-2100), 2593 Main St., Rangeley. All-terrain bike rentals.

Rangeley Region Sport Shop (864-5615), 2529 Main St., Rangeley. Fly tying supplies, instruction, and outfitting. More than 400 fly patterns in stock.

River's Edge Sports (864-5582) Rte. 4, Rangeley Lake Outlet, Oquossoc. Canoe rental and delivery; guide service.

Saddleback Fly Fishing (877-864-5441), Rangeley. 2-night, 3-day fly-fishing package includes lodging, casting instruction, and canoe.

Saddleback Marina (670-6100 or 864-3463), Oquossoc Cove, Oquossoc. Boat, water ski, tubes, and kayak rental. Tours aboard 1947 antique launch the "Oquossoc Lady" Memorial Day weekend-early Oct.

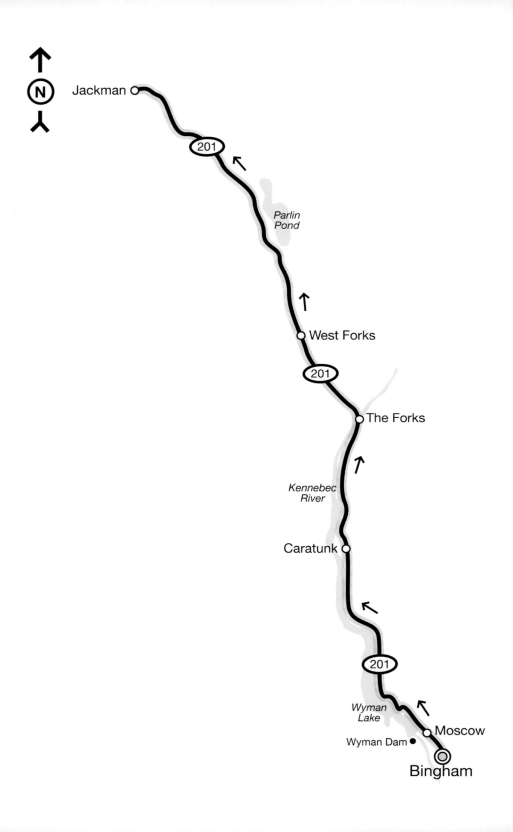

Into the North Woods

50 miles

major attractions

- Whitewater Rafting
- Canoeing
- Fishing
- Hiking
- Moose Watching

One of the loneliest corners of New England is also one of its most desolately beautiful. This drive traverses territory rich in wildlife – especially the lordly moose – and rich in the lore of old logging days. It also offers a chance to take to the river, shooting the rapids on exciting rafting expeditions.

Start in Bingham, "Gateway to the Maine Forest", a town located exactly halfway between the equator and the North Pole (3,107 miles in each direction). Bingham is a good place to gas up and get supplies: most of the next 50 miles between here and Jackman are dotted only with tiny settlements. **The entire drive follows Route 201**, also known as the Old Canada Road. In the 1800s, it was the primary link between Maine and Canada; now it's the **Old Canada Road Scenic Byway,** winding through the Upper Kennebec valley, and a portion of the Moose River valley, past some of the state's most magnificent vistas.

Moose are so common here that the road from Bingham to Jackman is nicknamed "Moose Alley." Most weigh between 800 and 1,000 lbs. and generally move pretty slowly. Don't assume they'll get out of the way when they see your car coming: they often won't. They're particularly active at dawn and dusk.

The 18th-century speculator, financier and politician William Bingham, for whom the town of Bingham is named, purchased 2,000,000 acres of North Country wilderness from General Henry Knox and his partner, Colonel William Duer, when they ran into financial difficulty. The parcel was described in *Maine: A Guide Downeast* (1970): "The Maine land was 'remote, rugged, uncleared, with its cold climate and short growing season, not well suited for farming. It had so little development or organization, and money was so scare in most of the communities that business, including that of prostitutes, was done by barter …' "

We're not sure about the prostitutes, but the description of the land is still accurate today – and that's what makes it so special. The North Woods is an untamed and unspoiled swath of wilderness so vast that even the moose wandering along Route 201 often appear a bit disoriented. But in the 1970s an enterprising group of businesspeople took this wilderness diamond in the rough and polished it into a recreation asset. Today, the upper Kennebec and Dead rivers offer some of New England's finest whitewater rafting (the umbrella organization **Raft Maine** provides information for seven of the outfitters that offer trips).

Most of the land in the North Woods is owned by timber companies and categorized as "working forest." The days of rafting logs downriver are over; today it's a common sight to see huge trucks laden with logs barreling down the highway.

The designation "plantation" – unique to Maine – refers to areas in sparsely populated areas to which the state legislature has granted a limited form of self-government.

Head north out of Bingham on Route 201, which follows alongside the Kennebec River and 13-mile-long **Wyman Lake**, created by the 155-foot-high Wyman Dam built in the late 1920s by the Central Maine Power Company. The lake is a popular spot to catch smallmouth bass, yellow and white perch, and sunfish.

Al Stuart was a native of Temple Flat in Moscow [Maine] and a log driver on the Upper Kennebec. In his book The River *(Pilot Press, 1981) he reflects on his days working construction on the Wyman Dam project: "It was with much regret that we watched the old saw mill and the cove disappear, as they prepared for the foundation for the dam. This area had been our playground for many years … We had long since moved the graveyards which were up in the basin … We made a large graveyard down at the lower end of Temple Flat. Many of the graves represented a sad story of the past, like the families who died on Pierce Hill with black diphtheria. There would be the names of the father and mother on one stone and the bodies of three or four children in the same grave with no markers. There was nobody to dig so many graves ... There were many epitaphs on the older stones of that day. One that I will always remember was on the stone of a young girl in the little graveyard on Pierce Hill on the Peter Pierce Farm. 'Death is Nature's honest due. I have paid and so will you.' How true."*

A state historic plaque along the road in **Moscow** tells of Benedict Arnold and his 1,150 soldiers, who fought their way up the Kennebec and Dead rivers in 1775 in leaky *bateaux* on their way to gain control of the British province of Quebec (see Drive #19). The journey was so rigorous that just 600 arrived, only to be defeated at the Battle of Quebec.

The first of several rafting companies along the Upper Kennebec are headquartered in **Caratunk**.

The **Appalachian Trail**, which stretches for 2,168 miles from Georgia to the summit of Maine's Mount Katahdin, crosses the Kennebec near Caratunk. The river at this spot is about 70 yards wide and has a swift, powerful current, often made even more dangerous with the release of water from hydro facilities upstream. A ferry once transported sportsmen across this stretch of river to Pierce Pond (famous for its trout fishing), and today, the tradition continues. Hikers (only) can hop the **Rivers and Trails Northeast Ferry** at designated hours between mid-May and early October.

Many of the area's whitewater outfitters are headquartered at **The Forks**, where two of the state's most beautiful rivers converge: the Kennebec, having descended from its source at Moosehead Lake; and the inaptly-named Dead River, which begins at Flagstaff Lake and offers the longest stretch of continuous whitewater in the East. For a true rafting adventure, sign onto a trip down the Dead just after one of the high volume dam releases that create 16 miles of class IV action (whitewater grades range from I, the easiest, to VI, the most difficult).

Side Trip

At The Forks, turn right onto Lake Moxie Road for two miles to the parking lot and stroll along a beautiful pine tree-lined trail through the wilderness to **Moxie Falls**. It cascades more than 90 feet, making it one of Maine's highest.

Continue north on Route 201 through West Forks (more rafting outfitters) and then alongside Johnson Mountain and then the southwest shore of lovely Parlin Pond. Just south of Jackman, stop at the Attean View Rest Area for a terrific view of Attean Lake, the ponds connected by the Moose River, and the mountains to the west.

Jackman, "The Switzerland of Maine," is the largest town in the region, yet it has the feel of an Alaskan outpost. Created as a stopping point for trains hauling lumber, it's now a premier destination for fishermen, hunters, snowmobilers, and canoeists who come to paddle the **Moose River Bow Trip**, a 34-mile loop through the wilderness.

German prisoners were housed at a POW camp in Jackman during WWII.

If you haven't yet spotted a moose, **take a "border and back" trip north of Jackman on Route 202** to the Quebec line. This part of the Moose River Valley *is* aptly named. From the border, there are views of the chain of lakes which stretch through Jackman to Moosehead Lake.

Planning to fish? The season lasts from April through September, with an extended release season in October.

information Area codes are (207) unless otherwise indicated.

The Forks Area Chamber of Commerce (663-2121), P.O. Box 1, West Forks 04984. forksarea.com

Jackman-Moose River Region Chamber of Commerce (668-4171), P.O. Box 368, Jackman 04945. jackmanmaine.org

Old Canada Road Scenic Byway (672-3971), 356 Main St., Bingham 04920. byways.org

Raft Maine (800-723-8633), P.O. Box 78, West Forks 04985. raftmaine.com

Upper Kennebec Valley Chamber of Commerce (672-4100), 356 Main St., Bingham 04920. upperkennebecvalleychamber.me

lodging

Attean Lake Lodge (668-3792), 105 Attean Rd., Jackman 04945. This family lodge (founded in 1900) is on Birch Island in the middle of an otherwise undeveloped lake. 15 log cabins sleep 2-6; all have porches, lake and mountain views, wood-burning fireplaces, and a full bath. Free use of kayaks, paddleboats, sailboats, and canoes; boat and motor rental. Rate includes 3 meals. atteanlodge.com $$$$

Bigwood Lake B&B (668-4461), 19 Forest St., Jackman 04945. "Pamper yourself in the rough" at this two-story lakefront home. Guests rent the entire house, and the owners provide breakfast fixings. Kayaks available. bigwoodlakebedandbreakfast.com $-$$

Bingham Motor Inn (672-4135), 89 Main St., Bingham 04920. 17 rooms in a classic motel; 3 in a renovated farmhouse include 2 with private decks. Also, mini- and full suites with kitchens. Swimming pool and hot tub. binghammotorinn.com $

Bishop's Motel (888-991-7669), 461 Main St., Jackman 04945. All units in this 2-story modern building have a/c, wi-fi, refrigerators, microwaves and coffee makers. Breakfast included. bishopmotel.com $-$$

Cedar Ridge Outfitters (668-4169), 3 Cedar Ridge Dr., Jackman 04945. 6 cozy 2- and 3-bedroom cabin with kitchens, porches, and gas grills on the side of a mountain a few miles from town. Hot tubs and a heated pool (closes mid-Sept.). Pets welcome. cedarridgeoutfitters.com $$-$$$$

Cobb's Pierce Pond Camps (628-2819 summer; 628-3612 winter), 4 Long Falls Dam Rd., Pierce Pond Township 04961. Since 1904 this traditional sporting camp outside Bingham has been attracting serious outdoorspeople. 10 cabins with woodstoves, baths and electricity accommodate 2-8; meals are served in a central dining room.

Inn by the River (663-2181), Rte. 201, The Forks 04985. 10 spacious and comfortably furnished rooms with private baths; 6 with whirlpool tubs and screen porches. Breakfast included. The pub is open nightly. innbytheriver.com $-$$

Last Resort (668-5091), 263 Main St., Jackman 04945. 70-acre resort established in 1902 has 8 rustic lakeside cabins (and 4 primitive tent sites), with their own outhouses, and generator-powered electricity from dusk to 10 p.m.; guests fill 5-gallon water jugs for use in cabins. Boat and canoe rental. Cabins rent by night off-season ($) and by week (6 nights) from July 5-Aug. 14; and Nov. 1-20. lastresortmaine.com

Mountainview Resort (668-7700), 263 Main St., Jackman 04945. 10 spacious, modern 2- and 3-bedroom housekeeping log cabins, all with 2 baths, fireplaces, and whirlpool tubs; and 10 1-bedroom lodge suites with full kitchens and private decks on a 40-acre resort with indoor and outdoor pools, a sauna, pool table, and fitness center. $$-$$$

New England Outdoor Center (800-766-7238), Rte. 201, Caratunk 04925. A full roster of 4-season adventures, and a variety of accommodations including lakeside cabins, campsites, private guesthouses, and the 17-room Sterling Inn. neoc.com $-$$$$

Pine Grove Lodge (672-4011), 823 Ridge Rd., Pleasant Bridge PLT (5 miles from Bingham off Rte. 16) 04920. Family-style, comfortable, inexpensive lodgings at a B&B/sporting camp. A large variety of accommodations include a bunkhouse that sleeps 14, 2 cabins with woodstoves, lodge rooms, and a 2-bedroom housekeeping cottage. Breakfast included. pinegrovelodge.com $

restaurants

Many of the outfitters along this route have restaurants in their lodges.

Bigwood Steakhouse (668-5572), 1 Forest St., Jackman. Steak shares the down home menu with BBQ ribs and a solid selection of fish dishes. Everything is made from scratch. D nightly. $$

Hawk's Nest Restaurant and Pub (663-4430), Rte. 201, Dead River, West Forks. Worth a visit, even if you're not hungry. Homemade soups, sandwiches, and burgers, along with more sophisticated fare in a hand built structure made from 100-200-year-old American logs. The carvings are by Jeff Samudosky, one of the nation's best carvers. B, L & D. $-$$

Maplewood Restaurant (672-3021), 418 Main St., Bingham. Casual dining with BBQ ribs, sandwiches, a free salad bar with all entrees, Sat. night buffet, and Sun. brunch. B, L, D, & Sun. brunch. $

Thompson's Restaurant (672-3330), 348 Main St., Bingham. A popular place since 1929 for diner-quality fare and homemade donuts. Mon.-Fri. 6 a.m.-6 p.m.; Sat. and Sun. until 8 p.m. $

activities

For Whitewater rafting adventures, see 'Raft Maine' in "Information" above.

Cedar Ridge Outfitters (668-4169), 3 Cedar Ridge Rd., Jackman. Guide service, rafting, kayaking, canoeing, hiking, biking, and just about anything else outdoors.

Cry of the Loon Outdoor Adventures (668-7808), P.O. Box 238, Jackman. Fully outfitted 1-7 day canoe and kayak tours, including the Moose River Bow Trip. Also, canoe and kayak rental and shuttle service. cryoftheloon.net

Hawk's Nest Restaurant & Pub (663-4430), Dead River, West Forks. 3-story, 36-ft. high indoor climbing wall.

Jackman Air Tours (668-4461), 7 Attean Rd., Jackman.

Maxx's ATV Rentals (668-4210), Jackman.

Moose River Golf Course (668-4841), Rte. 201, Jackman. 9 scenic holes at a par 31 course.

North Country Rivers (207-672-4814), 36 Main St., P.O. Box 633, Bingham (Nov.-Apr.: P.O. Box 47, E. Vassalboro, ME 04935). Rafting trips on the Kennebec, Penobscot, and Dead rivers; sea kayaking on Maine coast; wildlife safaris; cabin rentals.

Rivers and Trails Northeast, Inc. (663-4441), 1603 Rte. 201, The Forks. Transportation for hikers Mid-May-mid-July, 9 and 11 a.m.; mid-July-Sept., 9 and 11 a.m. and 2 and 4 p.m.; Oct. 1-early Oct., 10 a.m. and noon. Call for off-season schedule. riversandtrails.com

Photo Captions and Credits

Page 11: Marina on Echo Lake near Ludlow, Vermont
courtesy Donald Dill / imagesbydonalddill.com

Page 27: Mill pond, Weston, Vermont
courtesy State of Vermont

Page 45: Hot air balloon over Quechee, Vermont
courtesy Balloons of Vermont / balloonsofvermont.com

Page 59: Belted Galloway cattle near Rutland, Vermont
courtesy Rutland Region Chamber of Commerce

Page 73: First Baptist Church of Bristol, Vermont
courtesy Addison County Chamber of Commerce

Page 91: Church Street Marketplace, Burlington, Vermont
courtesy Lake Champlain Regional Chamber of Commerce

Page 109: Vermont State House, Montpelier
courtesy State of Vermont

Page 125: Stephen Huneck's Sally in bronze,
St. Johnsbury Welcome Center, Vermont
courtesy Darcie McCann, Northeast Kingdom Chamber of Commerce

Page 141: At the Montshire Museum of Science, Norwich, Vermont
courtesy Montshire Museum / Andrew Wellman photo

Page 155: Historic District, Harrisville, New Hampshire
courtesy Donald Dill / imagesbydonalddill.com

Page 169: Flume Bridge over the Pemigewasset River,
Lincoln, New Hampshire
courtesy White Mountains Attractions Association

Page 183: Conway Scenic Railroad train at North Conway Depot,
New Hampshire
courtesy White Mountains Attractions Association

Page 199: Step Falls, Wight Brook Nature Preserve, Newry, Maine
courtesy Maine Office of Tourism / Bethel Chamber of Commerce

Page 213: Lake Chocorua, New Hampshire
courtesy Greater Ossipee Area Chamber Of Commerce

Page 225: Fall foliage at Meredith, New Hampshire, taken from
M/S Mount Washington
courtesy Mount Washington Cruises

Page 239: Costumed interpreter at Sarah Goodwin Fountain,
Strawbery Banke, Portsmouth, New Hampshire
courtesy Strawbery Banke

Page 255: Portland Head Light, Cape Elizabeth, Maine
   courtesy Donald Dill / imagesbydonalddill.com

Page 273: Mare and foal, Pineland Farms, New Gloucester, Maine
   courtesy Pineland Farms

Page 289: Windjammer Angelique at the Rockland Breakwater Lighthouse
   courtesy Carol Latta / amazingmaine.com

Page 309: Little Cranberry Island, Maine
   courtesy Carol Latta / amazingmaine.com

Page 327: Bill Stevens' canoe *Field of Streams* awaits another day's fishing on Kennebago Lake, in Maine's Rangeley Lakes region
   courtesy Bill Stevens, Registered Maine Guide / George Rautenberg photo

Page 335: River rafting in northern Maine
   courtesy North Country Rivers

Maine Index

New Hampshire Index

Vermont Index